D0150976

THE ARGUMENT TO THE OTHER

American Academy of Religion
Academy Series

edited by
Carl Raschke

Number 42

THE ARGUMENT TO THE OTHER
Reason Beyond Reason in the Thought
of Karl Barth and Emmanuel Levinas

by
Steven G. Smith

Steven G. Smith

THE ARGUMENT TO THE OTHER

Reason Beyond Reason in the Thought
of Karl Barth and Emmanuel Levinas

WAGGONER LIBRARY
DISCARD

MACKEY LIBRARY
TREVECCA NAZARENE COLLEGE

Scholars Press
Chico, California

THE ARGUMENT TO THE OTHER
Reason Beyond Reason in the Thought of Karl Barth and Emmanuel Levinas

by
Steven G. Smith
North Carolina Wesleyan College
Rocky Mount, North Carolina

© 1983
American Academy of Religion

Library of Congress Cataloging in Publication Data
Smith, Steven G.
    The argument to the other.
    (American Academy of Religion academy series ;
no. 42)
    Bibliography: p.
    1. Barth, Karl, 1886–1968. 2. Lavinas, Emmanuel.
I. Title. II. Series.
BX4827.B3S54 1983   194   82–17031
ISBN 0–89130–597–1

Printed in the United States of America

CONTENTS

PREFACE

The "Other" is one of those words that is easy to say but hard to mean. Like its sister-word "transcendence," it belies itself every time it is used, for by means of it we comprehend quite nicely what supposedly exceeds our powers of comprehension. And this problem worsens as Otherness becomes a common theme of reflection and academic discussion. Familiarity breeds. . . familiarity. For this reason, only with trepidation may a new study dealing with matters Other be ventured. How could it possibly mean what it says?

Karl Barth and Emmanuel Levinas try strenuously to mean it. A certain movement has gotten into their thinking, and through theirs into mine, leading me to attempt to describe the ratio--tendentious supposition!--of this movement, this event. C. S. Lewis likened the decisive moment of his religious conversion to the frightening and at first disagreeable discovery that, whereas he had imagined his life to be a game of solitaire, the truth was that he was playing poker. That is the experience, if experience it be, of an Other. It is revolutionary. The revolution deeply affects intellectual practice, and if it is true, as I argue, that one's decision whether to acknowledge and how to behave toward an Other is determinative of all one is prepared to argue and to be persuaded of, there could hardly be a more important issue touching the nature of reason and the meaning of being.

The present work is a slightly revised version of a doctoral dissertation completed in 1980. Some recent publications were not available to me during the principal research and writing but have been taken account of in the notes and bibliography. I have made some improvements in my translations from Levinas' *Autrement qu'être ou au-delà de l'essence* after consulting the new Alfonso Lingis translation of 1981.

I am grateful to Joan Vinson for typing and to Elise Smith for help with last-minute amendments. For their valuable comments on various portions and states of the book, I would like to thank Professors Adrien Peperzak, Theo de Boer, Gerhard Sauter, and Edith Wyschogrod. I have been much stimulated and instructed by my fellow laborer in the Barth/Levinas vineyard, doctoral candidate Johan F. Goud. I must thank my teachers who put me in a position to write this work, particularly Professors Thomas Ogletree, Frederick Herzog, and my dissertation director, William H. Poteat, and also Edith Wyschogrod, the American Academy of Religion, and Scholars Press for help in publishing it. Finally, I wish to acknowledge my great debt to Professor Emmanuel Levinas, who gave me all the help I asked for and more. This study is dedicated to him, with respect and admiration.

S. G. S.
Rocky Mount, North Carolina
November, 1982

CHAPTER I

THE ARGUMENT

Karl Barth (1886-1968) was a Swiss Evangelical theologian who became famous for his criticisms of the liberal
theology of the schools of Schleiermacher and Ritschl, and for
his affirmation of the newness of God's Kingdom, the transcendence of God, and the freedom of theology with respect to all
philosophical presuppositions. In his major constructive work,
the *Church Dogmatics*,[1] he traversed almost the entire theological itinerary with an ever-increasing "Christological concentration"[2] whereby he refused to think beyond or apart from the
concrete event of God's revelation in Jesus Christ.

Emmanuel Levinas (1906-   ), a French philosopher and
a Jew, became known first for his role in the introduction of
Husserl's phenomenology to France, and later for his criticisms
of Husserl and Heidegger. He argued that both the transcendental idealism of Husserl and the fundamental ontology of
Heidegger follow an ingrained tendency of Western thought by
failing to acknowledge the other person as Other; and that, on
the contrary, my moral relation with the other person *as*
"Other" is more original than any knowledge or ignorance I
have of him, and more valuable than any value I could possibly
perceive in him or assign to him. Therefore the problem of
the *justice* of my relation with the other person takes over
first place from the problem of the *truth* of what can be
thematized in language or intuitively grasped in consciousness.
The ethical language that expresses or accomplishes the social
relation is prior to phenomenology and ontology, and opposes
the recurrent pretentions of phenomenology and ontology to
provide the foundations of ethics.

It may not be immediately evident why these two men
ought to be viewed side by side. What have they to do with
each other? They never met. There is no evidence in their
published writings that either is aware of the other's work.
The intellectual influences acknowledged by both--Plato, Kant,

1

and Kierkegaard, for example--register in different ways, at
different stages, and in the end with such important qualifications that we could place Barth and Levinas in no "school"
that would not include a large proportion of all modern
thinkers.[3] Moreover, the theme of God's or the neighbor's
transcendence is not at all unusual; it covers a multitude of
intellectual motives, strategies, and outcomes. We might more
naturally presume that a professional philosopher and a
professional theologian would mean very different things by
it. But the warrant for a joint investigation of Barth and
Levinas is more specific and urgent than this. The two men
share, beyond a preoccupation with transcendence, a very
distinctive way of describing it, arguing from it, and holding
consistently to it, which sets them far apart from their
contemporaries. The first clue to this shared distinction,
which offers the premise for the present study, appears in the
two books by which Barth and Levinas are best known.

Karl Barth's enormous theological influence began with
the publication of the second edition of *The Epistle to the
Romans*.[4] In this book the reader is arrested by Barth's
characterization of God as the "Wholly Other," *der ganz Andere,
totaliter aliter*. Paul's message of justification through
grace alone, of man's entire unrighteousness in all that he is
and does for himself, is restated by Barth as a denunciation
of church, culture, theology--of all man's efforts to deny or
conceal his unrighteousness by formulating his own terms of
relationship with God. To all "religion," conceived inclusively as man's reach for God (expressing his sinful persist-
ence in trying to justify himself), God's answer is No! God
is different from everything man knows; God is elsewhere than
where religious man seeks Him; God acts otherwise than as
religious man expects. We are unable to speak of God, for
only God can speak of God. Consequently the only legitimate
goal of theology is to announce its own inability to speak of
God. It can do this by using the negative concept of the
"Wholly Other," which locates God beyond everything man is
capable of knowing. Such a theology is appropriate in the
measure that it reflects the human predicament, in which we
wait in hope for God's Word to come from God Himself. The

rhetoric of the Other becomes a weapon to use against all attempts to speak of God apart from His own revelation. In *The Epistle to the Romans* we learn what can be done in theology with such a weapon. It is indeed surprising how far this No! goes; and it is disturbing how minimal and strange are the possibilities it seems to leave for valid theological discourse.

Emmanuel Levinas' major work *Totality and Infinity*[5] identifies two distinct spirits in the Western philosophical tradition. The dominant one is expressed by the Socratic dictum "Know thyself!" Philosophical inquiry is an exercise in which the free self masters the grounds of its own freedom by making clear to itself, so as to possess by knowledge, the meaning of its own being and that of the world. The world is something "other" than what the self is; but the formal "otherness" of the world (like the formal "otherness" of the concept of the *alter ego*, according to which the other person is a repetition of myself, only varying the spatiotemporal position) is made relative to an overarching structure of Being that includes both self and world. A philosophy is only considered adequate when it reduces plurality to unity, or "totality"-- the totality, say, of a graspable idea that satisfies the intellect, or of a finite discourse that closes discussion. *Adaequatio rei et intellectus* is the canon of rationality. The self measures everything by itself and denies that anything is fundamentally alien to itself. It follows that the self will, in the end, only allow criticism from itself. This is what its ideal of autonomy prescribes, and this is what commits it to a project of reducing all otherness to sameness, i.e. to a rejection of ultimate plurality in favor of intelligible unity.

There is another spirit, however, in this same tradition, which Levinas calls the "metaphysical" spirit of Desire for the absolutely Other.[6] Here philosophy, notwithstanding its quest for the intelligible idea or the finite discourse, avows the mystery of an ultimate plurality so far as it admits something Other than the self which remains unknown and unmeasured by the self. An example would be the Platonic formula locating the Good beyond Being: we do not measure the Good, because it measures us. The existence of the Other adds a new dimension in ethics, beyond the problem of how the free

self is autonomously to choose its own course. Because the
other person, merely in his plight as the hungry neighbor, is
more critical of me that I could ever be of myself--he questions
the right I have to the food in my own mouth--the other person
is the Other. The other person is "exteriority,"[7] the paradoxical possibility of true critique and thus of everything we
mean by critical reason. To do justice to this exteriority,
however, we must adopt and hold to a pluralistic way of thinking,
even if it requires us to renounce the priority of the intelligible idea or the finite discourse. The priority will belong
instead to my moral relation with the Other, in which the Other
has a kind of moral eminence which I address, not by knowing
him or choosing him, but by being subject to his claim, either
responsibly or irresponsibly. The only idea I can have of him
will be like Plato's idea of the Good or the Cartesian idea of
the Infinite, the "thought that thinks more than it can think,"[8]
a self-overflowing thought that makes a unique demand for an
eminent status. The only words I can apply to him will take
their place in a discourse without closure, i.e. a conversation
in which the Other is free to unsay and resay. Philosophy is
ethically transformed by allowing the idea of the Other to work
upon it and within it. The results of this transformation are
often surprising and disturbing; and it may be difficult to see
how, if the idea of the absolutely Other is given any credence,
it is possible to say the first word about it. How can we
speak meaningfully of something that is "Other" than any discursive theme?

Whether or not the basic intentions of these two books
are agreeable or readily understandable, it is impossible to
read either without being struck by two salient features. One
is the dominating position of a concept of total otherness, the
totaliter aliter. The other is the conviction that the ground
rules of thinking have somehow been irrevocably changed once
the posture that suits, or is suited by, this concept has been
adopted. The idea of the Other seems to represent an intense
critical fire through which all theology or philosophy must
pass, and beyond which theology and philosophy must be practiced differently. This suggests that neither Barth nor
Levinas can really be appreciated without reckoning with the

idea and seeing how it informs their arguments, even as they go
on to modify their usage or interpretation of the idea. Accord-
ingly, it is an essential task of either Barth or Levinas
scholarship to investigate the birth, formation, subsequent
career, and ultimate rationale of their arguments to the Other,
even apart from the independent interest that must arise in the
phenomenon of a shared "Argument to the Other."

The fact that Barth and Levinas both have the idea of
the Other and attach such importance to it is the starting
point of the present study, but only insofar as it favors the
presumption that a deeper logical commonality may be found than
this striking but, in itself, superficial coincidence. For the
"Other" is not, strictly speaking, *anything*: it is only a *way*
to speak of *something else*, something that may be quite definite but must remain, for one reason or another, out of direct
view. For Barth the "something else" is the God revealed in
Christ, the Creator incommensurable with the creature, who
nevertheless makes Himself known to us, in a manner lacking all
analogy in our experience. For Levinas the "something else" is
the other person--ultimately, the other man in his nearness to
God--who is the moral critic of the self and the prophetic,
eschatological critic of totalities like "Being" and "Spirit"
and "History." He must be proclaimed as Other because our
philosophical language, left to itself, will assign him a place
in an intelligible scheme of things, thus trespassing on his
right to make his own claim and speak his own truth. It is
obvious at the start, then, that the idea of the Other has to
be seen in the wider context of the argument in which it is
employed--and that the arguments of Barth and Levinas have
quite different purposes. There can be no pretense that the
Christian theologian and the Jewish philosopher are trying to
say the same thing; rather, they are trying to serve their
different objects in a similar way, viz. by employing a certain
kind of argument, which we call here the "Argument to the
Other."

The Argument to the Other that appears in a joint
reading of Barth and Levinas seems to be an argument about the
nature of argument itself. It contends first that we find ourselves in a fundamental situation of encounter with an Other

which is ruled by the problem of how we are to be justified
before this Other. Given the advent of the Other, we know ourselves to be *not alone*; consequently we cannot avoid the
problem of our relationship with the Other. Neither can we
"solve" it and put it to one side, for the otherness of the
Other cannot be mediated or suspended. The advent of the Other
reveals that our freedom, so far as it is related only to
itself, is arbitrary. We do not dispose of the meaning of our
own existence. This meaning is contingent upon our relation to
what is beyond us. Let us call this fundamental situation the
problem of justification, to show both that the starting point
is indeed a problem, and that it is a different sort of problem
than, for example, the problem of freedom which rules in
Kantian or "existentialist" philosophy. This is the negative
or critical phase of the Argument.

Given the problem of justification, and the intellectual strictures that it lays upon us, "reason" and "argument"--
hence, theology and philosophy--must be conceived in a new way.
If we argue within this situation, not pretending to resolve it
or escape it, we do not argue to conclusions that would dictate
the nature of the Other (or of a "Being" or "History" or
"Spirit" determining what the Other *could* be) or coerce the
response of the Other. That is, we do not argue on the ultimate presupposition of truth, because we do not possess the
truth of the Other. We argue instead on the ultimate presupposition of responsibility to the Other, produced as a good
relation with the Other. Whatever else we argue *for*, we argue
it *to* the Other, as a proposal for justice. The point is that
we do not, by this inversion, become sceptical regarding truth.
We still have concepts and intuitions and categories and everything traditionally needed for truth. But we have gained something that we lacked when the truth came first, viz. acknowledgement of our interlocutory responsibility which motivates,
orients, and criticizes our quest for truth. We can now
analyze conflicting truth-claims, not only in logical and
evidentiary terms, but also in terms of the seriousness of the
conflicting responsibilities underlying them. This seriousness
will not appear until our various pretentions to philosophically
or theologically control the meaning of the Other are put aside.

Having acknowledged the Other, we are free to welcome and to listen and speak to the Other. This is the positive phase of the Argument.

The analysis of the Argument to the Other bears directly on the individual interpretation of Barth and Levinas. A central question in Barth interpretation, to which theological criticism of him constantly returns, has to do with the nature of his reliance on philosophical principles. Is the second edition of *Romans* merely a particularly drastic form of idealism, a "new Titanism"[9] substituting the philosophy of the infinite difference for the philosophy of union or analogy? How much of the logic of *Romans* is carried over into the *Church Dogmatics*, and how influential is it there? Does Barth vindicate his own judgment that the theologian is free to make use of philosophical vocabularies and arguments as hermeneutical aids without thereby betraying his theological responsibilities? If it is true that the "Argument to the Other" names certain very characteristic and long-abiding tendencies in Barth's thought, and is implicated in the logic of its development, does the Argument amount to a philosophy? Does it compromise Barth's theology, or further it? We know (*ex hypothesi*, at least) that the Argument is not specifically theological, since it functions also in the non-theological context of Levinas' thought.[10]

A corresponding question in Levinas interpretation is: if phenomenology and ontology are false or inadequate to Otherness, how is it possible to talk about it? Specifically, what compass does Levinas steer by when he speaks of the Other and develops the logic of exteriority? If he is not a phenomenologist or an ontologist, what is he? By what standards of rationality are we to judge his claims? When Levinas emphasizes the continuity of his thought with phenomenology,[11] how are the analogies and disanalogies between his procedure and what is ordinarily called phenomenology to be evaluated? Is the Argument to the Other something distinct from phenomenology, which is nevertheless capable of cooperating with it? The parallel with the theologian Karl Barth would suggest that something other than Husserlian phenomenology is active in Levinas' thought.[12]

The first step in exploring the Argument must be an examination of how Barth and Levinas were brought to the point of defecting from their traditions. In Barth's case, we must look at the process whereby he abandoned liberal theology and eventually set new foundations with the idea of the Wholly Other, which began at the end of his school days in Marburg and culminated in the publication of the second edition of *Romans* in 1922. What made Barth change his mind? When did he change it? What continuity of intention exists between the first edition of *Romans* and the second? How does the idea of the Wholly Other function in second *Romans*--what does it accomplish? In Levinas' case the concept of the absolutely Other was elaborated in a much longer development, with anticipations in his doctoral thesis on Husserl and periodic advances throughout the thirty years leading up to *Totality and Infinity*. What was the reason for Levinas' discomfiture with Heidegger's ontological program? At what point did the theme of Otherness begin to carry the burden of Levinas' protest against Husserl and Heidegger? What is left of phenomenology for Levinas after its inadequacy to the idea of the Other is demonstrated?

Second *Romans* and *Totality and Infinity* represent the "crisis" stage of the Argument to the Other, the climactic acknowledgement of Otherness. In summarizing this stage by describing the problem of justification that it opens, it will be found that the supremely abstract idea of the Other brings other, less abstract concepts in its train, forming a characteristic pattern not merely in these two books but in the whole of Barth's and Levinas' work. Such concepts can also take on new meanings by virtue of their inclusion in the pattern. For example, Barth and Levinas both like to describe the revelation of the Other as an *event*, an unpredictable novelty calling forth an essentially adventurous response. In both cases the category of "event" critically opposes the category of "object" or "state of affairs," i.e. that of which there could be general knowledge, familiarity, possession, and security. Because "event" here refers to the advent of the Other, it takes on a more extreme contingency than would normally belong to the notion of occurrence. Against Schleiermacher, "event" is that which *interrupts* and cannot be contained by the pious Christian

self-consciousness. Against Husserl, "event" is that which
interrupts and cannot be constituted in the experience of the
transcendental ego. Now, it is only to such an extreme "event"
that the response of the self can be truly adventurous and
liberating, in that it involves a departure from self without
prospect of return--that is, it involves entering into relation
with what is absolutely Other even when one's own comforts and
certitudes can no longer be relied upon. Thus, despite the
fact that Barth and Levinas have in mind different events, they
are both drawn to place weight on the concept of "event," and
they jointly say something distinctive about the nature of
"event" in a way that is logically related to what they say
about other things.[13]

After their "crisis" formulations of the idea of the
Other, Karl Barth and Emmanuel Levinas both made far-reaching
changes in their procedures that involved, among other things,
a changed understanding of Otherness. Barth worked out this
change in the course of the 1920's and considered that he had
found his new starting-point (the ground on which the entire
Church Dogmatics was to be built) in his book on Anselm published in 1931.[14] Barth's interpretation of the ontological
proof of Anselm contains within it the critical concern of
Barth's negative theology, the positive capacity of his mature
dogmatics, and the transition between them. An analysis of this
book together with the first volume of the *Dogmatics* will show
how far Barth's shift from "dialectical theology" is consistent
with or even attributable to the Argument. The key texts to
read for the parallel development in Levinas are a number of
important articles written in the 1960's and 1970's, and his
second major book, *Otherwise than Being or Beyond Essence*,[15]
published in 1974. In this work the positive implications that
were already present in *Totality and Infinity*'s idea of the
Other as the Infinite bear fruit in a new methodic *via eminentiae* clearly distinguishable from the more negative method of
the earlier work. What is more, Levinas comes to apply the
idea of the Other consistently to *God*, who designates the
neighbor as moral claimant.

Church Dogmatics I and *Otherwise than Being* provide
solutions, of a sort, to the absolute problem of justification

created by the advent of the Other. In Barth's thought, the unique givenness of the revelation in Christ takes pride of place over the abstract non-givenness of the transcendent God. For Levinas, the presence of the third person, my neighbor's neighbor, makes both possible and necessary the comparison of incomparable Others; there must be logic, science, historical knowledge, and so forth, to weigh different moral claims and help construct the just order. Barth and Levinas come to mitigate the total chaos of Otherness in another way: by conceiving language and reason in independence of logical and experiential a prioris, they discover a possibility of rationally addressing the transcendent without reducing it to immanence. Just as the Other exceeds all experience, so human language can exceed experience by serving as the obedient gesture of *witness* to the Infinite. Our summary of the positive stage of the Argument must focus on this claimed innovation in rationality.

Finally, the important difference between Levinas and Barth must be brought forward. The Christian theologian and the Jewish philosopher do not merely have different interests; they have conflicting and competing interests. There is evidence that each recognizes and rejects something like the other's position. Does this discredit the supposition of an Argument that they employ in common? Or is the Argument implicated even in the form of their ultimate disagreement? I will argue at this point that there is a *ratio* of the disagreement between Barth and Levinas, and that what we know of their Argument to the Other is highly relevant to it. This will place the whole question of the right relationship between philosophy and theology in a peculiar light, for Barth and Levinas offer us, apart from any confrontation between Christian and Jew, an instructive confrontation between theology and philosophy--*if* the Barthian premises for theology and the Levinasian premises for philosophy are accepted. That is, precisely by means of what they have in common (an Argument that "reason" is constituted in encounter with an Other), Barth and Levinas oppose each other: reason based on obedient response to God's revelation in Christ competes with reason based on obedient response to one's fellow men. The competition becomes all the more acute when we discover how the two

arguments nearly converge to unity--as Barth finds the concretization of obedience to the divine Other in service of the
other person, while Levinas finds an essential reference of the
other person's Otherness to the distinct Otherness of God. Do
our two principals aim at the same object after all, the integral relation between the service of God and the service of
man? But the unmistakeable difference in the order of priority
according to which this relation is conceived gives rise to a
serious division between their worlds of thought, between
theology and philosophy. In this sense it is fair to say that
the two arguments or reasons "compete." It is the most serious
competition imaginable, that between two infinite responsibilities. In the light of this analysis it might be possible to
discuss the actual and perhaps even normative competition of
theology and philosophy on some basis other than accusing the
one of irrationalism and the other of faithlessness. This
would be ground worth gaining.

        Our joint reading will not directly involve the
entirety of the Barth and Levinas original literatures, but
only a portion of each, chosen to reveal the most important
movements of their arguments that lend themselves to comparison.
We will not follow Barth beyond the first volume of the
Dogmatics, even though the positive phase of the Argument might
find its richest documentation in the third and fourth volumes,
where Barth's emphasis moves from his polemic against the
analogia entis to his rich theological anthropology. The
crucial decision that enables this later turn is already made
in the book on Anselm, and finds its first application in
Church Dogmatics I. For similar reasons the Levinas exposition
ends with the 1975 article "God and Philosophy."[16] We will not
attend systematically to Levinas' aesthetics,[17] or to his
writings on Judaism,[18] even though they wrestle in illuminating
ways with the same problems, because (1) Levinas maintains a
distinction between his philosophical and religious literatures,
(2) our case can be made solely with reference to the (non-
aesthetic) philosophical literature, which has its own definite
continuity, and (3) our primary interest is in the philosophical paradigm that Levinas offers. Notwithstanding these
restrictions, it is our intention to present a coherent account

of the development of Barth's and Levinas' thought, and not
merely an analysis of the abstracted "Argument to the Other" as
an indifferent third thing. In following the thread of the
theme of Otherness we will, inevitably, present a less-than-
comprehensive account even of the works that lie in the middle
of our path. But this thread is chosen in the conviction that
it leads to the heart of the contributions that Barth and
Levinas make to theology and philosophy; and the presumption of
the Argument to the Other will be justified in the measure that
it produces convincing versions of the stories of Barth and
Levinas.

CHAPTER II

THE ADVENT OF THE OTHER: KARL BARTH 1909-1922

1. The First Turn

At the outbreak of the first World War, the German
academic establishment, including almost all of Barth's university teachers, not only failed to clearly oppose German involve-
ment in the war but seemed, to the scandalized Barth, to
support it.[1]

> The unconditional truths of the gospel are simply sus-
> pended for the time being and in the meantime a German
> war-theology is put to work, its Christian trimming con-
> sisting of a lot of talk about sacrifice and the like.
> Here is sufficient proof that the "truths" were nothing
> more than a surface varnish and not an inmost possession
> of this "*Christliche Welt*" Christianity. It is truly sad!
> Marburg and German civilization have lost something in my
> eyes by this breakdown, and indeed forever. . .[2]

Theologically Barth was a product of the very *Christliche Welt*
Christianity that he now believed to be discredited. He had
been an assistant editor of that liberal journal for a year
under Martin Rade.[3] In his early academic writings he argued
from premises supplied above all by his Marburg teacher Wilhelm
Herrmann. Barth's disillusion, therefore, was with a way of
thinking on which he still heavily relied. This and the war
placed him in a newly problematic position as a preacher, whose
theme must now be "*Dei providentia--hominem confusio*; round and
round that center do we turn now Sunday by Sunday and have no
other choice."[4]

Barth's earliest commitment to the liberal theology of
religious experience must be measured by the content of his
prewar academic articles. His later attack on experience-
theology presupposes an inside acquaintance with the motives
and strengths of this thought, which in his own version is not
simply the antipode of "crisis" transcendence-theology but in
some ways anticipates and provokes that development.

BARTH'S THEOLOGY OF EXPERIENCE. (1) "Modern Theologie
und Reichsgottesarbeit."[5] In this 1909 article written at the

13

end of his Marburg studies, Barth asks how a normative theology
is possible from Herrmann's starting point. The essence of the
"modern" theology represented by Herrmann is *religious individualism*, which secondarily entails *historical relativism*. That
is, Christianity becomes valid solely as it is effectively
realized in the individual existence of the believer, whose
action in the world is then determined by the divine norm. But
no one can supply such a norm to the believer from outside his
own purely individual experience, which is not in itself
generally valid or binding on others. The outworking of faith
does however require co-operation with others in the use of
generally valid methods, even in investigating such sensitive
matters as the historical grounds of the Christian faith, so
that the Christian cannot approach history otherwise than with
the relativistic presuppositions dictated by historical science.
Underlying historical research is a vital religious interest--
"The truth shall make you free."[6] Theology cannot dodge this
imperative.

The "modern" theologian who adheres both to Herrmann's
principle of religious individualism and to historical science,
with its implicit judgment of the relativity of the grounds of
that personal experience, will be utterly lost if he does not
at least have that experience. For him, "to be or not to be"
is the question: he must at least shine forth as one band in
the spectrum of historical religious phenomena. The "modern"
theologian does not surrender all rights to the mind of the
world, for his does have a duty to converse with the modern
culture-consciousness. But his modernity imposes on him certain important assumptions--for instance, that cognitive
primacy belongs to science, and that morality is the presupposition of religion.[7] He occupies an endemically problematic
position, but not an impossible one, since he can do no other.
He must speak out clearly in full cognizance of the relativity
of what he has to say.

In a defense of this article,[8] Barth expounds
Schleiermacher's principle of individuation to show that his
position is not normlessly subjective, and to argue at the
same time against orthodox objectivism. Herrmann himself had
varied the formula of Kantian-Ritschlian ethical theology by

incorporating Schleiermacher's idea that the content of indi-
viduated religious experience is more than any general, universal schema can account for. Morality remains the presupposition
of religion, in the sense that religion provides the answer to
the otherwise unanswerable moral question; but one cannot
derive from the moral law a complete account of religious
meaning.[9] With Herrmann, Barth rejects orthodoxy's premise
that Christian faith is based on the willed acceptance of a
doctrine as a denial of the primacy of personally realized
experience, and a travesty of faith. All religious discourse,
including dogmatics, can only be confession of faith to faith--
"because I can discover the essence of evangelical piety in
nothing other than the absolutely inner act of faith, inacces-
sible to all adequate conceptual formulation."[10] Theology
cannot prescribe to experience, because it is completely dependent for its content and validity upon the religious experience
it explicates. Theology's problem is latent in that experience.[11] There is a solution to it, but it is not discursive,
not available to theology. The two parts of the dilemma,
personal conviction and historical relativity, are brought
together within the single subjective existence of the Christian
believer. The individual is grasped by the Christian norm,
which then governs all his other judgments. But the superiority of the Christian norm can only be confessed, never
demonstrated.

(2) "Der christliche Glaube und die Geschichte."[12]
The relation between inner faith and outer reality is presented
again as theology's main problem in Barth's 1910 lecture
(published in 1912). How can a historically representable *then*
be normative for an immediately experienced *now*? Barth claims
not to offer any new proposal but only to show actual Christian
faith in its actual relation to history. The proper methodology
of theology (*Glaubenslehre*) must fit the methodology of faith
(*Glauben*), the idionomous reality of "God-experience, immediate
consciousness of the presence and force of the superhuman,
super-worldly, and thus absolutely superior power of life."[13]
Faith is the historical moment of consciousness par excellence,
since the problem of faith is the very problem of the actualization of culture-consciousness, i.e. of the reality-principle

determining personal existence. The *proprium* of Christian
faith is insight into the realized personality of Jesus, which
becomes the reality-principle of the believer's future. We
acquire it by the Spirit, which cannot be bound to an external
historical authority such as the Roman Catholic Church or the
"paper Pope" of Protestant orthodoxy. The Christ-insight does
have one presupposition: the fact that man is confronted with
his fellow man. To be religious, man must be in history.

Now a dilemma arises in attempting to do justice to the
objective aspect of faith as well as the subjective. In orthodoxy, with its notion of faith as assent to propositional
truths, the objective and rational Word of God seems to lose
its subjective correlate. Faith is misrepresented as a kind of
cognition. On the other hand, faith pictured as a non-cognitive
appropriation of salvation runs the risk of losing touch with
reality. Schleiermacher's solution is to see *Anschauung* and
Gefühl, the (subjective) apprehension of the reality of Christ
and its (objective) taking effect, as two sides of a unitary
process wrought by God. The process must *occur*; it cannot be
subsumed under the general concept of man; there is no religious a priori, either objective or subjective.[14]

Although we must emphasize the reality of Christ *in us*,
it is a great mistake to assume that "Christ in us" is a part
of our nature or culture-consciousness. Neither critical
philosophy nor Reformation theology allows this assumption. It
is also a mistake to abstract a Christ-in-Himself from faith's
appropriation of Christ, yet the objective *reality* of Christ in
us must also be emphasized. Christ is God's effect in us,
which is God Himself. Therefore the "objective" Christ *is*
Christ in us, confirming rather than contradicting the principle of religious individualism. The notion that the object of
faith is something simply exterior, which the believer as it
were reaches out and grasps, must be resisted: "You would not
have sought me had you not already found me."[15] Christian
revelation occurs when the believer is sympathetically affected
by Jesus' exemplary inner life, in which human self-consciousness is annihilated in favor of the perfect obedience shown
on the Cross. The way in which the first disciples experienced the risen Christ, like our own way, is historically

relative. Faith cannot be studied apart from history. The
church, made from the material of believing individuals, is the
historical vehicle of the realization of faith. The historical
method by which we study this phenomenon must be purely secular,
avoiding concepts like "revelation" and "miracle" in order to
prevent confusion between what pertains to theology proper and
what only pertains to the general culture-consciousness with
which theology is in dialogue. We must not look for necessary
laws by which faith is realized, however; we must respect its
contingency.[16]

(3) "Der Glaube an den persönlichen Gott."[17] Barth's
1913 lecture, which analyzes the concept of a personal God,
also re-examines the relation of words to experience and of
dogmatic theology to faith. Barth acknowledges a certain devaluation of words in comparison to experience in the Schleiermacherian tradition,[18] but he argues that in the very immediacy
of religious experience we are driven to think and speak, and
are thus engaged in dogmatics from the start. Dogmatics is a
secondary pursuit, but a necessary one. The question of God's
personhood is a question of better or worse dogmatics, which
while presupposing religious experience, must be free to develop
itself without continual interruption from the experiential
side. This does not mean that dogmatics is free to build fairy
castles:

> The scientific character of dogmatics cannot consist in
> the freedom from contradiction of the most harmonious sys-
> tem possible, but in the most exact interpretation possible
> of religious reality by its propositions, and in the great-
> est possible purity and completeness of thought. In this
> respect Calvin's *Institutio* is more scientific than most
> of what has been written in dogmatics since.[19]

The upshot of Barth's discussion of the reciprocal
implications of such concepts as the Absolute, the I, Spirit,
etc. is that an irreconcilable contradiction exists between the
finitude necessarily ingredient in the concept of personality
(as a thinking, willing, becoming "I") and the infinitude
required by the concept of the Absolute--or, in other words,
between a limiting anthropomorphic or psychologistic conception
of God and an idealistic neutrum. The problem is a genuine
one, imposing constraint on our religious discourse, because it
is based on an inner necessity to be found in religious

experience, and not on any projection of human conceptions onto the transcendent. That experience is of our created state of being, of "*living from God*, which is given to us in our *connection with history*. . . in this sense we have God and on this basis we are able to speak of Him."[20] The gospel of Jesus, where the value and task of personality stand at the fore, gives us our sharpest impression of the antinomy of the God-idea. Jesus' life, the purest example of personality, shows God as personality; and this personality contains an immediate reference to the personality of others, for unless there is peace with one's brothers there will not be peace with God. But beside this the gospel strikes the contrasting note of obedience, of the sacrifice of personality at Gethsemane and Golgotha, and of the superhuman work of the Kingdom of God. Here piety is driven to speak of the transcendent rather than the immanent, the superior, the "Sublime" (*das Erhabene*). "This double orientation of experience [*Erfahrung*], which indeed comes to unity in immediate lived-experience [*Erlebnis*]-- but also only in immediate lived-experience--is finally the mystery of all religion."[21] Discursive thought can posit but never fulfill this unity. Once again, an underlying paradox in religious experience produces an explicit paradox in theology.

In his early articles Barth accepts the results of the critical philosophy, of Schleiermacher's philosophy of religion (he regards the *Speeches on Religion* as the beginning of theological modernity[22]), of Schleiermacher's dogmatics so far as it takes as its starting point the Christian consciousness, and of Herrmann's stress on the existential point of Christian truth and the need for its personal realization. Perhaps the single most important idea taken by Barth from these sources is the principle of positivity--"Schleiermacher's discovery that there are no exemplifications, but only individuations, of religion."[23] In this sense Schleiermacher advances beyond Kant, but in a manner consistent with the critical import of Kant's philosophy, since faith is neither knowing nor willing nor judging, but an innermost determination of the believer's existence. Morality does remain the presupposition of religion. The Enlightenment condemnation of historical authority as

heteronomous remains in force. The problem of history is
directly addressed, but from the inside out; the meaning of
history is constituted as the outworking of faith, which itself
is a *sui generis* reality. These elements are brought together,
within a theory of the supremacy of personal existence, to show
how theology may take modern culture and historical science
seriously without losing its distinctive theme--at the price of
having to articulate its theme dialectically and circumspectly.

Looking toward the early Barth from the later Barth, we
recognize a characteristic propensity for centering attention
on *problems* taken to be constitutive of religious experience or
discourse. "It is my opinion. . . that an inwardly living
theology can endure and must indeed promote examination and
declaration of its problem."[24] "Modern" theology is defined by
the problem of objective history vs. individual experience; the
apprehension of God in religious experience is defined by the
problem of divine attributes that are not jointly thinkable.
Underlying all is the general problem: How can we speak of
God? How is theology possible? What decides the validity of
theological claims? Barth concludes that there can be no pat
answer to this question, that underlying the problem is--a problem. It would be a mistake, therefore, to imagine that the
Barth who wrote *The Epistle to the Romans* was awakened into
critical awareness from a sound "liberal" dogmatic slumber.
His earliest theology is a restless one. The incomparability
of Christian existence makes it resistant to the very theological expression it demands.

The principle of Christian truth, whereby we (1) know
what is Christian, and (2) are capable of challenging and teaching the general culture-consciousness, is the concretely given
experience of the Christian believer. This "immediacy," which
becomes a prime object of Barth's attack in both versions of
his commentary on Romans (the first edition speaking of a *new*
unheard-of immediacy, the second emphasizing that the new immediacy is indeed *unheard-of*), functions in Barth's early theology, as it functioned also in Schleiermacher's dogmatics, as
the critical reference point by which the mediations of philosophy and theology are to be judged. Barth writes in his first
article that his theology stands or falls according to whether

he *has* the experience in question. The irony of his position
in this period is that, while he was obviously very impressed
with Herrmann as an exemplar, he himself does not appear to have
attained sure possession of that "experience." Instead, his
interest in the objective social problem and the anti-pietistic
"religious socialism" movement increased.[25]

Barth's scattered references to Feuerbach[26] underscore
his interest in preventing a collapse of Christian revelation
into the general culture-consciousness. Such a collapse would
make superfluous any conversation between Christianity and culture, which for Barth would destroy the rationale of theology.
(Franz Overbeck's critique of culture-theology would later make
a profound impression on Barth.) Such a collapse would also
involve a theological misrecognition of faith, for Barth is
confident that a superhuman reality is indeed present in faith.
Talk about God is definitely something other than talk about
man. But too many theologians of the day give the game away by
defining faith as a category of general human experience, or
theology as a category of general science, thereby setting themselves up as the deserving victims of Feuerbach's argument that
theology dissimulates rather than reveals the truth of man.

THE STRANGE NEW WORLD. Numerous factors prepared for
Barth's change of mind,[27] but his theology began to crystallize
rapidly in a very different form after his encounter with
Christoph Blumhardt at Bad Boll in April of 1915.[28] Barth saw
in Blumhardt a biblical, eschatological hope for man no less
realistic and serious than the socialist hope, and thus the
possibility of a non-pietistic Christianity even more critical
of the established order than socialism could be.[29] Reviewing
a book of morning devotions by Blumhardt, Barth said, "I suspect
that he would have quite a few things to say about the conflicts
and problems that stir us nowadays. He will not say it, though;
it is not important enough to him because other things are more
important to him."[30] The biblical message overshadows even the
questions and answers of socialism; it is possible to reckon
with the concerns of socialism from God's own standpoint, but
not vice versa.[31]

> Another strong impression I get throughout. . . is how
> organic truth is, in the eyes of this man. He does not
> construe, or only playfully. He does not demonstrate or

engage in polemics. He sees the tragedy of life very
clearly, but he does not take it tragically, so to speak.
Not for a moment does the tragedy of life become an independent object of his interest; it lies embedded from the
very beginning in the peace of God as it were. Neither does
he stick things together, line them up, or glorify chaos as
God's creation. Instead he sees God creating life out of
darkness, one taking shape out of the other and growing in
the peace of God. The book is an unparalleled, joyful
triumph over our theses and antitheses. Again I ask myself
and my friends, is there anything mightier and more hopeful
in these times than when a man can and *may* think organically?[32]

The sudden appearance of "organism" in Barth's vocabulary may
be owing to his discovery of J. T. Beck,[33] whose "naturalistic"
idea of the Holy Spirit's work as a new "organism" later becomes
the hermeneutical centerpiece of the first edition of Barth's
Romans. Here it signals that Barth regards Blumhardt (as he
regarded Herrmann) as one who occupies the right ground--who,
in the sense of the modern theology question "to be or not to
be," is. The contrast of organic with mechanical thinking
points to the impossibility of hoisting oneself up to this
ground by any self-supplied artifice. "Organic" thinking proceeds entirely from itself or its subject matter, and thus is
objective (*sachlich*), or independent of subjective operations
of construal, in an eminent sense. The fact that a man like
Blumhardt can and may think organically is supremely hopeful
because it means that God is with us. Apart from God, that
ground cannot be occupied. No one can speak for the *Sache*
except the *Sache* itself.

The fundamental newness (hence, power of renewal) of
the Kingdom of God in Blumhardt's thought means that the usual
philosophical and political presuppositions of talk about God
are really irrelevant. Inspired by the freedom with which Blumhardt took God more seriously than either academic theology or
socialism, Barth and his friend and fellow pastor Eduard Thurneysen became progressively less attached to the reigning
theology and religious socialism. Thurneysen whispered to
Barth in 1916 that a "wholly other" theological foundation was
needed for their preaching and teaching.[34] Of course, that they
sought it meant that in some sense they had already found it,
although Barth could still speak in 1916 of God's righteousness
in terms of our "conscience" which is activated by the message

of the prophets, and could still appeal to religious individualism in saying, "One man may perhaps provoke another to
reflect upon 'the righteousness of God.' But no man may bring
another to the peculiar, immediate, penetrating certainty which
lies behind the phrase." Nevertheless: conscience "interrupts
even the cultivation of. . . religious thoughts and feelings!"[35]
Barth's vocabulary and method are not instantly transfigured,
but from this point forward his theology is dominated by the
problem of its free object, God, *in His freedom*. The work on
Romans tended to undermine Barth's confidence in his hermeneutical apparatus while it impressed him more and more with the
reality and unexpected import of his object.

> During the work it was often as though I were being
> looked at by something from afar, from Asia Minor or
> Corinth, something very ancient, early oriental, indefin-
> ably sunny, wild, original, that somehow is hidden behind
> these sentences and is so ready to let itself be drawn
> forth by ever new generations. *Paul*--what a man he must
> have been. . . and then *behind Paul*: what realities those
> must have been that could set this man in motion in such a
> way! . . . Right today I have a very strong impression of
> how discouragingly relative are all our devices "to let the
> Bible speak."[36]

For all his talk of "immediate certainty," Barth presents in his 1916 lectures a fundamental dualism between God as
we think of Him (as a "questionable figment of our own
thoughts")[37] and God as He really is, much greater than we ever
thought He would be. "His will is not a corrected continuation
of our own. It approaches ours as a Wholly Other [*als ein
gänzlich anderer*]."[38] In the Bible we find, if we read it
carefully with a desire to learn something beyond our own ideas
which we like to see mirrored in it, an "other" new world, God's
world as opposed to man's world, where God's sovereignty is
accepted.[39] We cannot justify our moral or religious positions
with reference to the Bible; we are always wrong, because the
Bible's world is always "other" than the world in which we take
our bearings. But God is not merely "other." We know Him precisely as the one who intends to establish a new world here on
earth, and who will therefore not allow life to be divided into
a "here" and a "beyond."[40] The deepest longing in ourselves
and the whole world is to be healed by this God. Yet the
answer in the Bible "is really much too large for us. . . since

it is a fruit which our own longing, striving, and inner labor have not planted."[41]

Barth is now ready to formulate the central problem of theology and the religious life in far more drastic terms than formerly. In his confirmation address of 1917, he tells his pupils:

> In religious questions there are no "experts" but only complete beginners, bunglers, and novices. . . The difference between you and us [Thurneysen and me] could at the most consist in the fact that this embarrassment burns our fingers quite differently than yours. . . because we are compelled to take the question of religion quite materially and seriously.[42]

It is the disturbed man, not the calm man, who is justified by God. "Religion" itself is no help to us; our need is for something different, the sort of thing we see mighty figures like Paul and Luther and Francis of Assisi wrestling with. "Religion" is a private concern for individual salvation; "life" passes it by. "Life" is war, deeds, class struggle, water, fire, electricity. Real biblical faith, like life, is much more powerful than any mere inner conviction: it is the power of a man's objective being committed to God's Kingdom. "Religion," on the other hand, is a kind of curse, part of the tribulation of the world. We must see our own solidarity with it so that we can accept the victory of "life" over "religion" attested by the Bible.[43]

There are hints in these wartime writings of a polemic against Schleiermacher, Marburg, and religious socialism, but what we find for the most part is a sudden vacuum in the place where these were taken for granted not long before. The interest has swung from the problems of religious experience and social justice to the problem of what God says. At the center of attention lies the Bible, or the voice in the wilderness of conscience witnessing to God's righteousness, rather than the issues of history and the divine value of personality. The Barth-Thurneysen correspondence from this period testifies to the excitement at the "discovery" of the Bible and a sense of mission in exploiting this discovery.[44] But it is not until the appearance of a work on the scale of *The Epistle to the Romans* that its larger dimensions are drawn in. Most importantly, the concrete actuality which Barth respected and sought as the basis of Christian discourse has now become something other than an experience—it has become the *news* of something wholly other than what lies in our experience. Once the real God is divided by His revelation from our own God, the questionable figment of our own thoughts, all important barriers are removed to the exercise of Barth's critique upon experience-theology.

2. The New Organism

Looking back on prewar Christendom, Barth commented on Romans 10:3 ("For, being ignorant of the righteousness that comes from God, and seeking to establish their own, they did not submit to God's righteousness") as follows:

> There arose profound "movements" and splendid working organizations for God's cause [*Sache*]; professors, writers, evangelists, and ombudsmen came forward radiating the enchantment of religious hypnosis. Religion had become such a "perceptibly potent force" in 1909 that there was a pressing need for a special reference book on its past and present [*Die Religion in Geschichte und Gegenwart*]. John Mott traveled with his speech on "The Hour of Decision" from country to country and we all more or less believed in him. Indefatigable world committees were at work. The socialists in Basel and the Christians in Edinburgh rejoiced at the approach of the Kingdom. . . but whether "the cause" was really *God's* cause. . . that was always a dangerous question. . . God was always good enough for the accomplishment and crowning of what men had already begun on their own. Objectively, the fear of the Lord did not stand at the beginning of our wisdom.[45]

Barth and Thurneysen had by this time been dissatisfied with the theological status quo for a good while, but they recognized that their dissatisfaction counted for nothing unless they learned a new and better way of doing theology. In June, 1916, Barth thought of himself as one still living on his private intellectual income, "which is nothing."[46] Beginning shortly after, Barth's interpretation of the letter to the Romans is a massive attempt to make use of the biblical income he has begun to receive from Paul. The new ground of Christian discourse is the new reality wrought by God in Jesus Christ, breaking through all human piety, church and morality. Barth frequently calls attention to the discontinuity between what God offers man and what man is even capable of conceiving, but also to a realized

identity between God's work and the human world. He speaks of
a new immediacy between God and man restoring their original
relationship, of a new "organism" effectively functioning in
human history, and of God's Kingdom as the actual fulfilling
content of the ideal empty forms of man's morality. Yet all of
these expressions of God-man unity are requalified in more
dualistic ways. First *Romans* has a kind of split personality,
formed by the tension between Barth's two great working principles: God as the Wholly Other, whom we dare not invoke, and
God as the present Victor, whom we dare not fail to invoke.
Possibly due to the proximity of Blumhardt's influence, the
positive aspect is here more striking and articulate. Consequently we associate in retrospect the "fear of the Lord" more
with second *Romans*, where Barth had much more to say about the
negative aspect, than with the "enthusiastic" first *Romans*.
However, the divine No is fundamental to the first edition just
as the divine Yes is to the second. A look at how Barth presents and qualifies the new organism of God's Kingdom in first
Romans will demonstrate this.

THEMES OF IDENTITY. Barth appears to remain firmly
attached to the Kant-Ritschl-Herrmann line which takes the
moral law to be the presupposition of the meaning of God and
what God does.[47] First *Romans* views God's revelation as the
answer to the moral question presented by the humanly knowable
but merely ideal and unfulfillable moral law. "The truth that
we know and proclaim as idealists is always a demand and a
promise, never a determination and creation, of a life from and
with God."[48] We can describe what is wrong with our life, but
we can never put it right. In some sense we come to genuine
fruitful knowledge of God merely by acknowledging our unhappy
moral consciousness. The standpoint that comes under discussion
in the Bible is not that of idealism, but it is the "filling in
of the empty space that idealism discovered and described."[49]
Barth sees Moses and Plato as representing the question and the
promise, Christ as the answer and fulfillment.[50] Despite the
incommensurability between the question and the answer--the
moral demand is essentially tragic, and therefore the solution
to it is a content that overflows the form, even as the horizon
of God's lordship extends to include the Gentiles as well as

the Jews--the force of the answer is still measured by the pathos of the question.[51]

The "morality" that Barth has in mind in this connection is more than the purely formal categorical imperative, or even the Decalogue: it includes socialism. Among the marks of the bankruptcy of modern Christianity is its insensitivity to the social question, as well as its perplexity over the war.[52] Over against the secular socialists, the church establishment is in the wrong. Not that the socialists are absolutely right; they have been imperfect servants. God may allow the socialism that has become "old and unsure" to leave the world without having brought what the world needed, but God *will* raise up a *socialist* church in a world become socialist.[53] The divine way of thinking is socialistic, not individualistic.[54] One's "deepest essence" is one's membership in the body of Christ, according to which the whole has priority over the members.[55] God brings men together, while "ideas" and religions divide them. However, although our social nature is determined by God, we may not identify God with anything we undertake ourselves to try to express this nature. Barth calls for "strike and general strike and street fighting, if necessary, but without religious justification or glorification"--and for "social democracy, but no religious socialism!"[56] The simultaneous embracing of socialism and rejection of "religious socialism" strikes a contradictory note, which can only be explained by Barth's conviction that God's cause points knowably and definitely in this direction, perhaps not in spite of its transcendence of all human causes but in virtue of that transcendence. That is, God's Word is the supremely critical word *as* a definite concrete social word. This can be acknowledged while the divine Word is at the same time distinguished from human words, including the human words that try to mimic the divine Word.

The problem of our knowledge of God and God's business is taken up by Barth on the model of the form-content duality that marks our moral aspirations. Just as we are already familiar with the good will, albeit only as an unanswerable demand, so, on the basis of an unbroken communion with God, we know about (have *Kenntnis* of) the truth. But *Kenntnis* is not

Erkenntnis; acquaintance with a conception of God is not the same as seeing the invisible nature of God. [57] Normatively and originally, we see as we are seen, living in a relationship of "immediacy" with God. [58] This is lost through sin, and no human effort can retrieve the situation. But in Christ the good will and the truth are again present and active. [59]

What is the nature of our "unbroken communion with God," if such there be? Barth characterizes God repeatedly as the "Origin," the transcendental ground which we presuppose even in our separation from it. [60] We do not have access to it; it gives itself to us in Christ. But even though it is radically non-given and thus "wholly other," it is ultimately thinkable, and in fact must be thought of, as something with which we are united, because our being is impossible without it. As spirit conquers flesh in our redemption, the presupposition of human life is changed; that is, its authentic presupposition comes into its own again, as the History of history, the Life of life. [61] Christians are henceforth only allowed to think according to this presupposition. [62] God's Kingdom, though it is not part of our history, becomes actual and active in our history. [63]

Reunion with the Origin and action from it is not a *mechanical* operation of combining discrete, basically unrelated elements in arbitrary fashion, but an *organic* process in which a single nature expresses itself through subordinate elements which it once again commands. God's cause is advanced by the new "organism," a new "organizing principle," which we join when we obey God. [64] Our relationship with God must be inward and necessary, i.e. organic, because it is a relationship founded on our new *nature* over and above all attitudes, programs, and inner convictions. [65] This nature, given us by God, expresses His will alone. The One is superior to the Many. On such a premise Barth seems committed to a totalitarian or monistic form of argument, in which the Whole is superordinated to the parts, and universalism is opposed to individualism. Barth goes so far as to say: "Let the differences between individuals, times, relations and forms be what they are: the surface of existence. As long as this is only known as difference, it is indeed only the evident nonsense of existence." [66] The history of the meaning of existence can only be written from a standpoint where variety is recognized as the variety of the One. This is the principle of the Old Testament's relevance to us; this is why Abraham concerns us, why Christ concerns us. Our alienation from God, if it were final, would give the right to all scepticism about the truths and values of this world.[67]

Clearly much of what Barth says corresponds to a certain philosophy of being, knowledge, and meaning, compounded principally from Plato and Kant and Hegel; but it is not at all clear that the philosophy, however it limits Barth's vision, constitutes his first commitment. On the contrary, the Bible message as Barth understands it seems to dictate which philosophies are picked up and which dropped in the theological enterprise. Examples may be found in his remarkable polemic against the "soul" [*die Seele*], by which he means individual spiritual existence as religiously or pietistically cultivated. According to Barth, to stand before God as a "soul" is to be against God, for *seelisch* existence is the root of that "boasting" condemned by Paul.[68] It gives the glory to self instead of God and looks inward when it ought to look outward to what God is doing in the world with the social body. To show the alternative to this sinful inversion, Barth employs a number of philosophical assertions: he argues for the priority of being (which is a function of the world) over knowing (which is a function of the isolate subject), and consequently for the priority of encounter (as real engagement with the world) over the "spectator attitude" (as detached contemplation of the world). A similar argument claims the superiority of God's *actual* accomplishment to the mere *possibility* described by idealism, as has been seen. Throughout first *Romans* the real and actual is associated with *world* history and *world* redemption, whereas the ideal and possible is associated with the individual subject, whose plight is tragic. However, this tragedy is superseded (*aufgehoben*) by God's victory, which becomes our new presupposition; therefore our thinking must be obedient to the Whole rather than to the parts, to identity rather than to difference.

THEMES OF DIFFERENCE. Barth takes over from the religious socialists the theme of the enmity between God and "religion." Further implications are drawn out under the

influence of Paul's doctrine of justification, which admits of
no valid distinctions of righteousness among men. For Barth,
this points to an absolute solidarity of all men in sin before
God, and forbids the notion of a saved remnant having nothing
in common with a fallen mass.[69] Within the human realm, everything is "religion," every program of thought and action is
equally futile. The decisive distinction is not between one
human viewpoint and another, but between the human viewpoint
and God's--which sets up the principal dualistic structure in
first *Romans*. The totality of God's world is opposed by an
inferior but still problematic human totality. If religion and
church have any privilege within this human totality, it is only
to the extent that they cry out: more than religion, more than
church![70]

Barth's apparent readiness to speak for God's point of
view, to think organically and positively the way Blumhardt did,
is balanced by a principled reticence. Christ *has* come, but we
are not *yet* wholly delivered from sin. Thus religion may not
point to itself, but only away from itself. We must approach
hungering and thirsting, not with full hands, for there is an
absolute discontinuity between God's world and the human
world.[71] Despite the fact that God is victorious, acknowledges
us as His own, and "has planted a seed in us that must grow,"[72]
the new possibility of life is no continuation or development
of what has been possible hitherto. Considered historically or
psychologically (i.e. humanly), it is not justified or even
interesting.[73] The struggle between the new world and the old
does not take place in the political sphere per se, because
God's revolution is absolute, more radical than Leninism, a
genuinely new creation of society.[74] Barth is capable of saying
that the Gospel tells us "nothing new, but the oldest; nothing
particular, but the most general; nothing historical, but the
presupposition of all history."[75] But this is only to emphasize
the disproportion between God's Idea and human ideas, and also
to prepare for the amazing import of the *revelation* in Jesus
Christ of this "nothing new" precisely as the newest, the most
particular, and the eminently historical event that founds a
new age. Human understanding is inadequate to this revelation.
It is a miraculous event.[76] It is not self-evident or logically

inevitable that the tragic seriousness of our religion and morality will be redeemed by God.[77] An inescapable part of grace, which gives us our new relation to the real, is judgment, which shows this reality as something we live at a disquieting distance from.[78] We may not reckon merely with how things stand absolutely with God vs. the reality of this world. We must reckon with how things stand for God *now*, i.e. as we are on the step-by-step way to the Kingdom of God, engaged in proximal, piecemeal tasks, in which we assume the incompleteness of God's victory.[79]

While Barth often speaks as though we now have God, he also often speaks as though this reunion maintains a unbridgeable divide. The new *Erkenntnis* of God is not "knowledge" as might be possessed by a soul. Everything of this sort (that is *seelisch*) remains doubtful and is superseded.[80] *We "have" God only in hope.* Hope is itself the fulfillment. Our new life is a sowing, not a reaping; a victorious struggle, not a restful peace. We continue to ask, rather than remaining content with any answer.[81]

> This is what we live from--not that we are spirited or spiritual, but that the Spirit is in itself Spirit--not from our deep, refined sighs, not from our need and hope, but from the unexpressed sighing of that by which we are moved, by the need and hope of the truth pressing toward liberation--not from our prayers, but from what drives us to prayer--not from our faith, but from that which moves us to cry: I believe, dear Lord, help Thou my unbelief! . . . God understands our sighing better than we do ourselves, because He hears in it and understands the speech of His own Spirit.[82]

Paradoxically, we "have" God while forswearing all "experience" of Him, because to "have" God is to forswear the mode of individualized existence (*seelisch* existence) that is capable of having knowledge and experience.[83]

Barth's rejection of "experience" is, however, not complete.

> We do not *build* on our experience, if we are conscious of being dead people with regard to sin. For experience (in contrast to hope, 5:5) leads to disgrace. But we are also not *without* experience; for God's Word cannot return to Him empty. We perceive in our lives the traces of our growth in the power of the new world, and these traces confirm. . . that the reality of grace, under which we stand, is in fact a reality, life and not a new idealism.[84]

There is a divine "psychology" of grace.[85] It is not to be confused with any human psychology, but it is a psychology, because it is a reality. The experience of grace is completely unlike experience of anything else; it belongs in a different category.

First *Romans'* main theme of identity--God's world as an all-determining, exclusive *totality*--is, at the same time, a theme of difference, in that God's world is a *new* totality opposed to the human world of sin (from which, humanly speaking, there is no egress). Both of these principles are implicit in Barth's notion of *Aufhebung*, "supersession" or "dissolution."[86] Barth thinks in terms of a dual impossibility: in human terms, God is impossible, His world being "wholly other," but in divine terms sin itself has become impossible, God's victory being irresistible and already accomplished in essence. God does not allow the duality between Himself and man (Christ and Adam) to stand.[87] Double predestination is not a fixed division of history but a "momentary expression of a *movement*, comparable to a bird in flight."[88] Hegelian phraseology lends itself to explicating this triumph of Christ over Adam. The efficacy of the triumph must not obscure the seriousness of the duality that caused the need for such a glorious overcoming.

The concept of *Aufhebung* sums up in a way the message of Barth's first *Romans* as well as its internal contradiction, of which Barth was undoubtedly conscious. We *do* have God (but only in hope); we *belong* to God (but only according to a prom- ise); we *must* speak of God (but it is impossible for man to speak of God). All these negative conditions are made relative to the positive premise. Later, Barth will come to be much more critical of man's ability to claim and respeak the divine Yes in spite of sin.

3. Transition

"We should like to be out of this society--and in another. But this is only a wish; we are still painfully aware that in spite of all the social changes and revolutions, every- thing is as it was of old."[89] In his 1919 Tambach lecture, "The Christian's Place in Society," Barth addresses head-on the ambiguity of the Christian life which first *Romans* had seemed, for the most part, to resolve by force of "enthusiasm."

> We may well remember that according to the gospels the seed is the word and the field is the world, but just what is the word? Which of us has it? May we not well shrink from the task of becoming sowers--from the task which at first brought consternation to men like Moses, Isaiah, and Jeremiah? Is our swift readiness to plant the divine seed in life more fitting than their hesitation to do so?[90]

After the publication of his commentary on Romans, Barth was subject to a variety of influences--Paul himself, Overbeck, Dostoyevsky, Kierkegaard, Gogarten, Grünewald, and Plato and Kant (in Heinrich Barth's interpretation)--which fortified his concern with the more critically extreme implications of the divine transcendence attested in the Bible. No doubt it would be inaccurate to say that an abstract "Idea of the Other" worked on Barth, changing his mind over the interval between first and second *Romans*; but it cannot be denied that his second thoughts as to whether first *Romans* had really begun from a fear of the Lord ranged themselves more and more around an interest in confronting the issue of the absolute Otherness of God.

A major change in methodology is suggested by Barth's characterization of the Tambach lecture as "a rather complicated kind of machine that runs backwards and forwards and shoots in all directions with no lack of both visible and hidden joints."[91] Such a "mechanical" picture of theological discourse contrasts pointedly with the "organic" power which Barth had appreciated in Blumhardt and which had contributed heavily to the positive approach of first *Romans*. Actually, on the organic standard any formal theology can only amount to a "complicated machine" doomed to failure.[92] Does a more resolute acceptance of Otherness, the ground on which we do *not* stand, entail a new priority for the "mechanics" of the discipline of theology? Looking ahead to second *Romans*, we see here an anticipation of "dialectical" method, predicated above all on the impossibility of speaking of God. It is more a reflection on, and less an emulation of, a witness like Blumhardt's. The pivotal Tambach lecture attempts to keep clearly in sight both the "great promise, a light from above which is shed upon our situation," and the "unhappy separation, a thorough-going opposition between two dissimilar magnitudes."[93]

If the Tambach lecture is more critical than first
Romans, it nevertheless continues to assume that the dualism
of God and man is superseded by God's victory. God is still
the Origin; His judgment does not annihilate us, it establishes
us. The Origin is the Archimedean point from which everything
is moved. While it is extremely dangerous to assume that we
have located this point and may speak of it--are we speaking
instead of another false transcendence?--yet God does not allow
us to take this "evil possibility" too seriously. After all:
"We *are* moved by God. We do know God. Divine history happens
in us and to us."[94] The Origin is the ground of both thesis
(the given reality) and antithesis (the protest on behalf of
what ought to be): therefore we are only entitled to protest
against the state of this world if we first affirm it as it is.
Barth, always a great respecter of actuality as a positive
critical principle, insists that we accept the world "as it is
given us and not as we dream it to be--and ask ourselves about
its relation to God."[95] In this sense, Barth can even accept
what Hegel says about the rationality of all that is real. It
is necessary to dwell on this to avoid the error, "made by some
Russian and many Oriental thinkers," of allowing the denial of
life to become the main object of interest.[96] While the Yes of
the thesis is overshadowed for us by the No of the antithesis,
the divine judgment going against our world as it is, neither
our Yes nor our No, "neither our rest nor our unrest in the
world, necessary though both of them be, can be final."[97] The
final word rests with God and is not humanly pronounceable.
Barth ends by emphasizing the transcendence of the synthesis:

> If I understand what the German theologian meant who
> during the war made the discovery that instead of saying
> The Life Beyond it would be better to say The Life Within,
> I can only trust that his dictum, more serpent-wise than
> dove-harmless, will not establish a school. No, no--we
> answer--begone from us, you psychics, with your Within!
> *Apage Satanas*! Beyond, *trans*: *that* is the crux of the
> situation, that is the source of our life. Our little
> within belongs to the realm of analogies, and it is from
> beyond that realm that we draw our life.[98]

In a 1920 lecture on "Biblical Questions, Insights, and
Vistas," Barth speaks extensively of the Wholly Other, shifting
the emphasis from resurrection to crucifixion.

> The only source for the real, the immediate, revelation
> of God is *death*. Christ unlocked its gates. He brought
> *life* to light out of *death*.
>   Out of *death*! The word cannot be spoken significantly
> enough. The meaning of God, the power of God, begins to
> shine upon the men of the Bible at the boundary of mortal-
> ity. . . The human correlate to the divine aliveness is
> neither virtue, nor inspiration, nor love, but the fear of
> the Lord, mortal fear, the last, absolute, perfect fear.[99]

Barth was learning from his brother Heinrich to understand
Socrates from the perspective of his "wisdom of death," and
Plato and Kant as philosophers of limits.[100] Reading
Dostoyevsky with Thurneysen, he saw God set up as the question-
mark against the totality of human existence, its problematic
but secretly redeeming boundary.[101] From Overbeck he learned
just how questionable even the most well-meaning theological
utterances are; Overbeck was responsible for an "inconceivably
impressive sharpening of the commandment 'Thou shalt not take
the name of the Lord thy God in vain',"[102] and for a strong
witness to the need for an eschatological transformation of
Christian theology.[103] Re-reading Kierkegaard, Barth was
impressed by his battle for the "infinite qualitative difference" between God and man.[104] The program of second *Romans* is
already announced in the "Biblical Questions" lecture:

> *The affirmation of God, man, and the world given in the*
> *New Testament is based exclusively upon the possibility of*
> *a new order absolutely beyond human thought; and therefore,*
> *as prerequisite to that order, there must come a crisis*
> *that denies all human thought.*
>   To understand the New Testament Yes as anything but the
> Yes contained in the No, is not to understand it at all.[105]
>
> *Qualiter? Totaliter aliter!* "That which is born of
> the flesh is flesh; and that which is born of the spirit is
> spirit." There are no transitions, intermixings, or inter-
> mediate stages. There is only crisis, finality, new
> insight. What the Bible brings us from beyond the grave is
> the perfect, the absolute miracle.[106]

Into this evolution of Barth's reflections there
intruded a decisive event, a turning point. Friedrich Gogarten
visited at Safenwil in October, 1920, he and Barth having "so
many good conversations by day and night."[107] After Gogarten
left, Barth suddenly realized that *Romans* could not be reissued
without fundamental changes. He began to write a completely
new version.

4. The Absolute Difference

"*We have the Spirit. . . we* means 'not we,' and *have* means 'not have.'"[108] Barth delivered this message in both first and second *Romans*, and both books can be fairly inter-preted as attempts to unravel its implications. Why then are they so dissimilar? How could Barth have travelled such a distance while holding to the same premise? Formerly Barth believed that we ought not to be ultimately preoccupied with the possibility that all our talk of God is only talk of a false transcendence. Because of what God has done in Christ, we know that we have this one Christian warrant for talk about God; *not* to talk from this warrant is to be disobedient to the revela-tion. By second *Romans*, Barth has come to believe that all men *are* liars, that their talk of God *does* miss its object, and that *true knowledge of God is not that knowledge which claims to supersede God's entire Otherness, but that knowledge which recognizes God as Wholly Other.*[109] As in the first edition, Barth wishes to emphasize the transcendence of the new man in Christ, in faith, over the old man--and the recaptured immediacy of the new man with his divine Origin. But one is no longer able to assume that one *is* this new man, for one has no capacity to talk directly about the new man's experience.[110] One may only speak on the presupposition, with the drastic limitations that go with it, that one is still entirely the old man, sun-dered from God. *None is righteous, no, not one; no one under-stands, no one seeks for God* (Romans 3:10-11). The Christian theologian does not exempt himself from this charge. He admits it. That is Christian theology.

THE ORIGIN. The neo-Kantian concept of the transcen-dental Origin is still applied to God in second *Romans*.[111] On this ontological premise Barth is able to speak, though not without paradox, of the genuinely autonomous recognition of absolute heteronomy, and of man's sinful rebellion as being against not what is ultimately strange but what is intimately man's own (Romans 1:19-21): "Disloyalty to Him is disloyalty to ourselves."[112] To this extent, knowledge of ourselves is knowledge of God, even if proceeding from the former to the latter can only yield a negative, critical judgment. God as the Other is by no means *an* "other," "no second, other Stranger,

side by side with those whose existence is independent of Him.
On the contrary, He is the eternal pure Origin of all things.
As their non-existence, He is their true being."[113] Because
God is superior to any merely formal pluralism that would
oppose Him to man, there remains an unbroken and indestructible
relation between God and man.[114] The One still controls the
Many. Commenting on Romans 12:17, Barth corrects Kierkegaardian
individualism with Kantian universalism in ethics by appealing
to this principle.

> The action which is properly ethical must not be direct-
> ed toward some hidden or secret happiness or unhappiness.
> Though the behavior of a given individual--for example, the
> work of an apostle (1:1)--may fail to be co-ordinated with
> the concrete behavior of human society, it must, neverthe-
> less, be co-ordinated with the truth by which human society
> is in fact constituted. That is to say, behind the apparent
> disharmony of the prophet and his environment there must
> exist a real and final harmony. We are justified in our
> refusal to submit ourselves to the judgment of the "Many,"
> but not for one moment dare we refuse to accept the judgment
> of the "All."[115]

A passage like this prolongs the totalitarian argument of first
Romans, in which the presupposition of the "One" seems to deny
the intelligibility or ultimate significance of plurality. But
plurality does turn out to be ultimately significant in second
Romans, because we only truly know the One when we know Him as
the Wholly Other than ourselves. The "One" is ground we most
certainly do not and never will occupy, according to our observable potential. It is not in our alienation from God that we
view Him as the Wholly Other: it is only in overcoming our
alienation from God that we so recognize Him. God's "Otherness" means His revelation. "In His utter strangeness God wills
to make Himself known to all of us. . . the predicate, *Deus
revelatus*, has as its subject *Deus absconditus*."[116] The significance of this revelation is that it corrects our chronic
delusion, which is at the same time our real and serious alienation from God, that God is *not* Other, that we have something
in common with Him that would be a warrant for valid, substantial talk about His nature or will. God has offered us a union
of divine and human love in Jesus Christ--"But when this is
said, we turn ourselves about, knowing that we are in no sense
competent to attain this identity or even to conceive of its
attainment."[117]

The pathos of man's separation from God is transferred to his loss of the realization of the infinite qualitative distinction, the "saving separation," between himself and God.[118] "Once the eye, which can perceive this distinction, has been blinded, there arises. . . between us and the 'Wholly Other,' a mist or concoction of religion,"[119] i.e. a false claim of continuity with God. When Paul asserts that faith upholds the law (3:31), Barth's interpretation is that the vast distinction between God and man "is their veritable union. . . in the veritable transcendence of the judgment and righteousness of God lies His most genuine immanence."[120] In newness of the Spirit there is no longer "any 'otherness' or opposition between God and men"[121]--but the man who recognizes himself as "flesh," thus as something wholly corruptible to be made into something wholly different, can aspire to speak of no other "union" than the union-in-disunion claimed by Barth. Man must love God *as* his judge, as the *deus absconditus* whose hiddenness is now not the same thing as His wrath. He will "recognize" God (in faith) in the divine incognito.[122]

THE OPEN QUESTION. First *Romans* interpreted the "grace" or "spiritual gift" of 1:11-12 as the active, creative inpouring of the divine into human history, which was the necessary condition of the intelligibility and force of the apostle's message.[123] But second *Romans* says: "The importance of an apostle is negative rather than positive. In him a void becomes visible."[124] This example shows how the identification of God as the Other leads to the conversion of positive premises to negative ones. A feature of the same movement is the replacement of the conception of God's revelation as the *answer* to the problem posed by religion and morality with a conception of revelation as the question, riddle, puzzle, or problem superior to all answers.

"The Gospel is not a truth among other truths. Rather, it sets a question-mark against all truths."[125] "As surely as no one is removed from the universal questionableness of human life, so surely is no one excluded from the divine contradiction that is in Christ, by which this questionableness seeks to make itself known to men."[126] "Thou failest to perceive that even now a question is being asked of thee to which thou canst give no answer."[127] "Religion possesses no solution of the problem of life; rather it makes of the problem a wholly insoluble enigma. Religion neither discovers the problem nor solves it: what it does is to disclose the truth that it cannot be solved."[128] God is the imponderable boundary of our existence who, as such, determines its meaning. The determination lies wholly beyond our grasp and can only appear to us as a question or seeming impossibility of justification. Overbeck's influence is discernible in the atmosphere of a comprehensive questionableness of human life in relation to an invisible point of reference, not so much in death as beyond death.[129] The meaning of the story depends on its ending, but between ourselves and the end of our story lies the opaque curtain of death.

RELIGION. I know myself to be entirely the old man, my judgments entirely those of the old man upon himself. I have a new identity in Christ lying beyond this world and the things of this world (church, culture, theology, "religion"), but only as a mysterious possibility which I do not "have" at all.[130] Therefore I do not transcend the things of this world in my relationship with God; God is in heaven and I am on earth. There can be no triumphal surpassing of "religion" (as was claimed in the first edition) for me. I must continue to acknowledge religion as the most serious possibility with which I have to reckon in this world.

> Moving within the sphere of human activity, religion is without doubt *holy*, because it points from humanity to divinity; it is without doubt *righteous*, because it is correlated with the will of God and parallel to it, being indeed the parable of it; and it is without doubt *good*, for it is that concrete, observable, mediated experience which bears witness to the immediacy which has been lost. Should we remove ourselves consciously or unconsciously from the dangerous ambiguity of religion, either we must take refuge in some other less exalted human possibility-- in some possibility that is ethical or logical or aesthetic or even lower; or we must side-step into some ancient or modern variety of religion; and, if we are not fully aware of the ambiguity of all religion, to do so will mean inevitably that the alternative variety we have selected will be a bad one. There is no human advance beyond the possibility of religion. . .[131]

Here Barth transposes the religious socialist theme of the reprobation of established church religion. The opposition is

not between God and religion, but between the religion of disturbance, tension, and critique, and the religion of comfort,
consolation, and self-satisfaction. Barth is now willing to
portray the great protesters Job, Paul, Luther, and Kierkegaard
as exemplars of the first sort of religion rather than (as in
"Religion und Leben") as exemplars of something better than
religion.[132] They do witness to something beyond religion, but
in the full realization that they remain this side of the
divine-human divide. Therein lies the profundity of their witness, which Barth attempts to match in his rethinking of Romans.

Barth's reasoning about the nature and status of "religion" is full of portent for his own future development, since
the same arguments apply to "theology." "The fatal prattle of
systematic theology, which we are bound to employ in speaking
about God, if we are not to become superficial and undisci-
plined, is a parable of the indivisible unity of the Truth."[133]

> [On "Perhaps there is one that teacheth," 12:7]--Can
> theology be a science? (!) . . . Kierkegaard has to say--
> "To be a Professor of Theology is to have crucified Christ."
> We know that Overbeck pronounced Theologians to be the
> "Blockheads of human society." No, the Word of God cannot
> be--taught! But once again we say: *Perhaps*. In spite of
> all this abuse, the longing for Theology still remains,
> precisely because of the mark of exclamation, which is the
> exclamation mark of resurrection. Omit the exclamation
> mark, and Christianity is betrayed not only by our speech,
> but also--which Overbeck forgets--by our silence.[134]

We find a rather startling prescription of what Barth later
called "theological existence" when he writes that theology
"can be not merely an ethical possibility, but the only ethical
possibility."[135] Paul's letter to the Romans is--theology.[136]
Barth himself is--a theologian.[137] The whole problem of second
Romans is theology. Barth tacitly rejects as inappropriate his
own past adulation of "organic" thinking--truly *sachlich*
thinking does not try to achieve some "divine simplicity"
(which is beyond its grasp) but reflects the dire complications
of the actual human condition.[138] Neither Blumhardt's Yes nor
Overbeck's No is possible any longer without qualification. In
between these two lies the realm of theology, where we attempt
to dialectically qualify the Yes and the No with each other.[139]

TOWARD PLURALISM. Theological discourse must conform
itself to the separation between God and man, which involves

more than announcing pluralism as a bare doctrine. The theological assertion of "pluralism" would be as false as the
assertion of identity, because all theology is, before God, a
lie. The pluralism that is operative here must be something
that possesses theology rather than a possession of theology,
i.e. an exigency or warning under which theology, as a questionable human effort, must labor. The divine No underlying pluralism is not a No that can be respoken by theology; it is a No
spoken *to* theology. Pluralism is thus a *project* for theology
of critical self-effacement before this No. The true radicalism
of second *Romans* lies in its willingness to undertake the project, beyond the bare assertion of the doctrine. A variety of
gaps and scars appear in the theological landscape, in which
the outworking of the pluralistic project may be traced. "The
road is most strangely defined almost entirely in negatives:
but it.is named the 'incomprehensible way of love' (I Corinthians
12:31). Can this rightly be named a road? It is no road--
which we can observe or investigate or even enter upon. We can
only pass along it."[140]

The *via negativa* generates a distinctive geometry of
the relation between time and eternity, earth and heaven, man
and God. The divine plane intersects the human plane from
above, in Jesus. But "the point on the line of intersection is
no more extended onto the known plane than is the unknown plane
of which it proclaims the existence."[141] The intersection
itself is invisible; what we do see is like the crater left by
an exploding shell, or a void where we would expect substance.[142]
This is the witness of the church, the negative apostolic work
pointing toward the invisible. Human conduct, especially when
it is disturbed and bent out of line, is a parable of the
eternal.[143] God wills to place us in a "new and true set of
co-ordinates" in which "God and man are drawn apart in order
that men may be drawn together in His presence."[144]

It is indeed a difficult program to get rid of "every
non-radical idea of transcendence."[145] Only by the extremest
radicalism, by a negation of man's negations as well as his
affirmations, may the pitfall of Gnostic dualism be avoided.[146]
The death of Christ "is not grace so long as it is a merely
relative negation; that is, so long as the attack upon the man

of this world peters out in mere criticism of, or opposition to, this or that concrete thing."[147] The death of Christ represents a silencing of man, which theology expresses by negating various aspects of the human frame of reference.

God is wholly other than the *human*; not merely other than this or that human possibility, but other than all human possibility; not merely other than life or death, but other than "existence." The man who apprehends the meaning of the gospel "is removed from all strife, because he is engaged in a strife with the whole, even with existence itself."[148] Thus Barth's talk of the "death-line" (*Todeslinie*)[149] refers to a problem more basic than human mortality.

God is other than the *temporal* or *historical*. History is not and cannot be its own judge. God's judgment does away with history, rather than altering it or prolonging it.[150] Barth repudiates his former claim that the divine seed is planted and must grow in human history:

> No doubt human love of God, the ordination of men to Sonship, and their calling to be witnesses of the Resurrection, are genuine occurrences, consequent upon God's knowledge of men and taking place in the knowledge of the true and only God. But this must not be taken to mean that His love has brought into being a particular temporal human being and having and doing, which is the result of a divine causation which took place concretely as the first of a series of temporal occurrences. Predestination means the recognition that love towards God is an occurrence, a being and having and doing of men, which takes place in no moment of time, which is beyond time, which has its origin at every moment in God Himself, and which must therefore be sought and found only in Him.[151]

The relevance, for faith, of an Abraham or Jesus is strictly supratemporal. Faith occurs in the "Moment," outside time,[152] in which all faith partakes of a simultaneity that is impossible within the historical order. The historical Abraham (or Jesus) is, as such, of no interest to faith.[153] But in the "Moment" eternity touches time along that undimensional line, and the believer's faith is contemporaneous with Abraham's.

God is wholly other than all human *experience* or possible objects thereof. That is, God's historical-objective inaccessibility is matched by His psychological-subjective inaccessibility. The "Moment" has no psychological content.[154] God is likewise other than the religion that would be a function of human experience. Gone are Schleiermacher's *Anschauung*, *Gefühl*, and *Einfühlung*. Along these lines, Barth now draws his basic diagnosis of the modern neo-Protestant theological situation, and his basic opposition to Schleiermacher. "[N]othing is so meaningless as the attempt to construct a religion out of the Gospel, and to set it up as one human possibility in the midst of others. Since Schleiermacher, this attempt has been undertaken more consciously than ever before in Protestant theology--and it is the betrayal of Christ."[155] Our encounter with God must not be romanticized into an "experience." What is it, if not an experience? An "open space, a sign-post, an occasion, and an opportunity," a question rather than an answer.[156] The great human desire to stabilize and possess revelation by setting up a religion of it or claiming an experience of it is futile, for the crater where the bomb once exploded has burned out, and the canal through which the water once flowed is now dry.[157] Does not religion "recognize that the place where God wills to reveal Himself cannot be identified with its own concrete and visible possessions, but is incomprehensibly more comprehensive?"[158] In this fashion Barth begins to articulate, not only his own opposition to Schleiermacher, but his own version of the Protestant corrective to Catholicism (where priority is given to the church's "concrete and visible possession" of grace and its own tradition) and the Calvinist corrective to Lutheranism (where priority is given to the believer's inward possession of Christ in faith).

God is wholly other than any possible *concept* we might have of Him. The God to which our concepts are adequate is the no-God of this world. Must this not involve us in serious difficulties, since concepts are our only means of thought?

> Explosions are the inevitable consequence of our bringing infinity within the range of concepts fitted only for the apprehension of what is finite. For, in so far as we admit infinity as a concept, that is to say, in so far as we make it observable to ourselves as infinity, since we are unable to rid it of its characteristic "otherness" in relation to what is finite, our concept of eternity emerges as an *almost* infinitely finite thing! But such an observed notion of infinity is in no way infinity itself; for when our notions are related to the Source of all that is ours, they are shown to be things that have been dissolved [*aufgehoben*].[159]

We see in this passage that at least one concept, the idea of
infinity, bears a significant relationship to God, even if God
never is captured in our employment of it. The idea of infinity
has this special status because it undoes itself, constantly
eluding our powers of conceptualization. Barth also assigns a
positive role to that philosophy which, conscious of its limits,
points away from itself toward that which exceeds it. He finds
such philosophy in Plato and Kant, a "genuinely critical rationalism";[160] for the infinite qualitative distinction between God
and man is the essence of philosophy as well as the theme of
the Bible.[161]

If something, this much, may truly be said of God, it
nevertheless may not be directly communicated in the normal way.
For the one true thing man can say is the paradox that he is a
liar. Hence: "The Church--if it be aware of itself and is
serious--sets fire to a charge which blows up every sacred edi-
fice which men have ever erected or can ever erect in its
vicinity."[162] In other words, theology must be dialectical.
Theology must lose any ambition to "succeed" in its "purpose,"
being instead content to swing like a pendulum in obedience to
the free act of God which dissolves all concrete positions
assumed by man.[163] Knowledge of the invisible is always dialectical, and we must never allow our dialectical presuppositions themselves to harden into theses.[164] This can happen if
we take the pendulum metaphor too seriously and imagine a purely
formal opposition between a qualitatively similar thesis and
antithesis.[165] We must forget neither the infinite difference,
nor that there is a synthesis of the opposed factors. The synthesis is not in our hands, but we are not allowed to retreat
into the "quiet and secluded nook of pietistic dialectic" which
takes the mere fact of conflict with sin as direct evidence of
salvation.[166] "Divinely simple" thought is ruled out.

> Only dialectical human thinking can fulfill its purpose
> and search out the depth and context and reality of life:
> only dialectical thought can lead to genuine reflection upon
> its meaning and make sense of it. For when our thought
> moves onwards direct and unbroken, when it is comprehensive,
> it is quite certain that we are not thinking about life; we
> are not thinking, that is to say, about the *Krisis* in which
> human life is in fact being lived.[167]

Theological dialectic is required by the dialectical character
of the *Sache* itself (the Yes of grace united with the No of
judgment in God's revelation). Second *Romans* seems to offer a
static, dualistic "Kierkegaardian" dialectic where first *Romans*
offered a dynamic, tripolar "Hegelian" dialectic. But this
contrast is misleading, since it suggests that a synthesis is
lacking in the former case--whereas God does victoriously rule
over the thesis and the antithesis, even in second *Romans*--and
that the synthesis is logically necessary in the latter case--
whereas God's victory in first *Romans* is "neither a necessary
truth of reason nor an accidental truth of history,"[168] and
Barth bases his dialectic on a *realist* ontology.[169] The more
"Hegelian" language of first *Romans* speaks of God's *victory*.
The more dualistic language of second *Romans* speaks of *God's*
victory.

Barth exercises the critique of the "other than. . ."
so far as to reverse himself on one of the main arguments of
the first edition regarding the social nature of man. Not only
is God other than *socialism*, as one among other concrete human
possibilities,[170] but the divinely justified new man is other
than the social body on which Barth earlier took his stand
against religious individualism. "God does not delegate His
claim upon men to any directly observable human formation, however spiritual. They encounter Him in their own particular,
individual tribulation and hope, and not through some notion of
the 'whole'."[171] Barth was never an individualist in Kierkegaard's sense, but he does lean toward Kierkegaard at this
point in order to criticize his former anti-individualist ex-
cesses. God is, of course, also wholly other than what Kierkegaard says about Him! Barth detects in Kierkegaard "the poison
of a too intense pietism," in Dostoyevsky "a hysterical world-fa-
tigue," and in the Blumhardts "a far too easy complacency."[172]
Overbeck, we have already seen, is criticized for his theological silence. Barth clearly believes that his hermeneutical
commitments, other than the central one to the Bible, are relative and dispensable.

ETHICS. Is the Wholly Other of Barth's second *Romans*
"other than" the Kant-Ritschl-Herrmann presupposition that the

moral problematic determines the meaning of religion? Or is this feature held over from the first edition?

On the one hand, Barth does continue to make very strong statements concerning the link between morality and religion. It is the problem of ethics which forces upon our attention "the great disturbance," "the Truth of God, which is never actually present or actually apprehended in our act of thinking, however sublime."[173] The problems of daily life bind us in a way that abstract thinking never does. We are not truly disturbed until we are practically disturbed. Ethical decisions determine whether "the impossible possibility of God. . . is not a mere phantom of metaphysics; whether, when we speak of the pre-supposition behind all things that are capable of analysis and description, when we speak of the outpouring of the Spirit in our hearts, we are or are not merely dreaming."[174] The whole riddle of existence is summed up by the "otherness" of my fellow man in a way that requires a solution in action. "God and man are drawn apart *in order that* men may be drawn together in His presence"[175]--might this not mean that the moral problem is, more than a reminder, the true rationale of the "infinite qualitative difference" and the revelation of God as Wholly Other? "[I]t is the lack of the glory of God which creates fellowship and solidarity among men."[176]

On the other hand, it is worth noting that Barth had dropped the idea of a divine content correlated with a moral form--the new life offered in Christ correlated with the unfulfillable, but knowable, moral law. Instead Barth points to a correlation of problem with problem: my encounter with God and my encounter with my neighbor. Furthermore, the ethical problem is not formulated in the idealist terms of the moral law, but in the concrete, contingent terms of the encounters of everyday life.[177] The newspaper, instead of Kant's *Critique of Practical Reason*, is the Bible's counterpart, in the spirit of his preaching and his confirmation address "Religion und Leben." Real life remains the eminent exception to his rule against the formula "religion and. . .," and "life" is, without doubt, conceived by Barth as a moral problem.[178]

The close connection between Barth's notions of God and of the problem of moral existence, in both editions of *Romans*, invites us to ask how much a theology of Otherness owes to the ethical inspiration of Kant or Herrmann or the religious socialists, rather than immediately to the Bible. Barth's theological seriousness is certainly ethical in tone. The failure of liberal theology in the war was, in Barth's eyes, above all an ethical failure.[179] There may also be a strong logical affinity between the gospel of the *deus absconditus* and that province of philosophical thinking most nearly ruled by an insoluble problem (the problem of my relation with the other person, transcending all problems of knowledge and taste). In this period, when Barth still considers himself free to appeal to "the essence of philosophy," he may wish to prevent any separation of the problem of God from the problem of existence, even if a free interplay between biblical and philosophical assertions be the means of union. But as long as Barth proceeds in this fashion the question can at least be asked whether the moral concern with the other person (in socialism, for example) motivates the conception of the Wholly Other, or whether God as the Wholly Other grounds the significance for faith of the otherness of the neighbor. Barth's explicit treatment of these themes in his later ethics lectures and the *Church Dogmatics* shows that he recognized this ambiguity and thought it needed resolving.[180]

5. Interpreting the Wholly Other

The relation between thought and action depicted by Barth in second *Romans*--according to which action has the greater critical significance, since practical problems remind us, in a way pure thinking never does, of God, the Problem of problems--may be the very type of the relation between theological *doctrine* and theological *comportment* which is maintained by second *Romans* and constitutes the true Copernican revolution of its argument. For Barth's argument is not that God *is* the Wholly Other. Such a statement, like any other direct theological predication, cannot stand before God. Barth's point is that *we* must speak of God *as* the Wholly Other because of the actual position in which we find ourselves, in the light of revelation. Not only do our thematic propositions fail to express God's nature; the very attempt to do so proceeds from

an illegitimate aspiration. Strict limitations are placed on
the theoretical dimension of our approach to God, which have
ultimately not a theoretical but a practical warrant, i.e. a
warrant in the inescapable problem of comportment toward an
Other who makes it impossible for any of us to justify ourselves. Barth's standpoint is more profoundly Kantian in this
respect than in any other, perhaps even more Kantian than Kant--
for, whereas Kant offered the doctrine of the primacy of practical reason, Barth presupposes and theologically *enacts* the
primacy of practical reason.[181] Barth's constant preoccupation
with the question "What ought we to do?" need not mean that the
strictly human moral problem was always uppermost in Barth's
mind. It can be explained by the fact that Barth's problem was
practical (though with reference to God!) rather than theoretical in nature.

If we are to stress the practical motivation of Barth's
theology, what then shall we make of the logic of the transcendental Origin, which Barth seems to adopt as a fundamental
epistemological premise determining everything else in the book?
The truth is that this epistemology is likewise determined by
the practical reality, and is often expressed in revealingly
practical ways.

> The truth concerning the limiting and dissolving of men
> by the unknown God, which breaks forth in the resurrection,
> is a known truth: this is the tragic factor in the story
> of the passion of the truth. When our limitation is appre-
> hended, and when He is perceived who, in bounding us, is
> also the dissolution of our limitation, the most primitive
> as well as the most highly developed forms of human self-
> consciousness become repeatedly involved in a "despairing
> humiliation," in the *Selbstironisierung der Vernunft* (H.
> Cohen). We know that God is He whom we do not know, and
> that our ignorance is precisely the problem and source of
> our knowledge.[182]

Barth's epistemology of ignorance suspends the normal epistemological rules by accounting this ignorance a fruitful problem
instead of a privation and dead end. The *Selbstironisierung* of
reason is the one appropriate way for reason to behave in face
of the righteous God. Furthermore, Barth's discussion of the
problem of ethics implies that pure reason, as pure thought, is
incapable of radically "ironizing" itself, that this is only
accomplished in the practical encounter.

Had the "Wholly Other" been a doctrine of God, rather than a device for placing theology in the right position before God, Barth could not have looked back on his *Romans* more than thirty years later with so much approval.

> Were we right or wrong? We were certainly right! Let one read also the dogmatics of Lüdemann, in its way so solid, or even that of Seeberg! If all that wasn't a blind alley! Beyond doubt what was then in order was not some kind of further shifting around within the complex of inherited questions. . . but rather a change of direction. The ship was threatening to run aground; the moment was at hand to turn the rudder an angle of exactly 180 degrees.[183]

Barth came to dissociate himself almost entirely from talk of the Wholly Other, but he never dissociated himself from the function that this talk served in its place in the theological discussion. He does not say that the concept of the Wholly Other presented a true picture of God for its time, but that the concept of the Wholly Other changed the *attitude* of theology right about.

Another indication of the relativity of the concept of the Wholly Other, indeed of the entire apparatus--that "strange incrustation of Kantian-Platonic conceptions,"[184] not to mention Kierkegaard's "Moment" and "Paradox" and Overbeck's much-modified *Urgeschichte*, which so sharply distinguished second from first *Romans*--is precisely the fact that Barth could write the second book within three years of the first, in the conviction that he was attempting to say the same thing better. Not only must first *Romans* be evaluated as an anticipation of second *Romans*, but second *Romans* must be seen as an extension of the earlier work, where "new advance positions" are occupied in a single offensive.[185] The common message is of the God who wills to make Himself known and to be known in no other way, of the God who is righteous and thus can have nothing in common with our sinful world, and of the God who triumphs over our sin by offering us a completely new life.[186]

These clarifications must be remembered in order to avoid making two fundamental mistakes in interpreting and criticizing Barth.

The first mistake consists in viewing Barth as a proponent of a doctrine of God as the Wholly Other. This view, if true, would render Barth vulnerable to the charge of logical

incoherence, since a *wholly* "Wholly Other" cannot be spoken of
with even minimal, negative, critical intelligibility. The Wholly
Other would slip past us like a ship in the night. Such a thing
as an absolute paradox cannot appear in human speech or thought,
and would in any event be absolutely irrelevant to us. If the
Wholly Other were a doctrine of God, Barth would agree with these
objections. He found the concept unserviceable to the extent
that it did unavoidably imply a (false) doctrine of God. But
theological discourse is *dangerous* (strange condition, if "logical" or "epistemological"!).[187] At this point Barth would
rather expose himself to the objections than join the objectors.

A second, related mistake would consist in viewing
Barth's theology as a philosophy in disguise, as a preoccupation
with the abstract transcendence beyond man's power of knowing,
or with the logically sublime negation of negation which, in
spite of its own denials, represents the highest stage of human
dialectics. On this view the dialectic as such would be the
true object of interest. Here we face a complex question, for
while it is amply evident in the context of his other work that
Barth's primary allegiance is to biblical revelation, he relies
on philosophical elements to shape and validate his argument
in second *Romans*. Much might be made in this connection of
Barth's avowal in the preface that his "system" consists of
recognizing what Kierkegaard called the infinite qualitative
distinction between time and eternity.

> "God is in heaven, and thou art on earth." The relation
> between such a God and such a man. . . is for me the theme
> of the Bible and the essence of philosophy. Philosophers
> name this *Krisis* of human perception--the Prime Cause: the
> Bible beholds at the same cross-roads--the figure of Jesus
> Christ. When I am faced by such a document as the Epistle
> of Paul to the Romans, I embark on its interpretation on
> the assumption that he is confronted with the same unmis-
> takeable and unmeasurable significance of that relation as
> I myself am confronted with, and that it is this situation
> which molds his thought and its expression.[188]

Perhaps as long as it is only a question of changing course 180
degrees, the theme of the Bible and the essence of (critical)
philosophy do coincide. That there is more to theology than
this is borne out by Barth's later development, and even by
second *Romans* so far as it dares to speak of the divine forgive-
ness lying on the far side of the critical negation. It does

prove at any rate to be the philosophy and not the theology that
is relative and auxiliary for Barth.

The extensive assemblage of philosophical arguments and
moods culled from Kierkegaard, Dostoyevsky, Overbeck, Nietzsche,
Plato, and Kant really forms only the background of second
Romans. It explains many points concerning the particular way
second *Romans* was written, but does not give the book its reason for being. The one truly determinative element in the book
that is not "biblical" in any obvious sense is the idea of the
Wholly Other, which does not come from Kierkegaard (though it
fits Kierkegaard's dualism of time and eternity) or Overbeck
(though it fits his somewhat ironic dichotomy between history
and eschatological Christianity). "Wholly Other" as a *name* of
God was probably suggested by Rudolf Otto's *Idea of the Holy*,
which Barth read in June, 1919, finding in it "ultimate insights"
and the possibility of "a basic surmounting of Ritschlianism"
despite its unfortunate psychologizing orientation.[189] Otto,
however, cannot be said to have seriously influenced Barth
beyond suggesting to him the possibility of systematically
arguing from this category.[190] The "Wholly Other" assumes a
unique character as it is mobilized by Barth in his work of
interpreting Paul. What Barth means by it is not readily separable from what he thinks Paul really means. Therefore if
Barth operates with a "philosophy" of the Wholly Other, it is a
philosophy that presupposes an encounter with what Paul encountered. Such a philosophy would not have a warrant distinguishable from theology's warrant, and thus would not be distinguishable from theology in the sense presupposed by the criticism
that Barth's theology was "only" a philosophy, or a philosophy
in disguise.[191]

According to Thurneysen, Barth has always been primarily occupied with the Bible, as its expositor.

> The tablets of Holy Scripture are erected before him
> and the books of the expositors from Calvin through the
> biblicists and all the way to the modern critical biblical
> interpretation lie open in his hands. Both then and now
> this has been the source from which his whole theology has
> come. . . Barth is no abstract thinker. . . and abstract
> here would mean liberated from the Scriptures. He does not
> project theological speculations out of his own mind; he is
> not concerned about a system; he is and remains a student

and teacher of the Holy Scriptures. Whoever tries to understand him as other than this will not understand him at all.[192]

Can Thurneysen's claim that Barth has never had a system be taken seriously, in view of the fact that Barth proclaims a "system" in his preface to second *Romans*? Only, it would seem, if there were something peculiarly anti-systematic about this "system" borrowed from Kierkegaard and all the other protesters--if this bombshell[193] had a liberating power to make room for something else. If Thurneysen is right, the "something else" is the Word of God in Holy Scripture, and we will not have understood Barth until we have witnessed the appearance of that for which room has been made with the exploding concept of the Wholly Other. But this means we must follow Barth on to the task of dogmatics.

Meanwhile, what can be said about the overall development of Barth's theology from 1909 to 1922?

For the early Barth, the religious experience of the individual was the given. It was not the possibility of the experience, it was the possibility of explicating that experience in objective, normative, theological fashion that was questionable and problematic. The fact that Barth himself did not have this experience, or at least did not have it to such a compelling extent as would have riveted his attention on the problem of correctly describing it, was an incidental irony that helps to explain Barth's readiness to disavow his Marburg background, as well as his attack, from first *Romans* onwards, on any "experience" as the proprium of theology. The Barth of 1922 has answered the question, how is theology possible? by denying the previously unquestionable premise of experience. He finds the possibility of theology in its impossibility, i.e. in its total contingency upon the grace of God. The concept of the Wholly Other creates a total vacancy where once there had been a collection of religious "givens" from which theology could more or less confidently proceed. Before God man is, has, and does nothing. But the vacancy of the human is occasion for joy, because into it will come--we hope--the divine Word.

CHAPTER III

THE ADVENT OF THE OTHER: EMMANUEL LEVINAS 1930-1961[1]

1. The Analysis of Existence

Emmanuel Levinas was born in Lithuania in 1906 and grew up in the Russia of world war, revolution, and civil war.[2] He emigrated to France and began to study philosophy at the University of Strasbourg in 1923. Teaching at Strasbourg then was a whole generation whose liberal ideals had been forged in the Dreyfus affair, providing Levinas with a "vision, dazzling to a newcomer, of a people equal to humanity and a nation to which one can be attached in heart and spirit just as strongly as by actual roots."[3] He studied phenomenology with Jean Hering starting in 1927, and made the pilgrimage to Freiburg to be with Husserl and Heidegger during two semesters in 1928 and 1929.[4] The fruits of this sojourn included a French summary of Husserl's *Ideas* published in 1929,[5] a co-translation (with Gabriel Peiffer) of the *Cartesian Meditations*, which appeared in 1931,[6] and his 1930 thesis on the *Ideas*, *The Theory of Intuition in Husserl's Phenomenology*,[7] which offers the first glimpse of Levinas' own philosophical posture.

THE CRISIS OF LIBERAL IDEALISM. Levinas' attraction to Heidegger is evident in *Theory of Intuition*, where the significance of Husserl's phenomenology is seen in terms of its preparatory role in the specifically Heideggerian project of fundamental ontology.[8] The attack on naturalism and psychologism in Husserl's earlier *Logical Investigations* meant, above all, a reopening of the ontological question, since the evidences and validities of the naturalistic view of the world were shown to be not original. They are relative and secondary to the absolute constitution of the world in consciousness, which is unveiled by the reductions of the *Ideas*. The new ontology is based on the absoluteness of consciousness--which Levinas prefers to call "experience," in order to minimize any resemblance to the epistemologically motivated subjective idealism that Heidegger criticizes.[9] "Intuition" is the main

event of experience, the presence "in person" (*selbstda*) of
objects to consciousness, neither as merely immanent in subjectivity (as naive idealism would have it), nor simply as things-
in-themselves (as naive realism would have it), but existing
strictly as given in the intentional, noetic-noematic correlation of experience. This absoluteness of experience implies a
fundamental ontology of *meaning*, and even that "all existence
is determined by the intrinsic meaning of our life,"[10] which is
the object of a new investigation. "What is the intrinsic
meaning of life which is manifested in the constitution of the
various regions of objects?"[11] This is, of course, the question
of Heidegger's *Being and Time*.[12] It is not really Husserl's own
question, although there is implicit in Husserl's work a certain
answer to it, which Levinas finds inadequate.

> [O]ne can reproach Husserl for his intellectualism.
> Even though he attains the profound idea that, in the onto-
> logical order, the world of science is posterior to and
> depends on the vague and concrete world of perception, he
> may have been wrong in seeing the concrete world as a world
> of objects that are primarily perceived. Is our main
> attitude toward reality that of theoretical contemplation?
> Is not the world presented in its very being as a center of
> action, as a field of activity or of *care*--to speak the
> language of Martin Heidegger?[13]

Husserl conceives philosophy as a universally valid
science, like geometry. Not that he requires a geometrical
rigidity for philosophical notions; but he adopts a fundamentally theoretical attitude, which "*seems as independent of the
historical situation of man as any theory that tries to consider everything sub specie aeternitatis.*"[14] The historicity of
"life," the specifically human mode of being, ought to be
studied in its own right as an original condition of the *sub
specie aeternitatis* attitude. Husserl does not appreciate the
historicity of consciousness because he makes the act of representation the paradigm of conscious life. "Intuition," the
event of the disclosure of being as experienced meaning, is then
biased toward the ideal of theoretical contemplation. The
phenomenological reduction, in which we look at life while no
longer living it, metaphysically assumes a freedom of man to be
theoretical, and begs the whole question of the historical and
existential meaning of the reduction.

The primacy of representation, i.e. of theoretical reason, is the point at which Levinas diverges from Husserl.[15] However:

> [I]ntentionality is not the mere representation of an object. Husserl calls states of consciousness *Erlebnisse*--what is "lived" in the sense of what is experienced--and this very expression connects the notion of consciousness to that of life, i.e., it leads us to consider consciousness under the rich and multiform aspects characteristic of our concrete existence. The practical and aesthetic categories are, as we have asserted, part of the very constitution of being, in the same way as the purely theoretical categories.[16]

Levinas' own philosophical program is marked at its origin by this interest in non-theoretical intentionality--to be studied later in "affectivity" or "sensibility," and the transcending intention of ethics--coupled with ongoing criticism of the primacy of representation that leads Husserl to construe the subject matter of philosophy as a realm of *objects* of consciousness. Heidegger's descriptions of the non-objective determinations of *Dasein* in *Being and Time*[17] blaze a trail for Levinas' later analyses of "escape," "fatigue," "laziness," etc.; and *Being and Time*'s displacement of the philosophical first principle from subjectivity to something (Being itself, or existence) by which subjectivity is *possessed*, could seem to enable a new appreciation, over against idealism, of the biblical view of man as essentially historical and creaturely.[18]

At the beginning of the 1930's Levinas was back in Paris, committed to Husserl's phenomenology in its Heideggerian development and active in the introduction of phenomenology to the French philosophical world. However, a long 1932 article on Heidegger already referred in a latently critical way to his "fundamental ontologism."[19] Hitler became Chancellor of the Reich in January, 1933. Heidegger joined the Nazi party and became rector of Freiburg University in May of that year. While the worst humiliations suffered by Husserl as a racially Jewish member of the Freiburg faculty took place after Heidegger's rectorship had ended, and the two men were seriously alienated long before 1933 on purely philosophical grounds,[20] it would still be difficult to overestimate the ominousness of these events for Levinas, who now had particularly strong reasons to find a path different from Heidegger's. The first indication of a new path is his 1934 article "Quelques réflexions sur la philosophie de l'hitlérisme,"[21] in which the crisis of anti-Semitic racism in Germany is seen as a function of the general crisis of the liberal ideals of Western civilization.[22]

Levinas joins Heidegger in criticizing the absolute, transhistorical freedom of subjectivity presupposed by Husserl's interpretation of the reductions of phenomenology, and by idealism generally. According to Heidegger, subjectivity belongs to Being and is ruled by Being's historical destiny, which is (primordially) to open itself for comprehension. But the typical aspiration of idealism is precisely to be free of the bond of finitude that history represents--to be able to make a true beginning in history, to be able to redefine one's identity. This aspiration is supported by the Christian conception of the soul as a freedom that transcends all worldly situations by its ability to start fresh, with the help of grace. Judaism too assumes a certain reversibility of time, in order that repentance and pardon be meaningful. While modern idealist philosophy does not have this dramatic sense of grace, it does free man from the world to the extent that it affirms the sovereignty of reason and theoretically reconstitutes the world according to rational law.[23]

Marxism is the first serious challenge in Western intellectual history to this conception of man.[24] For Marx, however, the break with liberalism is not complete, because the new awareness of the materially conditioned social struggle implies for him a certain freedom to consciously participate in it. The being of man is still assumed to be somehow independent of his situation. A conception truly opposite to liberalism would only be attained if man's situation were seen as the complete determiner of his being, from which it would be impossible for anyone to maintain any distance. But how could we identify ourselves totally with something we have not chosen? "The experience of our bodies seems to fulfill this paradoxical requirement."[25] One philosophical impulse is to regard the body as a tomb, an obstacle to surmount, an exterior, worldly object whose felt strangeness produces (for example) Socrates' alienation from it. But it is still possible to have a feeling of oneness with our bodies, which becomes a positive experience

when, say, a dangerous maneuver in sports is perfectly executed,
or when we suddenly find relief from suffering. So there can
be a philosophical adherence to bodily experience, even an
adherence that does not, like materialism, deny "spirit," but
understands spirit itself in terms of man's fated bodiliness.
Hitlerism trades on the cogency of this original sentiment to
support its contention that blood and race, the biological
elements of unfreedom, are the true basis of spirit. "Spirit"
becomes the spirit of a race, and authentic existence is proposed as the acceptance and affirmation of this historical,
biological condition.[26]

Compared with the rival ideal of the consanguine
society, the modern liberal ideal of society as a concordance
of free rational wills is precarious and false. It is undercut
by the difficulty it has in making concrete decisions in the
world, just as the free epistemology of idealism is haunted by
the option of scepticism. The free chooser can always go back
on his choice; the free knower can doubt what he knows. To a
society that has lost contact with freedom by retreating from
the responsibility it requires, the new Germanic ideal of man
promises sincerity, authenticity, and seriousness. The new
Germanic truth does not have the anonymous, public appeal of
universality, such as idealism would demand. It must expand
forcibly. It makes war and conquest inevitable, because it
cannot be separated from the people whose situation it expresses.
Their vindication, in *Lebensraum* and power-relationships, is
its vindication. Because of the violence of its truth, racism
is the enemy, not merely of liberal Jewish and Christian
culture, but of the humanity of man.[27]

Levinas is interested in the basic intention of liberal
idealism, but he does not believe that this intention can be
resurrected by reaching back behind Heidegger; for Heidegger's
"ontologism," his denial that Being as finite existence is
transcended, really expresses the root dogma of most Western
philosophy, which has always followed the advice of Parmenides
in confining its attention to what *is* and eschewing what *is
not*.[28] Even when idealism looks beyond the world of things to
the world of spirit, it is mainly interested in the possibility
of attributing a new kind of *being* to whatever it discovers.[29]

And yet, the value of European civilization undoubtedly lies in the aspirations of idealism, if not on the idealist path. In its first inspiration, idealism seeks to transcend Being. Any civilization that accepts Being, the tragic despair that it implies and the crimes that it justifies, deserves the name "barbarian."

Henceforth the only way that is open, to satisfy the legitimate demands of idealism without becoming involved in its errors, is to fearlessly measure the entire weight of Being and its universality. . . It is a question of leaving Being by a new way, at the risk of upsetting certain ideas which seem, to common sense and the wisdom of nations, the most evident.[30]

THE WEIGHT OF BEING. The 1935 article "De l'évasion" is the first major document of Levinas' philosophy of transcendence. He reiterates his judgment that Heidegger has changed the face of modern philosophy; but he intends to go beyond Heidegger.[31] Traditional idealism is no longer tenable, but the inhumanity of its contemporary alternatives, Communism and Nazism, invites a new inquiry into the real meaning of "humanity" and "civilization." A first clue is offered by the theme of "escape" (*l'évasion*), a disquiet running through the literature of the day which "appears as the most radical condemnation by our generation of the philosophy of Being."[32] The traditional revolt of philosophy against Being is motivated by the contradiction between human freedom and brute fact. The self is at odds with the world. But the self does not question *itself*. Its problems and conflicts are always caused by what lies outside it, in the world, but with itself it is at peace-- the self just *is*, in the same way that things, brute facts, just absolutely and identically *are* in indifference to the unknown and uncertain. "This conception of the ego as self-sufficient is one of the essential features of the bourgeois spirit in philosophy."[33] Underlying this bourgeois spirit is the unchallenged thesis of ontologism.

And in fact Western philosophy has never gotten past this point. In opposing ontologism--when it has opposed it--it has struggled for a better being, for a harmony between ourselves and the world, or for the perfecting of our own being. Its ideal of peace and equilibrium has presupposed the adequacy of being. The inadequacy of the human condition has never been conceived in any other way than as a limitation of being--otherwise the meaning of "finite being" would never have been considered. The transcendence of these limits, communion with infinite being, has remained its only concern.[34]

But the modern perception expressed in Heidegger's philosophy
is that finitude or the impossibility of transcendence pertains
to the very essence of what is, rather than to its existence
alone. We have the experience of being riveted to uninterrupt-
ible Being; in this experience we recognize that existence is
ultimately not a game, that there is no withdrawing from it;
its sheer facticity is its absolute seriousness. We feel the
whole weight of Being, but still we rebel against it. Our need
to overcome, not the world opposite to the self, not some particular mode or variant of Being, but *Being itself*, is our need
of "escape." This radical captivity to Being is given precisely
in the fact that I am and cannot stop being myself. *It is myself that I want to escape*.[35] My disquiet is not affected by
the fullness or harmony of the being I have, since the problem
is posed by the fact of being rather than by any limitation or
deficiency of it. How is *l'excendance*, the transcendence of
Being, possible--when Being remains the Alpha and Omega of
philosophy?

Actually, Being is the ground and limiting horizon only
of a certain philosophy. According to the ontologistic thinking
of this philosophy, the need to escape reveals to us that our
being is finite. The assumption is that an infinite being,
lacking nothing, would feel no such need. But is the need to
escape the sort of need that corresponds to a lack of being?

> Perhaps we will be able to show that in need [*besoin*]
> there is something other than a lack [*manque*]. . . the
> ideas of finitude and infinitude only apply to *that which
> is*; they lack precision when one attributes them to the
> *being* of that which is. *That which is* necessarily has a
> more or less extensive set of possibilities, of which it is
> master. Some properties can have relationships with other
> properties, and be measured by an ideal of perfection. But
> the simple fact of existing has reference only to itself.
> It is that by which all powers and properties are posited.
> The escape that we are considering must appear to us as the
> internal structure of this fact of being posited [*se
> poser*].[36]

Here Levinas makes an important use of the Heideggerian distinction between Being (*Sein*) and beings (*Seienden*).[37] The problem
of finitude, and thus of death, is a problem of the existent,
i.e. of that which is, and not properly a problem of existence,
i.e. of that by which the existent exists, since finitude is
not a privation of existence but simply its way. But the

originality of the wish to escape is such that it pertains to existence itself, and therefore has philosophical priority over the existent's problems of death and nothingness. The phenomenon of the need to escape is too hastily interpreted in terms of a metaphysics of fullness, according to which all need would reflect a lack and be satisfied by possessing something. This results from failure to distinguish existence from the existent, applying to the one an idea that could only have meaning for the other.[38] Need is a *presence* rather than a deficiency of Being.

Levinas measures the weight of Being by interpreting a certain group of experiences and emotions as events in Being, of ontological rather than psychological significance--affirmations of existence instead of the existent. When we suffer *malaise*, for example, we desire to be in a different way, but without reference to a specific goal. There is no particular satisfaction we desire, only deliverance. And *pleasure*, by the same token, represents not the filling up of a lack but always a kind of deliverance from Being, a lightening of its load. To the extent that pleasure is the answer to need, it shows that need is not nostalgia for Being or desire for fuller being, but the urge to "escape."[39] Pleasure is an escape that deceives, however, because ultimately there is no escape from Being. The self-defeat of pleasure registers in *shame*; its basis is our inseverable tie to ourselves. Levinas identifies our contradictory experience of the impossibility of escape together with the impossibility of continuing to be as *nausea*, the preeminent instance of malaise, "*the very experience of pure being*" in its "internal antagonism."[40] Seen in this light, the ideal triumph of Being traditionally named "eternity" represents no help for the existent. It is the worst curse of all. The same curse is on pure knowledge, *theoria*, the permanent attachment of thought to Being, "impotence before the accomplished fact. Knowledge is precisely that which remains to do when everything has been accomplished."[41]

"De l'évasion" presents a fundamental ontology that is Heideggerian in the sense that it inquires into events of affectivity which cannot be reduced to the categories of theoretical thought and free activity dominating Husserl's form of phenomenology. But it is already post-Heideggerian in the sense that its primary interest is in something Other than Being, the as-yet hidden destination of the flight from Being called "*l'évasion*."

Eleven years elapsed between "De l'évasion" and the publication of Levinas' next important original essay, "Il y a" (1946),[42] which was an extract from *De l'existence à l'existant* (1947). In the meantime Levinas had been naturalized a French citizen, called up into the army, captured by the Germans in 1940, held first in a prison camp in Brittany and then until 1945 in an East Prussian stalag for Jewish prisoners of war. His distinctive interpretations of Being, affective event, and consciousness continued to develop in this period, still guided by an overriding interest in "excendence" of Being. He writes in his foreword to *De l'existence à l'existant*:

> The present study has a preparatory character. It surveys and touches upon a certain number of themes, taken from wider-ranging studies devoted to the problem of the Good, Time, and the Relation with the Other Person [*Autrui*] as a movement toward the Good. The Platonic formula locating the Good beyond Being is the emptiest and most general sign guiding them. It signifies that the movement in which an existent is led toward the Good is not a transcendence by which the existent is raised to a superior existence, but a departure from Being and the categories by which Being is described: an *ex-cendence*. But excendence and Happiness must have a footing in Being, and that is why being is better than not-being.[43]

This first explicit linkage of the Good with the relation between men establishes the horizon of all of Levinas' subsequent work. By the wording of its title, *De l'existence à l'existant* also makes explicit the break and new polemical relation with Heidegger. The discovery of the "ontological difference" between Being and beings remains central; but the direction of philosophical movement, and the order of priority, is reversed. Levinas wants to show that the position of the existent, who as a separated entity defies and masters the weight of the anonymous existence by which it exists, points to a philosophical agenda of the personal and ethical, rather than to a "fundamental ontology" of a pre- or super-personal existence.[44]

Being, or existence, considered apart from things that exist, is characterized by Levinas by the objectless predication

"*il y a*," which is to say, "there is. . ." *nothing in particular*, just an utterly strange, unresponsive ambience which cannot be grasped by thought, for it is neither a thing nor a
purely absent no-thing, but an indeterminate, immediate
presence.[45] It impinges on our experience in certain pre-
conscious events in which our mode of being as individual
existents is threatened by an element that does not acknowledge
existents. The *il y a* of Being is thus a sinister phenomenon
(or rather non-phenomenon, non-showing) which, so far from
offering philosophy its ultimate point of reference, poses
instead the ultimate problem of the absurd, to which the constitution of existents is a (partial) solution. According to
Levinas we must seek meaning on the opposite side of Heidegger's
"ontological difference," the personal side.

De *l'existence à l'existant* offers a description of the
event in which the existent exists. The existent masters existence by possessing its own existence separated from the
existence-in-general of the *il y a*. This "hypostasis" (the
arising of the person) imposes upon the verb *be-ing* a subject,
the *one* who *is*.[46] But because hypostasis occurs as an event
and does not simply subsist as a state, the moment in which the
existent originates is "articulated": the existent arises by
asserting its own mode of existence, grasping existence in a
particular way.[47] The self-collection and self-identification
of the existent in the *instant* is an interruption of the general
historical time common to everything; without such an interruption of the process of all that is, there could not be this
particular existent. In this sense the "instant" is the pure
present, but not merely the present represented by an infini-
tesimal point on a time-line. The objective evanescence of the
instant is precisely its independence from the historical continuum; it has its own temporal locality, so that it can be its
own origin.[48]

Such pre-reflective events as "fatigue" and "laziness"
witness to the fact that existence is always a task to be begun,
a weight to be assumed, besides being the inescapable already-
given destiny of the existent. "Laziness" betrays an original
inhibition in Being, a failure of Being to perfectly accede to
itself.[49] The enterprise of existence can be at least

temporarily postponed "lazily"; and on account of "fatigue" the existence that has been grasped can be momentarily released.[50] Being is a problematic accomplishment, at its very core. "Fatigue" and "laziness" reveal an original distension (*déca-lage*) of Being in which place is made for the event of the instant, and thus the separate existence of the existent. The meaning of *consciousness*, according to Levinas, is not the making-present of Being but the power of suspending Being by going to sleep![51] The significance of sleep is pointed up by the affective horror of insomnia, which is a denial of privacy, an impossibility of escape from the presence of Being. Conscious existence is the freedom to close one's eyes. Cognitive consciousness of objects in the world is a power of retiring from those objects; one knows them without ceasing to be oneself, one can afford exposure to them; one has freedom to direct one's attention elsewhere.[52] With this interpretation of consciousness, Levinas tries to fill his own prescription for a new reckoning with the inspiration of idealism. Subjectivity, as "the power of infinite withdrawal,"[53] does not so much transcend Being as fall short of it or let go of it. There is no ideal realm over nature, but there is a dimension of interiority created by a sort of escape from Being, *l'évasion*.

In a second train of reflection, Levinas considers the relation of conscious existence to the *world*. To be in the world is to be attached to things.[54] The idea of intentionality--i.e. the ubiquitous correlation between objective meanings (*noemata*) and subjective acts of appropriating meaning (*noeses*)--arises from this attachment, but it is not originally the neutral, disincarnate relation to things envisioned by Husserl, but rather a spontaneous desire for enjoyment, a gusto for the things of the world. Levinas' "desire" is very different from Heidegger's "care" as the proposed horizon of being-in-the-world, for it is an utterly sincere absorption in things without any ulterior motive. "To be sure, we do not live in order to eat; but it would not be correct to say that we eat in order to live."[55]

The things of the world are given to be enjoyed by consciousness, and this givenness is equated by Levinas with *form*: "that by which a being is turned toward the sun, that by which it has a face, by which it is given."[56] Whereas the *form* of a thing is its relatedness to the system of references called the world, Levinas speaks of the *nudity* of things existing purely in their own unintelligible way, apart from that system. We encounter this sort of nudity (which is not to be confused with the "nudity" later predicated of the other person by Levinas) in art.[57] Artistic presentation, in fostering the "exoticism" of objects in the world, is concerned with detaching surfaces from the comprehended world; the artist uses forms to show "the very absence of forms, i.e. the non-transmutation of exteriority into interiority that forms accomplish."[58] "Exteriority," what is outside the self, is normally transmuted into "interiority," the comprehending knowledge and enjoyment of the self, but the artist reverses this reduction of the strange to the familiar. The self's position at the center, surrounded by other things which by their *forms* are given to the self to know and enjoy, establishes the "inside-outside" structure of the world. But this structure collapses in the *il y a*, which lurks behind all form as the absolute "matter" or indistinctness of the exterior world unrelated to interiority, the black night of insomnia, Pascal's silence of infinite spaces.[59] The *il y a*, pure Being, is as much a denial of the world (the "outside") as it is a denial of the self (the "inside"). Only because Being draws back from itself in the "retreat" of subjectivity is there a world.

In his descriptions of fatigue, effort, desire, and so forth, Levinas wishes to emphasize that these events in Being are not (contra Husserl) objects in intentional correlation, because they are not given to consciousness as phenomena. Moreover, the experiencing of them does not (contra Heidegger) retain any character of comprehension (*Verstehen*). For example:

> The *here* of consciousness, the place where it sleeps and escapes to itself, differs radically from the *Da* involved in Heidegger's *Dasein*. This latter already implies the world. The *here* we are starting with, the *here* of position, precedes every act of comprehension, every horizon, and all time. It is the very fact that consciousness is an origin, that it starts from itself, that it is an *existent*.[60]

Heidegger prolongs the traditional primacy of theory in Western philosophy, even though he criticizes its Cartesian subjectivist form by delivering the *ex*-istent over to the "opening" of Being.

> We oppose to the idea of existence in which the accent is placed on the first syllable the idea of a being whose very advent is a coiling upon itself, who is in a certain sense a substance, contrary to the ecstaticism of contemporary thought.
> The Heideggerian care, illuminated as it is by comprehension (even if comprehension itself is given as care), is already determined by the "inside-outside" structure which characterizes light. Without being knowledge, the temporality of Heidegger is an ecstasis, a "being beside oneself," not at all a transcendence of theory but already the departure of interiority towards exteriority.[61]

The inside-outside structure of the world of light—that is, the world of forms, which is the world-system of relationships—does not admit of radical otherness. It is a triumph of form (whether the immanent form bestowed by subjectivity in Husserl or the ontological form bestowed by Being in Heidegger) over "nudity," and therefore determines the very existence of the existent, since it will not allow anything to be merely itself: it requires that everything wear a mask and be for other things. It means that the One is ultimately intelligible, where the Many is not; and at the end of that avenue to the One, Levinas glimpses the subjective counterpart of the infinite cruelty of the *il y a*. From this come all the sinister overtones of "comprehension" (counterpart to the "horror of the *il y a*") in Levinas' analysis. The point is elaborated in a 1948 essay on Heidegger:

> Death—which for Heidegger is this absolutely new concept, finally contradicting thought or the *logos of the future*—is still thought, to the extent that it is comprehension, i.e. power. It is in terms of comprehension, of its failures and successes, that Heidegger finally describes existence. The relation of an existent with Being is for him ontology, i.e. comprehension of Being. . .
> But is the relation of man to Being merely ontology—comprehension or comprehension inextricably mixed with incomprehension, Being's domination of us in the midst of our domination of Being? In other words, does existence occur simply as domination?[62]

The inside-outside model of existence is a power model. All of its relationships are master-slave relationships, because it cannot escape thinking in a dialectic of activity and passivity, the giving and receiving of causes. But according to Levinas this model is not even adequate to the meaning of the self's pre-ethical existence. In measuring the whole weight of Being at the very point of upsurge of the existent's existence, we find that the load is lightened and thus far denied. The self's existence has meaning for itself; it does not depend on Being for meaning; in fact, Being depends on the self for meaning.

It still cannot be said that the existent-as-such transcends Being, because it only maintains a relative and temporary distance from it. The existent-as-such is still absolutely chained to Being and is always liable to the insomniac experience of being exposed to existence-in-general. Being and ontology are more fundamentally called into question by a different problematic than that of the Self: the problematic of Otherness, and specifically of the other person. The theme of the Other appears in the last section of *De l'existence à l'existant*, but belongs with *Le Temps et l'Autre* and later works, and must be discussed together with them.

Levinas said of the circumstances in which his philosophy was born that "the moral crisis brought about by the war of 1914 created in men an acute feeling of the inefficacity of reason, of the basic incongruity between rationalist civilization and the claims of the individual soul lost in the anonymity of the general."[63] The traditional aspirations of idealism were strongly represented by Brunschvicg in Paris[64] and even by Husserl, as Levinas emphasized in "L'oeuvre d'Edmond Husserl" (1940):

> Phenomenology, as a deepening of our knowledge of things and their being, constitutes for man a *way of existing* by which he carries out his spiritual destiny. It serves as a foundation for the moral sciences, as it grounds the natural sciences, but beyond this it is the very life of spirit recovering itself and existing in conformity with its vocation. It offers a discipline by which the spirit becomes conscious of itself (*Selbstbesinnung*), assumes responsibility for itself and, finally, its freedom. . . thus Husserl joins the great tradition of Western idealism.[65]

> In [Husserl's] theory of time, it is a question of the time of theoretical thought, of a formal time qualified only by the contents that fill it and participate in its rhythm, without creating it. Here again Husserl remains faithful to his fundamental metaphysical intentions:

spirit is the bond of meaning to thought, the freedom of intellection. Time accomplishes this freedom; it does not pre-exist the spirit and does not engage it in a history, in which it might be overrun. Historical time is constituted. History is explained by thought.[66]

But the academic year 1928-1929, in which Levinas studied in Freiburg, was the year of Heidegger's assumption of Husserl's chair. It was a year of unusual tension in which an avowedly post-idealist philosopher departed from the lines laid down by the master. Heidegger more or less turned phenomenology on its head by asserting that the primary philosophical task is to inquire into the meaning of Being, the very historical Being that is *bracketed* in the key act of Husserl's phenomenology, the *epoché*, by which critical detachment from the natural attitude is gained.

The new thought of Heidegger made a needed criticism of the rationalist assumption of the freedom of reason and consciousness from history. But the grave drawback of this thought, its "ontologism"--which was reflected, not accidentally, in its ethical and political insensitivity--showed that Heidegger's departure was not radical enough. After 1933 it became all the more urgent to understand the genuine spirit of civilization. Levinas undertakes this by accepting the Heideggerian reversal of phenomenology and reversing it in turn: that is, by accepting the ontological difference and the agenda of pre-conscious, pre-intentional events of existence for investigation, but going on to ask, instead of "What is the meaning of the *Being* of beings?," "What does it mean that in Being there are *beings* (persons)?"[67] In his analysis of existence Levinas has not yet described a true transcendence of Being, but he has discovered a sort of elision of Being in the articulation in the instant of the existent's existence.

2. The Theme of the Other

As soon as we consider that the existent is in a world, the otherness of what it finds in the world becomes an issue for it. Art offers a relation with the (ultimately horrifying) otherness of other things. But a new horizon of inquiry is opened up by the moral relation with other persons, whose otherness is of a different kind.

THE NEW HORIZON. The other person is never treated like a thing, but he is never separated from things--social institutions, manners, and (paradigmatically) clothing. Sociality is decency.[68] We co-exist not in our nudity but according to form, because our nudity is our private existence, our interiority maintained apart from the world. In society we do not surrender our own nudity, nor are we disquieted by the nudity of others. "One has to find something to say to one's companion, exchange an idea, around which, as around a third term, social life necessarily starts. . . All concrete relations between human beings in the world get their character of *reality* from a third term."[69] The real, i.e. the world, is fundamentally an arena of enjoyment and satisfaction for the self; desire for the other as other, love, reaches no worldly fulfillment and is thus ever-hungry. *"The very positivity of love lies in its negativity."*[70] Human otherness is a dimension without an object, an "unlimited, empty, vertiginous future."[71] Western philosophy and civilization, however, regard the problem of love and the Good as the problem of a term or goal;[72] and sociality is reduced to third-term relations, or to greater entities surpassing and controlling the persons involved, like "society" in the Durkheimian sense. Heidegger's category of *Miteinandersein* presupposes the third term of "truth" around which the authentic form of personal relation is revealed.[73] But all of these approaches avoid the question of relation with the other as other, the face-to-face relation without intermediary.

The relation with otherness acquires such urgency in Levinas' thought because of the essentially tragic situation in which the existent is placed, chained to Being and to itself. The subject's freedom with regard to things in the world is relative to the unfreedom of the spirit's bondage to existence: the power of withdrawal, of escaping definition, is ultimately not enough to escape selfhood and aloneness.

> The world and the light are solitude. These given objects, these clothed beings, are something other than myself, but they are mine. Illuminated by the light, they have a meaning and consequently are as though they came from me. In the comprehended universe I am alone, i.e. enclosed in an existence that is definitively *one*.[74]

The meaning of consciousness is freedom, but its primal condition is unfreedom; this is its tragedy. Being weighs on the present and precludes reasonable expectation of deliverance. But beyond any reasonable expectation there is *hope*, and beyond the tragic present there is *time*. For all its psychological familiarity, hope is really an infinite mystery, since the time in which a true deliverance from self and redemption of the present might occur is not thinkable in the self's own thought. The self is the problem, not the solution. Temporality, the advent of an *other* instant really other than the present instant (not the extrapolation of the present that thought inevitably posits), can only be produced in relation with an Other. The temporal dialectic is the dialectic of sociality. Actual time distinct from the eternally repeated instant requires the interval of nothingness that only occurs between the self and other persons. Traditional philosophers, and even Bergson and Heidegger, miss this by conceiving time as belonging to, or affecting, the self in its solitude.[75]

Now it is evident that the face-to-face human relation, transcending all worldly third terms, must be sought as the condition of temporality. This relation is asymmetrical; it is not based on an ethic of reciprocity, or of comfortably regulated charity; it forces us beyond the categories of unity and multiplicity that are appropriate to the constituted world. It is the locus of transcendence, Plato's *Eros*, according to which the subject has a possibility of remaining subject while leaving itself, being liberated from the fatal eternal return to itself. "To the cosmos, the world of Plato, is opposed the world of spirit, in which the implications of Eros are not reduced to the logic of genera, in which the self is substituted for *Same* and the other person [*autrui*] for *Other*."[76] This is the explicit transformation of Levinas' thought to a philosophy of transcendence, the "object" of which must be the Other.

TIME AND THE OTHER. How can the pluralism of temporality and the Other, different from all pluralism of things (founded in the unity of the existent's solitude), be thought? Levinas' 1947 lectures on "Time and the Other"[77] address the problem by recalling the groundwork laid in the analysis of existence.

Of course the present and the "I" turn into existents, and one can compose a time from this, having time as an existent. Any one can have a Kantian or Bergsonian experience of this hypostatized time. But that would then be the experience of hypostatized time, of time which is, and no longer time in its schematic function between existence and existent, time as the pure event of hypostasis. In posing the present as the mastery of existence by the existent, and in looking for the transition from existence to the existent, we find ourselves at a level of investigation which can no longer be characterized as "experience." And if phenomenology is only a method of radical experience, we find ourselves beyond phenomenology. The hypostasis of the present is, moreover, only one moment of hypostasis: it is possible that time indicates [yet] another relation between existence and the existent. It is this which will appear to us later as the very event of our relation with the other man, and which will thus allow us to arrive at a pluralist existence transcending the monist hypostasis of the present.[78]

Pluralist existence does not undo the monist hypostasis by making solitary existence relative to some collective existence (like Heidegger's *Miteinandersein*). Not for nothing has the hypostasis of the existent been shown to be an original event. But there is another event that transcends it. This transcending may not consist in a knowing, because in knowledge the subject absorbs the object; it may not consist in an ecstasis, because in ecstasis the object absorbs the subject; in both cases duality disappears. What is needed is an example of a relationship that maintains duality, and a paradigm example is furnished by *death*. The existent's relation to death is that of a solitude as such confronting a mystery as such.[79]

Our intimations of death, the unknown, come in suffering. Here the subject is in relation with something that does not come into the light where it can be seen and so in no sense proceeds from or is given its meaning by the subject. The "experience" of this mystery is so passive that it cuts through all experience proper. Death is never in the present, but in the future. The idea of an active assumption of death in suicide is self-contradictory, for we have absolutely no power-relation to it. It is not that we are powerless in the face of death, or that our powers are insufficient--the world of light is already full of things that surpass our powers--rather, death elides the whole question of power. By showing that an event of absolute otherness can happen to the subject, it

threatens the subject's innermost grasp of subjectivity. Death
shows us that existence is plural, and that plurality is not
simply a problem to be solved, e.g. by eternal life, but a
challenge to maintain a personal relationship with alterity as
such--in contrast to what Levinas calls the "supreme lucidity"
of Heidegger's being-toward-death, where death is assumed as a
possibility of *Dasein*.[80]

      Another prototype of relation not in the light is Eros--
not the "luminous" Eros of Plato, but the relation with mystery
that occurs in the irreducible duality of the sexes. Reality,
as sexual, is multiple, neither a contradiction (as with Being
vs. nothingness), nor a complementary duality forming a higher
unity, nor a fusion of two identities to one. The *pathétique*
of Eros lies in its irreducible twoness. Levinas finds in this
relation an entirely new way of existing, the *feminine*, which
retires from the light "modestly" in contrast to the beings
that face and rise toward the light of public evidence. The
feminine is, like death, a mystery, and thus love, like death,
is not a possibility to be freely assumed by existents: "it
does not depend on our initiative, it is without reason, it
invades us and wounds us, and yet the *I* survives in it."[81]
Love, too, is absolutely future; the caress is never satisfied
by sensation, because the Other is absent from the present.
The absence of the Other is the ground of time itself, i.e. of
truly new and different instants.[82]

      From Eros there finally emerges a concrete accomplish-
ment of our paradoxical relation to death, for in our *fecundity*
our being is prolonged in our children, who nevertheless remain
Other.[83]

> It is by my being that I am my son, not by sympathy. My
> return to myself, which begins with hypostasis, is therefore
> not without remission, thanks to the perspective on the
> future opened by eros. Instead of obtaining this remission
> by the impossible dissolution of hypostasis, one accom-
> plishes it through one's children. Thus it is not according
> to the category of causation, but according to the category
> of the father, that freedom and time occur.[84]

The "category of the father," not a category of cause and domination, cannot be reduced. The erotic and paternal relations
demonstrate that "alterity is not purely and simply the existence of another freedom alongside of mine. Over such a freedom

I have power, or else it is absolutely strange and unrelated to me."[85] The ethic of reciprocity that assumes equal, coexistent freedoms is a derivative complication of the original, asymmetrical relation with human mystery. Its logic grows out of the interior dialectic of these events of existence.

PLURALISM. The human relations described in *Le Temps et l'Autre* have a momentous implication for the logical foundations of Western philosophy.

> I do not *have* my child, I *am* my child. Paternity is a relation with a stranger who, even while being another person, *is* me; a relation between me and a self who is nevertheless not me. In this "I am," Being no longer has Eleatic unity. In existing itself there is multiplicity and transcendence.[86]

Over the decade and a half following *De l'existence à l'existant* and *Le Temps et l'Autre*, Levinas wrestles with the conceptual implications of his analysis of existence and alterity under the general heading of the issue of pluralism. The development of his philosophical position in the 1950's will be studied with reference to four important articles published in the *Revue de Métaphysique et de Morale*.

(1) "L'ontologie est-elle fondamentale?" (1951).[87] The meaning of reason has been revised by Heidegger's philosophy, which now sees the comprehension of Being as a function or accomplishment of existence itself, man's whole engagement with the world, even where this engagement is not in the mode of conscious theoretical cognition. Man lives the meaning of Being; his life is ontology. But this way of philosophizing still assumes that the truth of Being commands language—that men speak more or less rationally according to whether they speak more or less unforgetfully of Being. Precisely at this fundamental level it can be asked whether language is not in fact grounded in a relation prior to any relation of "comprehension," and thus whether *this* relation would not therefore necessarily precede and constitute "reason" rather than be constituted by it.[88] This is where Levinas takes his stand against Heidegger's fundamental ontology, by claiming that the interlocutory situation (our language conceived as a function of our sociality, i.e. our moral life together) is the presupposition that transcends Being and cannot be described within the

category of comprehension that still governs Heidegger's thought. Man's speech reflects a more primordial condition of his existence than his thought, one that can best be characterized (outside the sphere of comprehension) as "encounter." But, as Heideggerians might object, does not this attempt to correctly describe the relation with the other person constitute the appropriate comprehension of him, the letting-be (*Seinlassen*, *laisser-être*) of him in his own way? And is this letting-be not what ontology itself strives for?

To be sure, we still have to explain why the event of language is no longer placed at the level of comprehension. Why not simply enlarge the notion of comprehension, according to the procedure that phenomenology has made familiar? This seems to us to be impossible. The handling of ordinary objects is interpreted, for example, as their comprehension [by Heidegger]. But the enlargement of the notion of knowledge is justified in this example by the transcending of objects that are known. It is achieved in spite of all the pre-theoretical engagement that is involved in the handling of "tools." While being handled, an entity is transcended in the very movement that grasps it--and, in this "beyond" of transcending that is a necessary aspect of being "close to" something, the very itinerary of comprehension is recognizable. This transcending is not only tied to the previous appearance of the "world" each time we touch graspable things, as Heidegger would have it; it is shown also in the *possession* and *consumption* of objects. But there is nothing of this in my relation with the other person.[89]

"Man is the only being that I cannot encounter without expressing to him this very encounter."[90] No doubt we try to comprehend each other ontologically, by understanding each other's "being," and have no more original way to comprehend; but the yet-more-original context of this comprehension is established by the other *to* whom I speak even when it is he *about* whom I speak. The function of expression is first of all "to institute sociality."[91]

The relation with the other person, irreducible to ontology, Levinas now calls *religion*.[92] This is a religion without theology, connected with the Infinite (transcending comprehension) not as a positive revelation, nor as a dark, violent mystery of the "sacred," but as an ethical demand, the removal of the human face from the sphere of power. With this definition of religion, "we will welcome this ethical resonance of the word and all its Kantian echoes."[93]

> Religion is the relation with a being as a being [*avec l'étant en tant qu'étant*, i.e. with a person as end-in-himself]. It does not consist in *conceiving* it as a being--an act in which the *being* is already assimilated, even if this assimilation leads up to its release as a *being*, to *letting it be*. Neither does it consist in establishing some *belonging*, nor in coming up against the irrational in the attempt to understand the being. Is rationality nothing more than power over objects?[94]

Rationality ought not to mean the struggle and trickery by which the intellect annuls all particularity in favor of ideal generality, reducing all exteriority to interiority, but the (ethical) peace in which beings can be present to each other as singular, as what they are, unreduced. The other person is unlike the things of the world, which we more or less consciously know and master, in not being offered to our powers, in not appearing on the horizon of the ontological question. *Being, for Levinas, means power.*[95] Husserl's evidence and Heidegger's "opening in Being" mean givenness to a power--in the one case givenness of the world to the ego, in the other case givenness of the subject to Being. The unique phenomenon that escapes this horizon of power Levinas names the "face."[96] One trace of its uniqueness is the self-contradiction of the intention to murder the other person; certainly one can accomplish *a* goal in murder, but at that moment the other person escapes one's grasp definitively. The presence of the human face is the ethical impossibility of murder.

> The face *means* differently. In it a being's infinite resistance to our power is affirmed precisely against the murderous will that it defies, because it has meaning of itself, completely nude--and the nudity of the face is no figure of speech. It cannot even be said that the face is an opening [in Being]; that would be to make it relative to a surrounding plenitude.[97]

The otherness of the Other here implies an absoluteness of meaning, a total independence of horizon, that decisively alienates it from phenomenological procedure. The face is the *unconstituted*--a distinction granted by Husserl only to transcendental consciousness. In this radical interruption, phenomenology pays the price of pluralism.

Finally, Levinas raises the issue of the position in which the philosopher finds himself once the primacy of ontology has been rejected. He feels "particularly close" to Kant's practical philosophy;[98] the situation he has posed as an alternative to the realm of comprehension is ethical (if not "practical," insofar as the practical in Kant is still a matter of the free agent's exercise and self-limitation of power).

> Philosophical investigation cannot be satisfied in all cases with reflection on the self or on existence. Reflection only provides us with an account of the adventure of an individual, a private soul, returning to itself even when it seems to be fleeing.[99]

This remark provokes the question: If philosophy is not reflection or comprehension, what is it? If the philosopher himself belongs to the interlocutory situation that he takes to be his ultimate warrant for philosophizing, what sort of locution is his philosophy? The answer is for the most part delayed until *Totality and Infinity*.

(2) "Liberté et commandement" (1953).[100] Levinas considers the distinction between the ethical relation and power-relations of comprehension with reference to the traditional problem of how a plurality of *free* beings can coexist, acting on one another—the dilemma of autonomy and heteronomy. Just as intellection had been characterized as a "ruse"[101] by which the self substitutes its own being (in the form of the ideal generality of the concept) for the proper, particular being of what it knows, so here the event in which free beings attempt to act on each other is depicted as warlike; but the struggle is not a true encounter between two substances. It is only an "ambush" of one by the other. "Violence is a way of grasping a being by surprising it, by grasping it on the basis of its absence, on the basis of what, properly speaking, it is not."[102] Levinas' point is that in war, or competition generally, we oppose each other as forces, which is to say not humanly, not face to face; and that the specifically human relationship is completely different, because it is pacific. The neighbor does not appear as an obstacle to my freedom; his ethical opposition to me is *prior* to my freedom and is its condition. The Other does not meet me as an equal. "One being commands another, without this being simply a function of some whole that it embraces or some system, and without this happening tyrannically."[103] Pluralism is thus no simple multiplicity of indifferently

arranged beings all on a level. But neither is it a hierarchy in an ontological sense.

Modern man has had to face the fact that human freedom, "essentially non-heroic,"[104] does not guarantee its own continuance under torture, brainwashing, and so forth. We know that a soul can be made truly slavish. So the condition of freedom cannot lie in the rational capacity of the subject, which is irretrievably tainted by its own errancy and vulnerability. The foundation of freedom can only be provided by an *exterior* order of reason, a State, in which tyranny is anticipated and resisted. Here Levinas is not primarily interested in the theory of the State for its own sake, but in the fact that the self's freedom is founded in something outside it, something "heteronomous"; and the mediate heteronomy of the just state, with its exterior commandment of law, formally prefigures (but actually presupposes) the immediate commandment of the other person, the ethical impossibility of murder, which signifies of itself, absolutely exterior to consciousness. This exteriority is expressed by saying that the Other is prior to my freedom, where "freedom" is taken to embrace the whole intentional life of consciousness--the "infinite power (freedom) of withdrawal"-- so that, as we will find more explicitly later, the foundation of morality lies elsewhere than in any theoretical, practical, or axiological constitution in consciousness. This chain of implications leads Levinas to the notion of *creation.*

> If the face is not *known*, it is not because it lacks sense. It is not known because its relation with us does not trace back to its constitution, and (to speak in Husserlian terms) is prior to all *Sinngebung*. This sense before *Sinngebung*, this plenitude of sense prior to all *Sinngebung*, but which remains a relation with intellect-- a non-violent relation--describes the very structure of the creature.[105]

The created being is not its own author, does not possess its own starting point, and cannot sustain the ideal of autonomy. In moral terms, the self is the creature of the Other, because its starting point--the origin of the meaning of its freedom, and the unique possibility of liberation from itself--is the moral commandment prior (exterior) to all "conscious" meaning.[106]

(3) "Le moi et la totalité" (1954).[107] Levinas exhibits the self as primordially "innocent," unconscious of any

truth or value outside of its own enjoyment. *Le vivant* originally confuses its own particular life with all that is, i.e. with totality. It is only in taking thought that it distinguishes itself from the totality; this is in fact the very definition of thought, and the beginning of "experience" in the sense of relationship with exterior reality.

> The *vivant* is thus not without consciousness, but it has a consciousness without problems, i.e. without exteriority, an interior world of which it occupies the center. . . The identity of the *vivant* through its history is not at all mysterious: the *vivant* is essentially the Same, the Same determining everything Other, without the Other ever determining the Same. Had the Other determined the Same, had the *vivant* run up against exteriority, its instinctive being would have been slain. The *vivant* lives under the sign of "liberty or death."[108]

"Liberty or death" are the terms implicitly observed by life in its innocent upsurge, but this poses a problem: how can the totality ever criticize the partiality, how can true exteriority be present, in non-fatal fashion, to the self? This miracle does happen. It is the beginning of experience and thought: "In its beginning, thought finds itself before the miracle of fact. The structure of 'fact,' as distinct from 'idea,' lies in the miracle. Thought is thereby not simply reminiscence but always recognition of new things."[109] The miracle is the face-to-face encounter with the other person. Even the exteriority of the things of the world presupposes this exteriority par excellence of the human, for things as things are independent of me only because I do not possess them, meaning that someone else does or may possess them. "Thought begins with the possibility of conceiving a freedom exterior to mine. . . my relation with totality is a relation with human beings whose faces I recognize. With respect to them I am guilty or innocent."[110]

Guilt and innocence presuppose a being both free and tied to others, belonging to the totality but exceeding it. The revealed religions have offered an ontological scheme to solve this problem: guilt and innocence are assigned to the relation with a transcendent God, and the self remains sovereign in its own sphere, the world. But for the modern consciousness this scheme is defunct, even though many "pious souls," due perhaps to a psychological necessity, have returned to traditional faith.

> But is modern consciousness reflected in the pious soul?
> An important portion of humanity no longer finds the way of
> the spiritual life in religion or religiosity. Not that
> they feel themselves less guilty than past generations; they
> feel guilty differently. The fault they are accused of does
> not find pardon in piety; or, more precisely, the evil which
> weighs on them does not belong to the order of pardon.[111]

Pardon is a possibility within the *société intime* formed by two,
where there is always personal relationship with the wronged
party and a chance to start fresh. But the existence of the
third man—that is, the ramification of fault beyond our control, perhaps beyond intention, in any event beyond all possibility of "taking it back" and wiping the slate clean—institutes an order of evil yet more serious, because irreversible.
It demands a foundation of justice rather than love. "The
society of love is a society of two, a society of solitudes,
resistant to universality."[112] The ego grasps its own justification in the loving Thou; it is not held accountable to an
inassimilable, exterior standard, such as the law by which
"society" in the full sense (introduced by the third man) is
constituted. The third man, the one who is absent at the moment,
who may or may not be justly provided for in my treatment of
the Thou who is present, must be regarded as an original dimension of human life, not as an accidental complication of it.

Via the theme of the third person, Levinas criticizes
the modern philosophy that identifies religious existence with
love and the Other with the loved one. Such a conception is
not adequate to social reality. "Thus, the crisis of religion
comes from the impossibility of being alone with God and of
forgetting all those who remain outside of this loving dialogue.
True dialogue lies elsewhere."[113] The Other as Thou, in Buber's
or Marcel's sense, is not sufficiently exterior and critical.
If the full demand of moral society is taken account of, God
can no longer be conceived as a correlate of the self or as an
infinite reservoir of pardon. He must be "the fixed point
exterior to society, from which the Law comes"[114]--

> Yet by no means an allegorical personification of my
> conscience. Is there a "conscience" before "We" has been
> uttered? Is it certain that "conscience" could be separated
> from a "received commandment," from a certain heteronomy, a
> relation with the Other, exteriority? The Other, Exteri-
> ority, does not necessarily mean tyranny and violence. *The
> exteriority of discourse is an exteriority without violence.*

> The absolute that underlies justice is the absolute of the interlocutor. His way of being and manifesting himself consists of turning his face toward me, being a face. This is why the absolute is a person. To isolate one being among others, to be alone with him in the secrecy of the equivocation "*entre nous*," does not assure the radical exteriority of the Absolute. Only this unimpeachable, strict witness coming in "*entre nous*," making our private, secret life public with its speech, this demanding mediator between man and man, is a face, is Thou.[115]

The self's moral posture is no longer one of confessing its sins (to do which would call for an impossible overview of the moral ledger), but of standing under the accusation of others, even unknown, remote others. Exteriority determines the sense of interiority. Levinas carries out his characteristic rescue of liberalism by reversing its terms: the self does have irreplaceable dignity, because it has an illimitable liability to fault. The infinitude of this responsibility enters with the Third, who as it were throws open the moral circuit. For there to be public discourse there must be responsible parties to speak, expressive singularities--*justice* requires these singularities, so that the order of neutral reason or neutral language, spoken by no-one, does not go uncriticized. In "History" as such there is no responsibility and no justice.[116] The System, the objective whole in which the self is dissolved by biology and psychoanalysis, admits of no escape. Only in the encounter with an Other transcending this system can the self take its own distance from it and have its own separated being. Language is the miracle of this encounter, the original relation with the fellow man who is not controlled by the terms of a love-relationship, who will not accept merely poetical speech (which as such remains uncritical and dreamlike) but requires the public exchange value of prose.[117]

The equality which justice inevitably pursues is not based on a balance between what you and I deserve to get, but between what you and I are required to give in the service of justice. The "we" is not a plural of "I," because my position with regard to my "equal" is determined in an exchange of commandments--we command each other to command each other, we are co-responsible--rather than by any *conceptual* determination of who or what we are, what category we fall into, etc. Levinas' pluralism is not based on numerical multiplicity. The self and

the Other exceed the totality precisely because their relationship, the face-to-face encounter, interrupts the logic that
obtains in the totality (a logic of number and concept which in
itself only articulates the solidarity of consciousness with
the world whose meaning it constitutes). But the totality is
not opposed. Apart from this arena where free wills enter,
becoming causally conditioned, and encounter each other, with a
capability of perpetrating irreversible wrongs, there would be
no justice or injustice, and thus no moral meaning to attach to
persons. Consequently there is no question of dispensing with
concepts and quantities, but only of demonstrating their real
seriousness.[118]

The positive but relative significance of the "totality"
developed in this article must be borne in mind when *Totality
and Infinity*'s polemic against the philosophy of totality is
examined. "Totality" only becomes an evil when transcendence
of it is denied. Against "egoism," though, the System is in
the right.

(4) "La philosophie et l'idée de l'Infini" (1957).[119]
Philosophy has always searched for truth, but on two conditions:
(1) that truth be gained through *experience*, i.e. through relation with something absolutely Other that is not merely ingredient in our own nature, and (2) that the knower be free from
all compulsion, i.e. that the truth never alienate the seeker
from himself. But how can heteronomy and autonomy be reconciled? In this dilemma Western philosophy has largely opted
for autonomy, reducing everything Other to the Same rather than
risk losing the Same's self-mastery. But it is necessary to
appreciate the situation in which this decision was first made,
when the Greeks who distrusted "opinion"--that poison by which
the unwary soul could be insensibly influenced, altered, even
"eaten by others"[120]--searched for a way out of this insidious
flux, and found it in the ideal of the soul's irreducible freedom, anchored by immanent Reason. The individual was guaranteed
a being separated from the "participation" of all in all, as
Lévy-Bruhl used the word to describe the mythic consciousness
of primitives.[121]

The avowed primacy of the Same, however, Levinas calls
narcissism, because it is a commitment of the self to itself,

construing all knowledge as reminiscence and subsuming all particularities under neutral generalities. The power of consciousness over what it knows is assured, according to the relation of comprehension. Heidegger maintains the supremacy of the Same by studying all particular things via an embracing neutrum, "Being," which has no relation with the Infinite.[122] Represented in modern times especially by the Heideggerians and neo-Hegelians, this tradition in philosophy is "atheist" in that it denies "revelation," interruption of the world by something exterior to it. But there is a philosophical counter-tradition of relation with the Other, devoted not to some positive dogma but to what Levinas calls the "idea of the Infinite," the thought that "thinks more than it can think," Plato's thought of the Good "beyond Being." We are not adequate to this thought and must confess, like Descartes, that it has been placed in us from beyond.[123] Concretely, the "placement" of the Other in the Same occurs when the self is faced with its own injustice.

> The infinite does not block me as a force putting mine in check; it calls into question my naive right to power, my glorious spontaneity as a *vivant*, a *"force qui va."*[124]
> But this way of being measured by the perfection of the infinite is not in turn a theoretical consideration, by which freedom would spontaneously recover its rights. It is *shame* which freedom has of itself, finding itself in its very exercise to be a murderer and usurper.[125]

The moral life is "heteronomy through and through."[126] It bears emphasis that this is no passive heteronomy by which the Other has rights over against the Same which may or may not be infringed, but an active heteronomy, by which the Other already commands, and the Same already *is* unjust. The meaning that the self would provide for itself is disallowed, and moral responsibility is substituted for it.

Levinas now expands on his contention that there is no original equality between I and Thou: "It is necessary that the Other Person be nearer to God than I."[127] This establishes a "dimension of height" in Being,[128] an impossibility of domination through comprehension. The moral relation, alternative to "comprehension," is expressed as a desire aiming beyond all satisfaction, an infinite hunger addressed to something that cannot be nourishment. True Desire is goodness. But the openness to the Other that Levinas renders by "Desire" and "the idea of the Infinite" is presupposed by our very ideal of truth. We began by pointing out that experience par excellence is relation with the absolutely Other. The moral relation is, therefore, absolute experience (though not constituted experience in Husserl's sense, for "the face is pure experience, experience without a concept"[129]); the idea of the Infinite is "more *cognitive* than cognition itself," and all objectivity must participate in it.[130] The situation in which one is not alone is the situation par excellence.[131] The Good is not an exotic meaning remote from all others, but the meaning of all meaning. Its exigency occurs concretely as my neighbor's moral privilege with respect to me.

Levinas concludes by introducing an important distinction between the merely negative incomprehension of the Other Person that is implicit in the self's bad will, and the essentially positive incomprehension of the Infinite that is implicit in conscience. If the Other is not a phenomenon given as an *intentum* to consciousness, neither is it a mere phenomenal lacuna, a hole in the world. The Other is a noumenon, expressive of itself--yet, by which God commands the self.[132]

Many of the elements that will be marshalled in the master argument of *Totality and Infinity* (1961) have now been introduced--the Same and the Other, Desire, the idea of the Infinite, the ethical commandment, religion, creation, sensibility and enjoyment. Before proceeding to a discussion of how *Totality and Infinity* elaborates and adds to these themes, let us consider how several aspects of Levinas' philosophical orientation have evolved to this point.

The title of Levinas' first original treatise, *De l'existence à l'existant*, serves notice that for him questions of ultimate meaning pertain to personal existence rather than to Being. This must be remembered in order to understand the force of Levinas' identification of Self and Same, the thorough complicity, though not identity, he assumes between the knowable world as such and the (selfish) self as such, and the impossibility he asserts of giving "Being" any significance above and beyond the tyranny of the Same (unless it be the tyranny of the *il y a*). Worldly alterity is essentially surpassable. The transcendence of the intentional object is only posited in the process of getting to know the object, whereas the Other is absolved from the entire process and thus from phenomenology. But this detachment of the Other from Husserlian phenomenology does not contest that model (or only contests it in its claimed adequacy or primacy)--it adds something to it. With Heidegger the case is different. Heidegger has reversed Husserl, identifying Being as the agent of *Sinngebung* and the ego as Being's minion. But this "ecstaticism" is for Levinas a step backwards, an attempt to annul the real achievement of Western idealism in separating personal existence from the anonymous horror of the *il y a* and the cruelties of pagan rootedness. Levinas' appraisal of the *il y a* underlies his mistrust of "participation" and the violence of the sacred's demand for abandonment to a non-human experience. His analysis of consciousness as a power of withdrawal supports the liberal ideal or ethic of autonomy, so far as this is required by moral responsibility--but only that far.

Husserl's view of conscious life also lies back of Levinas' use of the idea of "the Same" as, quite literally, the realm of the same, the annihilation of difference. For Husserl the essence of meaning is given in the identification of ideal unity across a plurality of experiences; for example, the ideal object "this chair" is the meaning of the various perceptions of the chair from different angles, at different times, etc. insofar as they harmonize. The meaning of an idea may be conditioned by a horizon, as yet unsuspected, within which it appears--but the horizon is to be explored, to be made an object in turn.[133] The genius of consciousness is this reduction of plurality to unity, not necessarily a monolithic unity, perhaps rather a hierarchical whole or "layered" system, but in any event an intelligible totality. Levinas sees this totality as being in one respect a suffocating prison. The self surpasses everything it knows, by subordinating exterior singularity to interior generality; all worldly otherness is relative to its conquest in knowledge. The lack of absolute otherness in this realm means an impossibility of escape. Where is there to escape to? The world is thus a prison, albeit a spacious, interesting, and gratifying one, because it lacks access to any "outside." The battle within philosophy between monism and pluralism draws its seriousness from this sense of imprisonment and ennui, produced however only by moral exigence.

Levinas' attention to the "outside" Other, however, does not aim at reconstructing a second story of the universe, whether based on the human soul or on a divine being. His article "Le moi et la totalité" argues that the break with totality represented by the Other involves no removal from totality (the world) but a disturbance and redirection within the world. The only conceivable justice is economic, and its basis is money. His ethical "religion" is antimystical and does not, so far, invoke the name of God. His conception of the Self's transcendence of the System does not appeal to a detached intellective spirit (which would in any event be a wholehearted partner of the System), but to the pre-intellective sensibility of the existent, materially enjoying and being nourished by the world. Consequently the guilt of the self is the guilt of unshared food. Levinas presupposes that the God of the after-world and the heroic freedom of the human soul have both been demythologized. But precisely because of the destruction of the old metaphysics by Kant, Marx, and Heidegger, it is now necessary to ask in a new way about the spirit from which the meaning of our civilization derives.

3. Totality and the Infinite

In the preface to *Totality and Infinity*, Levinas immediately "concretizes" the abstract concepts juxtaposed in the title: totality means war, and the Infinite means peace.[134] Indeed, Tolstoy's *War and Peace* is a good introduction to the attitude of this work, for Tolstoy shows us the march of history as a juggernaut of evil from which no-one can keep his distance; we see the impersonal machine-like march of armies and events; we see the supposed master of events, Napoleon, as their most unfree puppet; and in the midst of all this we see the upsurge of humanity, whenever one man looks in another's face and sees him as a fellow man, perhaps only flickeringly and only for a moment. Levinas cites elsewhere the example of the crowd's hesitation to slaughter Vereshtchagin when urged on by Count Rastoptchin for his demented reasons of state: the doomed

young man's moral appeal cannot be silenced.[135] Thus Levinas
writes:

> Everyone will readily agree that it is of the highest
> importance to know whether we are not duped by morality.
>   Does not lucidity, the mind's openness upon the true,
> consist in catching sight of the permanent possibility of
> war? The state of war suspends morality. . . The art of
> foreseeing war and of winning it by every means—politics—
> is henceforth enjoined as the very exercise of reason. . .
> war is produced as the pure experience of pure being. The
> ontological event that takes form in this black light is a
> casting into movement of beings hitherto anchored in their
> identity, a mobilization of absolutes, by an objective
> order from which there is no escape.[136]

War "establishes an order from which no one can keep his distance; nothing henceforth is exterior. War does not manifest
exteriority and the other as other; it destroys the identity
of the Same."[137] Here we recognize the ultimate revelation of
Being as the denial of the existent, the *il y a*, from which
both the Same (as the separated existence of the existent) and
the Other must escape.

Totality and Infinity differs from Levinas' earlier
work by the frequency with which it discusses totality in the
guise of "universal history."[138] This means that Hegel stands
beside Heidegger as a model philosopher of totality;[139] and by
entering into a polemical relation with Hegel, Levinas steps
into the tradition of Cohen and Rosenzweig, for whom opposition
to the Hegelian system was a significant expression not only of
their philosophical principles but of their Judaism. Levinas
acknowledges in his preface the inspiration he received from
Rosenzweig's opposition to the idea of totality in *The Star of
Redemption*.[140] History is in a way the pre-eminent scheme of
Being, since its participants are judged only in terms of their
power or effectivity within the system. History is always written by the survivors, in whose third-person account the first
and second persons never appear.[141] Historical facts have
already happened and no longer answer for themselves.[142] In
historical terms both the separated being of the Same and the
exteriority of the Other are absurd. By starting from interiority and exteriority, Levinas reverses the primacy of history:
"Cronos, thinking he swallows a god, swallows but a stone."[143]
When the Other speaks, he does not merely provide us with a

text on which to practice an interminable work of interpretation. He *teaches*, which is to say that he is present interpreting his own text.[144] By virtue of this mastery he transcends any continuum of evidence.

The alternative to the ontology of war and the only vindication of morality is the eschatology of peace, or non-violent pluralism. Philosophers distrust this eschatology because it outruns the evidence and thus seems to belong to Opinion rather than to Knowledge; eschatology, in turn, does not try to fit itself into the system of totality by adding otherwise unknowable information to the evidence already amassed. The warrant of eschatology is rather that in Being itself there is "a surplus always exterior to the totality,"[145] for which the idea of the Infinite must be introduced.

> The first "vision" of eschatology (hereby distinguished from the revealed opinions of positive religions) reveals the very possibility of eschatology, that is, the breach of the totality, the possibility of a *signification without a context*. The experience of morality does not proceed from this vision--it consummates this vision; ethics is an optics. But it is a "vision" without image, bereft of the synoptic and totalizing objectifying virtues of vision, a relation or an intentionality of a wholly different type-- which this work seeks to describe.[146]

That something should signify of itself, independent of any system, means that the totality does not measure up to its own pretentions. The desire for the transcendent reality of the Other, which appears in religion as eschatology, appears in philosophy as *metaphysics*, a critical respect for the Otherness that cannot be mediated by the logos of ontology. Therefore, says Levinas, metaphysics is prior to ontology; the former does not oppose the latter, but questions its dogmatism, the claimed adequacy of the concepts by which it understands life.[147]

Totality and Infinity is "metaphysics." Our study of it will be guided by two basic questions: (1) How does it analyze or describe the Otherness of the Other at which it aims, and (2) How is it *able* to describe such a thing as the absolutely Other?

THE ABSOLUTELY OTHER. The formal aspect of the Other, its Otherness, is at the same time its content; that is, it is not other as a *result* of being one thing "other than" something else, but is from the very start and before all comparisons

Other.[148] It does not enter any system of "other than's"; the *absolute* Other is ab-solved from all relations.[149] Our metaphysical Desire is for something from which we are completely separated, "a country in which we were not born."[150] The journey to this country is without prospect of return. "To die for the invisible--this is metaphysics."[151] However, the Other does presuppose the Same as the absolute point of departure for the metaphysical relationship. The formal aspect of sameness or self-identity is at the same time the very content of the self: the self's complicity with the Same is total.[152] Merely formal relationships of identity and otherness occurring within the totality are not the model of the relation between Same and Other, between whom there is no simple opposition or apportioning of logical terrain. It is necessary that there be a self and a thought of the Infinite in order that Otherness be produced in Being, but this goes by the non-dialectical, non-logical "necessity" of goodness.[153] Goodness requires an irreducible pluralism in which the Same may not absorb the Other and the Other may not absorb the Same. It is important to recognize that Levinas proposes an egoism as well as an altruism, for even though the sense of egoism is ultimately determined by altruism, the egoism is not a "moment" to be eventually mediated, or a correlated antithesis to the Other.[154] That is why Levinas is at pains to reckon with the "secret" of the subject's interiority, which can never become public in the historical continuum or subject to the judgment of history[155]--the being so perfectly separated as to be "atheist," sufficient to itself in its life of enjoyment, not needing (in the sense of lack) anything Other.[156]

The Other is not *needed* because the Other does not belong to any economic system determined by the Same. Goodness is pure "luxury."[157] The impossibility of finding the Other within the structure of correlation that underlies the Same's comprehending transactions with relative others means that the Other is not a noema (intentional object) correlated with a noesis (intentional act), and therefore is neither an object of perception or cognition, nor a value, nor an object of volition toward which one could take an initiative.[158] The Other is not arrived at by negating the imperfections of man's condition.[159]

*not 9
Complete.*

We already know that the Other is other than all form and does
not "come into the light" where it would assume a place in the
world; and that no number or concept or *tertium quid* of any
sort can mediate the difference between Same and Other.[160] The
Other's Otherness is produced as a superiority to any such neutral third thing that, by claiming to rise above and encompass
Same and Other, would put them on a single plane, in a logical
opposition.[161] That would be only a relative pluralism, dis-
guising an ultimate monism based on the one frame of reference
within which things are opposed. The radical pluralism that
Levinas wishes to maintain presupposes an asymmetrical relation
between Same and Other, a "dimension of height" in which the
Other is situated as the incomparable and indomitable.[162]
Transcendence is trans-ascendence.[163] The idea of the Infinite,
at the same time the idea of perfection, exceeds totality up-
wards, beyond all phenomenal "givens" to a being that absolutely
reserves the prerogative of self-revelation.

All of these formal distinctions are integral to the
argument of *Totality and Infinity*, and it is a major purpose of
the book (subtitled "An Essay on Exteriority") to show how
other the Other is if the Other is really Other--so as to call
attention to the limitations of Husserlian phenomenology,
Heideggerian ontology, and Hegelian dialectic. But Levinas
considers this side of "pluralism" to be neither central nor
sufficient. Not a formal schema but an actual event in Being,
the irruption of the moral life, inflames the metaphysical
Desire within philosophy. The bridge between the abstract and
concrete aspects of this "ultimate situation" is the formula:
"*L'absolument Autre, c'est Autrui*."[164] The Other (non-concept,
non-phenomenon) is presented as the human face.[165] The relation
between the Same and the Other is language and hospitality.[166]
The Other is a stranger whose "nudity" or absolution from form
is at the same time his indigence, having nowhere to lay his
head, the helplessness and need of widows and orphans. His
"height" is his magisterial claim to express something absolutely new (himself); and the asymmetry that is formally indicated
by the idea of the Infinite is, concretely, the asymmetry of
intersubjective space in the master-pupil relation.[167] He is
not "*tu*" but "*Vous*," the one who commands rather than a familiar

or equal.[168] His "unforeseeableness" applies both to his
teaching speech and to his importunate plight, which can never
be assessed and budgeted.[169]

Levinas takes the line of Kierkegaard's *Philosophical
Fragments* in challenging the idea that all learning is reminiscence and all pedagogy maieutics.[170] The advent of the Other
means that the Same is apprised of something that could not
possibly be drawn from within the Same's own sphere.

> The absolutely foreign alone can instruct us. And it
> is only man who could be absolutely foreign to me. . .
> To approach the Other Person in conversation is to wel-
> come his expression, in which at each instant he overflows
> the idea a thought would carry away from it. It is there-
> fore to *receive* from the Other Person beyond the capacity
> of the I, which means exactly: to have the idea of the
> infinite. But this also means: to be taught. The relation
> with the Other Person, or Conversation, is a non-allergic
> relation, an ethical relation; but inasmuch as it is wel-
> comed this conversation is a teaching. Teaching is not
> reducible to maieutics; it comes from the exterior and
> brings me more than I contain. . . reason, without abdicat-
> ing, is found to be in a position to *receive*.[171]

In the human face, the revealer and the revealed coincide:
what is taught first is teaching itself, i.e. the fact that I
am in relation with someone "higher" than I.[172] My interlocutor masters even the temporal horizon with his magisterial word,
which never merely lapses into the past as a dead sign but
continually comes to its own assistance.[173] This living, paradigmatically spoken-in-person expression of the Other has (besides its own infinity) the entire world to teach me. "The
world is offered in the language of the Other; it is borne by
propositions. The Other is the principle of phenomena."[174]
Meaning itself now means teaching or being taught, i.e. being
taken up in conversation.[175] Such claims make up a calculated
overstatement on behalf of the Cartesian order of infinity
prior to the Socratic order of maieutics (the idea placed from
beyond vs. the idea drawn from within).[176]

The interruption of totality by the Infinite is disturbing, to be sure, because it opens a problem of justification for
the freedom of the Same that can never be resolved by the Same;
but Levinas departs from Kierkegaard and Hegel by insisting on
its peacefulness.

The Other is not for reason a scandal which launches it into dialectical movement, but the first rational teaching, the condition for all teaching. The alleged scandal of alterity presupposes the tranquil identity of the Same, a freedom sure of itself which is exercised without scruples, and to whom the foreigner brings only constraint and limitation. This flawless identity freed from all participation, independent in the I, can nonetheless lose its tranquility if the other, rather than countering it by upsurging on the same plane as it, speaks to it, that is, shows himself in expression, in the face, and comes from on high. Freedom then is inhibited, not as countered by a resistance, but as arbitrary, guilty, and timid; but in its guilt it rises to responsibility. Contingency, that is, the irrational, appears to it not outside of itself in the other, but within itself.[177]

The Other is not a paradox offensive to Reason, but the beginning of Reason. This is to conceive the rational as the just, the breath of air from "outside," the divine delirium of "winged thought" in the *Phaedrus*.[178] There are alternatives: the self can construct and fit itself into a totality, according to "the ancient privilege of unity which is affirmed from Parmenides to Spinoza and Hegel."[179] Its strategy is to overcome otherness, which it identifies as the cause of violence, by subordinating both I and not-I to an impersonal Reason.[180] Under these conditions, however, speech becomes a mere "pretext for an unintermitting psychoanalysis or philology or sociology, in which the appearance of a discourse vanishes in the Whole."[181] Under these circumstances there can be no truth, for there is no freedom of discrimination and no party responsible for it. Neither can there be truth if we grant freedom of the Same without an Other; under these circumstances the ego would share Descartes' plight, regarding the world as an unguaranteed, anarchic, insubstantial spectacle.[182] Only the world taken up in speech is meaningful, and only the proposition offered in conversation can be an objective truth. In this sense, then, "truth presupposes justice"[183] and reason presupposes the ethical relation between persons in which the self's position is, passively, an open reception of the Other, allowing him to come to the assistance of his own words, and actively, an apology seeking justification.[184]

The doctrine of reason is philosophy's Archimedean point, at which Levinas intends to apply a different lever. "The difference between the two theses: 'reason creates the

relations between me and the Other' and 'the Other's teaching
me creates reason' is not purely theoretical. The consciousness
of the tyranny of the State--though it be rational--makes this
difference actual."[185] Levinas' claiming of reason for ethical
metaphysics, and his careful analysis of the ways in which even
the scientific exercise of "reason" presupposes the face-to-face
language relation, provides him with some defense against the
charge that any philosophy of the absolutely Other must be an
irrationalism. But the Other seems to remain exterior and problematic to reason no matter how reason is defined. How can the
unthematizable be thematized? How can that which transcends
logic be incorporated in an understandable discourse? How can
the claimed condition of reason, lying beyond reason, be rea-
soned to? Levinas' suggestive but scattered remarks on the
problem of his method in *Totality and Infinity* call for inspec-
tion, inasmuch as a concept of Otherness cannot be made independent of the way it is sustained in an argument.

WHAT IS METAPHYSICS? Levinas claims that the development of his thought owes everything to the phenomenological
method, upon which he comments as follows:

> Intentional analysis is the search for the concrete.
> Notions held under the direct gaze of the thought that
> defines them are nevertheless, unbeknown to this naive
> thought, revealed to be implanted in horizons unsuspected
> by this thought; these horizons endow them with a meaning--
> such is the essential teaching of Husserl. What does it
> matter if in the Husserlian phenomenology taken literally
> these unsuspected horizons are in their turn interpreted as
> thoughts aiming at objects! What counts is the idea of the
> overflowing of objectifying thought by a forgotten experi-
> ence from which it lives. The break-up of the formal struc-
> ture of thought (the noema of the noesis) into events which
> this structure dissimulates, but which sustain it and re-
> store its concrete significance, constitutes a *deduction*--
> necessary and yet non-analytical.[186]

The "concrete" is what is as it irreducibly is, respected in its
own character, i.e. in its exteriority; the concept of "horizon"
means that the search for the concrete leads beyond what is only
naively or opinionatedly self-evident, in a critical movement;
and the concept of phenomenological "deduction" means that there
can be a philosophical procedure whereby the transition from
the naive to the critical, from Appearance and Opinion to
Reality and Knowledge, is effected. We already know that by

the "concrete" Levinas means the eminently exterior being of
the Other Person, who however is an abstraction beyond everything concrete (that could be held in thought's gaze),[187] and
that the ethical relation between men is the horizon of the
truth that philosophers of identity and totality naively seek.
It remains to specify the manner in which Levinas believes it
possible to move from the evidence of totality to the reality
of the Infinite.

The fact that Levinas appeals to the Kantian idea of
deduction as opposed to the Husserlian idea of reduction is
interesting in itself.[188] For Husserl, the reductions mean the
possibility of discovering a certain realm of objects (essences),
on the one hand, and a certain horizon of object-constitution
(the absolute consciousness of the transcendental ego), on the
other. But Levinas' metaphysics is neither an egology nor a
philosophy of objects. "For the way we are describing to work
back and remain this side of objective certitude resembles what
has come to be called the transcendental method (in which the
technical procedures of transcendental idealism need not be
comprised)."[189] Kant's transcendental deduction per se is not
a model for Levinas, inasmuch as it remains bound to objects by
seeking only the condition of the experience of objects.[190]
Levinas does not think that the signifying Other can be "deduced" from his signification, like a thing-in-itself from its
appearance, or that a purely absent ethical realm is demonstrably presupposed by the evident realm of totality. He maintains
that we are *already in* a situation in which totality and objectivating thought break up. We already do witness the "gleam of
exteriority" in the face of the Other Person.[191] "If, as this
book will show, ethical relations are to lead transcendence to
its term, this is because the essential of ethics is in its
transcendent intention. . . Already *of itself* ethics is an
'optics.'"[192] The deduction, therefore, consists in associating
ideas according to the non-analytic necessity of goodness
(which, for example, "warps" intersubjective space into the
asymmetry of which Levinas speaks) and then expressing these
ideas as a perturbation of the formal vocabulary and logic of
rational thought--the "concrete significance" of which is "restored" in the very perturbation. The non-objective ethical

relation of absolutely separated beings is the transcendental condition of the non-objective "concrete significance" of totality.

The key to metaphysics is the idea of the Infinite, which substitutes a commanding *non-adequation* for the principle of *adaequatio rei ad intellectus* governing the thought of the Same.[193] "[The] idea of the Infinite is transcendence itself, the overflowing of an adequate idea. . . The idea of the infinite is the mode of being, the *infinition*, of the infinite."[194] What is distinctive about this idea is that we know it only in the measure that we effect it; it is not a representation or a theoretical idea but a moral idea, a "practical" idea, which sustains activity itself.[195] To possess the idea is to have already welcomed the Other, submitting to his moral privilege.[196] Thus metaphysics is itself envisioned as the concrete accomplishment of the Infinite, in the social relation--the philosophical treatise moving in the same current as the rest of moral life.[197] The relation with the Other as Other cannot be theoretically depicted. We can only know the Other as Other without "touching," i.e. while facing him and engaging in discourse with him *about* something which he, as interlocutor, inevitably is not.

The Other is "faced" in philosophical language principally by the *via negativa*, to which Levinas constantly returns in order to exempt the Other from the false claims of totality--concretely, the tyranny of the State--which philosophy traditionally supports. Metaphysical method is "adequate" to its "object" only in avowing its inadequacy, acknowledging that its "object" remains beyond it. *Totality and Infinity* is most remarkable as an inventory of the philosophical predications that may not be attached to an admitted Other. But the import of Otherness does not have to do as much with the specific things I may or may not say about you, as with the fact that no matter what I say about you, I face you and cannot escape the problem of the justice of my comportment toward you. The activity of metaphysics, like all ethical activity, is oriented to the work of establishing justice. The philosophical opposition to totality is of a piece with political resistance to the totalitarian state. Metaphysics supports "true discourse"

against "rhetoric," in which men approach each other, not sin-
cerely, but by ruse--and opposes also the violence of the *mythic*,
in which persons abdicate from separation and responsibility to
immerse themselves in an experience whose ultimate meaning
remains hidden from them.[198] The method of metaphysics is fit-
ted to its end, the goodness of just relation that it aims to
serve, so that the metaphysical deduction produces a political
argument as well as a reorganization of concepts: it proclaims
the "politics" of feeding the hungry and clothing the naked.
Levinas wants to call our attention to this. "We shall. . . at
the risk of appearing to confuse theory and practice, deal with
both as modes of metaphysical transcendence. The apparent confusion is deliberate and constitutes one of the theses of this
book."[199] How could this confusion be avoided, if indeed it is
impossible to *say* thematically the Otherness of the Other, but
only possible to *show* the Other's Otherness by the act of refusing comprehension of him? What is the claimed "height" of
the Other, if not a gesture of self-abasement before him and a
preparation for his service?[200]

4. Interpreting the Absolutely Other

One central ambiguity of Levinas' philosophy is crystal-
lized in the formula of *Totality and Infinity*: "*L'absolument
Autre, c'est Autrui*." Does *Autre* come first, or *Autrui*? The
direction of movement expressed is from a philosophical category to a concrete reality; it is "the deformalization or the
concretization of the idea of the infinite, this apparently
wholly empty notion":[201]

> The method practiced here does indeed consist in seek-
> ing the condition of empirical situations, but it leaves to
> the developments called empirical, in which the condition-
> ing possibility is accomplished--it leaves to the *concre-
> tization*--an ontological role that specifies the meaning of
> the fundamental possibility, a meaning invisible in that
> condition.[202]

Philosophy inherits the idea of the Other from Plato and Descartes in a kind of dormant state; as an idea, i.e. as *l'Autre*,
it belongs to the totality, whereas in relation to the reality
of *l'Autrui* it accomplishes itself, "infinitizes," transcends
any philosophical doctrine of otherness. However, the only
trace left in totality by the event of the infinition of

Otherness is a chain of negations, which as such remain bound to the framework of ontology. Levinas' denial that the Other is a negation dialectically correlated with the affirmation of the Same, is itself dialectically correlated with the affirmation of correlation, as its negation! The system cannot be argued against, for to address it at all is to share a boundary with it and thus form a new system.[203] It is as though philosophy cannot but substitute *Autre* for *Autrui*, or a self-contradicting Other-formalism for metaphysics. Therefore the philosophical locution "*L'absolument Autre, c'est Autrui*" points the way out of the contradiction, by pointing the way out of ontological philosophy. *L'Autrui* is not to be understood as the empirical correlate of the logical category of *l'Autre*, but as the superlative reality (or as somehow associated with the superlative reality, if that reality turns out to be God) of which *l'Autre* is only a privative ontological or dialectical trace. As at the end of *De l'existence à l'existant* and *Le Temps et l'Autre*--where the I was substituted for the Same, and the other person for the Other--it is not a question of including persons in a neutral category, but of surpassing the neutral by the personal.

Regardless of intent, however, the surpassing of logic and Being can only be accomplished by understandable reasoning, and by predication with the copula "is," which immediately involves one in an understanding of Being. Whatever may have been the ethical significance of Descartes' discovery of the idea of the Infinite in the third Meditation--presumably Descartes was party to relations with God and his fellow men, before he wrote the third Meditation--the fact remains that he had an *idea* of the Infinite, and could ascribe to the Infinite no greater glory than necessary *being*. For Descartes, everything revolves around this unique theoretical event, as theoretical; and *Totality and Infinity* partakes of this orientation, even in exegeting implications from it that go beyond the theoretical. The idea of the Other is an irreducible component of the gesture beyond ideas, toward the other person, and is liable to critique as an idea. By what right does Levinas assume that totality is finite and "surpassable"?[204] Is not totality, or history, precisely the inexhaustible transcendence of the relations between Same and Other? The concept of *Aufhebung* in Hegel is bound to be misrepresented if it is forgotten that otherness is neither precluded nor mediated away, but presupposed and conserved, in Hegel's dialectic, which is set going and kept going by the upsurge of otherness. But Hegel recognizes that no Other can bear on the Same without violence. History is open, but "transcendentally violent." And to announce something Other than this violence, Other than history, can only be to irresponsibly flee toward unreality, to substitute for politics an art of the impossible. Perhaps the impossible "Jewish dream of heteronomy" must be thought alongside Greek ideas of Being and Logos, as a reflection of what Levinas calls the constitutive hypocrisy of our civilization devoted at the same time to the True and the Good;[205] but it is precisely Hegel who has tried to think this, whereas Levinas perhaps does nothing more than abdicate from the task.[206] Of him we might say, as Bosquet said of the charge of the Light Brigade, "*C'est magnifique, mais ce n'est pas la guerre*"--it is magnificent, but it is not philosophy. What meaning does peace have, except in relation to war; what is ethics except a movement *from* war *to* peace, in the play between war and peace? Neither pure war nor pure peace is conceivable.[207] And if pure peace were conceivable, it could give rise to nothing recognizable as ethics, because of its total abstention from history and power.[208]

Levinas cannot speak philosophically against Hegel (or Husserl, or Heidegger) without paying homage to Truth and thus confirming the Hegelian project of thinking all that is to be thought (or the Husserlian project of bringing everything to evidence in its own way, or the Heideggerian project of letting-be what is other in freedom of an imposed idea of Being).

> "It is. . . toward a pluralism which does not fuse into unity that we wish to make our way; and, if it can be dared, to break with Parmenides" (TA 20). Thus, Levinas exhorts us to a second parricide. The Greek father who still holds us under his sway must be killed; and this is what a Greek--Plato--could never resolve to do, deferring the act into a hallucinatory murder. . . But will a non-Greek ever succeed in doing what a Greek in this case would not do, except by disguising himself as a Greek, by *speaking* Greek, by feigning to speak Greek in order to get near the king? And since it is a question of killing a speech, will we ever know who is the last victim of this stratagem? Can one feign speaking a language? The Eleatic stranger and

disciple of Parmenides had to give language its due for
having vanquished him: shaping non-Being according to
Being, he had to "say farewell to an unnamable opposite of
Being" and had to confine non-Being to its relativity to
Being, that is to the movement of alterity.[209]

This is a fundamental criticism, to which the whole later movement of Levinas' thought responds, in an attempt to reckon with
the apparent bad faith of naming what is unnamable. But the
criticism shows up a methodic difficulty without coming to
grips with the broader movement and intention of this thought:
does Levinas really approach the king as an assassin, or are
his design and his perceptible accomplishments (his "concretiza-
tions") rather on the pacific side?

Philosophically, Levinas comes not to abolish the law
but to fulfill it. It is never a question for him of denying
or of posing an alternative to logic and evidence and Being,
but of discovering the original horizon of the meaning of logic
and evidence and Being, which is falsified when it is conceived
merely by analogy with these things. Truth is only truth in
the context of justice, which is not a truth. Ontological
philosophy, while not to be confused with metaphysics, does not
take on its right sense apart from metaphysics.[210] Since metaphysics accomplishes the transcendental condition of ontology,
Levinas reflects within ontological discourse the orientation
provided to it from without, so as to reveal or betray transcendence at the level of ontology. He calls the social relation "the logical plot of being,"[211] says that exteriority is
the essence of Being, and "Being is exteriority,"[212] says that
eschatology institutes a relation with *Being*, beyond totality,[213]
and that moral experience is the experience of Being par excellence.[214] The face is "the evidence that makes evidence possible."[215] But the hazard of linking the beyond-Being to Being
in this way, to show that Being depends for its meaning on the
beyond-Being, is that it requires an ontological expression of
the beyond-Being. The beyond-Being becomes, in short, Being
par excellence (how then is it beyond?). Moreover, this "tran-
scendentalist" procedure invites the suspicion that Levinas'
metaphysics only projects a sort of pre-Kantian intelligible
world in order to guarantee certain preferred values in this
world--such as the concept of objective truth, of which the

ethical relation is supposed to accomplish the very intention,[216] or the sincerity of personal expression.

Levinas' presentation of the idea of the Other is thus anything but incoherent. If anything, it errs at this stage on the side of ontological coherence, albeit often as the coherence of anti-ontology, by asserting that *Being* is *plural*. Nevertheless, a certain absolute incoherence is necessarily implied by the idea of the absolutely Other, and to retain a proper appreciation of this point it is necessary to identify possible misunderstandings of it.

First, the idea of the Infinite is an idea nonpareil. It is not distinguished from other ideas merely by what it is an idea *of*, but by the unique *way* in which it is an idea, which is not an idea at all in the normal sense. The deliberate confusion of theory and practice must be recalled in this connection. Levinas' idea is not Descartes' idea, whatever the precedent provided by Descartes. Rather, the idea of the Infinite is an interruption of the realm of ideas, a questioning of the assumption that the relation of the highest dignity is a knowing relation. Since the idea of the Infinite is not known, the metaphysics of Levinas is never to be confused with epistemology or ontology. To the question, Can an absolute Other be known? the answer is, Of course not! The purpose of the idea of the Infinite is to point or gesture away from things that are known (and unknown), toward something different, the personal order.

Second, Levinas' transcendental pacifism is not a rejection of politics. The fact that it rebels against taking politics to be the model of ultimate interhuman reality, as Hobbes' war of all against all (mitigated by prudence), does not imply that the war is unreal, or that there are not relatively better and worse ways to wage it. While war is irrefutable on its own terms, there is something beyond it that is unlike it, that is Other; and it is to this Other that we look in discriminating between the better and the worse. The face-to-face relation belongs to what Kant would have called the metaphysics of morals, rather than to *Sittenlehre* in the sense of psychologically and historically informed calculation of moral policy. In place of the immanently present law of Reason is the

transcendently presented "Thou shalt not commit murder" of the
neighbor's face, which unlike the categorical imperative is not
originally a qualification of practical initiative, but a questioning of initiative per se. Levinasian metaphysics of morals
is thus even further removed from "ethics" than is its Kantian
equivalent; and yet, as the prohibition of murder and injunction
of hospitality to the stranger, is far more concrete. It is
the primordial contestation of ontology's right to ground ethics
on a different basis than the acceptance of the other man as
Other, which always seems to be accompanied by a claim that
violence is necessary. What is this sort of argument ever used
to justify, if not violence? Left to itself, ontology does not
question the supposed necessity of violence and is thus a philosophy of injustice, the philosophy of the totalitarian state,
or of the colonialist continent Europe.[217]

The questioning of power is a different kind of movement
than the movement of power itself. This makes it ridiculous,
from the standpoint of power. But it would be more ridiculous
to accept the justification that power offers for itself, from
itself. That is why the Good, judge of Being, has nothing in
common with Being. To clarify the relationship between the
unequal beyond-Being and Being, while holding fast to the absolute and positive Otherness of the Good, even as the metaphysical trail leads beyond the neighbor to God, is the task of the
later work of Levinas.

The writings of Levinas examined so far make up a highly consistent corpus. The soil in which his original philosophy
germinated was the crisis of liberal idealism that dominated
especially the German intellectual scene between the World Wars.
In 1935 he identified the problem as the philosophy of Being,
and the solution (the recovery of the spirit of civilization in
face of the barbarity of Hitlerism) as a philosophy of the
beyond-Being. By 1947 the philosophy of beyond-Being had been
oriented to the two poles of the Same and the Other, each transcendent of the totality dealt with by ontology; in *De l'existence à l'existant* he gave a detailed analysis of the event by
which the self keeps its distance from anonymous Being, and in
Le Temps et l'Autre he considered both the conceptual uniqueness

of the idea of the Other and its concretization in sexual and
paternal relations. *Totality and Infinity* is an expanded and
matured treatment of these same themes, fairly evenly divided
in emphasis between Same and Other; the Same is commanded by
the Other, and the Other requires the Same, since only between
separated beings can goodness occur. His discussion of the
theses of *Totality and Infinity* at the Sorbonne recurred to his
earliest definition of his agenda:

> We search for a way out of idealism. We do not find it
> in a return to realism. The realism that satisfies Marxism
> or transcendental ontology is not realist enough to tran-
> scend idealism.[218]
> Idealism. . . is an egoism.
> To deny that being is *for me* is not to deny that it is
> for man, it is not to abandon humanism, it is not to sepa-
> rate humanity from the absolute. It is only to deny that
> the humanity of man lies in his position as the Self. Man
> par excellence--the source of humanity--is perhaps the
> Other.[219]

The great advance represented by *Totality and Infinity*
is its awareness of an essential equivocation between the theoretical and the practical, which is enjoined upon both the
philosophical medium and its message. The concept of Otherness
is a rule for comportment before the Other, specifically a
readiness to be taught by him and a generosity toward him
according to which the world is thematized and offered in language. This development consolidates the affinity with Kant,
which had been announced earlier in "L'ontologie est-elle fondamentale?" "Metaphysics" is Levinas' version of Kant's practical, ethical philosophy. Like Kant, Levinas wants to distinguish the root question "What ought I to do?" from the question
"What can I know?"--but, unlike Kant, Levinas finds the answer
to this question completely beyond the consciousness of the
Same, in the contingent, ungraspable justification represented
by the Other. Reason itself becomes a function of the social
relation. The revolution in reason that is brought about by
the advent of the idea of the Other is the most momentous consequence of the idea, for we find that the Other is more than
merely a problematic intruder on existing philosophy: it brings
its own philosophy, an ethical "metaphysics," with it.

CHAPTER IV

THE PROBLEM OF JUSTIFICATION

1. The Crisis

In spite of the obvious differences between the premises, procedures, and aims of Barth's and Levinas' arguments,
there are no less obvious similarities. The idea of the Other
belongs to a whole web of concepts woven through the two literatures; and it is now time to trace that pattern, as a way of
retrospectively summarizing what we have brought to light so
far, and also to anticipate further developments. It will be
understood that by discussing "the Other" as though the term
meant only one thing, we do not ignore the difference between
the theologian's and the philosopher's employment of it. We
abstract from this difference, for the moment, in order to let
the logical commonalities of the two arguments stand out in
relief. Only later will it be profitable to inquire into the
significance of the ways in which the arguments do not converge.

CRITIQUE. Barth and Levinas both make a point of
showing how their thought operates *critically*; their "metaphysics"[1] means to go beyond, not back behind, the modern destruction of "metaphysics." And this is at least partly owing to an
inner link between the idea of critique and the idea of the
Other.

> Critique or philosophy is the essence of knowing. But
> what is proper to knowing is not its possibility of going
> unto an object, a movement by which it is akin to other
> acts; its prerogative consists in being able to put itself
> in question. . . The knowing whose essence is critique
> cannot be reduced to objective cognition; it leads to the
> Other Person. . . The welcoming of the other person is ipso
> facto the consciousness of my own injustice--the shame that
> freedom feels for itself.[2]

> Genuine thinking is always strange to the world and
> unsympathetic.[3]
> The man who not only criticizes, disapproves of, and
> deplores himself, but is able finally to set his whole being
> in question and to be appalled at himself is, at any rate--
> not I! If we go on to ask: "Who then?" "What then?," we
> must be quite clear that, the moment we have--even though

carelessly or half in fun--asked such questions, there has already entered within our horizon something radically, irrevocably, and irreversibly Other.[4]

What does it mean for thought to be "critical"? Why should truly critical thought presuppose the totally Other? To "criticize" means to choose or judge. In a wide range of cases it is considered appropriate that people "judge for themselves"-- as only you can choose the clothes that fit you, the music you like, whom you love, perhaps by whom you wish to be governed, and so forth. But we consider it absurd and dangerous when people attempt to *judge themselves*. A reason for this lies in one's tendency to turn a fonder, less discriminating eye on oneself than on others; that is, we expect a self-measurement to be a less reliable measurement. But there is a further sense in which self-judgment, no matter how likely to be accurate, is not properly speaking a judgment at all. Self-justification is never quite a justification, but at best a well-argued petition for justification with respect to an exterior, "objective" standard. An honest person who has made a difficult moral choice may say, "I believe I did the right thing"; this likely indicates that the right thing has indeed been done; but the pronouncement does not constitute the justification. Similarly, a scientist of unquestioned integrity may witness by chance an occurrence that confirms his pet theory; but without controls and experimental repeatability, no one could accept his report as proof of his theory. His report would be a truthful account, but only of his own experience. A *critical* truth of science would have to be accessible to more than one investigator.

By paths such as these, the concepts of critique and justification lead to the concept of an Other. For criticism pertains, not to truth itself, but to how truth is gained, how truths are distinguished by the attitudes we adopt toward them, and how the discrimination of truth is a function of the relationship between those seeking it. Conventional agreement does not make truth, but the human way of having truth called "critical" presupposes some sort of open forum where one proposes the truth and is liable to have it questioned by others[5]--the most critical questions being asked by those most other, with whom we can take the least for granted. It is essential to the notion of objective truth that someone else may have it, that

I may be wrong.[6] Something like the same requirement applies
to our moral life, in that a deed put above all possibility of
reproach or question could only be a monstrosity. The moral
patronage of the Napoleon ideal does not get Raskolnikov through
Crime and Punishment; no action or project justifies itself.
Neither is there any truth or self-evidence so luminous that
the individual subject could say of it, apart from all criticism
by others, that it justifies itself as "objective" truth. However, the morally and theoretically sane person--whose sanity
consists in knowing that he is not alone and not a law unto
himself--not only acknowledges an exterior bar of judgment as a
negative check on illusion and folly, but seeks the Other's
judgment as something *better* than self-judgment, or the law of
the Creator as better than man's own law. "The absolutely other
not only refuses to be possessed, but contests possession, and
can by the same token consecrate it."[7] That is, only before an
Other does one feel shame and the impossibility of justification
(which is not even a problem for the self-satisfied, who thus
far is ahead of the game); but only in relation to an Other does
one have the *right* to anything, or the *responsibility* for anything. The "critical" order, based on a fundamental pluralism,
is at the same time the personal order. Therefore plurality is
not a mere privation of intelligible unity, but the fundamentally better situation in relation to which unity, as loss of
relationship, is the privation.

BEYOND EXPERIENCE. If the critical order is superior
to the uncritical, and if the specific difference of the critical order traces back to an original situation of plurality,
then the intellectual effort that means to serve the better
order must reckon with the Otherness by which the natural monism
of the theoretical consciousness is fractured. The idea of
critique leads to proclamation of a *Crisis*. The critical notion
of truth, for example, requires that my truth be the other's
truth as well. But I cannot possess the truth of this other;
if I did, that truth would have to be truth for yet another, a
third party; and so on.[8] Critical truth-seeking can never turn
into a truth that which makes truth critical, viz. the interloc-
utor/questioner, for interlocutors have a different role in
knowledge than the things that are known. But this means that

knowledge presupposes an ignorance without remedy; at least, the non-cognitive condition of knowledge presupposes something for which only a non-cognitive account may be given. In order to make way for a non-cognitive account, and perhaps before we even suspect what form such an account could take, it is necessary to proclaim a constitutive ignorance of the Other, a Crisis of knowledge and a problematization of our entire experience so far as it offers the material of knowledge.

The gap in experience opened up by the idea of the Other has already been documented in second *Romans* and *Totality and Infinity*; it remains as a permanent feature of Barth's and Levinas' thought. Man as *die Seele*[9] or *le vivant*[10] is at home with himself and godless, "atheist," the world of his separated life being so defined as to exclude the Other, whose epiphany calls it into question from beyond. Somehow the Other does enter our experience, but only as an "exploding concept" or "overflowing idea."[11] The interruption is never accomplished once and for all, so that it would become a dead issue: there never emerges a special experience that theology or philosophy could describe. Barth still said in 1962 that "evangelical theology is an eminently critical science, for it is continually exposed to judgment and never relieved of the crisis in which it is placed by its object, or, rather to say, by its living subject [the condition of knowledge that is not itself knowledge]."[12]

> Whoever believes, knows and confesses that he cannot "by his own understanding and power" in any way believe. He will simply *perform* this believing, without losing sight of the unbelief that continually accompanies him and makes itself felt. Called and illumined by the Holy Spirit as he is, he does not understand himself. . . The event of faith lies in no one's domain.[13]

When Levinas was asked in 1975 about the nature of "moral experience," he said: "I try to avoid the term 'moral experience'; it assumes a subject already established, who before anything else *is* and then at a certain moment has a moral experience."[14] In response to the suggestion that morality is founded on a fundamental intuition or choice, he replied, "Is there an initial choice? I would rather say: there is an initial question. . . because the question can be posed beyond any assurance of response."[15] The revelation of the Other is never a given.

It is *événement*, *s'accomplir* or *se produire*, *Ereignis* and *Geschehen*.[16] The question-event is critical of our experience not as an antithesis to experience, however, but as the "experience par excellence." "Actual experience begins where our alleged experiences cease, in the crisis of our experiences, in the fear of God."[17] The experience par excellence is, by the lights of the logic of totality, an impossible one, inasmuch as it belongs to no subject-object correlation. God's faithfulness and eschatological peace are the great impossibilities--but over against the good, sin is impossible in turn. There is no equilibrium between good and evil.[18] And because good and evil do not meet on one level, the revelation of the good is essentially equivocal. As it appears in this world it travels incognito.[19] While *Totality and Infinity* stresses the peacefulness of the disturbance of the Same by the Other, second *Romans* often refers to the encounter in Kierkegaard's language as the "Paradox."[20] But a much more nuanced account of Revelation as the incomparable communication of reason to reason is provided in the first volume of the *Church Dogmatics*.[21]

However broadly we define the concept of experience, whatever belongs to that experience still belongs to me, is cut to my measure. That which I belong to, that which measures me, would make an "experience" totally unlike any other, due to the impossibility of explaining it or resorting to it or standing on it the way I can stand on everything else I call my "experience." Ordinarily, experience is an increase in familiarity with things, an enhanced control of them or a reduced liability to being taken off-guard by them. Experience is cumulative. If I learn no lessons, dealing with every situation as though it were completely new, my being at the mercy of contingency counts as inexperience. Thus, if the Other belonged to my experience I would be able in some sense to look beyond him-- having mastered him, I could pay attention to something else. I would once more have gotten my responsibility to him under control. If my interlocutor belonged wholly to my experience, I would really be talking not to him but to myself, or to someone else beyond him. The God of experience becomes an object of theology without remaining subject; the experience-theologian is not responsible to God, but solely to other theologians, for providing a satisfactory account of the theologoumenon "God."

That which judges and justifies experience is not in experience, any more than the one who "has" experience (the transcendental unity of apperception) can become an object of experience. But beyond the logical point that I and the Other, who represent two dimensions of the constitution of experience, are not ourselves constituted, there is in Barth and Levinas the additional conviction that the locus of the Good must be elsewhere than in the evidently evil existence that all our experience teaches us.[22] Existence as we know it offers a spectacle of war: the repression of the State, the social aggression of the class struggle, the libidinous and resentful aggressions of individuals, and the encompassing violence of death. The new world we seek, our "eschatological certainty of peace," must be founded on a totally different premise. *Sollen*--a *Sollen* far more alien than the *Sollen* of idealism--appears to us as radical dissatisfaction with *Sein*. The concept of "value" is inapplicable to this hypercritical *Sollen*, for two complementary reasons: (1) unlike the Other, "values" belong to the world, and (2) unlike the Other, "values," whether or not simply bestowed by the subject, confirm the self in its enjoyment.[23] "Value" is *experienced*.

BEYOND MYTH. The just world, so different from our own, is not a "next" world. For there is no conceivable next world that is not an extension of our own experience. We design a mythic afterlife as a way of managing the future so as to assure the triumph of what is, after all, the problem rather than the solution, viz. the arbitrary freedom of self against neighbor and of man against God. The critique brought by the Other is not less critical than the Kantian thought that punctured metaphysics, or the Nietzschean thought that punctured the God of consolation. It confronts us with "the unique contradiction between life and death, between the things that are and the things that are not."[24] The seriousness instituted by the Other is of a different order than the individual concern for salvation, that "egoist cry of subjectivity";[25] it calls for objective justice and the forgetfulness of self in which lies the only possibility of liberation from self.[26] Both Barth and

Levinas reject the idea of immortality as a prolongation of the individual's existence.[27] The advent of the Other is a hyper-critical event calling into question *everything* to do with our existence. To respond to this call is to wake up from dogmatic slumber,[28] from the dream of self-sovereignty and from the delusion that the no-God of this world is the true God.[29] Onto-logical transcendence inevitably leads to some variant of what we already know and value, while the true transcendence is strictly a disruption of this world, an infinite proximity,[30] a question not remote but insistent. It is in fact a political question, but only on the paradoxical terms that while the Other subjects me to an infinite agitation for a materially just order, yet the Other is absolved from identification with any concrete version of that order. The Other, to whom there are no adequate means, is the only end that justifies them.

Desire for the totally Other may resemble a romantic *Sehnsucht*. But relation with the Other demands a sobriety that is incompatible with the ecstatic "participation" of mythic con-sciousness, or the romantic immersion in the ineffable or numi-nous.[31] "Indeed God rules, but He will rule in and through *you*. . . not through a magical-mechanical effect, but through a free act of your own will!"[32] The Other requires the separation (consciousness, discretion, will) of the Self.

2. The Plural Situation

There is a breach in the continuity of experience, not because experience is "finite," but because an Other has in some sense arrived and made an Other claim. The Other is not to be confused with a general questionableness of existence which would be a characteristic proper to that existence; rela-tion with the Other creates a new, different existence. Find-ing what we did not seek, desiring what we did not know we needed, we are placed in a certain position or situation from which we henceforth think and act. By itself, an interruption or limitation of our experience would create only a *problem*; but the presence of the Other makes it a problem of *justification*.

ENCOUNTER. It can be misleading to impose the idea of "relation" on the plurality of Same and Other, since that might imply an intelligible form, visible to a third party, embracing and defining the two.[33] The meaning of radical pluralism is that no such vantage point is available.[34] As I am faced by the Other, I do not rise in thought to a level where our "relation" becomes conceivable; I cannot determine my response to the Other (as Other) according to some idea about the nature or purpose of our relationship; the personal can never be translated into the neutral.[35] There is an irreducible contingency or pure responsiveness in truly facing someone else. Without belonging to a relation with the Same, the Other *encounters* the Same, furnishing from beyond experience a controlling term of the relation that ensues.[36] For Kant, the unrepresentable idea of moral freedom caused a crisis of the theoretical reason, the actual result of which was its subordination to the practical reason.[37] For Kierkegaard, the impossibility of speculatively mediating individual existence led to the subordination of theory to the practical matter of living one's life as "subjectivity" before God. The shift to the practical or existential standpoint corrects a kind of mad self-forgetfulness on the part of the theoretical systematicians; they are reminded of the actual shacks they live in, next door to their imaginary castles.[38] The idea of the Other functions as the reminder par excellence of the actual position in which we are placed, our problem of justification.[39] Our theoretical systems are not the absolute, but the relative; not the concept, but the Other (and the practical responsibility to which the Other calls me) is the concretissimum and ultimate horizon. This persistent superiority of the Other to the concept, which portends a superiority of the practical problem of just comportment (inasmuch as theory itself, never *of* the Other, is a form of comportment *before* the Other), is designated by the "height" of the Other, who always rises "above" my conception so as to face me "over" it. We cannot *assign* this height to the Other, for the Other rises above any hierarchy.[40]

Important consequences follow from the primacy of the practical for the method of philosophy and theology. One is no longer at total liberty to construct a world-view as one thinks pleasing or fit; Kant, for example, placed severe strictures on the possible meaning of theological propositions, not only as a negative result of his critique of metaphysics, but as a positive result of the moral law, which demanded a certain practical relation of the Omnipotent Being to duty. In so doing, he reflected the position in which he had been placed by the moral law--what it allowed and forbade him to say. In Barth and Levinas it is apparent that the problem of justification opened by an Other places man in a unique position, an ultimate insecurity that is no position.[41] "And the position is a lost position. Yes, a lost post which must nevertheless remain occupied. All posts which men occupy as men are lost posts."[42] The subject "already established, who before anything *is*" and then *has* experience, is undercut by this view of man. The necessarily unqualified openness of the *problem* of justification denies that the self has a position at all, as a secure possession; the heteronomous reference of the problem of *justification* replaces self-position with Other-position, and arbitrary freedom with responsibility. Responsible philosophical and theological discourse then becomes, before all else, a deferral to the Other. No rule limits the thought of the Other to the *via negativa* of absolving the Other from experience, myth, and concept in order to clarify the dimension of "height"--for obedience could also be offered positively (though it remains to be seen how). The crisis of theory-negation only shows a root principle by which responsible thought must differ from the irresponsible.

The movement of deferral can be seen, not merely on the battle-line of the argument for total Otherness, but throughout the writings of Barth and Levinas. Barth's idea of Scripture and tradition, for example, is guided by the consideration of our practical position here and now with respect to the there-and-then of Revelation, of the earliest witness to Revelation, and of the creeds and confessions which represent serious encounters of the church with Revelation.[43] There is no "pure reason" that transcends our historical situatedness with respect to these things, or at least no "reason" that would be theologically authoritative. In challenging the authority of any witness or interpretation, we must ask ourselves: where are we standing, when we criticize? What do we know that the Gospel writers did not? What in Revelation are we responding to (i.e. gives us a place to stand) that leads us to criticize a

particular dogma? The relative "height" of the authority of
the Bible and the church is not to be confused with the absolute
"height" of Revelation itself, but the lesser, like the greater,
is grounded in the impossibility of rising above a situation of
encounter to a superior third position from which that encounter
could be totalized and judged. The New Testament as a document
is only so "high," but it is "high" enough that one cannot peer
over it to independently acquaint oneself with Christ.[44] For
Levinas, the pluralism of the encounter with the Other Person
implies that philosophy is not an endeavor of the solitary
reflecting spirit to paint the best picture of experience, but
an "intersubjective drama" in which theses are offered and withdrawn, questions are answered and re-asked.[45] By accepting
philosophy as dialogue, the philosopher is freed from the ob-
sessive concern for transparency in method, from the "interminable methodological trampling" over his own footsteps[46]--from
trying to jump over his own shadow--in order to arrive at perfect clarity. While reflection turns ever inward in search of
its own foundations, the thought that obeys the absolutely
opaque Other can offer philosophy in public, can afford to
speak. Speech is the appeal to exterior justification.[47]

The "height" of the Other, which gives a meaning to the
idea of authority as an original dimension of personal relations,
reflects a particular understanding of wherein the Otherness of
the Other consists. It is not enough to say that the totally
Other is "elsewhere," for a purely elsewhere Other would be
fair game for speculation[48]--or silence. The Other is *here* in
a certain way, posing a question that does not simply equate
with the finitude of human existence. It is possible to answer
and serve the Other, even if not adequately, whereas an otherness like Death or Nothingness cannot be served but only addressed with some sort of anguish or resolve that is purely an
achievement of the self (or Being) and falls short of transcendence toward the personal. It is only by the personal, critical
claim underlying what we call "authority" that a radically Other
enters life, and a genuine transcendence of the self's life
becomes possible.

LEARNING. The authority of the Other, which we discussed as his "height," is directly related to the fact that we

have something absolutely new to learn from him. First, of
course, revelation reveals revelation itself (or teaches teaching itself):[49] that is, apart from the so-called "content" of
revelation (which is reduced in second *Romans* to the Crisis as
such), the primary content of revelation is that there is an
Other, with all the critical and positive consequences of this
fact. Socratic maieutics appears in this light as the pursuit
of ignorance rather than teaching--if, that is, the premise of
recollection is separated from the dialectical context in which
recollection is educed and criticized. But this means that the
relationship with the Other as Other may go on to be a teacher-
pupil relationship, from which one learns new things. The "experience par excellence" is not opposed to ordinary experience
in being empty, but in being adventurous, in being taught the
unheard-of. And the eagerness to learn that also belongs to
obedience to the Other determines our relationship with our
"fellow-pupils" the philosophers and theologians.[50]

The acknowledgement that we have something new to learn
puts us in a certain position with respect to religious texts.
Beyond the work of historical and textual criticism, we arrive
at a point where we sit at the feet of a writer to be taught by
him, to take him with as much seriousness as he speaks--to consider, when we fail to understand, whether the blame for failure
might not be ours--and in doing this we become more "critical"
than the "critics," as Barth said in his preface to second
Romans.[51] Only thus can the specifically theological sense
(i.e. the content of the particular question being put) be dis-
engaged from the dead letter of received documents. Levinas
adopts a similar attitude with respect to Talmudic interpretation.

> No-one can refuse the illumination of history. But we
> believe that this does not nearly suffice. We take the
> Talmudic text, and the Judaism manifested in it, as *teach-*
> *ings* and not as a mythogenic tissue of historical leftovers.
> We endeavor to read it with respect for its conventions and
> themes, without mixing up the meanings that proceed from
> this conjunction with the questions they raise for the his-
> torian and the philologist. Did the playgoers at a Shake-
> spearian theater pass the time showing their critical spirit
> by noting that where a palace or forest was drawn on the
> backdrop there were really only bare boards?[52]
>
> Pure philology, which is not enough to understand Goethe,
> is not enough to understand Rabbi Akiba or Rabbi Tarphon.[53]

But the respect we owe to what a text or person may teach us must not transform teaching into oracle, i.e. into a "given" revelation. At every moment our response to revelation is demanded afresh, so that personal relationship is maintained.[54]

The No by which the Other breaches our experience is the leading edge of his Yes, what he brings in his own way. The concept of authority remains empty without this affirmative content, for what difference would it make that I am forbidden to look "over" the face of the Other Person, or the privileged witness to Revelation, if there is nothing to learn in the relationship? What would the disturbance accomplish if it were merely a disturbance (except the destruction of the self)? Beyond the "Thou shalt not commit murder" is sociality; beyond death is resurrection. The service of the Other is a life completely unlike our life of sinful selfishness, but it is a new *life*, the life that overcomes the tragedy of self-bound existence.

SERVICE. Ulysses is a man of adventure, but all of his adventures are incident to a homeward journey. He represents that aspect of the Greek intellectual tradition that orders all speculation to the end of self-knowledge. But Abraham, called forth out of Haran, embarks on a different sort of adventure without prospect of return; a life of service rather than of self-knowledge.[55] Both adventures are actuated by a love of wisdom, perhaps, but for Abraham's part it is a question of the "wisdom of desire,"[56] of comportment in the sight of the Lord. To enter into relation with the absolutely Other, I must become a *stranger*, "hounded about, disturbed, stormed, shaken, humbled, the opposite of an assured man who has an answer for every question."[57] I am called out only to go noplace.[58] My fellow man appears, in his turn, as the unknowably other stranger in whom I encounter God's otherness.[59] These themes express the resistance of the "practical" (as determined by the problem of justification) to the recurrent efforts of the theoretical to be master once again. If justice, served in obedience, really is prior to "truth" (whereby what we know serves *us*)--if man is not the master--then it is incumbent upon the philosopher or theologian to vigilantly construe thought as obedience, to prevent the reduction of obedience to thought.[60] The "system" of the infinite difference is uniquely anti-systematic in this respect, for what it rules out is precisely the fortification of the familiar and useful that we call "systematic thinking." The practical disturbance of ethics breaches the ramparts of any system and reminds the theologian of the truth of God; henceforth dogmatics and ethics will not be allowed to separate, as though they were distinct disciplines.[61] Revelation's claim on existence makes an ethics without God as much of an absurdity as a God without ethics. Ethics is the "optics" of philosophy, too; not a branch of philosophy, but first philosophy.[62]

Both thinking and acting are forms of service, for the distinction between innocence and shame is more original than the theory-practice distinction. The person who has been subjected by the Other to the open question of justification has a different directionality, as it were, in all aspects of his being. His "service" is his going-out or transcending to the Other, by which he takes something more seriously than his own death.[63]

We have attended to a certain "logic" or relatedness of different ideas so far as they are associated with the Other. This is evidently not a coercive and self-subsisting logic that could be conceived independently of our two arguments, which each would then "have" to obey, in the way that one supposedly "has" to obey the logic of identity and non-contradiction; it is perhaps only the trace left by an eruption of certain Jewish and Christian notions within the framework of modern secular philosophy; but in any event a single pattern is discernible, and noteworthy. From the "axiom" furnished by the advent of the *totaliter aliter* are drawn the following theorems:

1. Institution of a relation that can only be accomplished, not conceived; hence, a new primacy of the "practical."

2. The moral "height" or authority of One who is Other than the self; hence, the superiority of the pluralist to the monist order, and the constitution of the personal order as one of appeal, command, and critique.

3. Displacement of the axis of the seriousness of existence from the tragedy of finitude or death to the existence-smiting (but blessed) exigence of an Other; hence a new life of service.

4. Absolute novelty, disturbing the maieutic presupposition of learning as reminiscence; hence a perpetual openness
to teaching, and the impossibility of satisfaction in knowledge.

What we have learned about the concept of Otherness
itself is that the Other *as Other* is not merely absent, but
equivocally present; not indifferent, but teaching; not something of which there is an experience, but an event that criticizes and reorients experience; not a neutrum or mediating concept, but an irreducibly positive, singular, personal self-revelation; not an abstract Questionableness, but an insistent and
concrete Question--which creates a continual movement from the
abstract "problem of justification" to the concrete problem of
justice, i.e. from the formal possibility or impossibility of
relation with the Other to the actual accomplishment of feeding
the hungry. All of these features are not mitigations or excep-
tions to Otherness; it is precisely these features that constitute *total* Otherness, the utterly strange and critical.

3. The Program

The transcendence of service is never accomplished once
and for all but always has to be re-enacted, even in the formal
disciplines of theology and philosophy. It is as though the
triumph of practical reason had always to be rewon in order to
be "practical" with this transcending signification. The Crisis
does not pass. Therefore the thought of the Other is placed in
polemical relation with many other thoughts dominant in modern
philosophy and theology which are not compatible with it; and
Barth and Levinas are both committed to polemics on a wide
front based on a diagnosis of the composition of intellectual
modernity. Their criticism is drawn by two motifs in particular.

The first motif is called by Levinas the "philosophy of
the Same" and is best represented by subjective idealism. Barth
understands the same thing broadly as Cartesian and Enlightenment rationalism, or as the thought of the "Renaissance man."[64]
The important element in any case is the determination of this
thought by the *problem of freedom* distinct from the problem of
justification, i.e. the problem faced by a free knower regarding
the reliability of what he knows (the epistemological problem
of Descartes, or Husserl), and/or the problem faced by a free

agent with respect to the rules by which he may act and the
structure of the world within which he acts (the existential or
practical problem of Kant, or the early Heidegger, or Sartre).
Credit is due this problem of freedom, because it *is* a problem;
as a critical questioning of the assumptions of knowledge and
action, it makes possible a break with mythic participation and,
through a sophisticated awareness of what the subject may *not*
claim to know or say, the fall of irresponsible metaphysics.
But the problem returns, like Ulysses, to the self. Its basic
strategy is to reduce otherness by making it relative to the
necessary conditions of the self's existence. It fails to
transcend experience to the degree necessary to truly distinguish "practice" from theory: Kant's "primacy of practical
reason" remains a doctrine of the one indivisible reason, and
the "I ought" and "I do" are conceived by analogy with the "I
think" as lacking any plural.[65] In the end I am only responsible to myself. The justification question deepens the problem
of freedom by commanding it instead of contradicting it. The
freedom that views itself as sufficient unto itself, a law unto
itself, is naive. Therefore the question to be put to the
theology and philosophy of the thinking or acting ego is: Do
you really believe you are alone, and that your certitude of
self (whether it be a serene confidence in Reason, or an existential anguish before Nothingness) is primary? Do you really
believe that you are the measure of the Other?

A second important motif in Western thought, which
Levinas calls the philosophy of totality, finds its apogee in
Hegel. It is the conquest of problems by a Solution, which
might be called the *solution of History* in honor of Hegel and
of the Troeltschian historicism and the historical-critical
school against which second *Romans* protests. Its basic strategy
is to solve the problem of otherness by making it relative to
an embracing whole, in which absolute meaning is located. By
denying that plurality is ultimate, the meaning of "justification" is transposed to the unanswerable argument of what is or
what does happen: *Weltgeschichte* is *Weltgericht*.[66] Now the
orientation to the objective All can have the salutary effect
of correcting the narrow perspective of egoist subjectivism,
and both Barth and Levinas are "objective" over against

Kierkegaard on this score.[67] The Self is less than the All.
But neither is totality the All, for the Other (unlike the Self)
really does interrupt the totality. In face of the eschatological judgment of the Other, it is a brutality to affirm that
the real is the reasonable; for the actual evidence that we
possess of the way of Being and History only fills in a picture
of wickedness and war. The solution of History misses the
order of the personal by confounding thought and speech with
the world, whereas the transcendence of thought and speech over
the world (not to Self, but to Other) is the only possibility
of personal, responsible life. The question to be put to his-
toricist theology and philosophy is: Do you really believe
that the totality you see, or conceive, is enough? Do you dare
to justify it, in face of the Other who is ground under its
wheel? Can you deny that the true life is absent?[68]

     The critique of the problem of freedom and solution of
History does advance the argument to the Other; it belongs to
the proclamation of the Crisis, the opening apart from which
the Other may always be confused with something less than Other.
But the fiery trail left by the meteoric theme of the Other as
it burns through the atmosphere of rationalism, existentialism,
and historicism, is not yet the Other. The Crisis in which the
pretentions of modern thought are rejected is a necessary and
enduring dimension of the argument to the Other, showing the
intellectual cost of obedience, but it cannot be the whole of
the argument. The service of the Other is a *new* life, but a
new *life*. Ought there not to be a proper method and description for this life, even within philosophy and theology--per-
haps as the very reconstitution of philosophy and theology--if
the thought of the Other is not to remain a purely formal or
even sophistical opposition to the things it is Other than?
We are brought to a two-sided quandary: (1) Can there be a
meaningful discourse about a veritable *totaliter aliter* (even
"about" being "to" the Other), or does discourse systematically
preclude mention of the Other and frustrate the attempt to
indicate the relative position of the Other? (2) If there is a
meaningful discourse in which the Other is implicated, will
this also imply that the problem of justification, which was
first portrayed as radically insoluble, does after all have a

"solution"? In other words, does the requirement of pluralism
admit of sufficient modification to bring about a real relation
between the Same and the Other, perhaps even a "givenness" of
the Other to the Same? If we must conceive of a givenness of
the Other, how will this affect our conception of the position
in which the revelation of the Other places the self?

In the following expositions it will be found that Barth
and Levinas do attend further to *election* as the way the true
Other is given and related to the Same. Our identity, as selves
and as church, is constituted by the fact that, before any
choice of our own, we are chosen. The theme of the *anteriority*
of the Other's claim to our own initiative will largely replace
the static concept of *exteriority* as the key to the Other's
concrete Otherness.[69] This shift in emphasis will enable Levinas
and Barth to pay more attention to the position in which the
Other places the self (and the church), and less to the *via
negativa* of "other than's," which always labors under the suspicion of being in logical bad faith. However, because the
Crisis does remain in force, both Barth and Levinas will adopt
a dialectical, saying-unsaying form of argument that attempts,
in faith or in a divine "folly,"[70] to cross the Red Sea of the
evidence and language of totality.[71]

> Is the approach, whose landmarks we have just pointed
> out, sufficiently sure? Is its starting point really
> approachable? Will we not be taken to task for failing to
> give adequate warning of the dangers of the route. . ?[72]

> It is no road--which we can observe or investigate or
> even enter upon. We can only pass along it.[73]

CHAPTER V

THE IDEA OF THE INFINITE: KARL BARTH 1922-1932[1]

1. Dialectical Dogmatics

In 1921, before Barth had written even half of the second edition of his *Romans*, he was offered on the strength of first *Romans* a chair at the University of Göttingen.[2] From this time forward Barth was to be primarily an academic theologian rather than a pastor. In the later chapters of second *Romans* and its preface there appears a keen interest in "theology" as a legitimate task.[3] Still, Thurneysen remained for the time being in his Leutwil parish, so that while Barth became ever more involved with the academic world, his relationship with Thurneysen reminded him of the activity of preaching as a relatively primordial form of church life presupposed by the second-order reflections of dogmatics.[4]

Barth's move, more specifically, was from the finger-burning embarrassment of preaching to the in its way no less questionable pursuit of articulating and criticizing doctrine. Just as the preacher is burdened with the impossible demand to speak of God to the congregation, so the theologian in the university is "expected not to whisper and mumble about God, but to *speak* of him: not merely to hint of him, but to know him and *witness* to him; not to leave him somewhere in the background, but to disregard the universal method of science and place him in the *foreground*."[5] At the time of second *Romans* Barth is willing and even eager to be considered a theologian, but only on the condition that his theology be seen, not as a system among the competing systems of the day, but as a marginal note to them all, a corrective comment on the overall situation.

[July 1922:] From the children's disease of being ashamed of theology, I think I have to some degree recovered. . . but I must frankly confess to you that what I might conceivably call "my theology" becomes, when I look at it closely, a single point, and that not, as one might demand as the least qualification of a true theology, a *stand*-point, but rather a mathematical point upon which one cannot stand--a *view*-point merely. With theology proper I

> have hardly made a start. Whether I shall ever get on with
> it or whether I shall even wish to get on with it, I do not
> know.6

The dialectical recognition of the perversity of theology is no
less in force later, when Barth does take up theology proper.
The path by which Barth reaches his dialectical dogmatics must
be examined in order to understand the link between second
Romans, which seems to explode all dogmatic platforms, and the
"Doctrine of the Word of God," the Prolegomena to Christian
Dogmatics of 1927. How does it become not only possible but
necessary for Barth to make doctrinal predications of the subject "Wholly Other"?

THE DOCTRINAL TASK. As a professor of systematic theology Barth now had to give lectures in the history of doctrine
and, eventually (1924), in his own dogmatics.7 For this reason,
if for no other, he had to get on with theology proper; but,
having renounced Schleiermacher and the theology of experience,
the apparent absence of an alternative to that theology (and
the apparent complicity of even the Reformation with some of
its unsavory fruits) meant that Barth could take nothing for
granted as a starting point or resource for getting on.8

> [Schleiermacher's] stuff is really brittle wherever one
> touches it, just one gigantic swindle, one is frequently
> inclined to cry out in wrath. However, the insight that
> the way taken by this undoubtedly very wise and honest
> religious man is a *blind alley* makes the situation quite
> clear, but the question: How then? is only the more alarm-
> ing.9

It is not surprising, given that Christian *subjectivism* was the
principal target of Barth's "Wholly Other" argument, that Barth
was relatively open to learn from the older objectivist orthodoxy, which he had earlier so vigorously attacked. Granted
that a simple return to orthodoxy is impossible, still, is there
not something suggestive in the idea of a theological validity
at least relatively independent of the believer's experience?
If the problem of Christianity revolves around the divine critique of human religious experience, might not the propositional
assertions of dogmatics have a significant critical role to play
over against that experience? Had not Paul himself wrestled
with the problem of the norm by which the church ought to choose

among the manifold spiritual uprushings within the Christian community--to govern the spirits by the Spirit?[10]

Finding himself without a teacher, "alienated increasingly from the good society of contemporary theology," Barth encountered Heppe's compendium of Reformed dogmatics in the spring of 1924.[11] "It was out-of-date, dusty, unattractive, almost like a logarithm table, dreary to read, rigid and incredible on almost every page. . . Fortunately I did not dismiss it too lightly."[12] The orthodox writers offered an improved access to Scripture through the Reformers and a model of scientific rigor, which moved Barth to incorporate orthodox objectivism, along with pietistic subjectivism, into his dialectical understanding of the work of the Holy Spirit. The mathematical point could remain supreme while a responsible dogmatics was carried out under its aegis.

> Orthodoxy doubtless has much to live down, but it has nevertheless a powerful instinct for what is superfluous and what is indispensable. In this it surpasses many of the schools that oppose it. And this, and certainly not the mere habit and mental inertia of the people, is the primary reason why it still continues to be so potent. . .
> We may also remark that there are times when even the most convinced heretic desires to depart from his customary psychologisms into positive statement, when, almost against his will, he wants to talk not of religion but of God; and on these occasions he can but employ dogmatic expressions.
> When the minister is given the final insight that the theme of the ministry is not man becoming God but God becoming man--even when this insight flashes only occasionally upon his mind--he acquires a taste for objectivity. And he ceases to view objectivity as a mere psychic instrument for use in analyzing the Bible and the dogmas. He finds a world which previously he had despised and hated as "supernaturalistic" slowly but surely becoming reasonable and purposeful. He understands it, so to speak, from within, from behind. He sees that what is written must be written. He gains assurance and freedom of movement in corners of that world so remote and strange that he had not allowed himself to dream he could ever be at home there. And at last he is perhaps able to find in the Apostle's Creed, with all its hardness, more truth, more depth, and even more intelligence than in any other that short-breathed modernism would put in its place.[13]

This evidently autobiographical statement was made in an October, 1922 lecture. It shows that Barth had acquired his taste for objectivity years before the encounter with Heppe's *Reformierte Dogmatik*, and consciously related this taste to the argument of *Romans* that the opening of the way from God to man places man

in crisis by terminating all illusions about a way from man to
God. Barth saw, however, that in the modern situation such a
taste was exotic. In 1923 he spoke on "The Nature and Purpose
of Reformed Doctrine":

> [T]he question of right doctrine cannot be opened up
> without the discovery and the acknowledgement of a great
> *perplexity* in modern Protestantism. Perhaps it is the
> greatest of all perplexities. Our disparagement of "doc-
> trine" is the fox's disparagement of the grapes. *Had* we
> something more essential and authoritative to say, had we
> a theology convincing to, and accepted by, definite and
> increasing groups of people, *had* we a gospel which we had
> to preach, we should think differently.[14]

The more or less abstract event of God's speaking from beyond
all experience in second *Romans* is replaced by the concrete
event of the preacher attempting to speak God's Word in the pul-
pit. The critical question is no longer "to be or not to be,"
"to have or not to have," but to *distinguish* the Word that is
God's from the words of men.[15] Dogmatics then becomes, instead
of the description of religious experience, the comparison with
Scripture of actual human utterances purporting to serve God's
Word. The contradiction in the fact that we must but cannot
speak of God, which had been positively resolved in first *Romans*
but accepted in its negativity in second *Romans*, once again
assumes a positive characteristic, but only within the boundaries of Barth's dialectic, i.e. with the "corrective" announced
and maintained. *Witness* emerges as the crucial category: "neither my affirmation nor my denial lays claim to being God's
truth. Neither one is more than a *witness* to that truth, which
stands in the center, between every Yes and No."[16] In Barth's
judgment, the Reformed understanding of the human relativity
and changeableness of dogma--that it is only we, here, now who
speak, albeit as seriously and bravely as we are able--embraces
the concern of dialectic and is still compatible with a zestful
commitment to the development of doctrine.[17] The outcome is a
stabilization of the pendulum that swings so wildly between the
first two editions of *Romans*.

Barth published in 1925 a lecture on "The Scripture
Principle of the Reformed Church," which reflected his own work
on dogmatics in 1923 and 1924.[18] It was Barth's first major
essay in dogmatics, summarizing his new attitude toward doctrine

and preparing for the full-scale dogmatics that would appear in 1927.

> Dogmatics is neither preaching, nor meditation, nor Bible exegesis. It obviously belongs to "life," but--let us say the fatal word right away--this part of life is *doctrine*. All the hostile considerations that usually come up when "theory" is spoken of, as opposed to "praxis," concern dogmatics more than other "theories." But one should no more be ashamed of this than of the gospel. It is the church's work of self-examination concerning what it ought to represent in its proclamation in order to be really *this*, the Christian church. . . [Dogmatics is] a task in which all sorts of unaesthetic and even unedifying smoke and dust is unavoidably raised, a task in which every presupposition does not stand intelligibly before the eye in every moment, but a task that must be taken up, precisely for the sake of the Gospel: because while the Gospel is indeed in itself pure and deep and divine, it is discovered ever and again by human beings as such, and thus must be protected against our own errors, confusions, and superficialities by rigorous conscious review of its unfathomable mystery.[19]

Dogmatics is a concern of the whole church, of everyone in it; although it has a craft aspect to be more or less mastered by specialists, acting as deputies of the church, yet to be a baptized Christian is to have a responsibility for guarding the link between the Bible and contemporary proclamation.

Barth the dogmatician had to sit once again at Calvin's feet. An important congenial point that he found in Calvin was the interpretation of God's complete otherness as His inalienable subjectivity in His revelation. "To speak of God can only mean to let God speak. To preach and to hear preaching means to make room and to let room be made for God's own Word."[20] But revelation of the transcendent is itself transcendent. Barth's 1924 commentary on first Corinthians had equated revelation with the "impossible possibility" of resurrection from the dead.[21] What then does revelation have to do with this all-too-human document, the Bible, in such a way that the critical question of talk of God can become the question of its relation to this particular book? Barth's handling of this issue in "Schriftprinzip" anticipates everything he says up to and including the treatment in the first volume of the *Church Dogmatics*. Its main features:

(1) The Bible accredits *itself* as the Word of God, and cannot be so identified on the basis of any human judgment. We do not choose the Bible; the Bible (i.e. God by means of the

Bible) chooses us. We know ourselves to be precisely the baptized, concretely God-designated community which confesses the
Bible as witness to revelation. To ask for a different reason
in support of the book's status would be to ask about a different thing, viz. a book that does not impose on us in this fash-
ion--a book perhaps of a certain antiquity, beauty, and prophetic character, with stirring episodes and deep insights,
which could be commended on historical or psychological grounds.
The Reformers did not disdain this sort of secondary apologetic.
But the Reformers were clear on the relativity of such an apologetic, and devoted their emphasis, lest there be any misunderstanding, to *the* reason, the "logical circle" in which Scripture
proves itself.[22] Barth's characteristic emphasis on the event-
character of revelation as a divine initiative--on *Offenbarung*,
as opposed to the Catholic or crypto-Catholic *Offenbartsein* or
Offenbartheit in which the Reformers saw the self-assurance of
Antichrist[23]--leads to the corollary that the question of the
makeup of the canon must be open in principle. The canon is
established by God; the church only confesses that in such-and-
such a location the Word of God is heard and witnessed in a
binding way. But no such discrimination on the part of the
church can be final, since the initiative in the encounter lies
with God.[24]

(2) The Bible is not to be confused with revelation
itself. The church's acknowledgement of the Bible is a secondary one, presupposing a primary acknowledgement of God's revelation, to which Scripture is a witness. The Bible writers do
not speak God's Word, they hear it. Only thus, because the
Bible is not identical with the object of its witness, does it
become a witness of theological import, relevant to the wholly
other object of theology, transcending any purely historical
interest it may also have. As this sort of "witness" it is
something more than a "source." It points away from itself,
being only too evidently a human document, but because it is a
witness, not a source, there can be no abstracting of revelation from it, no peering over it toward something that might be
established in another way.[25]

Scripture is a *privileged* witness because of the unique
position occupied by the biblical authors, at first hand to

revelation. *We* are not prophets and apostles. An essential characteristic of our relation to revelation is the temporal gap separating it from us, Lessing's ditch, which is bridged by the mediation of this third thing, the Bible. *God's* Word in Scripture does make us contemporaries of revelation, but only as God's Word in *Scripture*. The privilege of this document over against the church of today is a critical one, for the church finds itself continually confronted and measured by this particular standard. The Bible is "other." The Reformed Scripture principle implies the necessity of this opposition between the church and the criterion of its proclamation: the church never possesses its own validation, but must always await it as an ever-renewed miracle. The recurrent sin in the church is to seek an immediacy with God that is forbidden by the Scripture principle, i.e. to bypass that which maintains the distance between the Word of God and the word of man, as did the *Schwärmer* of Reformation times. "Ernst Troeltsch is seriously of the opinion that what is known in today's world as Protestantism owes more to the heirs of those *Schwärmer* than to the heirs of the Reformers, and this pleases him. In my opinion this ought not to please us."[26]

(3) It is indeed a paradox, but a central paradox of the Christian faith, that the word of God is concretely bound to this *particular* witness. "The proposition that the Bible is God's Word will be understood as a shadow or indeed a repetition of the high paradox of the Incarnation."[27] Barth conforms the relation between time and eternity, as it bears on the doctrine of Scripture, with his account of the Incarnation in second *Romans*, i.e. as a divine incognito related only miraculously to the temporal order. "Revelation is one. The Word of God has no history. It *occurs*, but it is the same yesterday and today." But: "Just as even revelation is, in the midst of history, itself history, the becoming *human* [*Mensch*werdung] of God, the entry of the eternal in the hiddenness of the temporal and precisely *thus* revelation, so also is the witness to it an earthly, relative, human occurence and precisely *as such* witness to revelation."[28] This represents an important change from the thinking in second *Romans*, which could only contemplate a (so to speak) sub-infinitesimal point where revelation left a

trace in history, the Cross as the point of human annihilation. The whole interest of second *Romans* was in the *Dasein* of revelation, its possibility/impossibility; here, the acceptance of the Scripture principle leads to an interest in the *Sosein* of revelation, its temporally and conceptually extended indirect identity with an entire book.

(4) Historically or experientially speaking, someone other than the biblical writers could be a more lucid or influential witness to Christ. Many might truthfully claim to have received more in the way of faith from their pious mothers than from the Bible.

> [C]oncerning the recognition of the Bible as the Word of God, it is a question neither of historical judgment nor of this kind of experiential value judgment of the accidental sources of Christian stimulation, but of the recognition of a *norm* of all such value judgments. . . That they are law, not that they enlighten us, is the reason for the priority of prophetic and apostolic words over others.[29]

The conception of faith as obedience offers Barth a view of the authority of Scripture that does not depend on the incidence or quality of certain experiences. To be sure, the internal witness of the Holy Spirit is still presupposed. In fact, Barth is now able to emphasize all the more the infinite qualitative difference between the motions of the Spirit and the autonomous motions of the human soul. "What if one is not 'religiously gifted'?" asks Barth. "Is it not almost refreshing. . . to read the admission of the Göttingen professor J. David Michaelis (died 1791) that, so firmly as he was convinced of the truth of revelation, in his entire life he never perceived such a witness of the Holy Spirit?"[30] The Holy Spirit is not a datum; what is given is an intuitively empty claim on our obedience which, lacking the Spirit, is impossible to fulfill. According to Alsted, this empty-handed reliance on the Spirit is the *basis totius theologiae*; according to D. F. Strauss, it is the Achilles heel of all Protestantism. We must understand both of these judgments and recognize the necessity for a decision between them.[31]

(5) The need for a *dialectical* theology can be inferred from the development of Protestant thought after the Reformation, which travelled down two roads: on the one hand, to the objectivist orthodoxy which turns the Bible into an oracle, a

historical artifact as such claiming divinity, following a
one-sided insistence that the prophets and apostles are speaking with the Spirit--on the other hand, to subjectivist pietism
which, by one-sidedly emphasizing the internal witness of the
Spirit, turns it into the psychological artifact called "religious experience." The Spirit-in-the-Bible and the Spirit-in-us
must always clarify and correct each other. The distinction
between them is only preliminary and relative; the Spirit is
one, God Himself, the Other; but, as such, the Spirit is not
given.[32] We have no call to replace our dialectical theology
with a theology of post-critical synthesis. The abstract second
Romans dialectic of Yes and No becomes here the dialectic of
inspired subject and inspired object, faith and obedience.[33]

  DIE CHRISTLICHE DOGMATIK. Barth's lectures from the
middle 1920's show, besides reiteration and refinement of his
dialectic, an increasing concern with specifically Reformed
doctrine and with his identity as a Reformed theologian in
relative opposition to Lutheran emphases and more serious opposition to Roman Catholicism.[34] This process began with the
assumption of his teaching duties at Göttingen. It reached a
climax in the outline of dogmatics Barth published in 1927. The
man who had dropped the bombshell of second *Romans* was widely
seen at that time as a prophet who had succeeded above all in
placing a gigantic question mark beside modern theology. Certainly this had been Barth's intention; but he had not failed
to point out that this questioning, itself theology, was itself
questionable. Barth's solidarity with the theologians and their
plight was clearly proclaimed in the forward to second *Romans*,
and so it is not surprising to find, in the forward to his 1927
Prolegomena to Christian Dogmatics, a somewhat impatient renunciation of the prophet's mantle. "I was and I am an ordinary
theologian who at best has a 'doctrine of the Word of God' at
his disposal and not the Word of God itself."[35] Those who
feared that a "scholastic autumn" would wipe out the fruits of
"the spring of the message of the Reformers,"[36] who had seen
Barth as a bell-ringing prophet of the Wholly Other, had simply
not understood the initial message.

  The object of second *Romans*, whom Barth had named the
Wholly Other, is likewise the object of *Die christliche Dogmatik*

in 1927. Barth regarded this dogmatics as a consistent development of his theology. Therefore we must ask how the *Dogmatik*'s
triune God, revealed in His threefold Word, is the Wholly Other
as wholly other, and how Barth now has to make this point very
differently than it was made in second *Romans*.

(1) *The theme of difference.* The infinite qualitative
difference between God and man is primarily discussed in terms
of man's incapacity for revelation (*finitum non capax infiniti*).
Barth's Reformed-dialectical appreciation of this point emerges
in a running polemic against Schleiermacher and the theological
"Cartesianism" for which he stands. "Cartesianism" becomes
Barth's generic term for thought which takes its starting point
in the certitudes and interests of the consciousness of the
human subject, an example being Descartes' proof of God from
the idea of God in man.[37] Schleiermacher's presentation of
theology as the explication of the contents of the religious
self-consciousness fits this mold. The category of "religion,"
to which neo-Protestantism is so much indebted for its answer
to the problem of the intelligibility of Christianity, is Cartesian in this sense, since it elevates a human reality to first
place and makes divine reality relative to it. "Being with God
and in God must be determined to mean: being with an absolute
[*unaufhebbar*] Other. God as the metaphysical extension of our
impulse to live, God as the original ground of our own *élan
vital*, is anything but God."[38] With Schleiermacher, on the
other hand, it seems that God, as a subject-person over against
us with whom we might have an encounter, is only a figure of
speech, since the height of religion is attained when "I am (in
this moment) the soul of the infinite."[39] The Schleiermacherian
religious man has no counterpart. His religion has no object.

Opposed to this, Barth restates his *Romans* view of religion as a human reality whose object is the Wholly Other.
The fearful confrontation with the Other is the highest expression of man's contradiction with himself and God. It is *not*,
for Christian theology, the subjective possibility of revelation; but God may nevertheless reckon this religion as fellowship
with Him and righteousness.[40] Barth includes the negative concept of religion in his dogmatics to witness against its exalted
role in the neo-Protestant tradition. Neither it nor the "Wholly

Other" addressed by it constitutes the starting point of dogmatics. But "Wholly Other" remains a normative theological concept
for Barth so long as he believes that the "Wholly Other" of
religion *is not wholly other*, and that the God who reveals Himself in His Word *is*, by contrast, *wholly* Other, true God and no
idol, not even the self-critical idol of the best form of man's
religion. However, to make exorbitant use of the phrase is to
invite suspicion that the object of discourse is this "Wholly
Other" of human religion, and for that reason the phrase must
disappear, except to draw this particular contrast.

If religion is a purely human reality, then Feuerbach
was right to deny the transcendent referent of Christian theology, for the theology of his day had by and large decided to
base itself on the phenomenon of religion. The distortions
that flow from this false starting point are legion: man claims
wildly exaggerated and romantic God-experiences (which no-one
could possibly have had, the way some books describe it!), theologians give their philosopher-neighbors the right to laugh at
their allegations of God's existence, a man-God idol is set up
in place of God, and finally, even by these means we are enabled
to say nothing that could not have been said just as well without setting off on the embarrassing Icarus-flight of "theology."[41] Theology loses and cannot regain its object unless, in
its reflection on the possibility of revelation, it once again
places confidence in the Holy Spirit rather than in any power
of man. Schleiermacher's man, who ultimately has no counterpart, does not wrestle with real sin but only, like Don Quixote,
with the windmills of what he imagines about himself. The real
struggle, Jacob's struggle with the Lord, is with the real sin
that we learn about only through the Holy Spirit.[42] Here we
discover that everything we tell ourselves is actually a lie,
an illusion of self-justification. The human reality of religion is not just a hapless quixotic ineptitude, an *Ohnmacht*, but
a sinful self-asserting *Eigenmacht*.[43]

On what basis can one speak of revelation, if not from
an experience of it? One *thinks* and *speaks* of revelation in
the form: "I believe, dear Lord, help my unbelief!"[44] Such is
the position occupied by *homo viator*, man on the way to God,
who listens, obeys, and hopes. Such also is the position the

theologian must occupy, represented by Anselm, whose theology
starts with prayer: "I search for Thy countenance, Lord. . .
You live in unapproachable light. . . You have made me and given
me all good things. . . Still I know you not."[45] Anselm prays
for the very possibility that neo-Protestant and Catholic theologies already assume they possess because of man's nature or
because grace has been made available to man as a secure com-
modity. Anselm assumes that God is *not* a content of his consciousness but unapproachably Other, based solely on Himself.
An object that is a content of consciousness is not based solely
on itself, because in the correlation of knower and known the
knower disposes over the known even as the known disposes over
the knower. The Word of God does not enter into this correlation, because God is the inalienable subject of His Word.[46]
"Man" as subject is exploded by the predicate of the fellowship
with God offered in this Word. The "I know" of theology is in
no sense a claim of human consciousness. God's inalienable subjectivity militates equally against the false objectivism of
orthodoxy,[47] for His *Word*, interrupting all subjective fantasy,
is exclusively *His* Word.

　　　(2) *The possibility of theology*. Just as religion is,
for Barth, the great need and tribulation of man, rather than
(as for Schleiermacher) the crown of humanity, so dogmatics is
the gathering place of all of theology's difficulties and inad-
equacies, rather than its proud culmination.[48] This is just
what makes dogmatics a serious business.

> Theology has a historical entrance and a practical exit.
> In both places, so long as they are sufficiently isolated
> from the middle that adjoins them both, it has an essen-
> tially harmless character. The troublesome and dangerous
> middle, owing to which all theology is troublesome and dan-
> gerous, is dogmatics.[49]

"Dogma" is an eschatological concept, referring to the conformity of the preached word with the revealed Word attested in
Scripture.[50] The fallible dogmatician cannot answer his own
questions, though; all his "knowledge" of God is only a dialectical pointer to God, and a reminder to the preacher.[51]

　　　Barth's taste for dogma extends this time as far as the
Chalcedonian Christology. The early church meant to rightly
express the miracle of the Incarnation, and a proper astonishment

at it; modern theology's rejection of the "intellectualism" of the early church only reflects on the failure of modern theology to engage its object.[52] Not to occupy ourselves with the Incarnation dogmas is not to take the Incarnation seriously.[53] Similarly, not to be concerned with rightly determining the concept of revelation is in effect to allow man to continue to delude himself about his own capacity for revelation.[54] There is no superior vantage point from which we could disparage the dogmatic enterprise: any such disparagement would itself be (bad) dogmatics.[55]

Revelation itself is, of course, the main critical resource of dogmatics, as the true but transcendent concretissimum. Humanly speaking, though, there are several concretissima by which dogmatics ought to be guided, including the witnessing activity of church proclamation--which is pre-eminent, because it is normatively "the pure form of Christian discourse"[56] and also, as a phenomenon ("*es predigt*," "there is preaching"), the factual given which provokes theological questioning.[57] Further, the theologian must acknowledge the concrete *authority* of (1) Holy Scripture as the divinely accredited witness to revelation, (2) the church's confession, and (3) our present existence,[58] on the one hand, and the concrete *freedom* of the human conscience responding to authoritative attestation on the other.[59] The meaning of "concretissimum" proposed here by Barth is, roughly, that which cannot honestly be gotten around, that which is irrevocably on the human scene posing a problem or claiming obedience. As has already been noted, for Barth "actuality" is a positive critical principle to be employed against the self-coddling and arrogance that he perceives in the pietistic-romantic and rationalist traditions.

All of these concretissima are binding upon theology, but they are relative to the Word of God and may not be set up as unconditional starting points for dogmatics. That would only be another Cartesian variation of the sort that the crisis proclaimed in second *Romans* has ruled out forever. God still stands over against all things human as the Question greater than all answers, the divine disturbance to which alone hope can attach.[60] But: "*Really to hear Christian preaching as talk about God and man means that man himself is called into question. That happens when those who have ears hear that God Himself has*

already answered them."[61] No longer is the Question presented
in abstraction from the Answer, i.e. from Jesus Christ. We
would not seek God had we not already found Him.[62] True, space
is only made for the answer when man is utterly insecure: the
thoroughgoing No is required along with the Yes. But the No
presupposes the Yes. In a purely logical sense, this point was
made also in second *Romans*, but there Barth spoke only abstractly of the divine synthesis beyond all human grasp. The concretissimum was the great God-problem rather than the answering
Word, because the Word was not actually on the scene. One could
recognize the necessity for an incognito, and still only specu-
late about the bearer of the incognito, under the rubric of
"Origin." In *Die christliche Dogmatik* it is no longer a question of the "Origin" but of the Word of God. This shift is not
at all calculated to introduce some "immanence" to balance a
one-sided "transcendence" in the earlier work, but to adequately specify and reap the dividends of the transcendence announced
earlier, with all its implications. Thus, of the various determinations of the object of theology that are discussed in *Die
christliche Dogmatik*, not one relativizes the transcendence of
that object.

(3) *The difference as uniqueness.* Second *Romans* drew
a connection between the Wholly Other and a particular historical event (the self-denial of Jesus on the Cross), but without
placing weight on the particularity of the event. In fact, the
Crucifixion in second *Romans* could be interpreted as an alle-
gorical or symbolic presentation of the timeless truth of the
relation between man and God.[63] The *Dogmatik* understands God's
Word as a contingent event spoken there and then in Jesus Christ,
heard here and now by the believer; Jesus Christ has become an
event of thirty years' duration instead of a deathly vanishing
point on the Cross. He confronts us not as a mere symbol of
the Word of God, but really as God's Word.[64] The Word is neither a "historical" event, nor a dialectically opposite anti-his-
tory. It is determined solely through itself rather than through
any conception of history—it is its own history, *Urgeschichte*.[65]
God's existence is only manifest in the revelation of *who* God
is, in the *Sosein* of revelation. Therefore the doctrines of
the Trinity and of the forms of the Word of God assume special

importance. By these doctrines we address the divine answer, lacking which the divine question is indistinguishable from a human question.

The importance of the doctrine of the Trinity lies in the fact that it binds human thinking absolutely to God, who as the *triune* God remains Lord insofar as His triunity (*dreieinig-keit*) forbids any objectivation by which man, in the correlation of knower and known, would become lord. God's mysterious tri-unity confirms that God grasps us rather than vice versa.[66] Consequently it is an appropriate doctrine to erect at the gate of all dogmatics, for God is truly the Other in *this* way, i.e. in a way incompatible with all of the other identities that man might project against the void opened up by the concept of the "Wholly Other." Theological truth does not aspire to be "uni-versal truth" (*Allgemeinwahrheit*) but the truth of *this* real-ity.[67] "God is a free Lord, not only over the principle of non-contradiction, but over His own Godhood," i.e. He is free to offer Himself as an object of knowledge without ceasing to be subject--He is free to be triune.[68] He makes Himself acces-sible to our thinking in His very inaccessibility, as Lord over our thinking.[69] Barth's doctrine of revelation is reinforced in two ways: by the assertion that God reveals Himself, i.e. is identical with His revelation, which is meant to preclude the possibility of locating and speaking of God on some basis other than revelation, such as in a natural theology;[70] and by the *Extra Calvinisticum*, the Reformed doctrine maintaining the reality of the Word outside (*extra*) of the God-man union so that this revelation/incarnation does not prejudice God's "majes-ty" (inalienable subjectivity).[71] This development of the Otherness of God is at the same time a confirmation of the war-rant of theology, for if there were no particular structure and content of revelation, there could be no distinctive intellec-tual obedience to it.

Barth speaks of the Trinity immediately in the charac-terization of revelation, "God speaks," in the threefold terms of the subject, predicate, and object of this speaking: *"He alone is the Revealer. He is completely Revelation. He Himself is the Revealed."*[72] Barth is encouraged by Schleiermacher's low estimation of the importance of the doctrine of the Trinity,

because if it is remote from Schleiermacher's starting point in
the religious self-consciousness it is all the more likely to
accord with the structure of genuine revelation.[73] The hard
paradox of the doctrine of the Trinity fits the mysteriousness
of the God who is not man, but became man. It is directly implicated in our confession of Jesus as Lord, and does not derive
from some antique metaphysical speculation. Can we renounce
this doctrine without ceasing to take seriously the Lordship of
Jesus as the answer to the question of *who* God is?[74]

Our relation to the revelation of the triune God is
determined by the different forms of the Word of God. The primary form is Revelation itself, God speaking in person, an
event in which the relation between God and man is itself instituted as Word, the Word before and over all words.[75] Church
proclamation, which serves this Word here and now, and Holy
Scripture, which serves this Word by attesting its having been
spoken there and then, are both forms of the selfsame Word. It
is the character of Word to be spoken by I to Thou, reason to
reason.[76] "The Word of God is not only a speaking [*Rede*] but
an address [*An-rede*]."[77]

> We are not speaking of the Word of God if we do not
> also speak of man's becoming aware of it, or, more concrete-
> ly, if we do not speak of how the perceiving man, the human
> I, here finally and conclusively encounters that without
> which he cannot exist, the Thou that is his origin. Thus
> the Word of God is a concept that is accessible only to
> existential thinking.[78]

This introduces the subject of man's "existence" as a
dogmatic category, which Barth was later forced to utterly renounce.

(4) *Existence*. Between 1909 and 1921 Barth was occupied by the preacher's problem of relating the message of the
Bible to the contemporary life of his hearers. This gave rise
to the idea of the correlated duality of "Bible" and "Life,"
which had found pointed expression in his addresses "Religion
und Leben" and "The Need and Promise of Christian Preaching"
(1922).[79] The same duality contributes heavily to the makeup
of *Die christliche Dogmatik*. We have already seen that the
actual existence of the believer is one of the concretissima
which serve as the norms of theology; in that connection, its
relativity to the supreme concretissimum of revelation itself

is apparent. However, "existence" as a *category* correlated
with the category of revelation, thus potentially on an equal
and independent footing with revelation, is another matter.
Since this is the principal issue dividing the 1927 and 1932
editions of Barth's Prolegomena, it is necessary to mark
exactly what Barth says about "existence" in 1927. And here we
must notice that Barth uses two very different approaches:
first, an adjectival qualification of theology or relationship
with God as "existential," not necessarily implying a special
philosopher's concept of "existence"; and second, a description
of the condition of man addressed by God's Word, often characterized as "man's contradiction" as well as his "existence."

For Barth, the word "existential" refers to the whole
being of the person in an actual encounter. An uncommitted
spectator attitude will not work in Christian theology because
the Christian revelation demands a decision and institutes a
relationship. The otherness of the Other secures the irreduc-
ibility of the encounter, in which the I does not dispose over
the divine Thou: God is only offered as an object of knowledge
to those who acknowledge His subjectivity. This calls for a
shift in theology from the "phenomenological" standpoint (compatible with mere spectatorship) to the existential.

> Everything we have discussed thus far must be under-
> stood as a concrete situation, as an activity in which we
> ourselves are implicated. For we only really involve man
> when we involve, at all points, ourselves. Only he who
> thinks of himself and his existence really thinks of man;
> and he only really thinks of circumstances and relationships
> who thinks of them as concrete situations, as activities in
> which he himself is existentially involved. . . Where it is
> really a matter of Man, then the subjective *is* the objec-
> tive. . . Therefore in the following we will speak no more
> of Christian discourse and preaching, but of *preachers* and
> *hearers*. . . We are changing from a phenomenological to an
> "existential" (one could also, in a more comprehensive
> sense, say: to an ethical) way of thinking.[80]

To speak of God to another man is not to propose some interesting theme to him, but to confront him, to "claim his existence
for God's Kingdom."[81] As a word of *address*, the Word of God is
only understandable existentially.[82] Barth discerns three
moments in the subjective response to revelation: (1) Reflection (*Nach-denken*), my perception and recollection of the message offered in words heard or read; (2) "Co-thinking" (*Mit-den-
ken*), in which I accompany what is said to me with my own

thoughts; and (3) "Self-thinking" (*Selber-denken*), in which the
Word becomes *my* word. The Bible calls on me to repeat with my
whole existence what is said to me.[83]

Thus far Barth's usage of "existential" indicates little
more than his already-familiar determination not to detach dogmatics from ethics. He makes the critical point against ration-
alists and romantics that something more is involved in faith
than mere logical consistency or inward poignancy. But that
Barth has a particular conception of existence in mind is only
suggested by the sequel to his account of self-thinking. Self-
thinking as such may come into play even in appreciating Homer
or Goethe. But the Bible's claim is uniquely incompatible with
pure spectatorship; it is a claim to witness to *the* Truth; and
it is a claim, not on a general readership, but on the conscience of the individual. "Of the individual! He is the correlate of truth, not mankind, not Christendom en masse. . . but
this man, I."[84] God's revelation places man in a dilemma of
decision, an Either/Or, rather than in any kind of state. The
being of faith is a becoming.[85] Behind this conception of
existence stands Kierkegaard, whose protest against speculative
rationalism Barth acknowledges as a model for his own, when he
says that man does not merely receive or think the question of
his existence but *is* that question--we are unavoidably the
interested perpetrators of our lives.[86]

Is Barth presupposing and offering a doctrine of man
conceived apart from revelation (or acquired outside revelation
and used to validate it), or is he only describing the situation
in which the believer is placed by God? Of the *Dogmatik*'s
twenty-five leading propositions, six contain a reference to
"man's opposition to God and contradiction with himself"--God
the Father is Lord over it, Jesus Christ is the victorious bearer of it, the Holy Spirit dissolves it, and the religion of the
Wholly Other is its most powerful expression.[87] Barth can speak
of the contradiction as follows:

[M]an is what he is, then, insofar as in all things he
is *not* what he is; he does not remain what he is; nothing
of what he has remains to him, except that what he is and
has is subject to alteration. . . Were his human being even
in the smallest measure, even for a single moment, Being
without Not-Being, he would be at home with God. But there
is no such measure and no such moment. That is the contradiction in his being at home with himself [*Beisichselbstsein*],

disclosed in the fact that he really hears talk of God and of his relation to Him, which turns his being at home into strangeness, *via*, and turns him into a *viator*.[88]

There is nothing more suggestive of abstract speculation about man's existence in all of the *Dogmatik* than this passage, but even here Barth makes it clear that the problem of "Not-Being" is but a gloss on the question that is put to man by revelation and revelation only. Once the question of God is heard, it becomes impossible to put a good face on the evil disorder of our life.[89] One might suspect, on seeing God characterized as the Answerer of the question of man's existence,[90] that Barth depends on a natural theology or theology of correlation (judging by "Barthian" criteria, that is); but here the question of man's existence has no autonomy or possibility of description apart from revelation. This consideration must also qualify Barth's claim that God *had* to become man in order to speak to man's contradiction.[91]

It is not to defend the phraseology of *Die christliche Dogmatik*, but only to understand Barth better in light of what we know of his intentions before and after this book, that we conclude: Barth's language of "existence" and "man's contradiction" is meant to convey an integral part of the biblical message, viz. that man is found by God to be lost in sin--and not that man, independently ascertaining and wrestling with his plight, hears God's Word as the correlated answer to his problem. There is no sign that Barth wishes "existence" to serve as the ground of the meaningfulness of the Bible; on the contrary. Nevertheless it is not difficult to see how a misapprehension could arise, in this year of the "Kierkegaard renaissance" and Heidegger's *Being and Time*, as to Barth's intention.[92]

Within the economy of revelation, however, "man's contradiction" is in one sense the subjective correlate of the objective Word, the question accompanying the answer, the No qualified by the Yes. Leaving aside the reasons why Barth's theology became dialectical: as long as it *is* dialectical it practically guarantees a place for such a thing as "man's contradiction." Thus the cautious retreat from dialectics in the 1932 Prolegomena coincides with the removal of the category of man's contradiction, as also of any independent conception of human existence. It may be said that the theological unruliness

of the concept of "existence," threatening always to become an
apparently autonomous category, contributed to Barth's decision
to go further in basing his theology solely on the Word as an
answer decisively superior to any conceivable question.[93]

(5) *Theology and philosophy*. Barth departs from his
statement in second *Romans* that the theme of the Bible is identical with the essence of philosophy. Theology's understanding
of the Incarnation is completely a posteriori; the Incarnation
is an "incomparable absurdity" a priori.[94] Man does not understand God unless he is addressed by God. This amounts to tacit
criticism of the concept of the Wholly Other in second *Romans*,
since that Other was an object of philosophy, negatively knowable a priori.

Barth maintains, however, that whether we know it or
not we cannot help thinking with the aid of more or less refined
philosophies of God, world, and man, ethics, epistemologies,
etc. One can no more sacrifice one's intellect than jump over
one's shadow. Luther and Calvin were Platonists; the anti-meta-
physical bias of the Ritschlians is itself a metaphysics; contemporary New Testament scholars are learning phenomenology at
school. Kierkegaard's anti-Hegelianism is a philosophy, and
Barth is certainly looking through these particular spectacles
at the moment. But we must not sanctify a system or method,
confusing our dependence with our freedom. We do not have to
be Aristotelians to appreciate Aquinas, or Platonists to respect
Augustine. It can happen, however, as in modern theology's
ensnarement with Cartesianism, that the relativity of our philosophical apparatus is forgotten, and man is given freedom in
principle to dispose over God. When that happens, theology must
consciously reject the intellectual scheme at fault.[95] Such is
the rationale for Barth's attack on Cartesianism, and for his
ease of conscience regarding his reliance on Kierkegaard. Kierkegaard's conception of existence represents a critical weapon
to use against false philosophical pretention.

BEYOND THE DIALECTIC. *Die christliche Dogmatik* is the
major monument of Barth's dialectical theology. Within five
years he completely rewrote it, as the Prolegomena to the *Church
Dogmatics*. But in 1927 he still believed strongly in the suit-
ableness of the dialectical method, as he confirmed in a remarkable parable set at the end of the work:

The people of Israel must cross the Red Sea to escape the Egyptians. The Red Sea is the multitude of unqualified human religious words about God. The people of Israel are God-fearing and God-loving and thus, like the man who is such, may and should know God. The Egyptians do not love and fear God, thereby denying, with full human justification, the possibility of knowing God. The passage is to the reality of such knowledge--but how shall this reality be reached? Now Moses reaches his hand out and the Lord causes a strong east wind to blow, i.e. revelation occurs and is proclaimed. "And the children of Israel went into the midst of the sea on dry ground, the waters being a wall to them on their right hand and on their left." Thus the God-fearing and God-loving ones dare to go into the midst of the sea, as if they would not drown there, because Moses reaches out his hand, because the Lord causes the east wind to blow--they dare to take religious words seriously in their complete unqualifiedness, as if knowledge of God were possible. And lo! Because Moses reaches out his hand, because the Lord causes the east wind to blow, the religious words separate into Word and Counterword, standing like walls on the right and on the left, and between which (threatened by the impossibility of Word and Counterword but protected by the possibility of both, so long as Moses reaches out his hand and the Lord causes the east wind to blow--thus by its only relative possibility!) Israel advances in peace toward its goal; knowledge of God becomes real for those who fear and love Him. And the admonitory epilogue should not be left out: if those who do not love and fear God imitate this supposed "dialectical trick" of Word and Counterword to know God, but appropriate this method without God, without knowing that it is the Spirit that gives life while the flesh, even here, is of no use-- try as they might, it will happen to them, as it is written: Word and Counterword will not remain standing like walls, their tensions and amphibolies will fall back together into the one word in which no knowledge is possible. "And the waters returned and covered the chariots and horsemen and all the host of Pharaoh that had followed them into the sea; not so much as one of them remained." The question is an open question for anyone, anytime, whether he belongs to Israel or to the Egyptians.[96]

Reconciliation is not redemption; the hearers of the Gospel still live under the Law; and our dialectical theology (*theologia viatorum*) reflects this state of affairs. It takes sin, the human impossibility, as seriously in a way as the divine certainty of grace. Revelation is not opposed here by non-revelation, but within our horizon there remains a balance between Yes and No, expressed for Barth in the eternal ambiguity of double predestination.

In his 1929 Dortmund lectures entitled "Schicksal und Idee in der Theologie," Barth provides the capstone and perhaps the concluding comment on dialectical theology. Once again his

central premise is the unconditioned transcendence of God; since
theology does not in any sense possess its object--which would
be the only evidence distinguishing it from other human intellectual endeavors--it has no other tools to work with than those
used by the philosophers.[97] Specifically, its thought cannot
help migrating between the two great end-points of reflection,
"Fate" and "Idea" (or "the Given" and "the Non-Given," "Reality"
and "Truth," etc.).[98] Theology is not justified by its position
on this spectrum, but by its obedient allegiance to the *Word* of
God, by which God distinguishes Himself from our realistic and
idealistic notions of Him. Considered apart from grace, our
theologies are simply philosophical realisms or idealisms. The
theological dialectic with which we attempt to compensate for
this condition can itself become a Trojan horse; it carries no
guarantee that we are starting with God instead of ourselves.[99]
Barth mentions two theological criteria, the doctrines of God's
free election (referring all theological "success" to God's
good pleasure) and predestination (which relativizes our thought,
defining it as *theologia crucis* rather than *gloriae*).[100]

The selection of these two principles as examples of
the doctrinal *proprium* of theology points back toward second
Romans, where they characteristically accompanied mention of
the Wholly Other. Barth considers again whether the concept of
the Wholly Other is just another *speculatio divinae majestatis*
such as Luther warned against, a *majestas diaboli* projected by
sin, or the *numen* of non-rational experience described by Otto:

> *This* "Wholly Other," the Wholly Other that is only a
> mirror-image of man, the keystone in the vault of his own
> construction and precisely for that reason no wholly other
> but only the last in a series of our own words--this Wholly
> Other can indeed bring man only to judgment without grace,
> because when he means to have his God in his own final word
> he plainly remains alone with himself, shut up in the prison
> of his distance from God, his alienation from God, and his
> enmity toward God.[101]

Here, then, Barth still regards God as the *wholly* other, with
whom theology has no given solidarity, before whom theology is
thoroughly embroiled with man's philosophical reflection on
himself. For that reason the dialectic is inevitable, for one
can only qualify the pretentions of realism with idealism, and
vice versa. For example, one can only prevent the idea of God

as the Wholly Other from becoming the purely non-given "Origin" of critical idealist philosophy by realistically emphasizing God's self-givenness in the historical Jesus Christ. But then one must always call attention to the transcendent non-givenness of the Truth distinct from any supposedly possessed and delimited Reality of God. In this way Barth tacitly invites us to regard the first two editions of *Romans* as a matched set, the first "naive" realist step followed by the second "critical" idealist step, each calling for the other's corrective but of course even together not adequate to God.

By making such a strong case for the visible solidarity of theology with philosophy, Barth verges on suggesting that whether or not theology is really occupied with knowledge of God is God's own secret. Dialectics per se are profitless. But something is on the scene Other than dialectics, viz. the Word of God which our thinking aims to serve, and this Word is *concretely* with us, in the there-and-then of Jesus Christ, in the here-and-now of church proclamation, and in the Scripture which mediates between them. However, for the purpose of these lectures, Barth treats revelation as *election*--"The Word of God means God's election"[102]--which is a way of absolving God from the human material of theology and ignoring the possibility that He Himself and His *ratio* might be, on His terms, available to theology. The predestinating Elector, *as such*, may remain eternally unavailable. The Otherness of God is still primarily a critical, negative otherness, and as a result Barth's theology is chained to the problem of its own possibility. "Dialectical theology" is a way of being obsessed with this problem, i.e. with the *sin* that actively opposes grace.[103] The non-givenness of God requires a continuing patient diagnosis of the relations between theology and philosophy. What then is the meaning of Barth's book on Anselm, which he called a "farewell" to "the last remnants of a philosophical, i.e. anthropological. . . foundation and exposition of Christian doctrine"? Why had Barth been "hampered. . . by the eggshells of philosophical systematics"?[104] Is the reason that philosophy had dictated a certain conception of sin, rather than sin dictating a close attention to philosophy? (Was Barth trying to cross the actual

Red Sea, or some other?) Had he been appreciating the Otherness of God too much, or not enough?

2. *Fides Quaerens Intellectum*

FEUERBACH'S QUESTION TO THEOLOGY. From "Modernes Theologie und Reichsgottesarbeit" (1909) through "Schicksal und Idee"
(1929)--perhaps least of all in the first edition of *Romans*--
Barth's central problem had been, not whether God exists, but
how, once God is acknowledged, theology is possible. His understanding of this problem was closely bound to his perception of
Feuerbach as the great unmasker of anthropocentric theology,
who rightly detected a devious anthropology in the theology of
his time. Because he specifically attacked theology,[105] Feuerbach is the foremost of the great critics of religion (Barth
acknowledges in similar though more limited ways Marx, Nietzsche
and Freud[106]) whose objections must be *granted*, forcing the
question: What then? How may we confess, notwithstanding all
this, that God is Other than, greater than, man--as we *must*?
How is this confession to be distinguished from the web of
wish-fulfillments that history, psychology, and philosophy can
better account for? Man does create God in his own image, and
cannot help doing so.

The fundamental strategy of Barth's dialectical theology in face of this question is based on the inalienable subjectivity of God in His revelation. This principle will not
permit the separation of the divine attributes from God, let
alone the sharing of these attributes with men such as we, and
directly opposes Feuerbach's idea that true divinity belongs
not to deity but to the attributes (really of humanity) that
are ascribed to deity.[107] And a true understanding of sin
reveals that Feuerbach's exaltation of mankind, not the theological attempt to speak of a God greater than man, is the real
illusion. Feuerbach is guilty of a double ignorance, which
applies also to all theology that is secretly or unwittingly
saying what Feuerbach said, of death and evil:

> Truly any man who knew that we human beings are evil
> from head to foot, and who bore in mind that we all die,
> would know that the illusion of all illusions is the notion
> that the being of God is the being of man. Even if he held
> the good God to be a dream he would certainly leave him
> free of any identification with such as we.[108]

The answer to Feuerbach is grace (God's freedom as the Wholly Other). But the apotheosis of man cannot be opposed with a mere idea of God, by the "Wholly Other," but only by the *wholly* Other who makes a concrete claim on us by revealing Himself. The alternative to theology of experience is theology of revelation, i.e. of God's self-givenness. However, dialectical theology will not allow itself to make too much of this "givenness," which can all too easily become one experience or object among others. While dialectical theology can point to revelation, and even ring it round with doctrines to confirm and defend the peculiar properties of revelation (as in *Die christliche Dogmatik*), it seems to remain beyond the interest or genius of dialectical theology to serve the material presence of God, i.e. to say concretely who God is. This could only be done if the problem of the possibility of theology were made secondary to a confirmation of its necessity and appropriateness--if the exclamation mark of second *Romans* were brought into the middle of the sentence. Barth's "discovery" of doctrine in the 1920's allows a certain openness to the *Sosein* of revelation, as we have noted, but the key aspects of this *Sosein*--for example, the location of Holy Scripture with respect to Revelation--have a conspicuously formal warrant, in this case the "necessity" that we be confronted by revelation in a particular testimony, that the canonical texts choose us so that it not be we who choose our own revelation. Barth was aware that all of these formal considerations could be interpreted in their turn as yet another projection of man, but he considered it right that theology submit to this ambiguity, as a function of its human distance from God. The answer to Feuerbach is, thus far, not a conclusive answer, nor does it intend to be. Theology does not claim to participate in God's own conclusive answer.

In his book on Anselm, Barth found a way to free Christian theology from preoccupation with its own relativity (its relation to philosophy) in a manner consistent with his ruling critical purpose expressed in the name "Wholly Other."[109] It is in this light that we view the argument of *Fides Quaerens Intellectum*--as the answer to Feuerbach, which as such contains both the positive possibility of theology and the decisive interpretation of the *totaliter aliter*.

ANSELM'S NAME OF GOD. Barth first explains Anselm's presuppositions regarding the conduct of theology, which make up the context of his proof.

Theology for Anselm proceeds from faith--concretely, faith under the authority of the church, the fathers, Scripture, etc.--and can in no case abstract itself from this ground. Anselm's proof may address the unbelieving "fool," but it declines to share his unbelief even provisionally. The eagle cannot argue with bats and owls about sunlight.[110] Thus Anselm's theology, considered as an apologetic, is strangely faulty, if the point of apologetic is to appeal solely to the unbeliever on the basis of the *noetic* rationality he may be presumed to share with all men, for Anselm's strategy is to exhibit (so as to conform the understanding to) the integral rationality of the *object* of theology. The faith of the inquirer implies, besides the humility of the seeker, the confidence of the finder.

> Anselm always has the solution of his problems already behind him (through faith in the impartial good sense of the decisions of ecclesiastical authority), while, as it were, they are still ahead. Therefore, his *credo ut intelligam* can as little imply an intellectual storming of the gates of heaven as it can a *sacrificium intellectus*.[111]

Anselm's faith is not in jeopardy when he confronts the unbeliever. He assumes that the unbeliever is seeking the same object and will welcome the illumination he has to offer.

> [P]erhaps he was daring to assume that disbelief, the *quia non credimus*, the doubt, denial and derision of the unbeliever are not really to be taken so seriously as the unbeliever himself would take them. Perhaps, while appealing to him "with proof," it was not in his lack of faith that he was trusting but in his faith. Perhaps he saw him standing at his side not only within the precincts of theology, but more important within the precincts of the Church.[112]

In short--and this is what allows Barth to take him so seriously--Anselm is content to rely on the self-vindication of the object of theology, i.e. on God's free grace, and only wishes to "prove" it on its own terms. His interest in *probare*, which issues from his wider interest in *intelligere* (the comprehensive enterprise of faith's joyous search for improved understanding of revelation), is only "rationalistic" in this objective sense, not in terms of some modern critical demand for presuppositionlessness.[113] The active solicitation of God's grace in the attitude of prayer in which Anselm begins his proof implies an unashamed acceptance of the relativity of theology, its reliance on contingent revelation as well as its inability to do justice to its object, and its circumscription by biblical and church authority as well as by the limits of its own development as a science. Dogmatic statements always await better instruction.[114]

The key concepts of Anselm's realist epistemology are *necessitas*, the impossibility that something should not exist or be other than it is, and *ratio*, the conformity of something to law. The terms are often used interchangeably, though for Anselm *necessitas* is the more fundamental. Now ontic necessity/rationality (pertaining to the object) precedes noetic necessity/rationality (pertaining to the subject's knowledge of the object), because knowledge *is* recognition of the basis and rationality peculiar to the object. Ontic and noetic necessity/rationality are of course subordinate to the *ratio veritatis* consubstantial with God, which sovereignly decides what is true reason in all cases. (This realism is thus not a *naive* realism.) The purpose of Anselm's proof is to find the subjective necessity that corresponds with the necessary existence of the already-given object of faith, i.e. to find the strongest possible form of the rationality of faith: to conceive "what is" as "what cannot fail to be."[115] Anselm's thought seeks to be mastered by its object. The actual, rather than the possible, is his ultimate critical principle. There is no question of proving the incumbency of the object on the mind, in virtue of the mind's own structure or resources, as later versions of the "ontological proof" attempt.[116]

The proof itself hinges on the Name of God discovered and used by Anselm: *aliquid quo nihil maius cogitari possit*, "that than which no greater can be conceived." As he describes the event in the prologue to the *Proslogion*, Anselm did not discover the Name as a result of his own ratiocination. It was revealed to him.[117] Granted the conceivability, or intramental existence, of the One named, and the priority of the objective vis-à-vis the subjective order, Anselm claims that something having only intramental existence without extramental existence is inferior to something having both, and thus may not bear the

Name. What does Feuerbach say about this? "The proofs of the existence of God have for their aim to make the internal external, to separate it from man. . . their result is to prove the nature of man."[118] "God is the highest that man conceives or can conceive. This premiss of the ontological proof--the most interesting proof, because it proceeds from within--expresses the inmost nature of religion."[119] The proof does seem a perfect example of wish-fulfillment when it is viewed in the usual way, as a conforming of the real to the ideal. The fact that Anselm's realism (understood by Barth as his reliance upon revelation) does not fit this interpretation but rather contests it, can only be dismissed by judging the realism (or the faith) itself to be a delusion. Barth, beginning with the faith premise, interprets the proof exactly otherwise, as the ultimate refutation of Feuerbach's thesis.

The man who reasons from his own idea of God to the reality of God assumes that he is in a position to be God's creator. But in Anselm's proof, man addresses God as creature to Creator, as one who, far from possessing substantive knowledge of God, stands under a critical *prohibition* against conceiving of God in the way other things are conceived of. The God who is the human wish, whose existence is accredited by our own thought, *is not God--unless* there is a pre-eminent objective existence to graciously ground this subjective existence. The Name does not say "God is the highest that man has in fact conceived, beyond which he can conceive nothing higher," nor "God is the highest that man could conceive."[120]

> This Name of God conceives God only in that sphere in which he can be conceived, not *in altitudine sua*, but with great hesitation and reserve--by conceiving the manner in which he is not to be conceived. He is not to be conceived in such a way--this possibility is ruled out by the revelation-faith relationship to him--that anything greater than him could be imagined or even imagined as conceivable. In the way of any thinker who has a hankering in this direction, the revealed Name of the Lord. . . stands as effective deterrent.[121]

Anselm wishes also to prove, besides the ordinary existence shared by God with other things, a unique existence peculiar to God which is impossible to deny even hypothetically. This he undertakes in *Proslogion* 3. It is an application of the same principle: just as something having both objective

and subjective existence is "greater" than something having
only subjective existence, so, between two things having both
objective and subjective existence, that thing the non-existence
of which is impossible to conceive is greater than another the
non-existence of which is at least conceivable. The non-neces-
sary existence would be a false God if it bore the Name.[122]
God's uniquely necessary existence is in fact the presupposition
of all existence, the reality of existence itself; that is why
it cannot be conceived as not existing.[123] The "nerve of the
proof," for Barth, is a parallel of the First Commandment: "by
what his Name forbids, God is fundamentally distinguished from
all beings that can be conceived as not existing."[124] Anselm's
own words confirm this interpretation:

> And this thou art, O Lord our God. Thou dost exist in
> truth in such a way that thou canst not be conceived as not
> existing. And that with reason. For if any and every mind
> were able to conceive of something better than thee then
> the creature would be rising above the Creator and judging
> the Creator. This would be most absurd.[125]

We know that this Name is indeed the Name of God because in
revelation we know ourselves to stand as creatures before our
Creator, in relation to whom our thinking is not free.[126] God
is the Infinite, not measurable by our thought.[127] Therefore
the problem of our theoretical attitude to Him is subsumed under
the practical problem of the obedience we owe Him.[128]

Anselm's proof addresses the fool of Psalm 14/53 who
says in his heart there is no God, but without taking his foolishness seriously. The fool represents the *other* attitude to
God, the odd possibility of disobedience. He stands under God's
wrath, while the obedient theologian stands under grace. He is,
for Barth, the old man, participating as such in the same universal double predestination in which the dialectic of second
Romans and "dialectical theology" began. The theologian is
himself the fool, even though he rejects the foolishness of
atheism in the act of theologizing:

> [Anselm] has not forgotten and has no intention of over-
> looking this other person who keeps on saying and is obvious-
> ly able to say and perhaps is bound to say, *"Deus non est."*
> He does not forget or overlook him just because he himself
> stands so very close to him and because by this opposition
> he himself is faced with the question that is now answered.
> *Unum idemque est quod quaerimus!* Did he not have to know

his opponent's case very intimately and expound it very forcibly in order to defeat him and so raise faith to knowledge? Is not he, who obviously was so well able to conceive and expound this opposite point of view, himself in some way and at some point an *insipiens* too? Or at least is the solidarity between him and his opponent not so entirely broken that he could always understand him as well as he understands himself?[129]

Here the more dialectical Barth begins to intrude on the more calm and positive Anselm. But only up to a point. For Barth appreciates precisely that in Anselm whereby he has virtually exorcized, or at least externalized, the foolishness of atheism (the non-givenness of God) from his theological program, giving rise to that "provocative lack of all doubt, including all 'philosophic doubt,' of all anxiety, including all apologetic anxiety" by which his inquiry is distinguished.[130] It is not that Anselm complacently believes himself to possess the truth; theology's truth must be petitioned for ever anew in prayer; but "it would be prayer devoid of faith in the hearing of prayer (and therefore not prayer) if theological thinking in the act of its fulfillment were not entirely sure of its case and so unwilling to venture forth at its own level with its unconditional demand."[131] The proof shows, in particularly powerful form, that *the question of the fool is excluded from theology.* Theology begins in the exclusion, i.e. in obedience.

In summary, the idea of the Infinite revealed to Anselm, "that than which no greater can be conceived," sets an independently based (ontically prior) God against and above any merely intramental, man-made God-concept. It is thus a denial of Feuerbach's thesis than which no more fundamental could be conceived, conceptually representing that which is more than any other concept could imply, the Infinite, in a way that depends on God's self-revelation, which is greater than the incomprehensibility-in-general that a purely secular gnosis (such as Gaunilo's) might attribute to God in order to object to the givenness of the Name. Anselm does admit the hiddenness of God, but only as God has given him to know it--and therefore this name has incomparably more critical power than the abstract objections raised by Gaunilo.[132]

Barth finds in Anselm an articulation of his own long-time conviction that the most serious critical questions are

posed by *actuality*.[133] This is implicit in the realism of
Anselm's theological scheme, which subordinates the subjective
to the objective, rationality (which has an original though not
exclusive affinity with the subjective) to necessity (which has
an original though not exclusive affinity with the objective).
The point is simply that we may not decide ahead of time who or
what or whether God *can* be, measuring Him by "possibility" (that
is, by ourselves): rather, God presents us with Himself as an
accomplished fact, as a reality which does not submit to the
confirmation of our sense of possibility but actually contradicts it, so long as we hold to the fool's position. The second
part of Anselm's proof makes the strong case for the manner in
which God, unlike all other objects, so totally dominates our
canons of possibility as to preclude even the hypothetical conception of His unreality. This domination establishes the pattern according to which, also in the realm of the relative and
finite, objective rationality has precedence over subjective.

In sharp contrast to Descartes, therefore, Anselm locates the uniquely indubitable reality with God. That is why
Barth, the opponent of Cartesianism in theology, alights on just
this proof and considers it the key to a new theological method.

THE ABSOLUTE DIFFERENCE BECOMES POSITIVE. Anselm provided Barth with an example of a theology basically different
from his own. Without losing sight of the relativity of his
effort, Anselm could think in undialectical realist fashion,
presupposing God's self-givenness in revelation and a spontaneous, even imperative desire of faith to perfect itself in
improved understanding of revelation. Because of Anselm's complete confidence in his object, he is not preoccupied with unbelief or its symptoms. Barth's dialectical theology, on the
other hand, is very much preoccupied with unbelief and its symptoms; it is premised above all on the continuing sinful state
of man whose enjoined obedience is, in important respects, *blind*
due to his alienation from God. The blind man spends much of
his time discussing his blindness, as for example the necessity
for dialectical Word and Counterword to hold back the waters of
the Red Sea of sin, or the necessity for theology to use and
try not to abuse the strictly philosophical conceptual resources
available to it. Both Anselm and Barth hear and continually

heed the divine Yes and No; neither attempts to derive the Yes or No from anything other than revelation. But Anselm addresses the No differently, not only by opposing himself as theologian to himself as fool, but by deriving the supreme No, the critical prohibition against all man-thought gods, directly from the supreme Yes, the revelation of God's Name. In this way the asymmetry that Barth had always ascribed to his dialectic, based on the real but transcendent superiority of the Yes to the No, is very elegantly exhibited. Had Barth ever succeeded in so clearly distinguishing the No of his theology from Gaunilo's idealist caveat against the knowability of God? Had he not in fact always been haunted by the resemblance of his "No" to the "Origin" of critical idealism, the "Absolute" of "Der Glaube an den persönlichen Gott," or the "Wholly Other" of Otto's religious psychology?

Barth said in "Schicksal und Idee" that theology is only possible as a dialectic between realist and idealist elements—presenting God as given and as non-given. He conceived God to be Lord over this dialectic, Other than either the realist or idealist theses, neither given nor non-given according to human thought. But this was still basically an idealist argument, premised on what God is *not* (*not* party to our dialectic). Anselm offers an equally critical conception of God based on what God *is*, a realist *totaliter aliter* expressing, instead of non-givenness, *unique* and *exigent givenness*. The concept of the Other as uniquely given, which the proof discloses as His necessary existence, provides for a new and more stable account of the unique warrant and task of theology. If theology adheres to its unique object, its scientific rationale will take care of itself. This perspective satisfies Barth for several reasons: (1) it allows a positive actuality to function as the critical principle in theology, vindicating the realist instincts (though not the naiveté) of first *Romans*, which Barth had suppressed in second *Romans* and only partially admitted in his dialectical theology; (2) it frees theology from inauthentic preoccupation with dialectic, philosophy, and what Barth called the impossibility of speaking of God, by accepting a God-given possibility of speaking of God; and (3) it provides theology with the proper starting point from which to authoritatively oppose Cartesianism and Feuerbachianism, because it may now indisputably *be* something different from Cartesianism and Feuer-bachianism. In this new theological existence, something like "organic" thinking again becomes possible for the theologian, to the extent that he abandons the repressive machinations of dialectic in favor of the distinctive *pulchritudo* of his object.[134]

3. Church Dogmatics

The two editions of Barth's Prolegomena are not nearly as different from one another as the two editions of *Romans*. The alteration of perspective in the first half-volume of *Church Dogmatics* is, however, of comparable importance, though of greater subtlety. Before the change is analyzed it will be helpful to catalogue the similarities. Dogmatics still begins as a Doctrine of the Word of God, of self-given revelation totally different from human knowledge and values; it is still the critical comparison of church proclamation with the revelation attested in Holy Scripture; it is still confessional rather than apologetic, having been chosen by revelation rather than choosing it; and the meaning of theology, as of Christian life generally, is still to obediently and "existentially" serve this Word, rather than to have, speak, or judge it for ourselves. The theologian still has only secular concepts at his disposal, and theology remains, in a way, necessarily dialectical. But there is also an important sense in which theology is no longer dialectical, which will be our main topic of inquiry, since it bears directly on the manner in which the otherness of God is conceived. The first volume of the *Church Dogmatics* proves to reflect the Barth-Anselm interpretation of the *totaliter aliter*.

MYSTERY AND DIALECTIC. Starting from his equation of the *deus revelatus* and the *deus absconditus* in second *Romans*, Barth consistently maintained that the concealedness of God is not to be abstractly inferred, but is itself part of revelation, inseparable from the revealed unconcealedness of God. The true Wholly Other, unlike Otto's "Wholly Other," is only acknowledged as such in His revelation. Thus the non-givenness of God is not a function of the absence of revelation, but the reverse.

Theological dialectic works with a Yes and a No that are both spoken by God, and both pertain to the inner movement of the *Sache*, revelation. However, in Barth's dialectical theology the divine No delivers the negative message that God is in heaven and man is on earth--man cannot speak of God--man is condemned to always be speaking of everything but God. Viewed under this aspect, theology misses its object, even though the merciful God may still reckon its exertions to it as righteousness. This is the meaning of the Crisis.

Church Dogmatics, acting on or at least consistently with the clue provided by Anselm, requalifies the divine No as a positively understood *mystery* ingredient in God's givenness. Barth still finds it necessary to warn against an overly "positive" attitude toward theological work, such as would give rise to an assured, undialectical command of Christian concepts and doctrines.[135] Theology must respect the mystery of God. But it must beware of the subtle pitfall of being too "positive" in its self-limitation.

> For it would be a highly refined way of becoming master of God's Word to think we could put ourselves in a position in which we have securely adopted the right attitude to it, that of servant and not master. Would not this be the loftiest triumph of human certainty? But would it not be a confirmation of the question and a fall into the temptation? For what would it imply if we had made, or were in process of making, that delimitation of the divine from the human? If we could do this, we should have said, or should be saying, what the Word of God is. The goal of all yearning in theology is to be able to do this, but this is the goal of an illegitimate yearning. . .
> Mystery thus denotes the divine givenness of the Word of God which also fixes our own limits and by which it distinguishes itself from everything that is given otherwise. Distinguishes itself? This means that we cannot establish its distinction. Otherwise it would not be a mystery.[136]

The mystery does directly involve the apparently ungodly aspect of revelation, i.e. its ubiquitous secularity, but we are in no position to do other than acknowledge the goodness and necessity of revelation coming to us in this way.[137] Unlike the other mysteries of the world, God is the permanent and eternal mystery.[138] God as Mystery is not to be confused with the Other of second *Romans*, although in both cases faith is called upon to acknowledge its normative relation to the concealedness of

God. In this case, God's mystery is the ambivalence or secularity of His revelation. It is conceived primarily as an aspect or quality of His givenness rather than as His pure non-givenness.

The necessary indirectness of our knowledge of the mysterious God generates a proper dialectical movement in theology. From the "twofold movement of the Word of God" come the familiar pairs Law and Gospel, letter and spirit, etc.[139] *Theologia crucis* has the twofold task of saying what can be said and warning against what cannot.[140] Barth continues to speak frequently of the transcendent synthesis of the theses of theology, which in our frame of reference are constantly alternating.[141] But this synthesis which we are incapable of finding for ourselves *is* found, in faith, in God.

> Committing it to God and seeking it in God, we really do find it; we hear the full and true Word of God, whether it be the divine content in its secular form or in the secular form the divine content. To hear the full and true Word of God does not mean perceiving the unity of veiling and unveiling, of form and content, and thus achieving Christian thought by the detour of faith. No, the thinking of faith will always be quite honestly a realistic or idealistic thinking, i.e., a thinking that in and of itself is most unchristian. As such. . . the thinking of faith is justified and sanctified thinking.[142]

Barth's dialectical reservations are evidently still in force, in that it remains impossible even in faith to grasp the complete truth; but he chooses now to emphasize that faith is nevertheless in a relationship with the truth, and that this (paradoxical) relationship dominates all reservations, since it is God-given. Taken together with Barth's sharpened attack on the "negative *theologia gloriae*" that would, like Gaunilo *contra* Anselm, fix a priori the limits of the knowability of God, this form of deference to theology's object signals a step beyond dialectical theology, though by no means a renunciation of it.[143]

The "mystery of God" appears in the fifth proposition concerning the Nature of the Word of God, at the point where *Die christliche Dogmatik* had announced its transition from "phenomenological" to "existential" thinking.[144] Barth inserts here a lengthy excursus on the impossibility of basing theology on existential philosophy, responding to Siegfried's misunderstanding to the effect that this qualification of theology as existential was meant to be constitutive and presupposed a philosophical interpretation of existence.[145]   On his other flank he perceives Bultmann, Gogarten, Brunner, and Tillich all to be demanding in various ways that philosophy or anthropology or culture be taken *more* seriously in principle.   Against Gogarten, Barth sees his demand for a "true anthropology" as the fundamental task of modern theology to be an expression of Schleiermacherian, man-centered theology which even in its polemical attitude toward the modern intellectual situation still allows that situation to dictate the ground on which theology will be based.[146]   The same objection applies to the "eristics" designated by Brunner as "the other [apparently more important] task of theology."[147]   And the concern of Gogarten and Bultmann with understanding the existence of the man who hears revelation, which is tied to their interest in clarifying the conceptuality with which theology works vis-à-vis philosophy--"and in Bultmann's proximity this certainly means to derive the possibility of theology from the relation perceived"[148]--impeaches the independence of theology by diverting attention from its object, revelation.[149]   Similarly, Tillich's disdain for the "concrete behest of God" in favor of "the infinite potentiality of God" deprives theology of its true basis in the church's concrete response to concrete revelation.[150]   The crisis in which man is placed by this revelation has nothing whatever to do with "even the most radical crisis in which man may find himself from the standpoint of general anthropology."[151]   Barth also rejects all abstract search for a method in theology, even a method based on the insight that no method is possible.   "Precisely by proclaiming the contents of the Bible and tradition we bear witness to the fact that we are in no position" to solve our problem this way.[152]   We bear *witness*, i.e. we refer the problem to that Other perspective in which it is solved for us. The concept of the Word of God means that the Church is not alone and is not referred back to itself.[153]

   THE KNOWABLE INFINITE.   God proves Himself to be the true Other by saying something to man that man is incapable of saying to himself.   God is concretely, not abstractly, incomprehensible; God is a mystery rather than a non-givenness; God precludes the *analogia entis*, man's presumption of a given

commonality between himself and God, *by* the *analogia fidei*,
God's merciful donation of a real relation between Himself and
the faith that He creates in man. The God problem is set, not
by what man does not know of God, but by what God gives man to
know. "Woe to me if I do not preach the gospel!" (I Cor. 9:16)[154]
--the impossibility of speaking of God must not be allowed to
interfere with the necessity of speaking of God. All along the
line *Church Dogmatics* treats the theme of God's Otherness in
this characteristic positive way, in the greatest contrast to
second *Romans*. The eminent reality of God's acts overshadows
(without displacing) the equivocal incognito in which the acts
of the Other are shrouded: God's speech is the uniquely true
speech,[155] "[t]his Word is the ground of our being beyond our
being; whether we hear it or not, whether we obey it or not, it
is in virtue of its superior existence that our existence is a
reality."[156] The Anselmian acceptance of the triumphant reality
of theology's object is operative here, as also when Barth discusses the eminent "personhood" and "fatherhood" of God,[157] and
the "historicity" of revelation.[158]

God says something to man. He positively commands the
proclamation of His Word.[159] Herein lies the need for proclamation and the God-centered confidence of theology--not "the
fact that certain circumstances and scales of value immanent in
the existence of man and things crave to be known and de-
clared."[160] God's Word is Other.

It is proclaimed to the degree that it presents and
places itself as an object over against us and the whole
world of all our objects, certainly in the unavoidable
medium of perceptual objectivity, but in this medium as the
object which can never in any sense be our possession, to
which we can never point back as to a datum, which is a
presupposition in the sense and only in the sense that it
sets itself where we cannot possibly set it. We have it as
it gives itself to us if we have it.[161]

The specific trait of otherness found in the proclaimed form of
the Word of God is also found in its written form. Just as
proclamation is the way in which God does not leave man alone,
so Scripture is the means by which God does not leave the church
alone with itself (as it is really free to listen only to itself
according to the Roman Catholic conception of unwritten tradition).[162] God would not be faithful to man if He did not

preserve the otherness of His Word, its incommensurability with all human words and systems.[163]

> Encounter with the human word as such is never genuine, irrevocable encounter, nor can it be. Encounter with the Word of God is genuine, irrevocable encounter, i.e., encounter that can never be dissolved in union. The Word of God always tells us something fresh that we had never heard before from anyone.[164]

Man's enmity toward God is his preference for listening to his own voice instead of God's. The meaning of Modernist anthropocentrism, the Catholic *analogia entis*, and dogmatic infallibilism and historicism is, fundamentally, that man will not allow something to be said to him.[165]

God's Word makes a claim on our hearing and therefore is somehow knowable. The first question of dogmatics concerning the subjective appropriation of the Word cannot be "How is human knowledge of revelation possible?" but "What is true human knowledge of divine revelation?"[166] It must proceed "on the assumption that revelation itself creates of itself the necessary point of contact in man," the *analogia fidei*.[167] Man does not have this gift to dispose of; it is loaned to him exclusively for use.[168] Epistemically as well as practically, man is allowed to enter only that "synergism" that advances God's will alone, based on a correct relationship of Creator and creature: as servants and witnesses, but precisely thus, as human, we have contact with God.[169] In our knowledge of Him His reality determines our existence.[170] The claim to Christian knowledge is justified by the event of God's self-giving, not by "even the most weighty stipulations" offered in advance of the event.[171] The Anselmian note is visible in places:

> Dogmatics as an enquiry presupposes that the true content of Christian talk about God can be known by man. . . The fulfillment of this knowledge, the event of human action, the appropriation corresponding to this address in which, through the stages of intuitive development to formulated comprehension, the revelation of the *analogia fidei* and the resultant clarity in dogmatics. . . take creaturely form, is, of course, a second event compared with the divine action itself, united with it in faith, yet also in faith to be distinguished from it. The second event, however, does not abolish the first. In, with and under the human question dogmatics speaks of the divine answer. It knows even as it seeks. It teaches even as it learns. In human uncertainty like any other science, it establishes the most certain truth ever known.[172]

The "intuitive apprehension" and "formulated comprehension" of
dogmatic science do not, however, mean that dogmatics is an
intuitive science striving for subjective self-evidence and
certainty. That would be a methodological Cartesianism incompatible with the Otherness of God. The purpose of dogma is to
serve the Word of God, which is not the same thing as to sub-
jectively replicate it. For example, Barth acknowledges that
the concept of *homoousia* is what philosophy would call an "empty
concept," since "we do not even remotely grasp the object to
which there is an attempt to respond in this concept."[173] But
Barth can still appreciate how the concept functions against
the Arian and polytheistic heresies. The dogmas of the Trinity,
despite their historical and philosophical questionableness,
have been vindicated by the service they have proven themselves
capable of performing in the struggle of the church to remain
loyal to its object.

The assurance proper to faith is not one of cognitive
possession but of hope, hungering and thirsting.[174] But because
we have this assurance from God, it is truly boundless and superior in every respect to the Cartesian thesis that human consciousness is the measure of this and all other knowledge.
Barth devotes a section of his paragraph on the Knowability of
the Word of God (§6) to "the Word of God and Experience," where
he attempts to define the normative concept of Christian experience, in the broad sense of the determination of the existence
of men by God's Word.[175] The specific character of Christian
experience is acknowledgement, a rational yet mysterious, personal, master-servant, contingent, decisional event in which
one is "letting oneself be continually led, always making a
step, always being in movement from the experience felt at one
time or the thought grasped at one time to the opposite experience and thought."[176] This is the dialectic-without-a-synthesis
of faith responding to the God it recollects and hopes for, without having. This "experience" is really "not experience but
more than experience."[177] Barth is willing now to let the
unique character of Christian experience, rather than some
claimed impossibility of Christian experience, oppose the distortion of Cartesianism.

> The saying *finitum non capax infiniti* cannot really prove what has to be proved at this point. If the real experience of the man addressed by God's Word is against this saying, then the saying must go, as every philosophical statement in theology that is in contradiction with this experience must go. As a philosophical saying it does not interest us in the slightest. We do not say *finitum* but *homo peccator non capax*, and we do not continue *infiniti* but *verbi Domini*. The real experience of the man addressed by God's Word is the very thing that decides and proves that what makes it possible lies beyond itself.[178]

It is still inappropriate to set up any experience per se as the proprium of Christian theology. For where within experience will be found the criterion by which to distinguish the valid from the invalid, divine from human?[179] That is why Christian experience is "more than experience"; like the church, it is not alone, not referred back to itself. The infinite Word of God eternally exceeds and masters this experience. It is axiomatic for Barth that our experiences and concepts in themselves express our resistance to God. Cartesianism is beyond any mere mistake, it is rebellion. "Unquestionably the image of God in consciousness is primarily and intrinsically and as such the image of free man. He who sees in this image as such the image of God is saying thereby that he knows free man as God."[180]

4. The Other Other

The first half-volume of the *Church Dogmatics* introduces the conception of the otherness of God, related to the principle of the analogy of faith, on which the "Christological concentration" of Barth's mature theology would be based. In order to see the corresponding resolution in his conception of the human other vis-à-vis the divine other, we must see how his way of discussing ethics changed in the period between second *Romans* and *Church Dogmatics*.

A 1922 lecture on "The Problem of Ethics Today"[181] does much to strengthen the suspicion that Barth's theology is grounded in a certain ethical definition of the problem of existence, which here is sweepingly drawn as the crisis or "sickness unto death" of man.[182] He analyzes the insufficiency of the Kantian theory of moral personality and of millenarian visions of the just state, and inserts into the breach the dialectic of the thought of God.[183] God is the answer to the

ethical question. God's answer is controlled by God's free
grace, and there is no way from man to God in seeking the divine
answer, but the crisis appears to be an existential aporia dis-
coverable in itself, apart from revelation. This would be the
"negative point of contact" type of natural theology of which he
later spoke disparagingly--for instance, in his 1934 controversy
with Brunner.[184] "The Problem of Ethics Today" contains no
explicit disavowal of this independent, though negative, significance of man's condition, although it does deny that the
problem points before revelation to God. The problem does
acquire a completely new seriousness in the light of revelation.[185] But Barth wishes to remind us that the Christian problem is the problem of existence, that ethics is no separable
department of theology.

By 1927 Barth is only willing to discuss Christian
ethics as a function of God's command to the believer.[186] In
this year, the year of his "existential" *Dogmatik*, Barth distinguishes, all along the line, the truth of the individual's
concrete situation from universal or general truth. Of equal
concreteness with the "existential I" is the "Thou" of the
fellow man, who in every case poses a particular rather than
general ethical problem. Barth casts the I-Thou relationship
in a distinctive light in his criticism of Feuerbach.[187] He
agrees with Stirner that Feuerbach's social "being of man" is
still an abstraction, and that Stirner's "single individual" is
a step nearer existential thinking--though still man without
God.

> But Stirner has put his finger precisely on Feuerbach's
> weak point, on the question of whether Feuerbach's man is
> *really* the *real* man. If Feuerbach's teaching on the "being
> of man" is to be recognized as the final priestly illusion,
> if the real man is always *I* for whom no human *Thou* at all
> can remove the burden of existence as an individual; if I
> am rather one on whom this burden is laid just by the
> unavoidably present human *Thou*, then the road to Feuerbach's
> God--and also the road to Stirner's "single individual"--
> is cut off. And then there is a possibility for the insight
> that the identification of God with man is impossible. More
> cannot be said.[188]

"More cannot be said," because Barth was sensitive to the danger,
which he saw represented by Gogarten, of even seeming to base
theology on an I-Thou philosophy.[189] But the train of reflection

is pursued in *Die christliche Dogmatik*, still with reference to Feuerbach. What is the *ratio* of the Incarnation? Why must God become man to reveal Himself? Because the problem of man can only be presented as the problem of the fellow-man. As Feuerbach showed, the way into the "inside of nature" by an uncritical absorption of the ego in the world is barred to us by the impenetrable limit of the fact of the fellow man. This limit is, in the final analysis, a limit placed on us by God. But since the limit is discussed in general terms it seems to belong to the order of creation rather than to the present action of grace, although Barth contemplates this action when he says, "No other creature than man can place on us (whether it happens or not is a question in itself) the limit determined for us by God."[190]

A new twist is given this question in Barth's 1928 ethics lectures at Münster, where he identifies the problem of the other man as the supreme problem of philosophical as opposed to theological ethics.[191] Neither philosophy nor theology can fulfill the claim to responsibility in which the reality of the Word of God places us regarding the other person. Only God "does ethics" in this sense. Philosophy does not have theology's responsibility to proclaim this reality, but it can remind the self that something is exterior to self-reflection and self-responsibility, viz. the wholly other. Philosophy can point toward the wholly other, so that what the other has to say may be heard. The "other" of philosophy cannot be God Himself; here, too, philosophy is distinguished from theology. The proper task of philosophy, concretely sharpened in ethics, is to remind the self of the *human* Thou, whom theology designates as the concrete locus of *God's* claim on the self. Philosophy's role (in its own sphere) is to upset the primacy of the imperative "Know thyself!" The claim of the other person attested by philosophy stands to the claim of God Himself as possibility stands to reality: "He *can* bring God's Word to us, if God wills to speak His Word through him."[192]

Barth's argument of 1928 assumes a Christian philosophy that recognizes and obeys the Word of God.[193] But in *Church Dogmatics* I/1 he rejects the possibility of a *philosophia christiana* and with it any interest in an independently posed examination of the moral significance of the neighbor. Even in

1928 he holds firmly that the other man is significantly "other" only as so designated by God--that we could not love the neighbor had God not loved us first. But he has a lingering interest in the human other as a dimension of "Life," as perhaps the last and weightiest desideratum of the basic correlation between Life and Bible that informs so much of Barth's earlier thought. The purely theological consideration of the problem (as Barth now understands "pure theology") within the framework of the *Church Dogmatics* does not appear until the second half of the first volume (1938). Here, in connection with his revised discussion of the *ratio* of the Incarnation, Barth repeats his comments on Stirner and Feuerbach, attributing to Feuerbach the possibility of "a surviving scrap of Christian insight" in his notion of the Thou as the rock on which the pride of the ego breaks--but the qualification is rigid. "If Feuerbach meant what the Bible calls 'our neighbor,' then we must agree with him."[194] "If we are aware of what we are by God's verdict, and thence aware also of what a fellow-man is, then he becomes for us a real other. . . His existence can thus become the means to divine revelation which is not only veiling but always unveiling as well."[195] Hedged with warnings that such analysis can only be made on the presupposition of the divine revelation, Barth is able to make this very strong claim for the unique Christian significance of the neighbor.

A clearer statement follows with reference to the relation between the First and Second Commandments (Mark 12:28-31).[196] God's love is first. Everything else must be interpreted as a response to it or consequence of it. Therefore, the Second Commandment to love one's neighbor as oneself has no meaning except as an expression of the love of God demanded by the First. Neighbor-love is praise of God; but "no praise of God is serious, or can be taken seriously, if it is apart from or in addition to" the Second Commandment, which is in effect the *definition* of "praise of God."[197] On the sole basis of this commandment--not because of "some inherent value in himself as such, or in the relation to him as such," or "the existence of certain original orders of human life in society"[198]--we perceive the other man, not standing alongside of God with an equal claim, nor as a merely secondary and relative claim on a

different level from the First Commandment, but as a uniquely
decisive token of the divine love.[199]

The other man is posited by God as other, i.e. as one
whom we do not choose. But the primary signification of his
otherness is, for the Christian, positive.

> The primary and true form of the neighbor is that he
> faces us as the bearer and representative of the divine com-
> passion. Where he is only Law, where he means confusion,
> accusation, the discovery of our wickedness and helpless-
> ness, wrath and judgment, we see him in a veiled form. . .
> he could not seriously claim and judge us unless he were
> primarily and properly set before us in quite a different
> way, as the instrument of that order. . . in which God wills
> to be praised by us for His goodness. . . That there is this
> instrument of the order is itself divine goodness which we
> ought to recognize and praise as such before we ever ask
> about the claim to which it gives rise.[200]

The positive meaning attaches to the divine reference of the
encounter with the neighbor, but when we ask who the neighbor
is or what kind of encounter best accomplishes the reference to
God, we find that the other man's paradigmatic form is the
wretched, repellent, sinful other who is as such our benefactor
because he is a sign instituted by Christ to represent Himself.
"For the sake of this misery, in His faithful actualization, He
became poor and homeless, tormented, dead and buried."[201] So
it is very definitely the aggravated otherness of the other
that counts in Christian ethics.

> [T]his neighbor will cause me a really mortal headache.
> I mean, he will seriously give me cause involuntarily to
> repudiate his existence and in that way to put myself in
> serious danger. In face of this neighbor I certainly have
> to admit to myself that I would really prefer to exist in
> some other [ganz anders] way than in this co-existence.[202]

The afflicted neighbor is so valuable to me because he shows to
me my own affliction: he will not allow me to forget my sinfulness. "The neighbor is indeed and necessarily a problem," to
our salvation.[203]

Barth's development between 1922 and 1932, which has
been presented here as a shift from a mainly negative to a
mainly positive conception of the otherness of God, involves a
change of attitude on a number of issues, the most important
being: (1) How is theological discourse warranted?, (2) What

is the right relationship between theology and philosophy, and
what might philosophy be able to contribute to Christian
thought?, and (3) What is the relation of revelation to the
moral problem of our existence?

We found ourselves continually entangled with the first
question, insofar as the revelation of the Wholly Other, which
at first called for no witness except to the impossibility of
a substantial witness, was later seen (by virtue of its givenness in *these* documents, proclaimed by *this* church) to encourage
some doctrinal formulations over others, within a dialectically
circumscribed theological scheme. The Wholly Other was ultimately seen to demand unconditional adherence of theological
inquiry to itself, in the form it chooses to give itself, so as
to preclude the possibility of taking the lostness of man as
seriously as his foundness with God. The starting point of
theology can be determined by nothing other than the way in
which God approaches man and the kind of response He demands.
Thus every alteration in Barth's idea of revelation gives rise
to a differently understood theological method, for the *reality*
of the object controls the *possibility* of knowledge of it.

The problem of philosophy lay constantly in our path,
not because Barth ever felt the need for a philosophical justification of God, but because all human thought remains on the
human side of the infinite qualitative difference. Theology
ought not to claim any special possession over against philosophy, for it has none. Philosophy is not the handmaiden of
theology; both theology and philosophy are the inadequate hand-
maidens of God.[204] In the Anselmian turn, Barth's theology
loses a bit of its handmaidenly modesty and leaves philosophy
to cleave unto God: that is, theology begins to shed some of
the conspicuous dialectical machinery of the 1920's in order to
let the Other be the Other as uniquely given.

Barth's conviction that the whole of man's existence is
claimed by God means that no separation of theology and ethics
is allowable. But he in fact presupposes their separation by
trying to show how they join together in "The Problem of Ethics
Today," where the reader learns first of the crisis of existence,
and then of the divine light shed on it in revelation. In this
he follows his "Religion und Leben" correlation of "Life" and

"Bible," which model is naturally suggested by the pastor's task of relating the message of the Bible to the modern existence of his hearers. Barth's conception of "Life" focuses more and more on the situation, not of modern man in general, but of the individual addressed by God's Word; and he finds under this regime of "concreteness" that the actual encounter with the neighbor as other counts for more than Kantian theory or socialist ideals. It is when theology finally steps clear of its philosophical eggshells that the very foundation of Christian ethics can become the otherness of the other person as a token of the absolutely Other.

CHAPTER VI

THE IDEA OF THE INFINITE: EMMANUEL LEVINAS 1961-1975[1]

The publication of *Totality and Infinity* in 1961 put
Levinas in a different position than he had been in hitherto.
He became famous as the "anti-Heidegger";[2] articles were written about him; questions were directed at him from all sides.
The process began in print with a discussion at the Sorbonne of
the propositions of *Totality and Infinity*, which he had submit-
ted as his thesis for the degree of Doctor of Letters.[3] In 1964
the serious and lengthy critique of Jacques Derrida appeared.[4]
Levinas became a professor at the University of Poitiers, by
1967 had moved to Paris-Nanterre, and to the Sorbonne by 1973.
Soon after *Totality and Infinity* there appeared signs of an
important shift in his approach to the analysis of the absolutely Other, and a largely new set of operating concepts is to be
found in his major work of 1974, *Otherwise than Being or Beyond
Essence*.[5] "Otherwise than Being" and "beyond essence" signal
that the philosophy of 1974 is devoted as much or more to the
idea of the Other as any of the work preceding, but its transformation of the theme indicates that certain aspects of the
earlier thought were more fertile than others: particularly,
the practice of metaphysics as an "infinition" or positive
welcoming of the Other, rather than as an anti-ontology. *Otherwise than Being* disrupts ontological language otherwise than
by opposing it antithetically.

Levinas first made systematic use of Descartes' idea of
the Infinite in "La philosophie et l'idée de l'Infini" (1957).[6]
The strangeness of enthroning Descartes in a philosophy dedicated to the primacy of the ethical was brought up by Jean Wahl
and Henri Gouhier, in response to whom Levinas noted that his
approval of Descartes' philosophy was confined to its "admirable
rhythm" in recovering the world only after encountering the idea
of the Infinite.[7] Descartes, like Husserl, is not only a philosopher of the *cogito* but an exemplary critical thinker who,
despite some equivocation,[8] manages to place the *cogito* itself

165

in question. Descartes writes, toward the end of the third
Meditation:

> Hence there remains only the idea of God, concerning
> which we must consider whether it is something which cannot
> have proceeded from me myself. By the name God I under-
> stand a substance that is infinite [eternal, immutable],
> independent, all-knowing, all-powerful, and by which I
> myself and everything else, if anything else does exist,
> have been created. Now all these characteristics are such
> that the more diligently I attend to them, the less do they
> appear capable of proceeding from me alone; hence, from
> what has been already said, we must conclude that God neces-
> sarily exists.
> For although the idea of substance is within me owing
> to the fact that I am substance, nevertheless I should not
> have the idea of an infinite substance--since I am finite--
> if it had not proceeded from some substance which was veri-
> tably infinite.
> . . . The idea, I say, of this Being who is absolutely
> perfect and infinite, is entirely true; for although, per-
> haps, we can imagine that such a Being does not exist, we
> cannot nevertheless imagine that His idea represents nothing
> real to me. . . And this does not cease to be true although
> I do not comprehend the infinite, or though in God there is
> an infinitude of things which I cannot comprehend, nor
> possibly even reach in any way by thought; for it is of the
> nature of the infinite that my nature, which is finite and
> limited, should not comprehend it. . .[9]

One does not arrive at the Infinite by negating the imperfections of visible existence or the finitude of the knower. It
is a reality, not a speculation. The idea makes a claim on the
one who has it, forbidding him to think that it could have
proceeded from, or be adequate to, interiority. It causes a
breach in the fabric of *cogito*-constituted reality, not by its
sheer absence--for while the *ideatum* must in a sense be sheerly
absent if the idea of it truly overflows the totality, yet the
idea itself is indisputably present in the form of this over-
flowing--but by its *already-given* presence prior to any possible
bestowal of meaning by the *cogito*. Levinas had previously
appropriated the idea of creation in "Liberté et commandement"
to express this anteriority of ethical meaning to *Sinngebung*;
the idea of the Infinite is simply Descartes' discovery that he
is a creature. His move in the last paragraph of the third
Meditation, "to consider, and admire, and adore, the beauty of
this light so resplendent,"[10] transmutes this cognitive infinity
into a personal Majesty.[11]

This is precisely the direction of the change in Levinas' thought, as may be found in comparing *Otherwise than Being* with *Totality and Infinity*: from a cognitive Other-formalism using the idea of creation to interrupt and limit phenomenology, ontology, and universal history, to a practical welcoming of the Other expressed in an "emphatic" language that *glorifies* the Infinite.[12] The rigorous pluralism of "separation" and "desire" gives way to the penetration of the Same by the Other, to "proximity" and "obsession." We will trace this change by surveying *Otherwise than Being* and certain of the intervening articles, with reference to the development of the theme of the Other and of the method and language employed by a philosophy devoted to the Other.

1. The Trace of the Other

The pluralism of *Totality and Infinity* is pictured for the most part spatially, as a simultaneous co-existence of separated beings who address each other in the present from a dimension of "height." Discourse is defined as an "incessance," a mastery of the present. Otherness is produced as the curvature of intersubjective space, and as the "exterior" with respect to the Same. Is this, as Minkowski objected, too static a conception?[13] If so, the reason may lie in Levinas' concordant interest in rehabilitating a certain mastery of subjectivity over time, in reaction to Heidegger's temporal ecstaticism. The subject installs itself in the present, which is its own time par excellence. But the Other commands the Same precisely at the point where the Same comes into its rights: the moral life is the reason for the Same's freedom, in fact the metaphysical requirement of that freedom. Levinas does not now retract this analysis, but he extends it to rule out the presumption that the Other's command intersects with, and is thus a part of, the present in which the Self is master. He adds a temporal metaphor of diachrony to the spatial metaphors of height and exteriority.

THE IMMEMORIAL. Already in *Totality and Infinity* Levinas indicated a temporal horizon of otherness in terms of the unforeseeableness or irreducible futurity of the Other, who creates genuine temporality by drawing the Same into ever-new moments. The Same can never arrive at the new instant and so cannot transform it into a present. In his 1963 article "La trace de l'autre" he opposes the motif of Abraham, who is called out of Haran to journey he knows not where, to the motif of Ulysses, all of whose adventures are on the way home to Ithaca.[14] For the movement of the Same toward the Other to be a true adventure without return, there must be an ingratitude on the part of the Other, a refusal to pay back on the risk of transcendence so as to render it prudent ex post facto. Eschatology is, in this sense, hopeless:

> The future for which work is undertaken should be represented from the beginning as indifferent to my death. . . To renounce being the contemporary of the triumph of my work is to have the triumph in a time without me, to see this world here without me, to see a time beyond the horizon of my time.[15]

Being-toward-death is commanded by what comes after death. This dimension of the meaning of what occurs in the present, which refers beyond all possible presents, "pierces" the present-- just as the epiphany of the Other Person as Other pierces his worldly manifestation, "like a being who opens a window in which his image has been reflected."[16] To take seriously the hopelessness of the beyond, to make sure it is not being transformed into an after-world, it is necessary to resolutely direct attention to this world, i.e. to Being's play of disclosure and dissimulation, in the search for the Other beyond either disclosure or dissimulation. The extraordinary Other is inserted, somehow, in the Same, as a unique disruption of it. The peculiar "evidence" of the Other's face in the totality is the *trace* left in totality by the Infinite.[17] Levinas' critique of false futurity thus points him, metaphorically, toward the past; for it is in the nature of a trace to *have been* left.

"The significance of the trace places us in a relation which answers to an irreversible past. No memory will be able to follow this past to the trace."[18] The trace left by the Other, who is absolved from all relation with a system of evidences or signifiers, is like the trace left by the perfect criminal who has deliberately effaced all traces of his crime. He has irreversibly upset the order of things precisely by vanishing from it.[19] Only an absolute being can leave a trace

in this sense. All signs made by such a being leave that trace.
"Over and above what the sign signifies is the passage of the
person who left the sign."[20] The whole realm of the ethical
thus deranges (though with absolute discretion!) the totalized
time of the Same, by refusing to synchronize with the Same,
either in the present of its intuition or in the ordered time
of its coherent accounts of what has gone before and what will
come. Transcendence is diachronic;[21] it is *le dire* distinct
from *le dit*, the *saying* of he who signifies distinct from *what*
he says and the appearance he makes, or the text he creates,
which are reintegrated into the totality. The totality's power
of reintegration is beyond challenge--except by a "maybe" or an
"if you like" that would acknowledge, under the incognito of
Being, the "enigma" of the beyond-Being, or eternity.[22] How,
in temporal terms, are we to conceive this extraordinary presentation of transcendence?

> For the possibility of the derangement a fissile present
> is required, "destructuring" itself in its very punctuality.
> The otherness that deranges order cannot be reduced to a
> difference revealed to the gaze, which compares and thereby
> synchronizes the Same and the Other. Otherness occurs as
> a digression [*écart*] and a past that no memory could revive
> in the present. . . In order that the uprooting from order
> not be ipso facto participation in order, this uprooting,
> this abstraction, must--by a supreme anachronism--precede
> its own entry into order. The past of the Other must never
> have been present.[23]

As an example of a great "experience" that is never actually
experienced, Levinas offers Moses' encounter with the burning
bush to which he does not raise his eyes, and with the God who
is "revealed" to him as having already passed by (Exodus 33).[24]
All this describes how the Other can remain equivocal and incognito, invading the Same without contesting it on its own terms.

ILLEITY. The Other who has passed by is different from
the *vous* of *Totality and Infinity* who, albeit from on high,
offers his countenance in a face-to-face encounter. Levinas
had already given the intersubjective relationship a reference
outside of itself by investing the second person with the dignity of *Vous*, who transcends and criticizes the *société intime*
of I and Thou alone with each other in the order of pardon.
The self's liability to judgment cannot be limited; the irreversibility of the mercilessly public moral order instituted by

Vous is, in fact, the condition of all moral seriousness. Now, in "La trace de l'autre," Levinas writes:

> Beyond Being is a third person who is not defined by the Self-Same, by ipseity: a possibility of a third direction of radical irrectitude, escaping the bipolar play of immanence and transcendence that is proper to Being, in which immanence always overcomes transcendence. The profile that belongs, by the trace, to the irreversible past is the profile of the "Il." The *beyond* from which the face comes is the third person. The pronoun *Il* exactly expresses this inexpressible irreversibility, which already lends itself neither to revelation nor to dissimulation. . . transcendence in an ab-solute past. The illeity of the third person is the condition of irreversibility.[25]

"Illeity" (*illéité*), formed on the third person pronoun *Il/Ille*, signifies "He who has passed by." The Other is absent from any discourse that would claim to be about him. He does not even enter into the correlation of the I-You encounter, so far as that encounter is structured as a correlation; that is, the *Il* is necessary, not simply to name a different person from the interlocutor, but to express the elsewhere and elsewhen of the interlocutor's Otherness. The idea of creation, the idea of a commandment prior to the self's freedom--i.e. the idea of the Other's Otherness as his anteriority to the Same, expressed increasingly now in temporal language as the immemorial past of the Other--culminates in this mutation of the pronoun by which he is called.

Levinas had opposed the *Vous* to the *Toi* of Buber and Marcel; now, he opposes the second person with the third.[26] And the third person--hence, the Other par excellence--is God.

> The God who has passed by is not a model, of which the face would be a copy. To be in the image of God does not mean to be an icon of God, but to be found in His trace. The revealed God of our Judeo-Christian spirituality retains all the infinity of His absence, which is in the personal order itself. He only shows Himself by His trace, as in Chapter 33 of Exodus. To go toward Him is not to follow this trace--which is not a sign--but to go toward the Others who stand in the trace.[27]
>
> In order to solicit Desire--a thought thinking more than it can think--the Infinite cannot be incarnated in something Desirable, cannot, as infinite, be restricted to an end. It solicits through a face, which is the term of my generosity and sacrifice. A Thou comes in between the I and the absolute He; the correlation [of relation with the Infinite] is broken.

It is thus vain to posit an absolute Thou. The absolute withdraws from the lighted scene. . .[28]

The first word says saying itself [*Le premier mot dit le dire lui-même*]. . . This first saying is, to be sure, nothing but a word. But the word is God.[29]

The problem of transcendence now points explicitly beyond the interlocutor to God. Levinas' idea of God is borrowed from religious tradition for strictly philosophical investigation of its meaning.[30] The task of *Otherwise than Being* is "to hear [*entendre*] a God not contaminated by Being."[31] The first important work to appear after *Otherwise than Being* is an article entitled "God and Philosophy."[32] We will try to account for this movement of his thought in our discussion of the relationship of his philosophy to revelation.[33]

The theme of the Third was introduced in "Le moi et la totalité" to found the order of justice, ethically superior to the order of love.[34] *Totality and Infinity*'s formula was: "The thou is posited in face of a [human] *we*."[35] But Levinas did suggest a connection between the Other and God when he wrote that the dimension of "height," the "curvature of intersubjective space," was "perhaps the very presence of God,"[36] and that "the other man, by his signification prior to my initiative, resembles God."[37] Nevertheless, he was also able to describe the fraternal moral solidarity of all men, as well as the triumph of the self over death through the creation of children,[38] solely with "horizontal" reference to other men. Now the trace and illeity represent a reorientation, a new direction proper to transcendence, for now God in a way dispossesses the Other Person of his Otherness so as to *confer* it on him from on high, where the human being is not. It would be hasty and oversimple to interpret this development as a transference of honor from the fellow man to God--as though Levinas had perceived and reacted to a danger of anthropolatry in his *Totality and Infinity* account. Nevertheless, the association of ethics and *religio* does assume a different aspect when, with the insertion of the idea of God, religion seems to contribute something original to the context of ethics. Is ethics no longer philosophy's "optics," or does this optics now reveal something new? Are the echoes of Feuerbach and Comte somewhat muted by the emergence of the theme of God, distinct (if not detached) from the theme of man, within Levinas' ethical discourse? We reserve discussion of this point for later.[39]

Meanwhile, the third man remains a topic in his own right in *Otherwise than Being*. His "tertiality" is different from that of illeity. The "anarchic provocation" of illeity directs me to approach my neighbor, as morally responsible for him;[40] but I necessarily approach, at the same time, my neighbor's neighbor:

> [T]he relation between the neighbor and the third cannot be indifferent to me as I approach. There must be justice between the incomparables. Thus there must be a comparison of incomparables, and a synopsis; an assemblage, and a contemporaneity; there must be thematization, thought, history and writing.[41]

In effect, Levinas now derives from the third what he formerly derived from the magisterial *Vous*, i.e. justice and cognitive objectivity. Ontology, the definition of man as the comprehension of Being, is given a warrant by the entry of the third,[42] for although the approach to the neighbor is still an accomplishment of "metaphysics" and the enigma of the beyond-Being, *immediately in that approach* it becomes necessary to compare, thematize, "know what one is talking about." Metaphysics precedes ontology, but does not live without it. (Indeed, the term "metaphysics" no longer appears in *Otherwise than Being*.) The relationship between the first and the second person is still infinitely asymmetrical, but with the advent of the third person the imbalance is balanced and reciprocity becomes possible. The third person also institutes a new relationship with God, for the grace by which I become the *Autrui* of others I can only acknowledge as His. "The 'passage' of God, of whom I cannot speak otherwise than with reference to this aid or this grace, is precisely this transformation of the incomparable subject into a member of society."[43]

Why does Levinas now link the rise of consciousness, i.e. the need to take thought, with the advent of the third, instead of (as in "Le moi et la totalité") with the advent of the second person, disturbing the innocence of atheist existence? How has his description of the relation with the second person changed?

2. The Other in the Same

In his 1967 article "Langage et proximité," Levinas begins to describe the non-thematizing intentionality peculiar to ethics as the *approach* of and to the Other, apparently in the conviction that the relation with the Other involves more than the standing off in "height" of a separated being named *Vous*.[44] The very idea of "proximity" occurring in association with "language" contrasts with the idea of "separation" which *Totality and Infinity* typically linked with "discourse"—though even there Levinas had noted the proximity created by the Other's solicitation of the self.[45] The Otherness of the Other is not originally an anti-concept; the anti-concept merely expresses what is originally the positive fact of the moral claim of one human being on another. The claim implies a relation—perhaps not a relation of number or concept, but in any event something other than bare separation. Now we read of this relation as proximity, and even contact.

> The *proximity* between Myself and the interlocutor [is] not our participation in a transparent universality. Whatever the message transmitted in discourse, speaking is contact. . . The exact point at which this change of the intentional to the ethical occurs and never ceases to occur, where the approach pierces consciousness, is skin and the human face. Contact is tenderness and responsibility.[46]

The Other is more than an ethical resistance opposing the innocent but unjust exuberance of the Self; the Other bears on the Same, pacifically but inexorably.

RESPONSIBILITY. *Totality and Infinity* determines the meaning of subjectivity as separation: its uniqueness, or absolution from the totality, derives from its ability to define itself by itself, acting as its own beginning and its own "atheist" end.[47] But the moral point of view supervenes in a new way in "Transcendance et hauteur":

> The absolutely Other is the Other Person. And the calling into question of the Same by the Other is a summons to respond. The Self does not only become conscious of this necessity of response as if it were a matter of an obligation or duty for him to deliberate; the Self is originally posited as responsibility through and through. . . To be a Self means henceforth to be incapable of fleeing responsibility. This surplus of being, this existential exaggeration called *being a self*—this upsurge of ipseity in Being is realized as a swelling up of responsibility.[48]

This is not a new theme--"Le moi et la totalité" had already traced the beginning of consciousness to the requirement imposed by the Other to take thought of the difference between the Self and totality--but it is a programmatic shift of focus.

"The Self before the Other Person is infinitely responsible."[49] Taken seriously, this idea is an outrage: it destroys all the balances and limitations that a "reasonable" ethic would posit to make the social world livable. No matter that moral altruism is the condition of reason, according to Levinas. Appreciated *in itself* and thought through to the end, it implies a fanatical zeal for the Other's well-being with a total disregard of self. It is indeed a gracious miracle that I am an Other for Others, that Others have responsibility for me just as I have for them. But only the advent of the third person makes even-handedness possible. Between the first and second persons, the "infinition" of the primary generosity of the Self toward the Other requires increasingly immoderate description. This infinite responsibility given prior to all choice is called "obsession,"[50] a permanent disquiet by which the self is torn from itself. Consciousness is the power of recoiling from things by knowing them neutrally (via ideal generalities), without being affected; but the nearness of the neighbor, the involuntary obsession of the self with the other, undercuts consciousness. It is (morally) impossible to keep one's distance from the moral claim.

> Language, contact, is the obsession of a Self "besieged" by others. Obsession is responsibility. But the responsibility of obsession does not proceed from freedom, for in that case obsession would only be a becoming-conscious-- that would be a Self obsessed by a fault committed in complete freedom, in which we would recognize the thinking subject in its splendid isolation, adopting intentional attitudes with regard to beings. . . Language is fraternity and thus responsibility for the fault I have not committed-- for the suffering and faults of others. Proximity, the very opposite of a game (freedom without responsibility) is a responsibility that does not refer back to my freedom. It is the condition of a creature in a world that is not a game. . . the condition of a hostage.[51]

The Self, held hostage by others, accomplishes its very egoity or uniqueness in the expiatory event of *substitution* for the sins and sorrows of others.[52] Thanks to substitution a being can be emptied of its being, can enter the non-being of the beyond-Being:

> The ethical event of "expiation for another" is the con-
> crete situation designated by the verb *to not-be* [*non-être*].
> It is by the condition of the hostage that there can be
> pity, compassion, pardon and proximity in the world--even
> the little that there is.[53]

My uniqueness is my irreplaceability. The whole weight of creation rests on my shoulders, and cannot be transferred; in this
way my moral responsibility confirms me in my selfness. But it
is a selfness completely opposite to the ipseity of the knowing
subject. Instead of coincidence with self and adequation to
self, my moral responsibility is the primordial non-adequation
and non-coincidence, or infinition, that carries me beyond
Being.

Levinas was asked at the Sorbonne why he had attached
the meaning of the human to absolute Otherness instead of the
actual solidarity in similarity which seems to underlie our
"human" life and make it possible. He answered that transcendence remained the essence of what he wished to say, and he
only regretted not having sufficiently clarified his idea of
it.[54] We must interpret this development of Levinas' thought
as the desired clarification, i.e. as an attempt to show that
transcendence *is* moral solidarity, and that the concrete relation with the *prochain* or *semblable* is produced as contact,
which transcends, not ordinary life, but the attempt to theoretically grasp ordinary life. Levinas continues to employ
ethics as an optics to show that Otherness is not an alien
predicate attached to the human, but an explication of the
human. The dangerous infinity of Otherness is precisely the
dangerous unlimitedness of responsibility to the neighbor,
which is allowed to express itself by its extravagant growth as
a theme in Levinas' philosophy. *Otherwise than Being* calls it
substitution, *"l'incondition d'otage,"* expiation, and *l'un-pour-
l'autre.*[55]

SENSIBILITY. How can the very selfhood of the self be
made, as Levinas claims, through the "persecution" of the Other,
in "absolute passivity"? "How can such a Passion take place
and time in consciousness?"[56]

The paradoxical requirement that the Other command the Same without intersecting with and thus submitting to the Same remains to be dealt with. The problem is persistently linked in Levinas' philosophy with the relation of consciousness to sensibility, the pre-theoretical life of the existent. The Self of *Totality and Infinity*, for example, has a being separate from the totality by virtue of its sincere enjoyment of a world that is not yet "intelligible." By the same token, the self has a primordial relation with *exteriority* in its worldly vulnerability; in suffering, the existent cannot keep its distance from what is other.[57] In either case the subject does not intend an object, but "lives from" (*vivre de*) what is other in an experience that always precedes and conditions thematization. Now the eminent Other, the Other Person, is lived-to rather than lived-from.[58] However, the transcendence of the self toward the Other is not a movement toward a spiritual super-world, but a movement for economic justice. For this reason the characteristic gesture of Levinas' thought is to find the transcendence that returns to immanence,[59] to find the idea of the Good that "commands me by my mouth,"[60] ordering my own sustenance toward the hungry Other. The transcendence of the neighbor affects me immediately, which leads Levinas to explore the possibility of a radical passivity, and a corresponding radical empiricism, at the heart of phenomenology.

Phenomenology shows that the condition of all intelligibility is signification, i.e. the conferral of sense on experience by subjectivity.[61] The essence of philosophy, going all the way back to Thales' "All is water" or Socrates' speculations about the Forms, is to find the ideal unities of appearance by which being takes on meaning. Being *appears*, is *manifest*, only through the application of generality to particularity, which is the rediscovery of the Same in the Other. The subject provides the "kerygmatic" judgment that sees "this" *as* "that," or takes "this" *for* "that," either in linguistic propositions or in the immanent signitive intentions of consciousness, by which (for example) successive perceptions of a chair are *taken for* presentations and contributions to the meaning of *one* ideal object, the chair. "'Taking for'. . ., positing as. . ., identifying the multiple is the property of thought insofar as

it is distinguished from mere sensibility."[62] Already active
and kerygmatic, sense-giving consciousness turns all experience
into discourse, for the identifying intention is the naming
intention.[63] The singular is only attained by the detour of
the universal.[64] Even "behind" language, in the so-called passive synthesis of pre-predicative experience prior to any conscious initiative of the subject,[65] we find that consciousness
presupposes some separation (in time) between feeling and the
felt: because it is temporal, consciousness always "loses" and
so has to "regain" meaning. This rhythm of losing and regaining
guarantees, even before the actual naming that goes on in discourse, that all meaning will be ideal, re-cognized. But we
must be careful not to interpret the *passivity* of consciousness
too hastily as a variant of the subject-object schema that
characterizes its *activity*. The original temporal upsurge of
consciousness is an opening of the distance between feeler and
felt, or knower and known, which as such is different from the
reclosing of that gap by the identifying work of consciousness.
The openness of this fracture of the present, this failure of
the knowing self to perfectly coincide with itself, is not to
be conceived in a merely negative way, as a privation of the
fulfillment of identified (ideal, universal) meaning. If we
can appreciate on its own terms the veritable passivity of consciousness, "a passivity more passive than any passivity simply
antithetical to activity,"[66] we have admitted a determination
of the Same by the Other, which would be truly heterological in
escaping the identification of the Same, yet peaceful in not
opposing or denying the work of identification but carrying its
own very different meaning in its own way. *Sensibility* presupposes such passivity.

The sensible is the immediate: that which provokes consciousness, rather than any possible object of it. At one
extreme, taste gives an example of an experience so intimate as
to "pierce" any intentional schematization of it. It shows the
different schema proper to our original solidarity with the
world, in which the world is consumed by us while it nourishes
us.[67] But the a priori of sensibility is set at the other
extreme, in approaching and being near what is *other*. Even
vision, the objectivating sense par excellence, has something

about it of the touch, for the eye approaches what it sees and
is caressed by it. Proximity par excellence is proximity to
the other person, the moral life. The presence-in-absence of
the other in the flesh escapes all consumption, because it only
"nourishes" perversely the insatiable Desire for the absolutely
Other. The impossibility of nourishment displaces and commands
all nourishment: in sensibility I am affected by a singularity,
without the detour either of universality (belonging to consciousness) or satisfaction (belonging to enjoyment). Enjoyment destroys otherness by consuming it; consciousness destroys
otherness by naming it; but the ethical relation is uniquely a
relation with the Other as Other. Unlike an object, the Other
provides his own non-ideal unity, by which multifarious experience of him is related to an identity.[68] This unity supervenes
on consciousness before its first act, requiring us to suppose
a "passivity more passive than all passivity."[69]

    Levinas describes in *Totality and Infinity* the "hospi-
tality" of the Same, welcoming the indigent Other into the home
it has made in the world. But just as responsibility has now
been immoderated into obsession, so hospitality becomes *fré-
missement*, "trembling," "shuddering," translating the divine
seizure of φρίκη in Plato's *Phaedrus*.[70] The Other in the Same
is a "touch of madness," a "psychosis,"; to have a soul is to
be "possessed."[71] The overflowing of the idea of the Infinite
formally indicates the overflowing of the self by the Other
that it paradoxically contains--which, as ethics, causes an
agitation of philosophy.

    INSPIRATION. Faced with the Other, the self of *Totality
and Infinity* takes the position in discourse called "apology";
for the problem posed by the trans-ascendent Other is an open
problem of justification. *Otherwise than Being*'s controlling
theme of the Other *in* the Same brings about a different situation, an inner agitation based on the immemorial subjection of
self to Other. It is no longer enough to say that the Self is
actuated by metaphysical Desire. Rather, the self is seized
and possessed by Desire, not as an "ecstatic" participation in
Being, but as the very movement of separation from Being. The
existent possesses existence as itself possessed; the relation
to Being is determined by non-being. Did the idea of apology

still carry the implication that the self is the master of itself, originally free of the Other (yet called to account), only
addressing the Other in a second movement distinct from separation? Once the interpretation of the Other's Otherness as his
precedence is carried from the precedence of "height" to the
passive genesis, we are taken beyond the pluralism of the Other-
than-the-Same to arrive at the "inspiration" of the Other-*in*-
the-Same. [72] The self's activity, including its philosophical
activity, consists of witnessing to the Infinite, which is given
in this particular way. The "original atheism" of separated
selfish being is *not* a symmetrical possibility of deafness and
disobedience to the Other; this "atheism" is originally overruled
in the *election* of the self.

> Prophetism would be the very psychism of the soul: the
> other in the same; and the whole spirituality of man would
> be prophetic. In witnessing, the infinite is not announced
> as a theme. In the sign made to the other, in which I find
> myself torn away from the secret of Gyges, "taken by a lock
> of my head" [Ezekiel 8:3] from the depth of my obscurity in
> the Saying-without-anything-Said of sincerity--in my "Here
> am I," present from the beginning in the accusative, I wit-
> ness to the Infinite. The Infinite is not in front of its
> witness, but is as though outside or on the other side of
> presence, already past, beyond any grasp: an afterthought
> too high to be pushed into the first rank. "Here am I, in
> the name of God!"--without referring myself directly to His
> presence. "Here am I," period! The word God is still
> missing from the phrase in which God becomes entangled with
> words for the first time. In no way does it state "I be-
> lieve in God". . . It is in prophetism that the Infinite
> escapes the objectivation of thematization and dialogue,
> and signifies as *illeity*, in the third person. . .[73]

The non-alienative, non-allergic presence of the Other in the
Same is at the same time the disproportion of God's glory,[74]
and thus refers immediately to illeity, bringing us full circle
with themes studied earlier. The idea of the Other in the Same
is not a manipulation of the relative positions of Other and
Same in order to solve the paradox of their relationship, but
an extension of the description of genuine Otherness, which
only aggravates the paradox. And the overflowing of inspiration
as prophetic witness once more places us before the question of
what philosophy does and how it does it--which must be taken up
next.

To sum up this section: in comparing *Totality and Infinity* with the thought of the succeeding thirteen years, we have traced the movement from responsibility to obsession, from hospitality to possession, and from apology to prophetism, all within the frame of a radicalization of the idea that the Other commands the Same. If there was once a distance maintained between the first and second persons, it has now collapsed, due to the inordinateness of infinite responsibility. It is still the advent of the second person that makes the *logos necessary*; but *logos* is not *possible* until the advent of the third. [75] The one, of course, may not be abstracted from the other. Levinas has not made a new distinction between discrete events; he has refined his analysis of the single event of subjectivity, distributing the aspects of it in a different way. The other person whom I actually face, *by himself*, obsesses me beyond all measure, but my obsession is qualified by the "tertiality" of *his* neighbors (which belongs directly to the meaning of my face-to-face encounter with him), and also by the tertiality or illeity of God, who has already passed by us, and in whose trace my neighbors stand, designated by God as moral claimants.

3. An-archaeology

Here we face a methodological problem. It consists of asking whether the pre-original Saying (the anarchic or non-original, as we call it) can be brought to betray itself by showing itself in a theme (whether an an-archaeology is possible)--and whether this betrayal can be reduced, whether one can simultaneously know and exempt the *knowledge* from the marks stamped on it by thematization in subordinating it to ontology. A betrayal at the price of which everything is shown, even the unsayable, and which makes possible the indiscretion regarding the unsayable which is probably the very task of philosophy. [76]

Levinas' later philosophy, as much as his earlier, is "about" something, or has a purpose. But what? The Other avowedly eludes all thematization. Granted that philosophy can then only be practical service rendered to the Other, by what presumption (as Derrida asks) is this service rendered *as philosophy*? And is there a properly philosophical justification for pursuing this particular course, or is "prophetism" a matter strictly for prophets? In *Otherwise than Being* Levinas makes an unreserved attempt to deal with these problems inherited

from *Totality and Infinity*. Besides assembling and developing
the many new themes we have noted already--most of which appeared
in articles of the 1960's--the 1974 work is, above all, Levinas'
Discourse on Method and his response to the questions raised by
Derrida. *Otherwise than Being* also redefines the break with
Husserlian phenomenology. To understand this it is first necessary to inquire into Levinas' relation to phenomenology, as
it is marked out in the writings of the intervening period.

ON HUSSERL. Levinas said that *Totality and Infinity*
owed everything to the phenomenological method. But it was
only possible to make this claim after the spirit of Husserl's
thought had been distinguished from its letter, which led to a
strained analogy between Husserlian and Levinasian phenomenology. Levinas searched for the "concrete"--as the ultimately
abstract non-phenomenon of the human face. Levinas moved from
meaning-objects to a "horizon" conditioning their meaning--but
this "horizon," besides being impossible to thematize, had
nothing to do with any operation of consciousness. Levinas'
"deduction," too, was unlike any other. So it was necessary
to conclude that the thought of *Totality and Infinity* develops
according to ethical rather than phenomenological rules. This
does not get rid of the problem, since it only substitutes the
question "What kind of ethical philosophy is this?" for "What
kind of phenomenological philosophy is this?" However, Levinas
does not wish to separate the ethics and phenomenology questions
completely, for he continues to speak of ethical "intentionality," i.e. the transcending ethical intention. The use of
this language assumes that phenomenologists can be asked to
respect the proper character of this whatever-it-is and not
impose a preconceived scheme, such as Husserl's intellectualism,
upon it.

What if the Other is a disturber of philosophical
method, any method, and Levinas' espousal of phenomenology
principally means that the idea of the Other has disturbed him
as a phenomenologist?

If the significance of the trace consists of signifying
without making to appear, if it establishes a relation with
illeity--a relation which, personal and ethical, obligatory,
is not disclosed--if, therefore, the trace does not belong
to phenomenology (the comprehension of "appearance" and
"dissimulation"), one could at least approach it by another

way, locating its significance in relation to the phenomenology that it interrupts.[77]

To the question, *what* is phenomenology interrupted by?, the
consistent answer of *Totality and Infinity* is that the question
is impermissible. Phenomenology is interrupted by a "who"
rather than a "what"; it is not a matter of something extra
appearing, but of all that has appeared being called into question. Phenomenology, or perhaps anti-phenomenology,[78] remains
a suitable procedure for demonstrating how originally different
this calling-into-question is from the realm of things called
into question. One uses the concept of phenomenon to say what
the "enigma" is not, and accepts the risk that "enigma" will
only be understood as a privation or variation of "phenomenon."[79]

Levinas does not simply adopt an anti-phenomenology,
however. He believes that phenomenology can free itself from
intellectualism, and that even Husserl is at times on the verge
of doing so. The true meaning of phenomenology lies in its way
of going about things: "Phenomenology is above all a method,
for it is essentially open" and applicable anywhere.[80] In
effect, Levinas rejects all of Husserl's more rationalist, systematic doctrines[81] in favor of a radically empiricist idea of
phenomenology as respect for exteriority and willingness to
deal with experiences of all sorts. He praises phenomenology
for its faithfulness in describing finite, ambiguous, or contradictory phenomena without measuring them for imperfections
against abstract ideals;[82] for bringing about the downfall of
the philosophical primacy of theoretical contemplation of objects, by showing the experience of reality that is already
"forgotten" in representation; for understanding the meaning of
an entity or notion strictly as a function of the way in which
it may be brought to evidence, which is an event implicating
both the seeker and the sought;[83] for granting sensibility a
primary role in the constitution of meaning; and for discovering
foundations of knowledge not themselves describable as knowledge, "more certain than certitude, more rational than reason."[84]
We have already noted the importance attached by Levinas to
Husserl's treatment of sensibility, to which several articles
are wholly or in part devoted.[85] Sensibility is a different
intentionality than the subject-object intentionality of theory

and representation, but it *is* an intentionality (in the sense that its meaning implicates the philosopher), and therefore there can be a phenomenology of it.

Given that phenomenology is essentially a radical experience and description of reality, what is Levinas' peculiar mode of experience and description? Further light is shed on this question by his 1964 article "La signification et le sens."[86] By "signification" he means *ceci en tant que cela*: "this proposed as, or offered to stand for, that."

> Reality, given to receptivity, and signification, which reality can assume, seem to be distinct--as though experience first offered contents, such as forms, solidity, roughness, color, sound, savor, odor, warmth, heaviness, etc. and these contents were given life only afterwards by meta-phors, as though they received a surcharge bearing them *beyond* the given.[87]

Signification often refers to what is absent; but does the absent have to be ultimately presentable, if signification is to have meaning? Is it true that for a God of unlimited perception there would be no distinction between signification and perceived reality? So intellectualism believes: "Figurative sense must be justified by literal sense, furnished to intuition."[88] And so Husserl believes. But pure receptivity without signification is only mythical, for no "given" simply drops into thought out of nowhere. The meaningfulness of perception itself depends on the illuminated horizon within which perceptions fit, and it is signification that provides the context, lighting the horizon. Words refer not only to intuitions but to each other and to the whole, language, culture, and history, in inexhaustible complexity--as well as to the positions assumed by those who speak and those who listen. Herein lies the value of Heidegger's departure from intuitionism toward a general hermeneutic of experience, dealing with each "given" only as embedded in a totality of significations. Language is the house of Being. Merleau-Ponty's analyses show, in addition, that signification does not pertain exclusively to an interior world of thought, but is rather the expression, the cultural gesture, of an active incarnate participant in being, expressing that being.[89] On this view language is at bottom the poetry that celebrates Being. While both Merleau-Ponty and Heidegger may be inspired by "the Hegelian vision of a subjectivity that

understands itself as an inevitable moment of the becoming by
which Being comes forth out of its hiddenness,"[90] in any case
both show that simple receptivity is not the original relation
to Being.

The consequence of the autonomy of particular systems
and histories of signification is the cultural relativism of
modern philosophy, or what Levinas calls its anti-Platonism.
We now lack the super-world of Forms by which real worlds could
be measured. We only get to know Being by surveying its many
scintillations, its inexhaustible richness.

> The political work of decolonization is thus found to
> be attached to an ontology, to a thought of Being, inter-
> preted on the basis of cultural signification, which is
> multiple and multivocal. And this multivocity of the sense
> of Being, this essential disorientation, is perhaps the
> modern expression of atheism.[91]

If neither intuitions nor Forms will function to offset this
"essential disorientation," what will? Materialism claims that
"economic" meanings based on human needs are serious enough to
have their own sense prior to any figurative, poetical sense, a
sense requiring technical, scientific expression. Poetry would
be only a deceitful game if it were completely divorced from
this foundation. Nevertheless, human need however serious is
still felt and expressed culturally, which is to say multivocal-
ly. The essential orientation must come from elsewhere.

> The needs that supposedly orient Being receive their
> sense from an intention which no longer proceeds from these
> needs. That was already the great teaching of Plato's
> *Republic*: the State that is founded on the needs of men
> cannot subsist or even arise without philosophers who have
> mastered their needs and who contemplate the Ideas and the
> Good.[92]

The Good, for Levinas, is the basic orientation of men who pre-
fer speech to violence. There is no master culture mediating
the French and the Chinese, but it is still possible for a
Frenchman to learn Chinese. Why should he do this? Why not
simply dismiss the foreign as barbaric? One meaning, the sig-
nification-without-a-context of the Other Person, orients all
meaning. Cultures are equally valuable, not because no standard of judgment exists, but because they are all human.[93]

The climax of this argument then occurs in *Otherwise
than Being*, where the themes of signification and proximity are

intertwined, and *ceci en tant que cela* is replaced by *l'un-pour-l'autre*, the commitment of "one for another" in moral responsibility and substitution.[94] Just as there is a "*sens unique*"[95] orienting the senses of Being, so there is a fundamental structure of signification orienting all significations. In this light, Levinas' history of modern philosophy reads as a progressive liberation from the domination of intuition (consciousness as the measure), leading to the generous gesture of "empty" signification (the signification that Husserl acknowledged, but regarded as an unpaid check[96]) offering self for the essentially absent Other.

These, then, are the hard terms by which Levinas maintains his connection with Husserl. He rejects his intellectualism and his intuitionism, and embraces a view of linguistic meaning that Husserl was never able to accept.[97] It can now be better seen just how important for Levinas is the power of language to signify in the absence of any corresponding experience, simply as a gesture. This is the key to the method of *Otherwise than Being*, which he says "ventures beyond phenomenology."[98] Phenomenology is the method practiced only as the point from which to depart.[99]

THE ETHICAL REDUCTION. Reviewing the logical incoherencies involved in the use of the idea of the Other, Derrida wrote:

> [T]he expression "infinitely other" or "absolutely other" cannot be stated and thought simultaneously. . . . the other cannot be absolutely exterior to the same without ceasing to be other. . . Or at least, cannot *be*, or be anything; and it is indeed the authority of Being which Levinas profoundly questions. That his discourse must still submit to the contested agency is a necessity whose rule we must attempt to inscribe systematically in the text.[100]

The most evident difference between *Totality and Infinity* and *Otherwise than Being* lies in the later book's effort to account for the fact that the Good can only be spoken of with the coherence of thematic language and thus only contests Being in the very event of submitting to it. Even ethics must use the copula "is." To be Other than Being, of course, cannot mean to be on the same level as Being, posed as an alternative to it. That would be to turn Being, and perhaps also the Good, into *a* being, an entity, to be grasped alongside of others. Heidegger

criticizes Platonism for this: to place the Good beyond Being
is already to have misunderstood Being as something of which
one could have an idea, i.e. to forget the primordial difference
between Being and beings.[101] Levinas now wishes to show that
his main argument does not depend on this kind of confusion,
even while he defends the Platonic formula against the Heideggerian attack. The "essence" of the phrase "beyond essence"
means Being distinct from beings, conceived verbally rather
than substantively.[102] The best English translation might be
"Be-ing." On this basis, Levinas gives a new account of language.

> Be-ing--temporalization--is the verbality of the verb.
> We want to suggest the difference of Being from beings:
> this strange temporal itching, modification without change
> (but in which one resorts to metaphors borrowed, not from
> time, but from the temporal, metaphors such as "process"
> or "act of being" or "disclosure" or "effectuation of being"
> or "flow of being")--Being is the verb itself. Temporaliza-
> tion is the verb of Being. Language, sprung from the
> verbality of the verb, would not consist solely of making
> Being understood [*faire entendre*], but also of making the
> Be-ing of Being to vibrate [*faire vibrer l'essence de
> l'être*].
>   Language thus does not reduce to a system of signs
> doubling beings and their relations--a conception which
> would be unavoidable if the word were the Name. Instead
> language would be the excrescence of the verb. And it is
> already as verb that it would bear the sensible life--tem-
> poralization and Be-ing of Being.[103]

Saying (*le Dire*), even though it is the pure verbality of language prior to the deposit of meaning in the names of the
already-said (*le Dit*), is yet teleologically oriented to the
Said. In Husserlian terms, the process of constitution, which
is not itself constituted, is yet strictly correlated with
objects that are constituted. In Heideggerian terms, it is the
destiny of language to create a text.

What if it were possible to "surprise" Saying before it
reaches its inevitable term in the Said? What if one could
systematically inscribe, in the ontological text of the Said
(or the dialectical play of the Said and the Unsaid, with which
Heidegger and the Heideggerians are occupied), the enigmatic
surplus of Saying conceived as the signification of one-for-
another? That would be to show--against Heidegger's "Language
speaks"--that one person offers language to another. Levinas

links his enterprise to this possibility of performing a "reduction" of the Said to Saying, in order to reveal Saying as
more than the correlated genesis of what is Said.[104] Saying
will produce an an-archaeology that is different from the
archaeology of ontological discourse, in which everything finds
a systematic place. The an-archaeology must of course be
written in a book, assuming the form of an archaeology; what it
shows, it shows only as an "indiscretion" or "betrayal."[105]
The unsayable can only be said diachronically, exceeding the
synchrony of the assembled Said.[106] Diachronic thought and
diction cannot be brought into one time, the synchrony required
by the teleology of Being; its teleology is different, leading
it to continually unsay what it says in service of the unsayable.

Levinas finds a parable of his own diachronic thought
in the diachrony of scepticism. Since it can be shown that the
sceptic contradicts himself, inasmuch as his act of denial presupposes the logic or experience he denies, reason is always
triumphant over him. Yet the specter of scepticism continues
to shadow the doorway of philosophy, as though the sceptic were
aware that his Saying had an origin or destiny beyond the Said.
"Scepticism is the *refutable*, but also the ever-returning."[107]
The return of the sceptical performance breaches the synchrony
of the Said by pointing to something outside the Said, which
cannot be said, but which can only register as this apparently
senseless disruption of what *can* be said.

Ethics is like the reverse side of scepticism, an addition to ontology instead of a subtraction from it. Where the
sceptic takes away, the moral self offers an overabundance.
But the parallel between the two holds to the extent that both
are refutable. Ethics, so far from being provable, is not even
statable according to the logical canons of statability. The
Other-than-Being has a perfect incognito in Being, leaving only
an invisible trace. Nevertheless we all stand in the trace and
have a seemingly impossible or gratuitous vulnerability to the
appeal of the Other-than-Being: we are commanded by it before
knowledge, theme, and *arché*. The paradoxical demands placed
on language by the Other signal that this Other is not a ruse
or persona of Being, but genuinely *better* than Being. Ethics
shows its difference from scepticism, too, in following the

via eminentiae rather than the *via negativa*--interrupting the
system by the superlative, an excess of meaning.

The ethical "reduction" of *Otherwise than Being* is only
negative in its outer movement of unsaying the Said, so as to
displace the argument to Saying. Within this outer movement,
though, is an inner movement by which Saying Says. Thus, while
much of *Otherwise than Being* is devoted to ingenious refinements
of the pluralist theses of *Totality and Infinity*, the heart of
the work and the token of a new direction in Levinas' thought
is the actual Saying of Saying, the communication or upsurge of
the original language before words. *Totality and Infinity* had
talked about metaphysics as an accomplishment of infinition,
but *Otherwise than Being* makes the riskier[108] attempt to itself
accomplish the infinition. Levinas describes this presumption
in different ways. A good example of the method being practiced while explaining itself is provided by the following passage:

> Thus for subjectivity to signify without reserve, it
> would be necessary that the passivity of its exposure to
> the other person not turn immediately back into an activity,
> but rather expose itself in turn: there must be a passivity
> of passivity and, in the glory of the Infinite, a cinder
> from which the act could not be reborn. This passivity of
> passivity and this dedication to the Other, this sincerity,
> is Saying--not as a communication of something Said, in
> which case it would be immediately recovered and absorbed
> or extinguished in the Said, but Saying holding its opening
> open, without excuse, without evasion or alibi, giving it-
> self without saying anything of the Said--"Saying" saying
> "Saying" itself [*Dire disant le dire même*], without thema-
> tizing it, but still exposing it. Saying is thus making a
> sign of this very significance of exposure; it is to expose
> exposure instead of maintaining itself as though in an act
> of exposing; it is to exhaust oneself in exposing oneself
> . . . [in a] pre-reflexive iteration in Saying of Saying
> itself.[109]

This pre-reflexive "iteration," this "exaltation" or benign
"abuse" of language,[110] this "emphatic" transformation of ontology's own vocabulary, producing within language the very dimension of height in which the Other of *Totality and Infinity*
appeared,[111] is in fact only a further aggravation of the process that began with the capitalization of *Autre* and *Autrui* and
the quest for the meaning of meaning. The journey without
prospect of return or absolute adventure of Abraham is enacted
by language trying, with a "touch of madness," to exceed itself,

precisely without knowing where the excess leads. The procedure is the reverse of arbitrary, however, since it responds to
the orienting "*sens unique*" of being by ex-posing itself, completely resigning its own initiative to the Infinite, to which
there can be a *witness* if not a thematization.[112]

   The emphatic method is not to be confused with transcendental method, which always seeks the foundations (in an architectural sense) of reality.[113] One justifies an idea by tracing
it back to the fixed condition of its possibility. But the
emphatic way of justifying one idea by another is to lead an
idea to its own superlative, as though by the final causation
of the Good. Levinas gives an example:

> [I]n a certain sense, the real world is the world which
> is posited [*se pose*]; its way of being is as a thesis. But
> to be posited in a truly superlative way--I am not playing
> with words--is that not to be exposited [*s'exposer*], posited
> to the point of appearing, *affirmed* to the point of becoming
> language [i.e. as "exposition"]?[114]

The method of emphasis is not a methodology. "I do not believe
that there could be a transparency as to method, nor that philosophy is possible as transparency."[115] This has particular
point with respect to the ethical reduction, since it reduces
the ethical speaker to Saying beyond any attempt to recollect
in the Said a thematizable justification of the manner of Saying.
Saying only justifies itself in the saying; the sayer, riveted
and shrunk to a point by infinite responsibility, can only say
on.

   RHETORIC, OR SWEET REASON. Levinas opposed philosophical discourse to "rhetoric" in *Totality and Infinity*, charac-
terizing rhetoric as a turning away from sincere face-to-face
encounter with the aim of approaching the neighbor obliquely,
by a ruse.[116] The antidote to rhetoric is not an impersonal
truth dominating conversation, however, but the bringing-into-
play of truth within the just relation of discourse. Poetry
too can be an approach to the Other,[117] a teaching,[118] but as
a thought that merely dreams it is to be "denounced."[119] Yet
Totality and Infinity is not a pure prose treatise in the traditional sense, and *Otherwise than Being* much less so. Derrida
(somewhat rhetorically) says that Levinas "forbids poetic rapture, but to no avail: in *Totality and Infinity* the use of

metaphor, remaining admirable and most often--if not always--
beyond rhetorical abuse, shelters within its pathos the most
decisive movements of the discourse."[120]   Leaving aside the
imputed pathos and implied rapture, it must be asked how the
undeniably "rhetorical" character of Levinas' philosophy affects
its rationality.

The meaning of ῥητορεύω is "to speak in public."[121]
The attempt to find the totally unreflexive openness of Saying
is, in a sense, a quest for the perfection of publicity, of
"exposure," since the self abdicates its very privacy to the
commanding Other. In any event, Saying is admittedly "only"
Saying, signification liberated from the measure of intuition
(though not, of course, from all relationship with intuition);
and a philosophy of Saying is "rhetoric" par excellence. Ethics
is only an "optics" by a very strained analogy, for ethics does
not present an object to vision or intuition, or demonstrate
the conclusion of an argument, but rather makes a gratuitous
appeal. The value of the human is always refutable. Ethics
cannot vanquish its sceptic, Cain, who does not obey the "gleam
of exteriority" in the Other's face. Not merely "ethics" in
the usual sense, but the entire range of human existence--
including the relations of eros and fecundity described in
Totality and Infinity as "beyond the face"[122]--is made up of
indemonstrable, non-phenomenal "experience" of which the human
meaning is, ontologically considered, an evanescent surplus,
mere icing on the cake. For instance, in answer to the question, "What does it mean to be a father?", Levinas looks beyond
biology, psychology, and ontology to suggest that paternity is
a particular relation with total alterity, the relation with
death established by the recreation of one's own self as an
Other, opening the human horizon of hopeful futurity. One does
not find this hope in the pages of *Being and Time*, by Heidegger;
there, no sense is attached to "beyond my death," but only to
facing up to nothingness as the Other.[123]

For Levinas, the non-coercive reason pertaining to the
ethical or the human--"*Raison, comme l'un pour l'autre!*"[124]--is
not a deficient reason. The non-coerciveness of moral reason
is the very rationality of genuine reason distinct from mechanical necessity. The rhetorical appeal of a discourse is again

distinguished from logical structure, but as a donation instead
of a privation, i.e. as "sweet" reason--the sweetness of which
reflects obedience to the Good rather than the deceptive sugar-
coating of ill rhetoric. Unlike the monolithic Reason formed
by logic, or by the one Being or Spirit or History, the sweet
reason proposed by Levinas is the positive production of *plurality*, on the assumption that plurality is better than the One.
When I see a hungry indigent, do I do better or learn more by
reasoning from myself to him ("I earn a living, why can't he?")
or from him to myself ("Why should my belly be full if his is
not?")? The first form of reason, generalizing or universaliz-
ing the Ego, is always a reduction of the Other to the Same, an
imposition of rules by which the Other should be constrained;
but the second form of reason, the opening of the Same to the
Other, is fundamentally a discovery of the absolutely new, a
discovery of the Other's unassessed need and of myself as one
who can come to his aid. Language, work, sexuality, etc. all
have this power of surpassing themselves in becoming a gift.
Reason as one-for-another *is* the meaning of reason. On this
view "rhetoric" is rehabilitated and even enthroned in the
intersubjective drama of philosophy.

How reason, or rhetoric, actually functions for Levinas
must be illustrated by his characteristic ways of arguing. The
superlation of "emphasis" we have already examined. Two other
patterns seem especially important: some statements, or statement sequences, contain a claim of necessity (*Il faut que. . .*);
and some other statements unite distinct concepts by saying that
one is the other, or that one is the condition or meaning of the
other.

The "*il faut*" is clearly an ethical *il faut*, drawing on
the same necessity by which one "must" feed the hungry. It
often appears to defend the originality of ethics against the
pretentions of ontology--"*Il faut penser l'homme à partir de la
condition ou de l'incondition de l'otage*"[125]--or in defense of
the propositions that are essential to ethics.

> The interiority that assures separation. . . *must*
> produce a being absolutely closed over upon itself, not
> deriving its isolation dialectically from its opposition
> to the Other. And this closedness *must* not prevent egress
> from interiority. . . In the separated being the door to
> the outside *must* hence be at the same time open and closed.

> The closedness of the separated being *must* be ambiguous
> enough for, on the one hand, the interiority necessary to
> the idea of the infinite to remain real and not apparent
> only, for the destiny of the interior being to be pursued
> in an egoist atheism refuted by nothing exterior. . . But
> on the other hand *within the very interiority* hollowed out
> by enjoyment there *must* be produced a heteronomy that in-
> cites to another destiny than this animal complacency in
> oneself.[126]

These "musts" do not refer to eidetic necessity, since no intuition is being described, nor to logical necessity, since the
described requirements are paradoxical. The door to the outside
must be closed, *because* the Good is better than anything that
could satisfy a lack; the door to the outside *must* be open,
because the Good, better than my own will, commands me. However, the argument does employ an ontological vocabulary of
being, reality, interiority, and exteriority, and sets up its
own logic as a variation on ontological logic. "Ontological
pluralism" is one response to the command of the Good. *Otherwise than Being* provides an example of a more immediate response,
and thus a more obviously ethical appeal:

> In any case, no less than this [hearing of the Good] is
> *necessary* for the little humanity that adorns the earth, be
> it only simple politeness and polishing of manners. For
> this, there *must* be a de-regulation of essence, bringing
> about more than a mere aversion to violence. This aversion
> only witnesses to a beginning or wild stage of humanity,
> given to forgetting its dislikes and turning itself into an
> "essence of de-regulation," gathering round itself like all
> essence, inevitably jealous of its perseverance [in Being],
> of honors and military virtues. For the little humanity
> that adorns the earth, there *must* be a slackening of essence
> to the second degree: *to tremble--further, to shudder--at
> every moment, in the just war waged against war, for the
> sake of this justice* itself. There *must* be this weakness.
> This slackening (without being slack) of virility *must* have
> underlain our repudiation of cruelty, even to the small
> degree that we have repudiated it.[127]

The ethical necessity represented by "*il faut*" advances Levinas'
argument as a whole, while the breadth of the argument is explored in terms of the overlapping and echoing possibilities of
concepts such as "maternity," "vulnerability," "expiation,"
"substitution," and so forth. [128] Statements like the one that
"the proximity of the Other Person. . . is only possible as
responsibility for the other person, which is only possible as
substitution for him,"[129] are examples of the ethical emphasis:

it is not conceptually possible in ethics to keep the idea of proximity from turning into its superlative, responsibility, nor to keep responsibility from burgeoning into obsession and substitution, responsibility even for the other's responsibility.[130] Concepts make claims on each other just as people do.

TRANSCENDENTALISM. At the Leiden colloquy of 1975, Levinas accepted de Boer's characterization of his thought as an "ethical transcendental philosophy," provided his transcendentalism was not understood as an architectonic search for the foundations (which, if found, would have to be the foundations of the Same).[131] But what transcendentalism does not seek the foundations, in some sense? If Levinas' philosophy is transcendental or "first" philosophy, then it must search for what is (in some sense) unconditioned, to which all else is (in some sense) relative or obligated for its meaning. We do know that Levinas claims to find the meaning of all meaning in the *sens unique* of moral responsibility; it remains to be seen how the philosophy of responsibility conditions all other philosophy, thus perhaps proving itself to be philosophy, after all, rather than an eccentric comment imposed on philosophy for the nonce.

Levinas provides a transcendental philosophy of *time*, for example, by understanding time as an upsurge of genuinely new instants, as a function of the relation with the Other. This means that the Other is in some sense the transcendental condition of everything we understand by and through temporality, viz. our entire experience. However, the *ethical* interpretation of our experience is refutable in any given instance, for rights and wrongs can be shown to be relative; guilt can be shown illusory; hope derisory. "Justice" and "truth" reduce all too easily to power and guile. Therefore, while the Good is the transcendental condition of our entire moral experience, our moral experience is not demonstrably an experience, in the sense that one could point to it as a datum. Our truly moral "experience" is not *of* anything at all, that could appear in the Same; it is precisely transcendence of the Same. But it is not without relevance to the Same, since it transfigures it as the meaning of its meanings. The truths of the Same are themes to offer in conversation; the nourishments of the Same are food for the hungry Other.

Like *Totality and Infinity*, *Otherwise than Being* presents the beyond-Being as a horizon conditioning the meaning of Being, and it can no more stay clear of entanglement with the language of ontology, by virtue of this relationship, than could the earlier book. However, *Otherwise than Being* more consistently avoids the pitfall of uncritically deducing the metaphysical from the ontological, because it consistently deduces the ontological from the metaphysical. The intention to do this appears already in *De l'existence à l'existant*, where Levinas writes that ex-cendence and the Good must have a foothold in Being, and that is why Being is better than non-Being.[132] *Being*, whether or not it requires the Good (and the Good is beyond anything Being would require), *is required by the Good*. "The seriousness of responsible speech retains a reference to Being."[133] By beginning with the responsible speech, one sets oneself the strange task of finding one's way to Being from it, and can even say:

> The way of thinking proposed here does not consist in disregarding Being, nor in treating it with the ridiculous pretention of a disdainful manner, as though it fell short of some superior order or Disorder. But it is from proximity, on the contrary, that Being takes on its just sense.[134]

Levinas salutes Kant for having found a meaning of the human beyond the horizon of ontology: "The fact that immortality and theology could not determine the categorical imperative, shows the novelty of the Copernican revolution: a meaning unmeasured by Being or not-Being, Being being determined, on the contrary, by meaning."[135] Being as Being is a function of Justice.[136] Ontological thinking, in search of origin and *archê*, is *forgetful* of the pre-original upsurge of signification and an-archic responsibility.[137]

> The fact that one could not philosophize prior to monstration,[138] where sense is already a Said, a something, a "thematized," does not at all imply that monstration is not justified by signification, which would motivate monstration and be manifest in it, [though as] betrayed and to be reduced--that is, would be manifest in the Said. The fact that one could not philosophize prior to the manifestation of something does not imply, moreover, that the signification "Being," correlated with every manifestation, is the source of this manifestation and of all signification--as one would think from Heidegger--nor that monstration is the foundation of everything that is manifested--as Husserl

thinks. It is appropriate to reflect anew on the very meaning of the psychism, which in the Western tradition is placed in the play between Being and its manifestation, or in the correlation of Being and its manifestation.[139]

These statements on the priority of signification to Being show that ethics is first philosophy and the condition of all philosophy. The passage from ethics to the rest of philosophy is effected by deductions of theory from subjectivity as one-for-another,[140] of the universality of truth from the responsibility of the self for all neighbors,[141] of the cognitive function of sensibility from its meaning as vulnerability,[142] and of consciousness as a modification of obsession by the advent of the third person, who makes thematization and ratiocination necessary and possible by requiring the comparison of incomparables, the search for justice amid the conflicting claims of Others.[143] The benefit of this procedure rests on the choice of starting point, for the *sens unique* leading from beyond-Being to Being is not reversible. For example, a free will's engagement of responsibilities can be understood as a response to the pre-volitional approach of the Other, or as a modality of Saying; but neither the approach nor Saying can be understood on the model of freely chosen engagements.[144] *Otherwise than Being* builds up a vocabulary of words drawn from outside the tradition so that, whenever possible, Levinas can say "approach" instead of "initiative," or "exposure" instead of "evidence,"[145] or the "maternity" according to which the Other is "gestated" in the Same, instead of the open window of the monad.[146] The process is not original to *Otherwise than Being*—the key term of "De l'évasion" was drawn from outside philosophy—but it reaches a climax there.

Ethics passes into philosophy as a philosophy of subjectivity, thus as a revision and continuation of Husserl's project.[147] From the one point of affection by exteriority that Husserl allows, the "passive genesis," Levinas turns the meaning of subjectivity upside down, from an agency of knowing and judging to a *subjection* or exposure to the suffering of Others. "Interiority," the separated and free life of consciousness, is reconstructed on this basis only: one must take thought and initiative in the service of justice. The uniqueness of the ego is brought about by its condition of being

unable to shift the burden of responsibility to other shoulders. The ego is given the whole world--as Atlas, rather than
as Archimedes.[148]

Ethics also passes into philosophy as an attempt to
think the difference between Being and beyond-Being, thus as a
revision and extension of Heidegger's project, which stopped
short at the difference between Being and beings. The initial
problem is not forgetfulness of Being, but of God. When *Totality and Infinity* announced that it would risk seeming to confuse
theory and practice by dealing with both as modes of metaphysical transcendence, it proposed an ethical transformation of
Heidegger's attempt to think Being in a more original way than
that represented by an idea of Being.[149] For Heidegger, too,
is in search of the beyond-Being, in the sense that for him the
use of the term "Being" tends to falsify Being by portraying it
as a namable entity.[150] In effect, Levinas criticizes Heidegger
for not going far enough, i.e. for still being a prisoner of a
totalization of Being based on the primacy of the relation of
comprehension, which prevents an opening of his philosophy to
the genuine "pre-origin" of meaning. By the fruits of Heidegger's philosophy, which are pagan and sub-ethical, it can be
seen that he has failed to escape ontology. All his scrupulous-
ness for letting-be the different ways of Being does not avail
to reckon with the Good.[151] *Being and Time* opened philosophy
to the Other, but to the Other of nothingness; and the fundamental mood it determined was anxiety. Levinas' response is
readiness to suffer for an issue that is indifferent to the
death of the self.[152] The perspective of the beyond-Being does,
however, mean that Being is not alone; it is "limited" by what
exceeds it. In a kind of Platonic revenge, Levinas can talk
about Being with a positiveness that Heidegger could never
assume. For Heidegger, the talking itself is a production of
Being; for Levinas, of beyond-Being via Being, *judging* Being.

Finally, ethics possesses the rest of philosophy according to the traditional claim of *humanism* to ground and orient
all knowledge and discourse, in the context of the modern crisis
of the meaning of the human. With the critique that reveals
Reason to be ideology, and the science that removes the traditional exteriority of the knower to the known by making the

knower a known object in his turn, modern man is caught in a moral vacuum, his Good reduced to the goods he happens to want-- and in the theoretical ennui of "nothing new under the sun." The play of *esse*, Be-ing or "essence," is produced as the politics of *inter-esse*, of the *conatus essendi*; human beings are merely agents of interest, striving to persevere in their being and finding it impossible to escape from the norm of war that this perseverance perpetuates. But the responsibility of one for another is an undoing of "essence" and "interest," creating the very possibility of disinterestedness that the liberal ideals of truth and justice have presupposed without being able to sustain.[153] Transcendence, or disinterestedness, already is in the modern world as its hunger for social justice:

> One day in Louvain, after a lecture on these ideas, I was taken to a house of students (called there a "pedagogy"); I found myself surrounded by South American students, nearly all of them priests, all mainly concerned with the situation in South America. They spoke of what is happening there as a supreme test of humanity. They asked me, not without irony: where, concretely, have I found the Same concerned for the Other to the point of undergoing a fission? I answered: here, at least--here in a group of students and intellectuals who could very well have been preoccupied with their inner perfection and who have nevertheless talked of nothing but the crisis of the masses in Latin America. Were they not hostages? This utopia of conscience was historically accomplished in the room in which I found myself.[154]

But ontology is also in the world in the form of capitalism and colonialism[155] and in the political cruelties of our age represented above all by Hitler.[156]

A line from *King Lear* appears at the beginning of *Humanisme de l'autre homme*: "I should e'en die with pity/to see another thus."[157] Each new death of a fellow man is a new *premier scandale* for thought;[158] exposure to the suffering of others gives rise to thought, not only in the pages of *Otherwise than Being*, but in the world. The response is the "hemorrhage" of the self for the Other--in philosophy, the logical hemorrhage of Saying overflowing the Said.[159]

The humanism of the other man is the answer to the problem posed by the crisis of Western liberalism, inasmuch as Western philosophy has otherwise failed to find a humane

alternative to its idealist tradition.[160] Modern man is reduced
to an object of sociology or psychoanalysis, a plaything of
technology, and a pawn of ideology. In the world wars human
life is shown to be eminently extinguishable, anything but eternal; human freedom is unmasked as non-heroic. The loss of transcendence is the encompassing of man by the totality, and his
victimization by the characteristic effects of totality: violence and ennui. When exteriority speaks, it does not promise
an afterlife or guarantee an eternal order, but demands material
justice in the present. This "prophetism" uses a language of
verbs and nouns, but not merely to produce Be-ing or beings.
Neither does prophetism accept a position outside or alongside
of the philosophy of logic and categories, as one among many
possible pre-philosophical "inspirations." As *the* inspiration,
it is imperious. The Good claims to rule philosophy and reveal
to it its own deepest intention, and it does this in the philosophical fashion par excellence, by determining the meaning of
Reason itself. Philosophy is transformed into "an-archaeology."
It is in this sense that the more method-conscious *Otherwise
than Being* represents the key achievement of Levinas' cumulative
argument. To be sure, methodology is not the end of philosophy,
and when Levinas renounces a terminal preoccupation with method
he makes clear that more than methodology lies in and beyond
Otherwise than Being. But the claim of this philosophy *to be
philosophy* is justified by the explicit conquest of Reason by
prophetism that is carried out in *Otherwise than Being*, which
enriches the argument of *Totality and Infinity* without fundamentally changing it.

Responsibility's frame of reference is not a world, but
the Kingdom of an invisible God.[161] When we look beyond *Otherwise than Being*, we find that Levinas continues to address the
special problem of transcendence associated with the idea of
God:

> It is the meaning of the beyond, of transcendence and
> not ethics, that we seek in this study. We find it in
> ethics. . . For the formula "transcendence to the point of
> absence" to mean more than the simple explicitation of an
> ex-ceptional word, this word should be restored to the sig-
> nification of the entire ethical intrigue--the divine comedy
> apart from which this word ["God"] could not have arisen.[162]

4. Philosophy and Theology

The philosophy of the Other in *Totality and Infinity* is an ethics, or metaethics; the Other is the Other Person. When the word "God" appears its meaning is strictly determined by ethics.

> I do not wish to define anything by God, because what I know is the human. I can define God by human relations, not the other way around. God knows, I am not opposed to the idea of God! But if I should say something about God, it is always on the basis of human relations. God is the inadmissible abstraction. . . the abstract idea of God is an idea that cannot illuminate a human situation. The reverse is true.[163]

But even in *Totality and Infinity* the Other is not *simply* the neighbor, for it is said of him that he is nearer God than I, that he resembles God, and that his face is "the manifestation of the height in which God is revealed."[164] The themes of illeity and the trace develop later this referral or displacement of glory from the neighbor, who is its designee, to God. If the idea of God is assigned no meaning that is not ethical, it is nevertheless true that God is an irreducible reality, distinct from the fellow man, who signifies differently, as the One who has passed by.

Any discourse that addresses or is oriented to God is in some sense a theology; or at least, in Levinas' case, no less a "theology" than a "philosophy," i.e. a disturbance of theology as much as a disturbance of philosophy. His definition of ethics as *religio* is certainly no arbitrary gesture. But he rigorously distinguishes between *religio* and the positive religions, and also between philosophy and positive theology. Talmudic studies seem to occupy a third place, neither philosophical nor positively theological, though religious.[165] The commentaries and commentaries on commentaries of the Talmud belong to a discipline separate from philosophy, but their truth may still be reflected in the mirror of philosophy; the philosopher need not regard this literature as a folklore, but may be taught by it. However, it is not true for Levinas that philosophy is in a superior position, capable of assimilating and rationalizing the whole import of the Talmud. The one important bridge between the two is the fact that the Talmud names God by exploring relations with beyond-Being, rather than by

proposing knowledge of a quiddity or essence--and the holiness
of God is found to refer directly to the constitution of a just
society.[166] For philosophy, too, the concepts of theology are
completely empty except insofar as they draw on ethical content.[167] The revelation of the Infinite does not lead to any
dogmatic content, and its "eschatology" is different from the
revealed opinions of the positive religions, because, as the
original breach with totality, revelation and metaphysics precede either negation or affirmation--revelation of exteriority
as such provides the precondition of the meaningfulness of any
affirmation about God.[168] The claimed transcendence of positive
religion is still a participation in Being.[169]

> The metaphysical relation, the idea of the infinite,
> connects with the noumenon which is not a numen. This
> noumenon is to be distinguished from the concept of God
> possessed by the believers of positive religions ill dis-
> engaged from the bonds of participation, who accept being
> immersed in a myth unbeknown to themselves. The idea of
> the infinite, the metaphysical relation, is the dawn of a
> humanity without myths. But faith purged of myths, the
> monotheist faith, itself implies metaphysical atheism.[170]

Theology, in turn, is criticized for treating in ontological
terms the relationship between God and the creature.[171] On the
one hand, Levinas gives monotheism credit for the idea of creation ex nihilo, an idea which certainly belongs to theology,
but on the other hand he denies that the idea of the Good need
be sought anywhere outside of philosophy. It is to be traced
to Plato, not to some "oriental wisdom."[172]

The harsh treatment of theology in *Totality and Infinity*
can only be understood as a function of other polemical objec-
tives in the book. Levinas aims to bring philosophy under the
command of the Good by pointing to the breach or embarrassment
of totality in which the Good imposes itself. The claim is
that the totality cannot be understood if the gleam of exteriority that interrupts it is not also understood, i.e. if its
totalizing pretentions go unchecked. Now, while the fact that
the man Plato responded to the Good is by itself no more a
proof of the Good than the fact that the man Moses responded to
it, still it calls into question the assumption that our philosophical discourse, based on a Greek heritage ("Athens"), is
historically and necessarily deaf to this particular theme of

the Good or creation ex nihilo, which would be referred to a completely non-philosophical Hebrew heritage ("Jerusalem").[173] The case of Plato--and later Descartes, and Kant, in different ways--shows that at the very heart of the West's devotion to the *logos* there is a divine disruption and redefinition of *logos*. Thus, while Levinas accepts the obligation to "speak Greek" and believes that the true enthusiasm is rational sobriety,[174] he finds that even speaking *Greek* is *speaking*, Saying. Neither Platonism nor "oriental wisdom" are parochial on this point.

Only with care can one speak of the "Jewish inspiration" of this philosophy, since for Levinas "religion" is on the whole defined by its function of consolation,[175] and to that extent is as defunct as the divine Being and afterlife to which that consolation is normally pinned. The Judaism that finds its way into the philosophy of Levinas does so as a "religion of transcendence" which, like Hermann Cohen's "religion of reason," is based on the general human condition and is basically indifferent to the authority of a certain history or scripture, if not indifferent to the importance of history and scriptures in suggesting meanings to the philosopher. Levinas seems to occupy a position similar to Cohen's, in that he is able to give a strong positive valuation to both philosophy and Judaism, the latter remaining separate but attaining its real dignity by the share it attains in Reason (transcendence). Judaism itself is normatively the ethical "religion of adults," transcending the primacy of consolation and thus the philosophically deprecating notion of "religion."[176]

Notwithstanding the distance Levinas keeps with regard to theology and religion, from *Totality and Infinity* onward the "Good" is named "God." In *Otherwise than Being* he writes:

> But egoism is neither first, nor ultimate. Jonah's adventure, the impossibility of escaping God (and I utter the word God without suppressing the intermediaries that led me to this word or, if I may say so, the anarchy of its entry into this discourse--just as phenomenology states concepts without ever tearing down the scaffolding that allows it to climb up to them)--the impossibility of escaping God (who, in this at least, is not one value among others) lies at the base of me as self, as absolute passivity.[177]

Might this God be the biblical God? Would the mentioned inter-
mediaries then belong to a positive religion? God is introduced
as "the God of the Bible" and "the God of whom the Bible speaks"
in the 1975 article "God and Philosophy,"[178] which asks how this
God can become part of a discourse governed by the ontological
philosophy of the West, which aims at ultimate comprehension.
God can only enter this discourse as a supreme Being; thus,
"rational theology," submitting to the rules of ontology which
can confer no higher honor than "being," destroys God's "improb-
able" transcendence of any analogy or criterion.[179] On the
other hand, it is possible to declare the God of Abraham, Isaac,
and Jacob out of bounds for philosophers, lacking a sense, beneath intelligibility. But what if there *is* meaning beyond
Being?

> To ask, as we will attempt to ask here, whether God
> cannot be expressed in a reasonable discourse that would be
> neither ontology nor faith [the faith that speaks the lan-
> guage of Being, 101], is by implication to doubt the formal
> opposition established by Yehouda Halevi and taken up again
> by Pascal, between the God of Abraham, Isaac, and Jacob,
> invoked without philosophy in faith, on the one hand, and
> the god of the philosophers on the other hand: it is to
> doubt that this opposition offers a real choice.[180]

Faith (in this sense) fails to offer an alternative to philosophy (in the sense of ontology), because it claims to *know* something or to have a special *experience*; by referring to an experience, faith fails to breach the immanence of the Same within which nothing is alien to philosophy. Faith as experience
delivers itself over to philosophy; religious "revelation" is
assimilated to the "disclosure" on which philosophy thrives.[181]
But God as the idea of the Infinite breaches the unity of experience,[182] creating an insatiable desire for a Desirable that
remains separated and holy while directing the self to the
supremely undesirable, non-erotic neighbor.[183] And from this
analysis it appears that God "is not simply the 'first other
person,' or the 'other person par excellence,' or the 'absolutely other person,' but other than the other person, differently
other, other with an alterity prior to the alterity of the
other man. . . transcendent to the point of being absent" and
possibly being confused with the *il y a*.[184] The subject does
not experience or prove the Infinite, but witnesses to it--

witnessing being the very modality of its glory.[185] Witnessing
is Saying, prophecy of the Infinite: "The Lord God has spoken;
who can but prophesy?" (Amos 3:8).[186]

Is this argument philosophical, theological, both, or
neither? On the one hand, God is distinguished from the God of
ontology--because He transcends the Same. On the other hand,
God is not the God of "belief," because belief, as a kind of
participation, has not gotten as far as the critical destruction of the "supreme Being" which even Heidegger's thought of
the difference between Being and beings accomplishes. "Philosophy" thus has a relative right over against faith, but it still
falls absolutely short of transcendence, since the constraints
of logic and Being rule it unchallengeably. Levinas' God is
not said to be *not* the God of Abraham, Isaac, and Jacob. The
fact that *Otherwise than Being* makes no apologies for the "anarchic entry" of God into its discourse may signal that this
God is or could be suggested to the would-be philosopher of
transcendence by a particular scripture or tradition. Indeed,
the growth of this philosophy of God out of ethics may be the
required gesture of respect for the scaffolding by which the
sense of that ethics was gained--an explication of the monotheism on which the ethics was based. But however the idea of God
entered philosophy, it did not then justify itself by the authority of a scripture, but only by its call to witness its
glory via the service of the neighbor.[187] (Similarly, Levinas
does not claim that Descartes' idea of the Infinite is "innate";
here, too, the contingent history of philosophy does not apologize for the order in which its ideas appear.) The idea of
God or the Infinite, wherever it comes from, gives a universal
possibility of thought thinking more than it can think. For
this philosophical theology, the significance of revelation lies
in the event of revelation itself, i.e. as a breach of totality,
but the "scaffolding" by which one approaches the idea of revelation may be bound up with a historical revelation, even the
revelation of the Torah.[188]

The development of Levinas' thought between 1961 and
1975 does not entirely lend itself to schematization as a series
of changed positions, or even as a single shift in position.

Most of what is written in *Otherwise than Being* could find a place, and often does find an anticipation, in *Totality and Infinity*. But *Totality and Infinity*'s dominant themes of separation and pluralism are transfigured in *Otherwise than Being*. It is as though the idea of the Infinite (the in-the-finite) overflowed the mainly negative, critical analysis of Otherness, or anti-ontology, of the earlier work and served as the springboard for a positive Saying of transcendence in the later. The absolute difference becomes absolute "non-indifference."[189] The election of the Same by the Other, prior to any initiative of the Same, is a revolution in Being preceding the revolution by which the existent masters existence, of which Levinas said, in *De l'existence à l'existant*, that it "precedes every act of understanding, every horizon and all time."[190] The elect consciousness is called out into time *before* its absolute self-beginning; the origin is already in relation with the pre-origin. Jonah cannot escape God.

Levinas was told at Leiden that the face of the Other in *Totality and Infinity* seems to emerge out of nothingness, giving his philosophy a phantom-like character. He answered: "The other must be welcomed independently of his qualities, if he is to be welcomed as other. If there were not that, a certain immediacy. . . the rest of my analyses would lose all their force."[191] The negative movement is not superseded by the positive; it remains the presupposition, because it reflects the very abstraction of the non-evident face, the very indigence or unloveliness of the other to whom God sends me. How much is a diseased derelict "worth"? Is there any destiny of Being or scheme of value that does not exclude or oppress someone in the world?

The infinite thus absolves itself from all horizons. But it also produces or infinitizes itself, overflowing its idea and eventually overflowing the proprieties of discourse by the total exposure and immodesty of Saying, "Saying" saying "Saying" itself. The argument relies not on an alternative to ontological language but on a divine ambiguity that can be induced in it. This positive presentation of the Infinite, which is also to be found in *Totality and Infinity*, is the mounting religious urgency of Levinas' later argument which becomes the

glorification of God. As in Descartes' case, the Good is too
Good (and too Other) not to call God; analysis yields to adora-
tion. The analogy holds only up to a point, for the God of
Levinas is adored only in the third person, never face to face.
That may be the difference between a Catholic and a Jew.

Levinas' philosophy of transcendence, and of meaning as
the meaning of transcendence, does not become less ethical as
it is devoted to God; ethics remains its optics as well as its
mode of production. "[T]he non-presence of the Infinite is not
a figure of negative theology. All the negative attributes that
state the beyond-Being become positivity, in responsibility."[192]
But the question arises more insistently as to whether this
philosophy is a theology, and if it is, whether it is a natural
or revealed theology. According to the ordinary meaning of
those terms, it is neither. It might be called a revelation
philosophy, i.e. a philosophical theology of the event of revelation distinct from all possible contents of revelation. The
"contentless" event is only apparently abstract, since it is
after all the concrete irruption of the moral life in my relations with others. In His own way, not to be confused with the
way of men, God has spoken in passing by my neighbor and me,
leaving the trace in which prophetic man stands.[193]

CHAPTER VII

LANGUAGE AND REASON

1. Reality as Impossibility

The "emptiness" of the concept of the *absolutely Other*
continues to raise the specter of its ultimate meaninglessness.

> [I]s there a conception of the world, a basic view of
> existence which can include what we have called God? If
> the general conception of the world and the general pattern
> of human thought are the criteria, can such a thing as
> revelation in the Christian sense exist as all? Does this
> God exist, of whom we have spoken as the subject of this
> revelation? What are we in fact talking about? Are we
> possibly talking nonsense, talking about a non-ens? There
> are theories of knowledge which can account for what we
> have called the self-revelation of that which exists, and
> there are ontologies which can embrace the gods correspond-
> ing to these revelations. But as far as one can see there
> is no theory of knowledge and no pattern of thought which
> can embrace revelation in the Christian sense of the term.
> We can work through the whole history of philosophy from
> Thales to Martin Heidegger, and we shall be forced to the
> same conclusion. . . if a purely human conception of the
> world is the measure of all things, then neither revelation
> nor God in the Christian sense exist at all. We would in
> fact have been speaking about "nothing" when we were speak-
> ing about revelation and God.
> We have not, however, been speaking about "nothing,"
> but about a reality, something incomparably more real than
> anything that can be called real in the sphere of human
> thought and knowledge.[1]

> One can also, to be sure, claim that the God of the
> Bible does not have a meaning, that is, is not properly
> speaking thinkable. . . "The concept of God is not a prob-
> lematical concept; it is not a concept at all," writes
> Mme. Delhomme in a recent book, in continuation of a great
> tradition of philosophical rationalism which refuses to
> accept the transcendence of the God of Abraham, Isaac, and
> Jacob among the concepts without which there would be no
> thought. What the Bible puts above all comprehension would
> not yet have reached the threshold of intelligibility!
> The problem which is thus posed, and which will be ours,
> is whether the meaning equivalent to the *esse* of Being,
> that is, the meaning which for philosophy *is* meaning, is
> not already a restriction of meaning, a derivative or diver-
> sion of meaning: whether the meaning equivalent to essence--
> to "Being's move," to Being qua Being--is not already en-
> countered in presence, which is the time of the Same. This
> assumption can only be justified by the possibility of going

back from this meaning that we claim is conditioned to a
meaning which could no longer be put in terms of Being, or
of beings. We must ask if beyond the intelligibility and
rationalism of identity, consciousness, the present, and
Being--beyond the intelligibility of immanence--the significance, rationality, and rationalism of *transcendence* can be
understood. . .[2]

The idea of the Other, in the form either of Anselmian
or Cartesian infinitism, overflows the boundaries of the possible. It is *im*-possible because it is not *in* any statable set
of possibilities. The Barth-Anselm idea of the Infinite, which
argues the priority of the reality of the event of revelation
to noetic possibility, is like the Levinas-Descartes idea of
the Infinite in showing that the Other's antecedence to any
frame of reference in which the subject would be at home implies
a redrawing of the limits of possibility by the Other. Whenever
it is the subject, or Being, or History that guarantees a given
extension of "possibility," the Other is inevitably excluded.

Since the eminent reality of the Other is an excess
over the possibility of the Same, the reach or gesture to the
Other must be veritable transcendence of the Same. But what in
the Same has the uncanny ability to do more than it can do,
effecting the "thought that thinks more than it can think"?
The gesture that exceeds the Same, instituting relationship with
the Other as Other, is nothing more or less than *language*, which
is uniquely able to make "contact at a distance, relation with
the non-touchable, across a void."[3] The Other interrupts our
dreams, our "reflection," by speaking. "It is possible to turn
our eyes in different directions or shut them, but not our ears.
It is the ears which are here involved. When we hear God we
are not free, but are completely chained and bound in our
thoughts and words."[4] "The *immediate* is the interpellation
and. . . the imperative of language."[5] The imperative "chains"
us and "binds" us because, invading us through the ears,[6] it
cannot be intercepted and filtered through our ideas of what
can happen and what can be demanded. The Infinite is in-the-
finite already. "To hear a voice that speaks to us is ipso
facto to accept an obligation with respect to the one who
speaks."[7] The order of language is the personal or spiritual
order, therefore, because the event of speaking is immediately
the event of appeal and response, authority and obedience. In

speaking and hearing, persons are present to each other in person, not competing with each other's freedom, soliciting rather than coercing each other,[8] transcending through speech any vision or image by which one would belong to the "experience" of the other.[9] "Language is the incessant surpassing of the *Sinngebung* by the signification"[10] inasmuch as the very structure of signification is one-for-another, an extroverted *Sinngebung* that no longer gives sense for the self but for the Other. Speaking is a true giving of sense and hearing is a true reception of sense, a totally passive suffering of sense, a *Sinnerleidung* or "passive genesis" prior to any initiative of the subject. Only in his word is the teaching Other sovereign, differing fundamentally from a disclosed thing by coming to his own assistance in mastery of his revelation.[11]

The advent of the Other and the personal relation between self and Other is inseparable from the event of language. It is obviously not accidental that speaking and hearing fit so well the requirements of the concept of the totally Other by spanning the void that separates the Other from the Same. Language is the event on which the category of event is modelled; language enacts that primary relationship which the concept of the Other tries secondarily to explicate by placing its logically peculiar aspects in relief.[12] Speaking is a transcendence: to propose the world to the other, seeking his agreement, is in itself an unthinkable adventure and a fatal hemorrhage from the standpoint of the self-sufficient *cogito*. And hearing is a transcendence: to know the truth of the starry heavens as it is taught from beyond the stars, from no-place, by a teacher who imposes a rigor, an awful obedience, but the absolute excitement of novelty. Speaking and hearing constitute the personal order of pacific interaction between freedoms, reason-to-reason, commanding without dominating. A dysfunction of language is inseparable from a dysfunction of the personal. The dilemma of the modern world, what Barth calls its "short-breathed modernism" and Levinas its "impossibility of speech, which is perhaps the most incontestable experience of our age,"[13] is the derangement of the personal. The accountable speaker drops out of language in Heidegger's "*Die Sprache spricht*," Language speaking itself.[14] In modern science man becomes the object of a discourse that is so much *about* him it is almost no longer *by* him or *to* him; his interiority (or whatever it is about him that transcends the system) has vanished, and discourse is de-stroyed.[15]

The personal order exceeds the order of things known by its *timeliness*. The realm of possibility par excellence is the present, where the self, posing as transcendental unity of apperception, is unchallengeable. The past is only known as a reconstituted present, obeying the laws of the present, in memory. The future is only reckoned as an extrapolation of past and present, i.e. our "experience." But language, rela-tion with the Other, draws the self out of the present and consequently provokes a critique of the philosophical or theo-logical primacy of the present. As an alternative to Schleier-macher's Christian self-consciousness, Barth fixes his points of reference in the recollected commission and promise of God and the expectation of the promise's fulfillment.[16] This "ex-pectation" and "recollection" do not reduce to "knowledge" in the Cartesian or Kantian sense. There is such a thing as Chris-tian knowledge, but it is determined by the critical question of *which* recollections and expectations are authoritative and to be confessed. "What ought I to do?" and "What may I hope?" retain the upper hand over "What can I know?," prolonging and confirming the triumph of practical reason--in this case, right theological reason. For Levinas, moral responsibility causes an explosion or "fission" of the present, i.e. an opening up of the ego to something that is not in the present, never has been, and never will be. The Other is always more ancient than the memorable, has always passed by, preceding one, so that the relation with the Other is determined by a commission (the "anarchic provocation" to goodness) rather than a knowing. The commission aspect is permanently superordinated to the knowing aspect. The horizon of futurity opened up by one's children likewise creates a hope irreducible to any knowledge or predic-tion.[17]

Because language is an excess over experience, anything that can be regarded as a teaching is an excess over any pos-sible object of theoretical knowledge. After the critical historians have done their work on the Bible, the question remains: "What does it mean?" "Meaning" in this sense refers, on the one hand, to that which is being witnessed to, which lies elsewhere (such that one would disrespect the pointing-away intention by studying the psychology of the one pointing or the "influences" on him), and on the other hand to the fact of witnessing itself, which is no phenomenon. To witness is to obey and to solicit the obedience of others. Thus beyond all history, and beyond all the ontological or cosmological criteria that might be adduced to help decide whether or not God *can* exist, a claim is made. What is the meaning of this claim? Its meaning is not establishable in the way that the existence or nature of an object (its place in the intelligible economy of Being) is establishable. One perceives or recognizes or otherwise experiences an object, but one does not *learn* from it, one is not put on the spot by it, in the personal way implied by this extra demand "What is the meaning?" Exactly like G. E. Moore's open question "Is it good?," the question of meaning cannot be closed. There may yet be an orderly, prosaic science of this meaning; there will have to be rules for its investigation and presentation; but the appropriate obedience to the Other will be an axiom of this science, just as differently appropriate attitudes of response to phenomena constitute the other sciences.[18]

The "meaning of meaning" contemplated by the open question of meaning is beyond Reason as ordinarily conceived. It shows its difference from logic and evidence by travelling incognito and refusing to coerce obedience. It has, in a sense, no answer to the moral sceptic, Cain, or to the fool who says there is no God--except to offer a way of being that excludes Cain and the fool as impossibilities. Murder and atheism are ethically or theologically (but not physically or psychologically) impossible. The empty signification of the Other has to be empty to be generous and gracious, but its emptiness also makes it refutable. This is perhaps only to state the tautology that because of its impossibility it is impossible. The Good is miraculously Good because it is different from the evident way of Being.

2. From Crisis to Argument

Immediately upon the proclamation of the crisis of the *totaliter aliter*, both Barth and Levinas had to deal with the inevitable misunderstandings that their ideas of transcendence evoked. To clarify their meaning, they were drawn into what has been called here the positive phase of the Argument to the Other, the phase in which the Argument becomes active as an argument, i.e. as a dialectical Yes- and No-saying, or as "Saying" saying "Saying" itself. They had to show that the crisis applies to their own language as much as anyone else's, and that the idea of the Other can only be advanced in an Other-serving manner--that one cannot argue *from* the Other as though the Other were a premise, but only *to* the Other as transcendent Justifier. At stake is the risky crossing of the Red Sea, which here signifies the this-worldly teleology of language, its inability to show that which it is not *about*, that which its themes fail to capture.

What thematic language fails to capture is the speaking or hearing performer of language. Therefore the Argument becomes, conspicuously, a performing or ongoing practicalization of Reason. The principal object of the Argument is to call attention to itself as a performing distinct from a thematizing, but since it is language it is always a thematization also, and so must divide itself as a performing from itself as the specific performing of thematization with a gesture of oversaying: for example, by forcing a verb into the place of a subject, as in the formula "'Saying' saying 'Saying' itself," or by putting the subject in the place of the object (on behalf of that Subject) in saying that the Revealer Reveals Revealedness, i.e. Himself.[19] Language resists these moves by inviting us to read "Revealedness" or the second "Saying" as things; the Red Sea continues to wash over the trail. The bear trap of thematization snaps shut. In order to prop it open it is necessary to *go on* unsaying and oversaying, just the same as one has to go on counting out infinity. The willingness to go on is obedience itself, staking out a different dimension than that occupied by the inevitable thematization--of which, in fact, thematization is the material, but never the form.

We have noticed a tremendous volatilization of the language of theology and philosophy by the fact that the Other is a point of reference outside the thematizable realm. Since no approach to the Other contains its own justification, the vocabulary used becomes fluid and dispensable. According to Barth, what elects a term or a reasoning is not the immanent logic of a system, for all systems are shattered upon the advent of the Other, but the totally contingent consent of the inalienably subject "object" of theological reasoning.[20] For Levinas, the "emphasis" on ontology is not justified by an inner drive of ontology's subject matter but by the Other dimension one has attained by running the emphatic risk.[21] Philosophy cannot define in advance the kind of experience or language that will prove hermeneutically important.

At first glance, the motives behind Barth's dialectic might seem very different from Levinas'. For Barth the problem is not in the nature of word, but in the sinfulness or finitude of human words.

> [E]ven in the simplest occurrences of my life, His will has not been done. . . not even at the most exalted moments of my life do I fulfill His commands. Does any single thought of mine express the all-compelling power of the Spirit? Does one single word of mine formulate the Word after which I am striving and which I long to utter in my great misery and hope? Does not each sentence I frame require another to dissolve its meaning?[22]

But the nature of the obedience that man falls short of is itself dialectical—just as the lost knowledge of God, according to second *Romans* (disagreeing with first *Romans*) is the knowledge of God *as* Other.

> Obedience means that there is encountered in the known man of this world an irruption, where the new man is able to breathe and move. Obedience is the sense for the specific peculiarity of the Divine and for the Wholly-Other-ness of God. . . a readiness to retreat from every concrete position which we have occupied, from every undertaking, alliance, compromise, or daring venture upon which we have embarked; in fact, from every method of thought or manner of behavior. Obedience means that the pendulum is allowed to swing to and fro, freely and without interruption, from its point of suspension; and that we are free to. . . move along the same road backwards and forwards again without ever standing still. . . This is the obedience congruous to the Gospel of Salvation. But who is competent for such obedience? Speaking soberly and very obscurely, we answer— *not all.*[23]

"Not all" means not the Church of Esau, not the known man. The obedience from which Sin divides us is the obedience of a dialectically fragmented discourse and action. Religion's problem is not that it falls short of a noblest form, but that it fails to do away with itself, to absolve God from itself.[24] Like the "diachronic" thinking of Levinas, dialectic is *witnessing*, redirecting attention to something beyond the language being uttered to, in Barth's case, the God who is jealous of His own Word, who intends to speak it Himself. This God and this grace are, of course, anything but dialectical. The "purposelessness" of free-swinging human dialectic responds to the Purpose of purposes, God's. Even politically, the Christian is saved from his own interests not to be indifferent but to be (in Levinas' term) non-indifferent.[25]

The power of dialectics and diachronics to unravel the thematic coherence of language is already present in speech, which continually undoes itself, absolving both speaker and hearer. "The face is a living presence; it is expression. The life of expression consists in undoing the form in which the existent, exposed as a theme, is thereby dissimulated."[26] The enigma of speech is not one of the phenomena mediated by speech; it deranges the order of phenomena, leaving an invisible trace.[27] That is, the trace is invisible if one *looks* for it. But one must rather follow it. Unlike the "given" phenomena, speech and personal relation go on. It is as against the nature of speech to think of stopping it as it is to be satisfied with having attained a certain level of moral virtue; it is like trying to stop time itself.[28] The "sincerity" or youthful innocence (*jeunesse*) of speech, according to Levinas, is its ever-readiness to surge up afresh, to be "unseasonable," to never be captured by the Said.[29]

Levinas' "original Saying," like Barth's original Revelation, ties a knot of responsibility, establishing an order more serious than Being and anterior to Being.[30] Why, then, is language in action so perverse as always to falsify Saying by reducing it to a Said, or reducing the Word of God to a doctrine of the Word of God? If "Saying" is really the authentic character of language, if the Word of God is really the event that creates faith, why is it necessary to say this so strangely?

Does the perversity of language lie with the particular activi-
ties of philosophy and theology, which always want to state the
case, establish the *logos*, even of realms where there might
perhaps be no "case"? On the other hand, if philosophy and
theology are unavoidable, if they reflect merely the escalation
of argument or discussion between people who care about what
shall jointly be said or done, is the betrayal of Saying by the
Said in fact the symptom of that moment in an argument when one
person makes the winning move, the coercive move predicating a
human or divine *nature* or saying what the unsurpassable *possibilities* of discourse are?

3. From Beyond Reason to Reason

Man entrenches himself in the realm of possibility to
repel the claim of exteriority that exceeds possibility. "Modern" man entrenches himself according to certain intellectual
patterns, which determine the polemical moves made by Barth and
Levinas (against "Cartesianism," Hegel and Heidegger, etc.).
It is said that the meaning of God is unclear until the meaning
of Being has been thought, or that the meaning of the other
person is impossible to ground apart from exposing the operations of transcendental consciousness. How *can* I know anything
of which I am not conscious? How *can* a God be spoken of whose
Otherness defeats the logical rules of coherent, non-contradic-
tory discourse?

The aim of the Argument to the Other is to set these
relationships right side up, not to violate consciousness and
logic. It is not a dysfunction of language to operate according
to rules, or to appeal to intuition and judgment. The dysfunction lies in setting up the rules and intuitions as the supreme
court of justification. The reach to the Other, language, becomes an argument, the Argument to the Other which holds itself
open, contorted into an active acknowledgement of transcendence.
The obedient performing of the argument then "establishes" (not
architectonically) theological and philosophical reason; it
provides the context within which the other materials of reason,
such as evidence and logic, can be reasonably marshalled. The
holding-open of the Argument superior to all evidence and logic
does not, however, imply a perpetually unfinished conversation

that would never conclude anything, any more than the absolute pacificism of morality implies that history is abstained from and never made. History is made, but does not justify itself. So too evidence is offered and logic employed, but neither do they justify themselves. They must become the material of personal relationship. The sense of any enterprise is determined by the fact that we face an Other; that is why, faced the wrong way, backwards, the Other is nonsense, not a concept at all, etc. Theoretical reason makes nothing of this "practical" reason. But the elect self, facing the right way, no longer asks whether God makes sense--recognizing that it is a categorical mistake to adjudge the meaning of the meaning of meaning.

Modern man's growing speechlessness reflects his forgetfulness of the right standing of consciousness and logic, the former as mobilized in the apology of argument, the latter as the trace left by living discourse. The rational is consecrated by the reasonable, the appeal or signification of one to another; but the reverse does not occur. Justice does not derive from consciousness and formal logic. Injustice--atheism, racism, capitalism, colonialism--comes from consciousness and logic when they are set up uncritically as the ideology of Reason. The meaning of Reason is determined otherwise. The Argument to the Other claims to be the only right argument, the argument that keeps arguing--its argue-ing characteristic kept in the foreground by dialectical or diachronic presentation. The crucial distinction between argument as mere evidencing or demonstrating, and argument as transcending appeal, is contained in the concept of *witness*. "Witness" designates a normative mode of "with-ness": the prodigious index finger of Grünewald's John the Baptist pointing away from himself toward Revelation.[31] The Other is invoked, not evidenced; invited, not coerced; appealed to, not disposed of. To secure the irreducible character of "invoke," "invite," and "appeal," it is necessary to show the *total* Otherness of this Other, the away-ness from self of the pointing to him, and the absolute void that must be crossed to "get to" him.

Barth's concept of *dogma* seems initially to be an attempt to *fill* this void. Does he believe that the theological

conversation does have a terminus, that there is one statement
of the nature of the case that will be adequate to all persons
involved--but that the statement can only be made by God, so
that dogma is an "eschatological concept"?[32] Or does he rather
believe only that of the many things that may be said, some are
more just than others and thus deserving of investigation and
commemoration? "Dogma" for Barth can be the very paradigm of
the empty signification, the "non-knowing knowledge"[33] that
fails to comprehend the Other--like the dogma of the *homoousia*
which conveys not the faintest idea of God as an object, but
criticizes those statements (Arianism, etc.) which pretend to
do so.[34] Descartes' idea of the Infinite is a philosophical
dogma, a "principle," yet for some reason Levinas considers it
important and apt to put it above other principles. One cannot
dispense with principles altogether and continue to speak responsibly. The motto of Levinas' autobiographical essay "Signature" is taken from a conversation overheard in the subway:

> "The language that tries to be direct and name events
> is unjust after all. Events tempt it to be prudent, to
> compromise. Men are grouped by their commitments into par-
> ties, without realizing it. Their talk turns into politics.
> The language of commitment is calculated."
> "Who speaks straightforwardly of what really is? Who
> speaks from the heart about men? Who shows them his coun-
> tenance?"
> "The one who expresses himself in terms of 'substance,'
> 'accident,' 'subject,' 'object,' and other abstractions. . ."[35]

The most abstract idea is the idea of the Infinite. By means
of it, Descartes pointed away from himself, over and above the
fabric of philosophical assertions. Therefore this particular
assertion or "dogma" is just, worthy of remembering and mar-
shalling again in the contemporary discussion. The church dogma
of Christ's eternal deity "antecedently in Himself" also functions to strike all standards out of our hands; it says to us
that the knowledge of Christ's deity can only be the beginning
and not the result of our thought.[36] The one justifiable system
is the anti-system of Kierkegaard's infinite qualitative difference.[37] The one just war is the war against war.[38]

The Argument places us in a position ("that is no position") *beyond Reason* in the sense of a canon of principles or
categories or ideas; and from this position we make our way to
Reason. According to the movement of the Argument, Reason is

not something we start with but something we get to, and the
establishing of this sequence is the justification, the mak-
ing-reasonable, of Reason. Reason is fundamentally reasonable
when it functions as obedience to the Other. The movement to
it is already reasonable insofar as it follows the *sens unique*,
the one-for-another structure of signification.[39] Theology as
a science presupposes obedience to God, which means awaiting
his gracious justification.[40] *Knowledge* itself in the normative
theological sense becomes transfigured by the dimension of responsibility to the "known" Word of God:

> By the knowledge of an object by men we understand con-
> firmation of their acquaintance with its reality in respect
> of its existence and nature. But confirmation of their
> acquaintance means that the reality of the object concerned,
> its existence and nature, being true in themselves, now
> become in some way, and with some degree of clarity and
> distinctness, true for men too. Their acquaintance with it,
> instead of being a contingent and outward determination of
> their own existence, now becomes a necessary and inward
> determination. Knowing, they are affected by the object
> known. They no longer exist without it, but with it. In
> so far as they think of it, with the same confidence with
> which they dare to think in general they must think of it
> as a true reality, as true in its existence and nature.
> Whatever else and however else they may think of it, they
> must begin by thinking of the truth of its reality. Face
> to face with this truth they can no longer withdraw into
> themselves in order to affirm, question or deny it thence.
> Its truth has come home to them, has become their own. And
> in the process they themselves have become the truth's.
> This event, this confirmation, in contrast to mere cogni-
> zance [*Kenntnis*], we call knowledge [*Erkenntnis*]. Cogni-
> zance becomes knowledge when man becomes a responsible
> witness to its content.[41]

According to this "epistemology," which is more than an epistemology to the same extent that true knowledge exceeds mere
cognizance, the subject loses his power of withdrawal from what
he knows. It invades him and claims him; he is responsible to
it. "Experience" of the Word of God is necessarily decision,
and is thus immediately also either obedience or disobedience,
with no liberty of indifference.[42]

> We pursue dogmatics because, constrained by the fact of
> the Bible, we cannot shake off the question of the obedience
> of Church proclamation. The question of its obedience in-
> cludes that of its truth. But the question of its truth
> can be put only as the question of its obedience. As the
> question of its obedience it is the question of dogma.[43]

To place truth in the context of obedience is to make the journey from the beyond-Reason to Reason, in the prescribed way that
rights Reason. The phrase "right Reason" is not redundant. It
reflects awareness of the sinful alternative. The sense of this
alternative pervades Barth's notion of dogma.

> The dogma of the Holy Spirit means recognition that in
> every respect man can be present at God's revelation only
> as a servant is present at his master's work, i.e., follow-
> ing, obeying, imitating and serving, and that this relation--
> as distinct from that of any human servant and master--
> cannot be reversed in any way or at any point. This devel-
> oped recognition of the unconditionality and irreversibility
> of the lordship of God in His revelation is what makes the
> dogma of the Holy Spirit difficult, difficult, of course,
> intellectually too, but difficult intellectually only be-
> cause man does not want the very thing that it states to
> be true.[44]

Compare Levinas: "The shame for oneself, the presence of and
desire for the other are not the negation of knowing; knowing
is their very articulation. The essence of reason consists not
in securing for man a foundation and powers, but in calling him
in question and inviting him to justice."[45] The beginning of
intelligibility for Levinas is the commandment of the face, of
language.[46] "The truth of being is not the *image* of being, the
idea of its nature; it is the being situated in a subjective
field which deforms vision, but precisely thus allows exteriority to state itself, entirely command and authority: entirely
superiority."[47]

The idea of the Infinite is the Other in the Same, which
is to say, the impossibility of atheism. In *Totality and
Infinity* and second *Romans*, however, it seemed that atheism was
not only part of the message but the very essence of the message.
Barth and Levinas consummated the critique of false gods so as
to clear the field for the true God. The gratuitous, unheard-of
surplus of the Other belongs to no correlation with the Same--
the eye has not seen and the ear has not heard, which means that
man is objectively godless--and disobedience is the constitutive
feature of the evident world. But in the infinitization of the
Infinite, i.e. in the upsurge of an Argument to the Other out
of the critical idea of the Other, an "emptily" signifying discourse reaches out from disobedience to obedience. Obedience
is possible, after all, though only under extraordinary

conditions; and language, as theology and ethics, is its body.
Theological language, understanding itself as service of revelation rather than description or judgment of it, comes pouring
out of the Crisis as a recurrent divine Yes overshadowing the
No of the Crisis. The "otherwise-than-Being" becomes, concretely, the ethical "emphasis" of philosophical language, arising
not from a problematic gap in the totality but from the divine
necessity of inspiration. Both the Cartesian and the Anselmian
version of the idea of the Infinite have the primary effect of
placing the one who has the idea in a certain position, a drastically self-critical position; it is the shame and disobedience
of being in an atheist world that does not contain the Other.
But the very shame implies that the Other is somehow present,
infinitely close; somehow one has already been transposed into
the Other frame of reference in which atheism or disobedience
is impossible. One is possessed, elect. The inaugural decision
has already been made against disobedience, and thus the gesture
of one's attempt to describe one's position is transformed from
the negative indication of what the totality cannot contain to
the positive indication of the totality's real meaning, oriented
by the meaning of meaning--just as, at the end of his third
Meditation, Descartes' self-critique moves as though by an inner
logic to the adoration of Majesty. The danger that the meaning
of meaning would reduce to non-sense is only in force in the
negative moment of Crisis, the moment of shame in which disobedience is taken more seriously in a way than obedience. The
positive moment begins when this danger becomes meaningless, or
rather is reoriented to the dangerous but inevitable adventure
of *given* goodness, election. Now theology or ethics becomes
the sole possibility of language, instead of something beyond
language's last possibility. "God has spoken; who can but
prophesy?" Now metaphysics is no longer glimpsed through the
gaps in ontology, but ontology is deduced from metaphysics; now
theology breaks free of its philosophical incognito and conforms
to the commission of its Subject.

To the extent that the Crisis is conserved but surpassed
in the positive production of the Argument offered in service
to the Other as the prototype of all arguments, the so-called
"problem of justification" is solved. It is solved from the

side of the Other. Looked at from the side of the self, it
remains a crisis and an insoluble problem. But regarded from
the side of the Other, the maintenance of the problem for its
own sake is a kind of selfish reserve, the last resort of idealism, the extremest form of dialectic which assumes that the
Ursprung or synthesis is non-given (so that it may be kept at
arm's length). The existence of theology and ethics is living
proof of the solution in this sense. The problem of justification, viewed as insoluble, is the "hard" logic of the Other,
for the sheer unavailability of the Other necessitates an absence of significant talk about him. As a mere problem, the
problem of justification continually subsides into the problem
of freedom, as a paradox or check on freedom, a general Questionableness of freedom. Therefore the presence of purportedly
significant talk about or to the Other expresses a position on
the "sweet" side of logic and evidence. By obeying the Other
it is no longer necessary or inevitable that one should be constrained by the impossibility of relation with the Other, according to the possibilities of the Same. Obedience means exactly
that that canon of possibility is no longer canonical. On the
other side of the Other's incognito is the gracious personal
presentation of the speaking Other, and on the other side of
Crisis and logical impossibility is the sweet reason of argument as pure rhetoric, soliciting assent on the basis of freedom,
not less serious for that but moreso. The Argument to the Other
represents the sweetest reason and the purest rhetoric. We will
have entirely failed to understand it if we can only assign a
negative, privative sense to this beyond-Reason that makes
Reason reasonable. To the pure performing or pure practical
freedom of language, not divorced from experience but orienting
it and transfiguring it, making an offering across the void
entailed by the absolute pluralism of personal relation, we
give the name of "argument" irreducible to experience.

    If the Other were susceptible of indication and descrip-
tion in the way things are ordinarily indicated and described,
there would be no question of Other-talk being "nonsense" or an
impossibility. But the philosophical and theological ostension
of the Other is completely blind, groping as through a fog
toward the absent, the exterior, and the different, which is

never on view. What is on view is the groping, or "witnessing";
and in the absence of the object, the form of the gesture toward
the object is all the more noticeable. This is what has allowed
us to discuss Barth and Levinas as arguers of one Argument.
While it is plain that their objects must be different, yet the
unique conditions under which they attempt to speak of their
objects seem to impose on them the necessity of a certain kind
of gesture of language, with its own logic. The idea of the
Infinite states in a nutshell a central feature of this logic,
since the Infinite is not a representable idea but at most a
performative rule--"Keep counting," in the case of the numerical
Infinite, or "Look higher" in the case of Anselm's proof or
Levinas' curvature of intersubjective space--arriving at no conclusion. It specifies a performing that never rounds off into
a performance. Barth and Levinas perform this performing, "witnessing" to the Other, betraying the presence of a hidden body
by dialectical and diachronic perturbations in their own tra-
jectories. But to ascribe a "logic" to their performing in any
sense is to envision a checkability or repeatability that would
be the condition of the relevance for the reader of the Argument
to the Other. If the gesture beyond Reason is not arbitrary,
there must be something reasonable about it; it must somehow
embody or repeat or appropriately respond to the pacific appeal
of the Other, which is allegedly the condition of Reason. Barth
and Levinas write for an audience. How do they offer their discourse to be judged? We know that it does not aim to coerce,
but how positively is it to be persuasive or convincing?

The presupposition for the intelligibility and cogency
of the Argument to the Other is the "impossible" event of *election*. God has already called us. He has already passed by and
left His trace. The fact of election is strictly unestablish-
able, impossible to apologize for; having already cut the Gordian
knot of the logically open question "God could be, or God could
not be," this pure (though not brute) *fact* of the system-shat-
tering advent of the Other creates that situation we have called
the problem of justification, which has, if not the architectonic distinction of being more "fundamental" than any other
situation, at least the theological and ethical distinction of
being more *serious* than any other conceivable situation.

Election is the given: it determines the sense of "reason" as obedience, so that the reasonableness of the arguing performance toward the Other, which determines the sense of reasonableness in all other cases, is a function of that argument's capacity to serve the Other. The only way to check the gesture of service is to repeat it, to go ahead and be obedient, bending the knee so that faith may come. The arguer does not take unbelief, the liberty of indifference, as seriously as belief and non-indifference. The auditor of the argument, himself an Other, is invited to come into it. But he is not appealed to as though the event of election had never happened. He is treated as though he himself were elect, for *he is*. This is the "kerygmatic" element of the argument,[48] witnessing to a Good to which we are all actually subject; and this is what we have also called the transcendentalism of the Argument, its claim to find the uniquely necessary meaning, the condition of the possibility of all meaning.

The auditor's discovery of his own election can only take the form of the Argument's performing. His trajectory, too, must be perturbed by the hidden body. His experience must be reoriented by what is beyond all experience. There is nothing in his experience to appeal to him by; therefore he must be drawn out of that experience, and the drawing out is the teaching of the reasonable gesture of obedience to the Other. The gesture is justified, not by its intention, not by its shape or feel, but by the Other whom it solicits. The only way to teach the gesture of reasonableness vis-à-vis the Other is to evoke it; it is like the truism that one can only learn to swim when one has been put in the water. Levinas can argue that we are all already in the water, already swimming, insofar as we are human; it is only a question of giving the right account of that moral performing which already determines the whole range of human meanings. Barth for his part does not accept the "apologetic" problem of addressing men who are standing dubiously around the pool, unready or unwilling to enter. The audience of dogmatics is made up of those who are already swimming, those whose seriousness is the seriousness of the church. We may not assume in any case that the Other is at our disposal, for the presupposition of the Argument is that we are at the Other's

disposal. This being-at-the-Other's-disposal, our infinite
liability to critique, transcends any fixed Reason; but only
through ethical and theological seriousness does Reason become
serious, and Unreason an evil. Only because the Same meets the
Other does the apparatus of the meeting (including the trace
left by past meetings and the projection of possibilities for
future meetings) become significant. That is Levinas' "significance, rationalism and rationality of transcendence."

Against the objection that this alleged gesture is not
repeatable and thus not reasonable, Barth can reply that there
is a church, and even acknowledge that without this community
of obedience dogmatics would be senseless; Levinas, meanwhile,
can point to the South American priests concerned for the masses
and say that *here*, for example, the gesture is accomplished,
whether or not knowingly. We have been faced throughout the
present study with a remarkable repetition or echoing of certain
gestures by *two* thinkers, a theologian and a philosopher, which
prima facie argues repeatability and supports the presumption
of something like a "logic" or "reason." In addition, we have
repeated and tried to extend some of their gestures for our-
selves--since this is the meaning of regarding their thought as
a *teaching*.

The problem of evoking obedience is complicated by the
fact that man does not want to serve. Something else tempts
him. Is the temptation linked to the teleological correlation
of Saying with the Said, the destiny of language to objectify,
or with the coercive moment in which an argument is "won"? Is
it that man--Promethean self-willing man, or the self-knowing
Cartesian *cogito*--has a freedom that makes him lighter than air,
a freedom superior to responsibility and thus a weightlessness
superior to weight, so that he *rises* to a height higher than
the "height" of any Other? Having reached the pinnacle, a law
unto himself, man becomes deaf and dumb. He cannot hear the
biblical witness, because he is too "high" to be placed in a
position beneath what the biblical writers are pointing to; he
can only study their "experiences," their psychology, their
interaction with other writers, with history, and perhaps even
with deity, so long as all of these things are objects laid out

before the supreme knower's "leaning-over" gaze.[49] He cannot
speak to anyone, because he is masterless and has no necessity
(or possibility) of justification; what need is there to speak
any more? Why thematize, why express? In fact, though, he
continues to speak. His most beautiful and airtight arguments
are still offered to Others, not wholly with the intention of
coercing desired behavior from them, but in hope of appreciation,
soliciting consent. Otherwise this "Reason" which is supposed
to be the alternative to violence becomes itself a violence.
The peacefulness of Reason as a mode of relationship derives
from the peace of the beyond-Reason.[50]

Still, we remain violent creatures. Because of our
hunger for experience we fill in the empty signification and
thereby make it a signification of something other than the
Other. The transcending gesture of language becomes reflexive;
we want to know just where we stand over against this fearfully
contingent judgment of the Other, and we can only know this by
knowing enough about logic or nature to predict what *has* to be.
The desire for certitude, which is often taken to be a founding
decision for the rational attitude, is not only not itself
rational, it is anti-rational: it denies the possibility of
rationality by affirming the self's guilty freedom as blameless,
placing it beyond question so that it can question everything
else, lording it over everything else. The self's basic confusion and sin is its failure to recognize that the Other is
Other. Perhaps the Argument to the Other is an "eschatological
concept"--does the Argument actually occur, that we can tell?
What we do find is language perverted to the uses of war, political language, speech as manipulation, speech without hearing.
A shadow of falsity lies over all our encounters with each
other and all our claims about God. The most thorough-going
devaluation of human existence is fully justified. But there
is enough peace in the midst of war, and enough language above
the howl of the wind, to know what is meant by the notion of
the personal order--of commanding, obeying, teaching, promising,
loving, and their various distortions and negations--and to
distinguish that order from the order of Being. We may become
confused when we try to tell how we know it, but we do know it.
Finally, we know that we would be incapable of even imagining

the negative logic of the *totaliter aliter* if a concrete claim were not already made on us, driving us on to have this impossible and otherwise unwarrantable idea. For these reasons, all the negativity witnesses to the positivity, albeit through a glass darkly.

No doubt it is owing to the darkness of the glass through which we look that the two arguments in which we have been able to discern one Argument do not, after all, agree in their estimations of where the Otherness of the Other leads.

CHAPTER VIII

THE DIFFERENCE

1. Two Versions of Transcendence

In the preceding chapters we have discovered and endeavored to describe the "good risk" run by Barth and Levinas in their use of theological and philosophical language to witness to the Other. Meanwhile we have been running our own risk in venturing to learn from Barth and Levinas simultaneously, so as to attain a synopsis of an "argument to the Other." The risk has paid off. There was something to be learned in just this way. But what we have learned is clearly not the whole of what Barth and Levinas respectively teach, for behind the Argument lie two rich, serious, and divergent arguments, a strictly philosophical "phenomenology" and a strictly Christian theology. Once this divergence is recognized, there is an important question to ask: to what extent is the divergence itself comprehensible in relation to the Argument or the idea of the *totaliter aliter*? Is the separation of the two arguments as instructive as their commonality?

A difference between Barth and Levinas already appears in formally comparing their articulations of the Argument. The progress of the Argument has been represented as a movement between different conceptions of the Other as a function of the Other's non-givenness, givenness, and different ways of being non-given and given. In the first, "Crisis" stage of the Argument opening the problem of justification, the salient feature of the Other, the "first principle" of second *Romans* and *Totality and Infinity*, is absolute non-givenness. But the non-givenness of the Other of *Totality and Infinity* is far more concrete in its way than that of second *Romans*, for it is tied to the encounter of the self with the neighbor; it belongs to the "phenomenology" of the eminently everyday event. It is *here*, facing me on the spot, that the Other Person is Other, absent. But in second *Romans* the divine Other corresponds to nothing concrete (in spite of its claimed reference to human relationships).

227

The Other is announced in Christ, to be sure, but in Christ
shrunk to the point of the Crucifixion, the annihilation of the
human. Then, in the second "infinitizing" stage of the Argument, whereas Levinas and Barth both suppose a new givenness of
the Other (the Other "in" and inspiring the Same, the *analogia
fidei*), this givenness takes a highly abstract form in Levinas,
as the radicalization of the absence of the Other in the mutation of the You to the He who has "passed by," while in Barth
the highly concrete givenness of Christ in the attestation of
Holy Scripture sets the stage for dogmatics as, essentially,
Christology. Thus the spirit of Barth's conception of Otherness
is tied to the strangeness of particular things--this church,
this book, that first-century man. But the spirit of Levinas'
conception of Otherness is tied more to the alienation from
particular things of moral "utopianism"; the Other is the
Stranger who uproots one from all identity and place, to serve
all men. This difference is reflected throughout their thought.

According to Barth, the Christian is distinguished from
the non-Christian, and the Church's language is distinguished
from the world's language, by a particular *knowledge* of a certain *truth*, and an interest in the consequences of that knowledge. The meaning of the premise "God speaks" is that God
rather than man speaks; God says something different than what
man could say, so that the critical question is to recognize
the Word of God in the midst of human words--not to pick it out,
but to be obedient to it in its purity once it has picked us
out. This knowledge is not merely theoretical knowledge, and
it is not something one could have in the absence of the Holy
Spirit (*Dei loquentis persona*), but it is still a cognitive
determination of the human subject that claims priority as such.
Christian ethics, for example, is determined not by the immediate claim made by the other person, but by Christian knowledge
of the meaning of the other person.

> What is the meaning of "conscience" in Christian ethics?
> Very simply it means that we may know what God has done for
> us. And we may therefore also know about ourselves, and
> know about ourselves as God knows about us, so choose and
> determine ourselves and our acts as God has chosen and
> determined us. Good or evil action is simply being obedient
> or disobedient to this knowledge of ours about God and our-
> selves.1

The immediate moral claim of the Other person is significant as a reminder of what God has done for us. But our knowledge of the revelation is the reference point and context of the reminder. For Barth, the issue in the German church struggle of the 1930's is not the openness of "Saying" but *what shall be said*, which truth shall be witnessed to.[2] Does Barth advocate the very "collectivity of truth" that Levinas criticizes?[3] Does not the subordination of morality to a supreme Truth simply reconfirm the violent domination of beings by Being, and thus represent a defection from the personal order?

According to Levinas, the genuine transcendence is a derangement in Being prior to any dogmatic affirmation or negation, which has the positive importance of uprooting the self from any fixed position so as to pin it under the *other* weight of moral responsibility. The relation between man and man is the sole valid warrant for theological discourse. There is a God not reducible to man, but this Levinasian "Extra" is an extra of ethics--just as Barth's *Extra Calvinisticum* is an extra of the Incarnation, i.e. a reserve of non-givenness associated with a concretely given revelation. Levinas explicitly reverses the order adopted by Barth: a God prior to man is an abstraction.[4] The One who has passed by has the priority of infinite anteriority, but we can speak of Him only because of the encounter with the neighbor in the trace left by His passing. By witnessing to the glory of the Infinite, Levinas' later philosophy moves in a different direction than the Feuerbachianism that Barth opposes, in the sense that it makes a point of associating the divine properties with God instead of man. But the meaning of the divine is controlled by the meaning of the human. Does not God become here a dimension of an "order of creation," the sort of I-Thou moral or spiritual order that Gogarten and Brunner adapted from Ebner, Buber, and Grisebach?[5] Would not the Incarnation reduce on this view to a prime illustration of a philosophically ascertained truth?

Each of these positions out-Others the other, so to speak. The theologian falls short of transcendence of Being; the philosopher falls short of listening to God's own Word. The fact that the Christian theologian begins with the Incarnation of God, while the Jewish philosopher assumes no such thing, must of course be an important reason for their divergence. This point must be alluded to, although it is not here necessary to bury Barth, Levinas, and ourselves under all the centuries of the Jewish-Christian controversy. The primary interest of their difference is not the difference between Jew and Christian. But the difference between Jew and Christian is part of the background of our problem. Therefore what Barth has said about Judaism and what Levinas has said about Christianity merits our attention, at least in passing. Probably the most significant statement made by Levinas in this connection is his avowedly philosophical appreciation of the idea of Christ published in 1968, "Un Dieu homme?"[6] As a criticism of the Incarnation, this piece attests the solidarity of Levinas' philosophy with its Jewish background.[7]

The first philosophically suggestive aspect of Christ concerns the way in which God's transcendence occurs in the world. Pagan conceptions of divinity are caught in a dilemma: either the gods sojourn among men and take an interest in their affairs, thus becoming less than divine, or divinity is preserved at the price of any condescendence. "As the world absorbed the gods in the poets, the world is sublimated in the Absolute in the philosophers. Then the infinite is manifested in the finite, but not to the finite."[8] Order is restored, denying "the extra-*ordinary* surplus of proximity between the finite and the infinite"[9] which is the meaning of our life, albeit a surplus over the meaning that can appear in logically coherent discourse.

> Would not the idea of a truth whose manifestation is not glorious or brilliant, the idea of a truth manifested in its humility. . . a persecuted truth, be the only possible modality of transcendence? Not because of the moral quality of humility, which I would not deny in any case, but because of its *way of being* which is perhaps the source of its moral value. To be manifested as humble, as allied with the defeated, the poor, and the outcast, is precisely not to restore order. . . Humility and poverty are a manner of being in Being, an ontological (or mé-ontological) mode, and not a social condition. To be presented in the poverty of exile is to interrupt the coherence of the universe.[10]

Transcendence appears in this ambiguity or incognito, in face of which the soul alternates between belief and atheism, taking the risk of transcendence instead of the satisfaction of certitude. One can ask whether the true God can ever raise His incognito to enter the history of the historians. "One can ask whether the first word of revelation should [rather] come from man, as in the ancient prayer of the Jewish liturgy in which the faithful give thanks not for what is received but for the very fact of giving thanks."[11] Is it not too much for God's poverty and too little for His glory that he should become *present* as a Thou? Doesn't the true God always withdraw, so that the face of my neighbor is inserted between me and Him? God excites an infinite Desire and so cannot be incarnated in something Desirable.[12]

Secondly, the Christian idea of the transubstantiation of Creator to creature in the man-God suggests the idea of substitution, which Levinas regards as the meaning of subjectivity. Incarnation means exposure, being hostage to the suffering of others to the point of revoking the identity of self, emptying the self of being.

> But the analysis that leads to my conclusions does not start from a God, or from a spirit, person, soul, or *animal rationale*. Each of these terms is an identical substance. But the business of the self is to revoke its identity. How can an other be expected to sacrifice himself for me without requiring the sacrifice of still others [for him]? How can his responsibility for me be admitted without immediately finding myself, by my hostage's condition, responsible for his very responsibility? To be a self means always to have an extra responsibility.
> The idea of the hostage, of my expiation for the Other—in which relations grounded on exact proportion between fault and punishment, freedom and responsibility (relations which transform collectivities into a society of limited responsibility) are upset—cannot be extended beyond me. The fact of being exposed to the burden imposed by the suffering and fault of others posits the selfhood of the self. I myself am the only one I can victimize without cruelty. The Self is the one who, prior to any decision, is elected to bear the whole responsibility of the World. Messianism is this apogee in Being, an overthrowing of the being that "perseveres in its being"—which begins with me.[13]

Levinas thus draws limits beyond which the Christian conception is an infringement of transcendence. The first forbids the surpassing of God's incognito, the unveiling, the Resurrection and Gospel: the idea of a face-to-face relation with the Infinite. The second forbids the shifting of my own responsibility to other shoulders, a fulfillment of messianism in someone other than myself. Christ is Messiah in a way other men cannot be; the grace that occurs in him interrupts the moral order. But the Other is not the gratification of a pious wish, or relief from the moral burden. Beyond all "opinions of faith" regarding who Christ was and what he did, true messianic seriousness is the critical imposition of the moral burden above every lesser seriousness. Morality rejects the idea of God's infinite pardon, which only invites infinite evil.[14]

As a Christian, Barth must ascribe negative significance to the Jewish rejection of the Incarnation.[15] To scruple over the proper form of transcendence can be a way of not listening to God.

> Has not the rejection of Jesus by the Jews made it shatteringly clear that it was possible to accept the God of the Old Testament in what seemed to be the most profound reverence and the most zealous faith and yet in fact to deny Him to the extent that His form, now become quite concrete, became an offense to the righteous? Or what other objection could Israel bring against Jesus apart from the divine self-unveiling which now, not for the first time, but for the first time quite unequivocally, encountered it, making, as it were, bodily contact with it?[16]

The Old Testament that poses only an unsolved problem, knowing only an unknown and hidden God--divorcing the expectation from the fulfillment--is a Jewish abstraction.[17]

> We will, therefore, if we sink to the level of the Jewish attitude to the Old Testament, again regard Christ as a mere sign or symbol, a mere witness to the real togetherness of God and man. . . Just because the signs and witnesses of the Old Testament point to the real togetherness of God and men, unlike the symbols and symbol-bearers of heathendom, they do not point to the empty space of metaphysical ideal truth, but to coming history.[18]

Because Israel rejects Revelation, what it does point to is the "void,"[19] to "metaphysical ideal truths."

Israel rejects God and is rejected by God and stands as a sign of His judgment; but the concept of Israel, like the concept of the church of Esau, pertains to Barth's all-inclusive understanding of double predestination. We have to become Jews to become Christians; we too reject and are rejected. This puts (in 1938) the burning issue of anti-Semitism in an ironic light. It is characteristic of the bad conscience of the Christian that he avoids the necessity for becoming a Jew by joining in the judgment of Israel, instead of joining Israel the judged--as if the Christian could judge any sin but his own!

Salvation means alienation, and "salvation is of the Jews" (John 4:22). And because man will not be alienated, even for his own salvation, he rolls away the alienation on to the Jew. In that way it all becomes so simple. We can find so many grievances against the Jew. Once we have raised even our little finger in Anti-Semitism, we can produce such vital and profound reasons in favor of it, and they will all apply equally well to the Bible, not only to the Old but also to the New Testament, not only to the Rabbi Paul but also to the Rabbi Jesus of Nazareth of the first three Gospels. And we have to ask: What offence that we can take at the Bible is more pressing and goes deeper and is more general than the offence which it offers here? For if the liberal solution ["occasional pleas for humanity"], which is no solution, collapses, how can we not be Anti-Semitic? At this point we need the miracle of the Word and faith if the offence is to cease, the perversion to be overcome, the Anti-Semitism in us all eliminated, the word of man, the Jewish word of the Bible, heard and accepted as the Word of God.[20]

Barth proposes a Christian solidarity with Jews in their sin, because it is part of the truth of man's situation; but that does not remove the undesirableness of the role. In second *Romans* Barth writes that the highest form of religion is the religion of the prophets and psalmists of Israel, "which is nowhere excelled, certainly not in the history of Christianity, and not even in the so-called 'Religion of Jesus'";[21] but this is in the context of the condemnation of all religion. God suffers religion in spite of itself.

Barth and Levinas are not to be seen as the archetypal Christian versus the archetypal Jew. No doubt better examples could be chosen for that purpose. But one *is* a Christian, and the other *is* a Jew: the accepter of Incarnation is defined by his acceptance and the rejecter by his rejection, and these definitions must control to some extent the development of their respective conceptions of Otherness.[22] But we must remember that Levinas speaks as a philosopher, proposing a universal sense. It is more pertinent and suggestive to consider the difference between Barth and Levinas as a function of the new ways in which they respectively establish theological and philosophical reason. How do the idea of the Other and the Argument to the Other affect the relationship between *theology* and *philosophy* on the models provided by Barth and Levinas?

2. Theology and Philosophy

Barth and Levinas both argue to the Other. For both, the lynchpin of the argument is an especially radical idea of the totally Other whose very Otherness becomes a heuristic key to questions about the ultimate presuppositions of theology and philosophy, as well as the principal gesture by which the argument is deflected from its return to self-certainty and pointed outward to the Other, as an apology for self. For both, the idea of the totally Other must be more than an idea in order to be totally Other--it actually represents the calling-into-question of the self (especially the self posed as the theoretical subject) by an Other *One*, a person who is on the scene without further apologies, and who in his complete superiority to any challenge turns the tables on the self and opens the problem of the self's justification. The "idea of the Infinite" is concrete, not a checker to be jumped arbitrarily across the intellectual gameboard. But this means that the thinker who has the idea of the Infinite is not at liberty to construe its content; it is "formal" not in lacking a matter but in evoking the "empty signification" that transcends any fulfilling intuition, i.e. the language that exceeds experience. That *is* its matter.[23] But the empty signification is not launched into the void of a general Questionableness of human freedom. It belongs in the context of a vis-à-vis, a personal relationship established by the claims of God and the neighbor. The theologian and the philosopher are bound by particular responsibilities. They both begin, albeit in different ways, with a *revelation*, which is to say: with the concrete (in the sense of primary, underivable, irreducible meaning) as the personal. The event of revelation that grounds Barth's theology is the church's proclamation of God's revelation in Jesus Christ. The event of revelation that grounds Levinas' philosophy is the appeal of the human face; more precisely, the face in the trace of God.

Barth and Levinas are not free to alter or adjust their starting points, and neither are we free in interpreting them to adjust their arguments so as to produce a desired juxtaposition. But a significant juxtaposition does appear, nevertheless, in taking Barth and Levinas purely on their own terms. *There are different revelations. Election and obedience may be differently determined. And a normative divergence and even competition between theology and philosophy* (by which we mean Christian theology on the one hand and philosophy in the European tradition on the other) *may be established by the advents of different Others, imposing different problems (and solutions) of justification.* There is divergence in the fact that the theologian begins with God while the philosopher begins with man. But Barth cannot give sense to the divine revelation apart from its practical determination of human existence as moral existence; and Levinas cannot give sense to the moral life without pointing beyond the human to the divine. So there is competition, too. The different accounts bear on the same topics. Both gestures of obedience are ultimately serious, and for that reason neither can accept a position subordinate to the other. Both are driven to speak of the two incommensurable but allied magnitudes of the personal order, God and man.

Levinas' philosophical theology, from Barth's point of view, is perhaps a particularly sophisticated, attractive, and biblically informed thought, but a backwards thought nonetheless. It endeavors to give sense to God on the basis of the sense of man, to reverse the right theological order from above to below. The interhuman transcendence of the moral life is a part of creation, to be distinguished from the Creator. Even the "infinitization" of the moral order signifies in a wider context, the truth of man's divine determination in Jesus Christ. Barth's affirmation that the Other Person is a sign instituted by Christ directly contradicts Levinas' claim that the Other Person's face is a "signification without a context," notwithstanding the profound affinities between the two claims in their background, their impact, and the behavior they require. The contradiction is the more remarkable for the fact that Barth at one time occupied a position extremely close to that of Levinas. The statements in second *Romans* about the essential hiddenness of God and the essential link between this hiddenness and the "practical disturbance" of human life and the neighbor's Otherness confronting me daily are very suggestive of rapprochement between the two. But Barth must be viewed in his whole development, which he understood to be a gradual disentanglement from *mixophilosophicotheologia,*[24] including the Kantian

ethical religion mediated to him by Cohen and Herrmann at Marburg, as well as the Wholly-Otherism compounded from Kierkegaard
and Overbeck. This is the burden of his discussion of the relation between the First and Second Commandments in *Church Dogmatics* I/2: to show (as he believed) that the Christian takes
the moral life no less seriously than the non-Christian, not
despite but because of the context or perspective in which it
is placed by the Christian revelation. The particular Other to
whom the Christian theologian strives to be obedient *particularly* requires "infinitization" in life and in theology.

In 1960 Barth contributed an article on "Philosophie
und Theologie" to a festschrift for his philosopher-brother
Heinrich.[25] Here he emphasizes the difference in priority by
which philosophers and theologians pursue the indivisible truth,
philosophers thinking from creation to Creator and theologians
from Creator to creation.[26] When philosophy attempts to reverse
its order, it becomes crypto-theology; and the confusion of
crypto-philosophizing is the fate of a theology too interested
in, say, "orders of creation" for their own sake. The theologian, commanded by the whole truth in Jesus Christ, can only be
objectively (*sachlich*) intolerant of the philosopher's claims,
but his intolerance is relative to the fact that neither he nor
the philosopher possesses the truth. Neither can speak from
heaven. They are *Mitmenschen*, co-responsible, needing to learn
from each other and to remind each other that they have their
differences.[27] Barth does not envision a philosophy of Levinas'
sort, unless it would qualify as crypto-theology by virtue of
its movement from above (the Good) to below (Being). The one
point at which Barth does address and even prescribe a philosophy like Levinas' is in his ethics lectures of 1928, where he
says that the proper role of philosophical ethics is to call
attention to a Wholly Other in the form of the human other (so
that the ego may be critically reminded that it is not alone in
the world).[28]

Levinas no more disdains God or scripture than Barth
disdains ethics. The idea of God is philosophically incumbent
upon he who would understand the meaning of the moral life; the
scriptural witness to human relations with the transcendent may
be an irreplaceable scaffolding by which one climbs out to

awareness of this meaning, to be respected and conserved. But
there is no divine revelation that is not primarily a moral
revelation. As is true for both Judaism and philosophy, beyond
this-worldly morality "everything else is chimerical."[29] Levinas
does not necessarily deny all legitimacy to theology. He is
critical of ontologism in theology, but not of the possibility
that a religious discourse would "know more" than a philosophical discourse could.[30] Barth's theology certainly does not
presuppose the selfish concern for one's own eternal happiness,
the infantile unworldliness, the "participation" in Being or in
a drama whose real meaning remains unknown to the participant,
or the anti-rational "violence of the sacred" that Levinas criticizes in religion. But Barth does "know more." One who does
not know what Barth knows can hardly accept it and bear witness
to it, but neither need he rule out the seriousness of the
election and responsibility involved in Barth's enterprise. Has
not Barth done more than most to point out the questionableness
of the phenomenon of "religion"?

One cannot apologize for the Other; one has to apologize
to the Other. The primary accountability in the game of giving
reasons has already been pinned down, according to this irreversible relation of "height," which defines the good existence.
This is as true of Levinas' ethical existence as of Barth's
theological existence. This is precisely why there is incom-
patibility and competition between the different conceptions of
God and man, because they are existence-determining--and each
of us has but one existence to determine. The great interest
in this particular opposition between Barth and Levinas is that
it suggests a certain interpretation of the actual tension that
we do find between theology and philosophy, and also within
theology insofar as theologians account to man as well as to
God. Let us treat this interpretation as a normative model.
The model departs from the stereotyped opposition of "faith" to
"reason," because both Levinas' philosophy and Barth's theology
require "faith," in the sense of a surpassing of experience,
and "reason," in the sense of an enactment in language of
acceptable service of the Other. Instead the conflict is between Incarnation-faith and ethical faith, between Christ-reason
(or God-reason via Christ) and man-reason (or God-reason via

the neighbor *tout court*). The difference between Christ-reason and man-reason, which is between two responsibilities--not between two interpretations of "responsibility," since "responsibility" does not occur as a general thing awaiting specification, and the subjective initiative of "interpretation" is always preceded and commanded by an actual responsibility--highlights the true seriousness of the difference between theology and philosophy, which underlies their manifold disagreements about the structure of reason and the nature of reality. Barth's Christianity and Levinas' humanism, perhaps unlike some other Christianities and humanisms, do not quietly compare notes in a joint quest for a more adequate or inspiring or socially progressive picture of the universe. With Barth and Levinas we are nearer in spirit to Luther and Marx, i.e. to an earnest Christian rejection of humanism and an earnest humanist rejection of religion, based in both cases on non-negotiable principles of responsibility.

Our Christian believes in the event of God becoming a man, in spite of the improbability of the fact of it and the moral or religious questionableness of the idea of it, because, having heard God speak in this way and being unable to pretend that he has not heard God speak, he is bound to take the event and its implications more seriously than the various reasons that are advanced against it. Of course, he is also an unbeliever: but he confesses that his belief is a better possibility than his unbelief, so far better that his unbelief is excluded. It is better to believe that God will redeem the world than that only human efforts will avail to improve it; better to believe that only God reckons righteousness than that good and evil are humanly assignable predicates; better to believe that Christ rose than that all things pass away; and so forth. God's purpose is superior to the most well-meaning human purposes arrayed apart from it and thus against it. The best humanism is but a variation on the pride of man by which he rejects God and attempts to justify himself. Man without God simply cannot be concerned for man, even the other man, except with the sinful distortions that mark his whole life of disobedience to God.

Our philosopher, on the contrary, believes in an event of man meeting man that transcends Being and interest, an availability of man for man so radical as to constitute a hostage's condition, which is presupposed by everything that passes for civility and peace in the violent world--even the little civility that obtains between philosophers and theologians. This humanism is the concretissimum against which all theological abstractions must founder; the moral a priori of human justice disallows any claimed priorities that would direct our ultimate interest and attention elsewhere. No recollection of a past event or expectation of a future life can justify material oppression of the other person. One must acknowledge the truly serious reasons that philosophers have had for denying God-- such as (for example) Marx's belief that religion impedes the evolution of a just society and the cultivation of man's humanity. Now Levinas does not deny God. But he only allows himself to speak of God under the control of these moral, humanistic presuppositions. In either case, philosophical seriousness analyzes into a way of caring for man, the putting of a certain responsibility first, a prior election by the problem of man as the problem of goodness. Theologians too are men and speak to men. Whatever they say is subject to critique, for their speech inevitably serves certain worldly interests, at the same time that it presupposes the pacific disinterestedness of the moral relation if it is speech at all. The theologian cannot argue that something is superior to that relation without violating it.[31]

Our model does not allow an abstract opposition between Reason and Faith, or Value, or God. Either an Other makes a claim or not; either a person is on the scene (or leaves a trace on the scene) or not. If so, a condition of seriousness exists. Reason then arises, according to Levinas, in the balancing of claims, in the fact that I cannot serve all my neighbors equally and at once, but must somehow decide which responsibilities come first. "Reason" is a modification of the infinite obsession of one man with the welfare of any other. The language with which men address each other is a modification of witnessing and glorifying the Infinite. Theological reason, according to Barth, arises in the critical comparison of the church's proclamation

with the authoritative witness of Scripture to Revelation, i.e.
as a modification of the infinite accountability of man to God
by the specific terms of the commission given by God, as we
have it in this witness, to proclaim His Word. Neither of these
conceptions of Reason is "epistemological" (tied to an alleged
necessary structure of knowing) or "ontological" (tied to an
alleged necessary structure of being). Both knowing and being
are brought into line with the curiously empty but transcending
concretissimum of relation with the *totaliter aliter*.

The Argument to the Other is, therefore, not one but
many. Because the Other is not an abstraction, it matters *who*
the Other is, who is on the scene. And the fact is that more
than one Other is on the scene. There is a plurality of neighbors, toward whom the transcending gesture of service takes the
form of the reasonable arguments of philosophy; there is God in
Christ, toward whom transcending language becomes the reasonable arguments of Christian theology, heard differently by
believers and non-believers. Theology in turn reaches toward
humanity, as theological anthropology and ethics, while philosophy reaches toward the infinity of God in responding to the
enigmatic goodness of just relation with the neighbor, in the
form of philosophical theology. The emphasizing and discounting
and agreeing and disagreeing between the different viewpoints
fits a pattern and acquires its seriousness in relation to the
primary responsibilities to which the different thinkers are
elected.

It really is our everyday practice to analyze reason in
this fashion, as a matter of seriousness and responsibility.
There are people who believe that no astronaut has travelled in
space or landed on the moon--that the whole enterprise was a
television stunt. There are people who believe the earth is
flat. It is theoretically possible to argue with a flat-earther
forever without being able to convince him that the earth is
round, if he is not willing to accept the authorities and rules
by which such a thing is provable. In the end one is driven
back on the question, *Why* is it important to you to argue the
way you do? What is at stake for you in denying that the earth
is round, or that astronauts have left it and stood on the moon?
That is, if I am not to dismiss your contention as capricious,

unserious, and irresponsible, I must have something to go on other than the logical non-absurdity of your counter-position; as far as I can see there is no *reason* for you to fly in the face of publicly acknowledged fact. You are perhaps "rational," but ultimately unreasonable (stubborn, resentful, cantankerous?).

With disbelief in God the situation can be very different. It may be claimed that belief in God is against "Reason," going by a conception of Reason that is considered indispensable for the maintenance of theoretical sanity and practical justice in human affairs. For example, if scientific intelligibility is thought to depend on the possibility of unlimited causal explanation, it may be thought contrary to science, and thus intellectually incoherent and damaging, to assert the existence of Someone not subject to the observable causal network. Or the idea of a God superior to any human conception of the Good may be considered a license for violence. Conceptions of Reason are to a certain extent open to discussion, but they partake of the seriousness of our human life together; Reason generally means peace, and non-reason war, and the menace of the latter produces the urgency of the former. When it is specifically claimed that belief in God's incarnation in Jesus Christ is against moral reason, because it entails an unjust limitation of the responsibility of every man for every other, a dishonest reliance on the efficacy of the Atonement, etc., the conflicting seriousness is plain to see, and the conflict is correspondingly more difficult to debate. There is no alternative model the superiority of which one could demonstrate. There is no theoretical bias to criticize or clear up. One either hears and obeys the Holy Spirit on this point, or one. . . doesn't.

The formal undecidability of a pure conflict between responsibilities (even if any two men can only suggest, never perfectly execute such a conflict) reflects the non-coercive "sweet" reason of the arguments that we have tried to show. The personal is the order of appeal rather than demonstration. When Christ says, "But who do you say that I am?" (Matthew 16:15), he does not expect arguments to be marshalled or evidences to be weighed. He expects the Word of God to be hearkened to. That the Word is not hearkened to by the world is not a neutral fact but the scandal of sin, and the world's sin does not reduce to the possibility that its view of itself could be improved, could be more nuanced or comprehensive. It is a mystery of the heart.

The presumption by which we set up Barth's and Levinas' arguments as irreducibly competitive paradigms of theology and philosophy is really a corollary of the presumption of their shared Argument. Only by virtue of their common gesture of arguing to the Other can they think from such purely irreconcilable starting points for theological and philosophical reason, viz. differently identified personal Others. If the Others were only relatively other, it would be possible to consider neutrally which has the precedence, based on logical possibility or empirical probability or axiological impressiveness. But they are *wholly* Other, which means they are absolved from that kind of weighing and comparing. They are that by which we weigh--that which weighs.

Barth and Levinas are unusual figures with which to exhibit the normative relationship between theology and philosophy, since their arguments go against the grain of most theology and philosophy. They represent a counter-movement to many of the main trends of modern Western thought. An index of the magnitude of the counter-movement is the inordinateness of the concept of the *totaliter aliter* and the disturbances that seem to flow from it in the arguments of Levinas and Barth. We have tried to show what is at stake with this idea in different ways: as a triumph of a species of practical over theoretical reason, as a problem of justification superior to the problem of freedom or the solution of History, as an appreciation of the personal order in its difference from the ontological, and as the grounding of theology and philosophy. Finally we have considered the divergence between the theology of the one and the philosophy of the other as a function of the fact that the direction of the Argument to the Other is utterly dependent upon the unforeseeable identity of the Other and the nature of his claim. To go farther, to truly be taught by Barth and Levinas--which means to be referred to the Others to whom they witness--would involve a redirection of our attention from the formal similarities of their gestures to the objects of their gestures, from "scholarly existence" to theological and/or ethical existence, to actual service. John the Baptist becomes impatient if one stares too long at his outstretched finger.

LIST OF ABBREVIATIONS

1. Works of Karl Barth

"Antwort"	"Antwort an D. Achelis und D. Drews," 1909
CD	*Die christliche Dogmatik*, 1927
CGG	"Der christliche Glaube und die Geschichte," 1912
FQI	*Fides Quaerens Intellectum*, 1931
GPG	"Der Glaube an den persönlichen Gott," 1914
KD	*Die kirchliche Dogmatik*, 1932-1967 (*Church Dogmatics*)
MTR	"Moderne Theologie und Reichsgottesarbeit," 1909
"Nachwort"	"Nachwort" to *Schleiermacher-Auswahl*, 1968 ("Concluding Unscientific Postscript on Schleiermacher")
R^1	*Der Römerbrief*, 1st ed., 1919
R^2	*Der Römerbrief*, 2nd ed., 1922 (*The Epistle to the Romans*)
RTM	*Revolutionary Theology in the Making*, 1914-1925
TFA	*Theologische Fragen und Antworten*, 1957
TK	*Die Theologie und die Kirche*, 1928 (*Theology and Church*)
WGT	*Das Wort Gottes und die Theologie*, 1924 (*The Word of God and the Word of Man*)

2. Works of Emmanuel Levinas

AE	*Autrement qu'être ou au-delà de l'essence*, 1974 (*Otherwise than Being or Beyond Essence*)
DEHH	*En découvrant l'existence avec Husserl et Heidegger*, 2nd ed., 1967
"Dieu"	"Dieu et la philosophie," 1975 ("God and Philosophy")
DL	*Difficile liberté*, 2nd ed., 1976
EE	*De l'existence à l'existant*, 1947 (*Existence and Existents*)
HAH	*Humanisme de l'autre homme*, 1972
LC	"Liberté et commandement," 1953
"Moi"	"Le moi et la totalité," 1954
OF	"L'ontologie est-elle fondamentale?," 1951
Q&R	"Questions et réponses," 1977

TA   *Le Temps et l'Autre* (1947)

TH   "Transcendance et hauteur," 1962

TI   *Totalité et Infini*, 1961 (*Totality and Infinity*)

TIPH   *La théorie de l'intuition dans la phénoménologie de Husserl*, 1930 (*The Theory of Intuition in Husserl's Phenomenology*)

NOTES

Chapter I

1. *Die Kirchliche Dogmatik* (KD) (Zurich: EVZ, 1938-1967 [1st ed. of I/1 published by Chr. Kaiser in Munich, 1932]). Citations of literature in this study will uniformly be of the original-language editions, followed in parentheses by page numbers for the English translations that are used (otherwise my translation). The English editions are listed in the Bibliography.

2. *How I Changed My Mind* (Richmond: John Knox, 1966), p. 43.

3. It is possible to argue that both were influenced by Hermann Cohen, but not too much can be made of this. In Barth's case the influence is patent, since Cohen taught him at Marburg and seems to have determined his conception of philosophy, at least through second *Romans*, where Cohen's idea of the Origin (*Ursprung*), interpreted as the radically non-given presupposition of all knowing and being, is frequently cited and contributes to the notion of the Wholly Other. Levinas is almost completely silent regarding Cohen, however, and there is no evidence that Cohen's Origin influenced him. But Levinas does pay homage to Franz Rosenzweig, who in turn had great respect for Cohen as "the master." Rosenzweig saw himself allied with Cohen in his own opposition to Hegelian totality (which so impressed Levinas in *Totality and Infinity*): "Thus even if Cohen, the master, would be far from admitting it, we are continuing to build on the great scientific achievement of his logic of origins, the new concept of the Nought. For the rest he may have been, in the execution of his ideas, more of a Hegelian than he admitted--and thereby as much of an 'Idealist' as he claimed to be. Here, however, in this basic idea, he broke decisively with the idealistic tradition. He replaced the one and universal Nought, that veritable 'no-thing' which, like a zero, really can be nothing more than reality. There he took his stand in most decided opposition precisely to Hegel's founding of logic on the concept of Being, and thereby in turn to the whole philosophy into whose inheritance Hegel had come"--*Der Stern der Erlösung* (3rd ed.; Heidelberg: Lambert Schneider, 1954), p. 30f. (21). Levinas simply takes Cohen at his word, i.e. as an idealist; cf. "Le nom de Dieu d'après quelques textes talmudiques. Discussion," in *Débats sur le langage théologique*, ed. E. Castelli (Paris: Aubier, 1969), p. 69. But Edith Wyschogrod finds Levinas in "significant [albeit mainly tacit] conversation" with Cohen, especially his later views--"The Moral Self: Emmanuel Levinas and Hermann Cohen," *DAAT*, No. 4 (1980), 35-58.

4. *Der Römerbrief* (R²) (2nd ed.; Munich: Chr. Kaiser, 1922).

5. *Totalité et Infini* (TI) (The Hague: Martinus Nijhoff, 1961).

6. TI 3 (33).

7. TI is subtitled "An Essay on Exteriority." "Exteriority" signifies both the beyondness of the absolutely Other and an eminent sense of objectivity that does not depend on subjectivity for its meaning--cf. TI 266 (290).

8. "La philosophie et l'idée de l'Infini," in *En découvrant l'existence avec Husserl et Heidegger* (DEHH) (2nd ed.; Paris: Vrin, 1967), p. 174.

9. "Die Menschlichkeit Gottes," *Theologische Studien*, No. 48 (1956), p. 8 (43).

10. But Levinas' philosophy is a philosophy of God, as becomes increasingly clear in his later thought; so it cannot be ruled out that the context of his thought is theological, though it is surely not theological in the same way that Barth's thought is.

11. "In spite of everything, I think that what I do is phenomenology, even if it is not according to the rules laid down by Husserl, even if the entire Husserlian methodology is not observed"--"Questions et réponses" (Q&R), *Le Nouveau Commerce*, Nos. 36-37 (1977), p. 72.

12. Unless Barth is interpreted as a phenomenologist-- cf. H. J. Adriaanse's comparison of Barth and Husserl in his thesis *Zu den Sachen selbst* (The Hague: Mouton, 1974).

13. See below, Chapter IV.

14. *Fides quaerens intellectum* (FQI) (Munich: Chr. Kaiser, 1931).

15. *Autrement qu'être ou au-delà de l'essence* (AE) (The Hague: Martinus Nijhoff, 1974).

16. "Dieu et la philosophie" ("Dieu"), *Le Nouveau Commerce*, Nos. 30-31 (1975), 97-128.

17. Primarily represented by "La réalité et son ombre," *Les Temps Modernes*, 4 (1948), 771-789, and by the articles collected in *Sur Maurice Blanchot* and *Noms propres* (Montpellier: Fata Morgana, 1975 and 1976).

18. Primarily represented by the collection *Difficile liberté* (DL) (2nd ed.; Paris: Albin Michel, 1976), and by the three series of Talmudic lectures, *Quatre lectures talmudiques*, *Du sacré au saint*, and *L'au-delà du verset* (Paris: Minuit, 1968, 1977 and 1982).

Chapter II

1. The following exposition of Barth's thought between 1909 and 1922, like the other expository chapters on Barth and Levinas, is selectively oriented to the development of his concept of the Other, though on the assumption that this development has very much to do with the progress of his whole theology and cannot be described in isolation from this progress. For a more complete survey of this period and evaluation of influences on Barth, see Henri Bouillard, *Karl Barth* (3 vols.), Vol. 1: *Genèse et évolution de la théologie dialectique* (Paris: Aubier, 1957); two books by Eberhard Busch, *Karl Barth und die Pietisten* (Munich: Chr. Kaiser, 1978), and *Karl Barths Lebenslauf* (Munich: Chr. Kaiser, 1975); Peter H. Monsma, *Karl Barth's Idea of Revelation* (Somerville, N.J.: Somerset, 1937); and James D. Smart, *The Divided Mind of Modern Theology* (Philadelphia: Westminster, 1967). An especially good study of the crucial shift between the two editions of Barth's *Römerbrief* is Nico T. Bakker's *In der Krisis der Offenbarung*, tr. W. Bunte

(Neukirchen-Vluyn: Neukirchener Verlag, 1974). See also James S. Walker's Claremont dissertation *The development of Karl Barth's theology from the first edition of Der Römerbrief through the second edition of Der Römerbrief* (1963).

2. Barth to Thurneysen, Sept. 4, 1914 (RTM 26). Citations of the Barth-Thurneysen correspondence will be by date, so that they may be found either in the complete edition--*Barth-Thurneysen Briefwechsel* (2 vols.) (Zurich: TVZ, 1973, 1974)-- or in the portions published earlier in Barth and Thurneysen festschrifts, collected in *Karl Barth-Eduard Thurneysen: Ein Briefwechsel aus der Frühzeit der dialektischen Theologie* (Munich: Siebenstern, 1966)--ET *Revolutionary Theology in the Making* (RTM), tr. J. D. Smart (Richmond: John Knox, 1964). An RTM page reference will be given when that translation is available.

For an investigation of the actual effect of early war events on Barth, see Wilfried Härle, "Der Aufruf der 93 Intellektuellen und Karl Barths Bruch mit der liberalen Theologie," *Zeitschrift für Theologie und Kirche*, 72 (1975), 207-224; and Jochen Fähler, *Der Ausbruck des 1. Weltkrieges in Karl Barths Predigten 1913-1915* (Bern: P. Lang, 1979).

3. Busch 57-63 (46-52).

4. Barth to Thurneysen, Sept. 4, 1914 (RTM 27).

5. (MTR), *Zeitschrift für Theologie und Kirche*, 19 (1909), 317-321.

6. MTR 318.

7. MTR 317.

8. "Antwort an D. Achelis und D. Drews" ("Antwort"), *Zeitschrift für Theologie und Kirche*, 19 (1909), 479-486.

9. Cf. "Die dogmatische Prinzipienlehre bei Wilhelm Herrmann," in *Die Theologie und die Kirche* (TK) (Munich: Chr. Kaiser, 1928), pp. 248f. (244f.), for Barth's discussion of this point.

10. "Antwort" 484.

11. "Antwort" 485.

12. (CGG), *Schweizerische Theologische Zeitschrift*, 29 (1912), 1-18, 49-72.

13. CGG 5.

14. CGG 54.

15. CGG 57.

16. CGG 71f.

17. (GPG), *Zeitschrift für Theologie und Kirche*, 24 (1914), 21-32, 65-95. Cf. Barth to Thurneysen, May 4, 1913.

18. See Barth's articles "Schleiermachers 'Weihnachtsfeier'" (1924) and "Schleiermacher" (1926), where the devaluation of words is taken to be symptomatic of the fundamental intention (and mistake) of this theology--TK 133f. (156f.), 138f. (161).

19. GPG 23f.

20. GPG 89.

21. GPG 94.

22. "Antwort" 484. The war threw a different light on Schleiermacher as the founding father of modern theology: "Had not even he in the first edition of his *Speeches* from 1799 written impossible things about the British and the French? Had he not also been a leading Prussian patriot from 1806 to 1814? Would he also perhaps have signed that manifesto [the 'Manifesto of 93 German Intellectuals' defending Germany's part in the war; see Härle, *op. cit.*]? . . . According to what I

know of his letters from the period after 1815, I remain convinced that, no, he would not have done that. Nevertheless, it
was still the case that the entire theology which had unmasked
itself in that manifesto, and everything which followed after
it (even in the *Christliche Welt*), was grounded, determined,
and influenced decisively by him"--"Nachwort" to *Schleiermacher-
Auswahl*, ed. H. Bolli (Munich: Siebenstern, 1968), p. 294 (120).
 23. "Antwort" 480.
 24. "Antwort" 486.
 25. Cf. Monsma (*op. cit.*), pp. 32-35.
 26. E.g. CGG 72 and GPG 87.
 27. His 1911 lecture "Jesus Christus und die soziale
Bewegung," in *Der freie Aargauer*, 6, Nos. 153-156 (Dec. 23, 26,
28, and 30, 1911), shows that the confrontation with the practical problem of industrial poverty in Safenwil had put academic
theology in a place of only secondary importance for him compared with the issue of socialism (cf. "Nachwort" 292 [119];
see Friedrich-Wilhelm Marquardt, *Theologie und Sozialismus:
Das Beispiel Karl Barths* [Munich: Chr. Kaiser, 1972], for an
investigation of the links between socialism and the different
stages of Barth's theology). Härle has even suggested that the
death of Fritz Barth in 1912 gave rise, in Freudian terms, to a
"deferred obedience" of the liberal son to the anti-liberal
father!--cf. the preface to R^1, "Nachwort" 294f. (121), and
Barth to Thurneysen, Jan. 20, 1915. Thurneysen, who was instru-
mental in Barth's deepening acquaintance with the Swiss religious socialists, also knew the younger Blumhardt personally and
was able to introduce Barth to him.
 28. See Busch 96ff. (83ff.).
 29. See Barth's article on Naumann and Blumhardt,
"Vergangenheit und Zukunft," in *Anfänge der dialektischen Theologie (Anfänge)* (2 vols.), ed. J. Moltmann (Munich: Chr.
Kaiser, 1963), Vol. 1, pp. 37-49 (35-45), and Thurneysen's book
Christoph Blumhardt (Munich: Chr. Kaiser, 1926), for the Barth-
Thurneysen view of Blumhardt. For an appraisal of Blumhardt's
influence on Barth see J. Berger, *Die Verwurzelung des theologischen Denkens Karl Barths in dem Kerygma der beiden Blumhardts
vom Reiche Gottes* (Berlin: Humboldt U. Inaugural Dissertation,
1955), for a strong claim; and for qualifications of that claim,
see G. Sauter, *Die Theologie des Reiches Gottes beim älteren
und jüngeren Blumhardt* (Zurich: Zwingli, 1962), pp. 235-267.
 30. "Auf das Reich Gottes warten," in *Suchet Gott, so
werdet ihr leben!* by Barth and Thurneysen (2nd ed.; Zurich:
Evangelischen Buchhandlung Zollikon, 1928), p. 176 (21).
 31. Barth said in 1934, "Once I was a religious socialist. I discarded it because I believed I saw that religious
socialism failed to take as serious and profound a view of man's
misery, and of the help for him, as do the Holy Scriptures"--
"Der Christ als Zeuge," *Theologische Existenz Heute*, No. 12
(1934), p. 21 (125).
 32. "Auf das Reich Gottes warten" 177f. (23).
 33. Attested in a letter of July 27, 1916, to Thurneysen
(RTM 38) about the same time as the writing of the Blumhardt
review--Busch 104 (92).
 34. "Nachwort" 294 (120); Busch 109f. (97).
 35. "Die Gerechtigkeit Gottes," in WGT, p. 5 (10).
 36. Barth to Thurneysen, Sept. 27, 1917 (RTM 43). A
similar awe appears in a comment on Calvin in 1922: "Calvin is
a cataract, a primeval forest, a demonic power, something

directly down from Himalaya, absolutely Chinese, strange, myth-
ological; I lack completely the means, the suction cups, even
to assimilate this phenomenon, not to speak of presenting it
adequately"--Barth to Thurneysen, June 8, 1922 (RTM 101).

37. WGT 14 (23).

38. WGT 15 (24). Horton's translation relies on hind-
sight, inasmuch as the sloganistic usage "*the* Wholly Other"
does not precede Barth's 1919 reading of Otto (see below, p. 50).
The more casual usage of the phrase "*ganz andere*" is common in
Barth at all times. Here it is somewhat pointed, and worth
emphasis; but even in his prewar sermons Barth habitually contrasted the ways of man with the "*ganz andere*" ways of God:
"Es ist ein Glück, daß Gott ganz anders ist, als die Menschen
gewesen sind und noch sind. . . Gott ist and will etwas ganz
Anderes als ihr denkt! . . . *Gott ist anders*, als wir alle
bisher gedacht, anders, als im Gesetz und in den Propheten
beschrieben ist, anders auch, als der gewaltige Täufer ihn beschrieben hat"--*Predigten 1913*, ed. G. Sauter and N. Barth
(Zurich: TVZ, 1976), pp. 168, 249, 305.

39. "Die neue Welt in der Bibel," in WGT, p. 25 (39).

40. WGT 31 (48).

41. WGT 21 (32).

42. "Religion und Leben" (Lecture given on October 9,
1917, in Safenwil), first published in *Evangelische Theologie*,
10-11 (1951-1952), pp. 437f.

43. "Religion und Leben" 450.

44. In the first letter we have after Barth's sojourn
with Blumhardt of April 10-15, 1915, he says "it is a comfort
to have the firmest ground basically under one's feet and not
to be wholly alone" (April 22, 1915, RTM 29). He begins to
discuss the "tactics" of their "separation from the 'Others'"
(i.e. their fellow pastors) (May 5) and to worry about the
danger of adopting Gnostic airs (May 14, signed "*dein Mitpil-
ger*").

45. *Der Römerbrief* (R¹) (1st ed.; Bern: G. A. Bäschlin,
1919), p. 299.

46. Barth to Thurneysen, June 26, 1916 (RTM 37).

47. Barth's departure from this line in the second
edition of *Romans* is praised by Bultmann, who sheds light on
what Herrmann taught his pupils: "Herrmann--not exclusively,
but yet with strong emphasis--answered this question [of how
the believer comes to faith] by reference to a psychologically
understandable 'experience' ['*Erleben*'], to a process, a psychic
historical procedure, and in this he was not free from a trace
of pietism. His answer consists in the well-known theory of
rationally grounded obedience under the moral law, of the despair which is the end of this road, of the intervention of the
forgiving grace of God, revealed in Jesus, for which this is
the preparation. To ask and to answer the question of the way
to faith in this sense is false--Barth was right here. Even
Herrmann's students were often not fully satisfied with this
schema, which does not fit Paul at all"--"Karl Barths 'Römerbrief' in zweiter Auflage," in *Anfänge* I, p. 135 (114). Although Barth has attempted to purge this schema of its "trace
of pietism," it is still an important element of R¹. Cf.
Herrmann's *Ethik* (4th ed.; Tübingen: J. C. B. Mohr, 1909).

48. R¹ 52.

49. R¹ 57.

50. R¹ 69.

51. When Barth says, "At the beginning of all history stands a completely and consistently good will, as the ruling principle of the whole" (R[1] 279), the question naturally arises whether Barth means by "God" nothing other than the (Kantian) Good Will. Commenting on Romans 5:15-17, Barth portrays the divine way as human moral freedom: "Thus it is here simply a matter of whether the will shall be free and active, whether it shall become will. . . Where is the will that does not actually will this? Where is the conscience or soul that would not say Yes to the divine freedom? Has not the decisive word already been spoken in all of us, that freedom is greater than slavery?"--R[1] 142.

52. R[1] 330.
53. R[1] 332.
54. R[1] 338.
55. R[1] 357, 405.
56. R[1] 390.
57. R[1] 26.
58. R[1] 14.
59. R[1] 193.
60. E.g. R[1] 105, 227, 271. The neo-Kantian philosopher Hermann Cohen is the source of the "Origin" terminology--see Bakker (*op. cit.*), pp. 87-93; cf. George S. Hendry, "On Barth, the Philosopher," in *Faith and the Philosophers*, ed. John Hick (New York: St. Martin's, 1964), p. 213.
61. R[1] 43, 107.
62. R[1] 93f.
63. R[1] 83.
64. R[1] 62, 70, 155, 357.
65. R[1] 357.
66. R[1] 101.
67. Man as sinful has no "reason" that cannot be accounted for psychologically (R[1] 22); the power of historical-psychological relativism is the only power to be taken seriously under God's wrath (119, 164); the old Adam used his "freedom" to create the industrial order--"Have we not really seen through the teleology of the Adam-level, the radical worthlessness of our liberalism?" (177).

68. R[1] 206.
69. R[1] 326.
70. R[1] 88.
71. R[1] 292.
72. R[1] 105.
73. R[1] 118.
74. R[1] 379.
75. R[1] 7.
76. R[1] 48.
77. R[1] 10.
78. R[1] 51.
79. R[1] 388f.
80. R[1] 113.
81. R[1] 24, 113, 150f.
82. R[1] 252.
83. R[1] 79, 100, 124, 128f., 148, 153, 184, 227, 237, 250.
84. R[1] 156f.
85. R[1] 157.
86. E.g. R[1] 83, 95.
87. R[1] 137.

88. R^1 286.

89. "Der Christ in der Gesellschaft," in WGT, p. 33 (253).

90. WGT 36 (276f.).

91. Barth to Thurneysen, Sept. 11, 1919 (RTM 47).

92. Barth referred in R^1 to the embarrassing resemblance between the dully mechanical workings of the judgment of death and the construction of dogmatic textbooks—139.

93. WGT 39 (281f.).

94. WGT 49 (296), my translation.

95. WGT 51 (299).

96. WGT 51, 58 (300, 310). "Dialectical theology" was often charged with exactly this.

97. WGT 65 (320).

98. WGT 65 (321).

99. "Biblische Fragen, Einsichten und Ausblicke," in WGT, p. 86f. (77).

100. Busch 129 (116); cf. Heinrich Barth's lecture "Gotteserkenntnis," in *Anfänge* I, 221-255. The "wisdom of death" is associated also with Overbeck—WGT 91 (83). The superficial Platonism of R^1 (original existence in the Idea—separation therefrom—return thereto) owes more to Kutter and Kutter's view of Schelling, according to Bouillard (*op. cit.*, p. 104).

101. Thurneysen's book *Dostojewski* (Munich: Chr. Kaiser, 1921) was an inspiration to Barth as he wrote second *Romans* (Barth to Thurneysen, Aug. 3, 1921: RTM 59), and he reported that it was "read eagerly" in Göttingen even before second *Romans* appeared (Dec. 11). Barth has said that apart from his acquaintance with Dostoyevsky he could not have written either the first or the second draft of *Romans*—Introduction to Thurneysen-Barth correspondence 1921-1925 (RTM 72).

102. "Unerledigte Anfragen an die heutige Theologie," in TK, p. 3 (57).

103. T. F. Torrance (*Karl Barth: An Introduction to His Early Theology, 1910-1931* [London: SCM, 1962], pp. 71-80) sees Barth as the inheritor of the Schweitzer-Weiss-Overbeck "thoroughgoing eschatology" interpretation of Christianity, converting their sceptical minus into a plus.

104. Busch 128f. (116).

105. WGT 89 (80).

106. WGT 95 (91).

107. Barth to Thurneysen, Oct. 27, 1920 (RTM 53).

108. R^2 256f. (273).

109. While writing the second edition, Barth perceived a catastrophic shift taking place from Osiander to Luther (i.e. from "effective" to "forensic" justification)—Barth to Thurneysen, Dec. 3, 1920 (RTM 55).

110. "The word 'humanity' means unredeemed men and women; the word 'history' implies limitation and corruption; the pronoun 'I' spells judgment"—R^2 59 (85).

111. R^2 4, 21f. (28, 46)—cf. 56f. (82), the "Origin" *of the Crisis*. "The truth has encountered us from beyond a frontier we have never crossed; it is as though we had been transfixed by an arrow launched at us from beyond an impassable river"—220 (238).

112. R^2 21 (46).

113. R^2 52 (78).

114. R^2 271 (288).

115. R^2 453 (468f.).
116. R^2 44f., 408 (70, 422).
117. R^2 313 (329).
118. R^2 75 (100).
119. R^2 25 (49).
120. R^2 88, 91 (114, 116).
121. R^2 280 (297).
122. R^2 18 (42); 79f., 262 (105, 279).
123. R^1 5.
124. R^2 9 (33).
125. R^2 11 (35).
126. R^2 15 (40).
127. R^2 34 (58).
128. R^2 241 (258).
129.   Cf. pp. 287-300 of Overbeck's *Christentum und Kultur*, ed. C. A. Bernoulli (Basel: Benno Schwabe, 1919), and "Unerledigte Anfragen an die heutige Theologie," TK 4-8 (58-60).
130. R^2 177f. (197f.).
131. R^2 236f. (254).
132. R^2 240f. (257ff.); cf. above, p. 23.
133. R^2 317 (333).
134. R^2 432f. (447).
135. R^2 433 (448).
136. R^2 514 (530).
137.   Preface to R^2, p. viii (4).
138. R^2 ix (5).
139.   Barth tries to show a dialectical partnership between Overbeck and Blumhardt in "Unerledigte Anfragen"--"Blumhardt and Overbeck stand close together; back to back, if you like, and very different in disposition, in terminology, in their mental worlds, in their experience, but essentially [*in der Sache*] together. Blumhardt stood as a forward-looking and hopeful Overbeck; Overbeck as a backward-looking, critical Blumhardt. Each was the witness to the mission of the other"--TK 2 (56).
140. R^2 221 (239).
141. R^2 5 (29).
142. R^2 5, 12 (29, 36).
143. R^2 445f., 420f. (461, 435).
144. R^2 369 (385).
145. R^2 82 (108).
146. R^2 90 (115).
147. R^2 174 (194).
148. R^2 11 (35).
149. R^2 86, 96, 103, 136f., 144, 147 (111, 121, 127, 159f., 167, 169).
150. R^2 34, 51f. (58f., 77f.).
151. R^2 308f. (324).
152. R^2 83ff., 91, 114, 514 (109ff., 116, 137, 530). R^2's "Crisis," "Moment," "Decision" etc. stand in sharp contrast to the timely horizon of R^1 (the *past* of the old man, the *future* of God's Kingdom, the *present* struggle); compare the two treatments of Romans 8.
153. R^2 124, 185 (148, 205).
154. R^2 101 (125).
155. R^2 207 (225).
156. R^2 26 (50).
157. R^2 40, 49 (65, 74).
158. R^2 103 (127).

159. R^2 273 (290).
160. R^2 118, 370 (141, 386).
161. R^2 xiii (10).
162. R^2 359 (375).
163. R^2 514f., 370f. (530f., 386f.). Ethical action is "purposeless," too--467 (483).
164. R^2 111, 141 (135, 164).
165. R^2 155 (177).
166. R^2 244 (262), my translation; cf. 316 (322).
167. R^2 411 (425).
168. R^1 223.
169. This observation is made by Walker (*op. cit.*), p. 160. Cf. Gerhard Krüger, "Dialektische Methode und theologische Exegese," *Zwischen den Zeiten*, 5 (1927), 116-157.
170. Cf. R^2 28, 112, 202, 394 (52, 136, 220, 409). But for all that Barth wants to distinguish once and for all between Christian revelation and socialist doctrine, he continues to indicate quite clearly that Christianity sides with socialism--448f. (463f.).
171. R^2 427 (441).
172. R^2 259 (276).
173. R^2 412 (426).
174. R^2 478 (494).
175. R^2 369 (385), my emphasis.
176. R^2 319 (335).
177. In this respect there is an affinity between R^2 and the prewar articles (cf. CGG 54, GPG 90) and sermons.
178. R^2 250 (267).
179. "Die Menschlichkeit Gottes" 6 (40).
180. See below, pp. 158ff. Cf. Ulrich Dannemann, *Theologie und Politik im Denken Karl Barths* (Munich: Chr. Kaiser, 1977), Chapter 1, for a detailed discussion of the politico-ethical dimension of R^1 and R^2; cf. also Marquardt (*op. cit.*).
181. Krüger notes that for Kant, philosophy remained a contemplative enterprise, even though it concluded to the primacy of the practical. The philosopher *as critic* is not subject to his critique. But the dialectical theologians go farther by subjecting themselves to the very crisis they proclaim--"Kant und die Theologie der Krisis," *Theologische Blätter*, 3 (1924), pp. 104f.
182. R^2 21 (45).
183. "Die Menschlichkeit Gottes" 6f. (41).
184. *Credo* 159 (185).
185. R^2 vi (2).
186. In view of Barth's persistent claim of continuity in his own development, it is impossible to argue a fundamental cleavage between R^1 and R^2, as Stadtland does, without giving up all sympathy with Barth's self-interpretation, which Stadtland also does--Tjarko Stadtland, *Eschatologie und Geschichte in der Theologie des jungen Karl Barth* (Neukirchen-Vluyn: Neukirchener Verlag, 1966), p. 56. Cf. Barth's criticism of Stadtland-- Barth to Stadtland, Jan. 18, 1967, in *Briefe 1961-1968*, ed. J. Fangmeier and H. Stoevesandt (Zurich: TVZ, 1975), pp. 373-379 (232-236). On the other hand, Bakker is right to maintain, against von Balthasar, that the common premise is the *discontinuous* newness of the divine over against the human, rather than God-man *identity*--Bakker 103; Hans Urs von Balthasar, *Karl Barth: Darstellung und Deutung seiner Theologie* (2nd ed.; Cologne: Jakob Hegner, 1962), pp. 77f. (55f.).

187. "In the moment when we dare to say we believe, we remain always under suspicion. The necessity and possibility of passing through the narrow gate which leads from life to death and from death to life must always seem utterly strange . . . to try to take even one step forward, dangerous in the highest degree. The comfortable, easy and assured manner in which men advance toward this critical point is the primary curse which lies upon all, or almost all, dogmatics"--R^2 126 (150), my translation.

188. R^2 xiii (10). Barth's mind changed drastically on this point. Cf. KD I/1 411f. (391): "Jesus' message about God the Father must not be taken to mean that. . . Jesus had in mind what all serious philosophy has called the first cause or supreme good, the *esse a se* or *ens perfectissimum*, the universum, the ground and abyss of meaning, the unconditioned, the limit, the critical negation or origin, and that He. . . baptised it by means of the name 'father'. . . In this regard we can only say that this entity, the supposed philosophical equivalent of the Creator God, has nothing whatever to do with Jesus' message about God the Father."

189. Barth to Thurneysen, June 3, 1919 (RTM 47).

190. Bultmann classed R^2 with Otto's book (and Schleiermacher's *Speeches*!) as an attempt "to prove *the independence and the absolute nature of religion*"--*Anfänge* I, 119 (100); and there certainly is a philosophy of religion in R^2, which is explicitly stated at 225 (243): "We are able to see that, compared with other things of which we are aware, religion is a distinct and quite peculiar thing. A numinous perception of any kind has an alarming and disturbing effect upon all other perceptions; a divinity of any kind tends to bring men into a condition which is more or less ambiguous; a cleavage of some form or other is made between their existence and a contrasted and threatening non-existence [etc.]. . . Something of this *Krisis* underlies all religion; and the more insistent the tension becomes, the more clearly we are in the presence of the phenomenon of religion, whether or no we ourselves are conscious of it."

191. I mean to leave open the possibility that a Christian philosophy distinguishable from Christian theology is at work, because Barth took this possibility very seriously over the following decade. Cf. *Die christliche Dogmatik* (CD) (Munich: Chr. Kaiser, 1927), pp. 403-407 on *philosophia christiana*.

192. Introduction to Barth-Thurneysen correspondence 1914-1921, RTM 13.

193. T. F. Torrance called R^2 "an extraordinary work, for just as a bomb can only have its intended effect if it explodes and shatters itself, so the *Romans*, as it were, blows itself up and the reader along with it"--Torrance, *op.cit.*, p. 50f.

Chapter III

1. For more information and analysis of this period, see Jacques Derrida, "Violence et métaphysique," in *L'écriture et la différance* (Paris: Seuil, 1967), 117-228 (79-153); Daniel E. Guillot, "Emmanuel Levinas. Evolución de su Pensamiento," in E. Dussel and D. Guillot, *Liberación Latinoamericana y Emmanuel Levinas* (Buenos Aires: Bonum, 1975), 47-124; and

Edith Wyschogrod, *Emmanuel Levinas: The Problem of Ethical Metaphysics* (The Hague: Martinus Nijhoff, 1974). An important recent addition to this literature is Roger Burggraeve, *Emmanuel Levinas' metafysisch-ethische herdefiniëring van het subject vanuit joodse en filosofische achtergronden* (Leuven U. dissertation, 1980).

2. All biographical information is drawn from Levinas' brief piece "Signature," in *Difficile liberté* (DL) (*op. cit.*), 373-379--in English: "Signature," ed. A. Peperzak, tr. M. E. Petrisko, *Research in Phenomenology*, 8 (1978), 175-189.

3. DL 373 (175f.).

4. It was in this period that Heidegger took over Husserl's chair at Freiburg, amid growing awareness of the disagreements between the two. One could hardly study phenomenology in Freiburg at this time without becoming embroiled in the controversy as to the direction phenomenology should take. Cf. Herbert Spiegelberg, *The Phenomenological Movement* (2 vols.) (2nd ed.; The Hague: Martinus Nijhoff, 1976), Vol. 1, pp. 275-283, and Vol. 2, p. 402; and see Levinas' reminiscences in "La ruine de la représentation," DEHH 125f.

5. "Sur les *Ideen* de M. E. Husserl," *Revue Philosophique de la France et de l'Etranger*, 54 (1929), 230-265.

6. *Méditations Cartésiennes* (Paris: Colin, 1931). Levinas translated the fourth and fifth Meditations. This was an important publication inasmuch as Husserl did not allow the *Meditations* to appear in German in his lifetime--Spiegelberg, Vol. 2, p. 403.

7. *La théorie de l'intuition dans la phénoménologie de Husserl* (TIPH) (Paris: Alcan, 1930).

8. TIPH 14f. (xxxiiif.).

9. See the "Conclusion," p. 216 (153).

10. TIPH 217 (154).

11. *Ibid.*

12. It is also the question (though asked in a different way) of Bergson's "life" philosophy, then influential in France and always esteemed by Levinas, as shown by his frequent references to it--in TIPH, see e.g. p. 219 (155); cf. the English "Signature," p. 180, n. 23.

13. TIPH 174 (119).

14. TIPH 220 (155).

15. TIPH 86ff. (53ff.).

16. TIPH 86 (53); cf. DL 374 (178f.): "In showing that consciousness and represented Being emerge from a non-representational 'context,' Husserl showed that representation is not the exclusive site of truth. The 'scaffolding' required by scientific constructions must be kept in service, if one is careful about the meaning of these edifices. The Ideas that transcend consciousness cannot be separated from their genesis in consciousness, which is fundamentally temporal. In spite of his intellectualism and his assurance of the pre-eminence of the West, Husserl thus called into question the Platonic privilege--until then, uncontested--of a continent that believes it has the right to colonize the world" (my translation). Levinas often mingles his blame of Husserl's intellectualism with praise of Husserl for providing the means of overcoming it.

17. §29 *et seq.*

18. The idea of creation becomes central in Levinas' philosophy, although it is associated with Descartes' "idea of the Infinite" rather than anything in Heidegger. Levinas

continues to admire some of the speculative gestures of *Being and Time*, and at Leiden in 1975 linked his own idea that the self is constituted and assumed by moral responsibility (rather than vice versa) with Heidegger's progress to the self from the event in Being of "mineness" (*Jemeinigkeit*)--Q&R 77f.

19. "Martin Heidegger et l'ontologie," *Revue Philosophique de la France et de l'Etranger*, 57 (1932), 395-431. A modified version appears in DEHH, 53-76. He wrote in 1932: "The progress toward the eternal that Western consciousness believes itself to accomplish with the supratemporal perspective of science, is not a victory carried off by the Spirit over concrete, temporal existence, but a moment in the very drama of this existence. The Spirit's leap toward the eternal does not transcend this drama to give a new birth to persons, it does not transfigure them by an act of grace entering from outside. But by virtue of the integrating element of existence it is completely dominated by the leit-motif of this drama. It has seemed interesting to us to emphasize this reduction to time . . . of everything one would be tempted to call supratemporal, the reduction to existence of everything one would want to call *rapport*. This is his fundamental ontologism; our concern in this study is to highlight it"--419f., DEHH 70f. The opposition of "ontologism" to transcendence announces the problematic of Levinas' philosophy.

20. See Spiegelberg; L. Kelkel and R. Schérer, *Husserl: Sa Vie, Son Oeuvre* (Paris: Presses Universitaires de France, 1964), p. 15ff.; and Jean-Michel Palmier, *Les écrits politiques de Heidegger* (Paris: L'Herne, 1968), pp. 49-64.

21. *Esprit*, 2 (1934), 199-208.

22. Our flexible usage of "liberalism," "idealism," and "liberal idealism" reflects Levinas' own flexibility and generality. What he thinks are the important characteristics of "liberal idealism" will appear in his analyses.

23. "Quelques réflexions" 201f.

24. Heidegger attached this importance to Marxism; cf. the "Brief über den Humanismus," in *Platons Lehre von der Wahrheit. Mit einen Brief über den Humanismus* (Bern: Francke, 1947), p. 87 (287): "Because Marx, in discovering [the alienation of man], reaches into an essential dimension of history, the Marxist view of history excels all other history. Because, however, neither Husserl nor, as far as I can see, Sartre recognizes the essentially historical character of Being, neither phenomenology nor existentialism can penetrate that dimension within which alone a productive discussion with Marxism is possible." In the *politics* of the 1930's it was racism that took history seriously, and it was the racist Nazis rather than the Weimar liberals who "met" (and prevailed over) the Marxists in Germany. Levinas does not accuse Heidegger of racism now, or ever; but he will make clear that he regards Heidegger's way of taking history seriously as a philosophy of rootedness (*enracinement*), of pagan adoration of worldly situatedness and power, which is as such unjust--for the same reasons that are brought forward in this article against racism. Cf. DL 183, 301.

25. "Quelques réflexions" 203.

26. *Ibid.* 206. Cf. TI 93 (120).

27. "Quelques réflexions" 208.

28. G. S. Kirk and J. E. Raven, *The Pre-Socratic Philosophers* (Cambridge: Cambridge U., 1957), passage No. 344: "Come now, and I will tell thee. . . the only ways of enquiry that can be thought of: the one way, that it *is* and cannot not-be, is the path of Persuasion, for it attends upon Truth; the other, that it *is-not* and needs must not-be, that I tell thee is a path altogether unthinkable. For thou couldst not know that which is-not (that is impossible) nor utter it; for the same thing can be thought as can be." The ghost of Parmenides thus haunts any attempt to think or utter the beyond-Being, and will return later, in the form of Jacques Derrida, to question the achievement of TI.

29. "De l'évasion," *Recherches Philosophiques*, 5 (1935-1936), p. 390.

30. *Ibid*. 391f. We will often capitalize "Being" in token of its philosophical and polemical significance for Levinas.

31. Cf. the "Introduction" of *De l'existence à l'existant* (EE) (Paris: Vrin, 1947), p. 19 (19): "If at the beginning our reflections are in a large measure inspired by the philosophy of Martin Heidegger, where we find the concept of ontology and of the relationship which man sustains with Being, they are also governed by a profound need to leave the climate of that philosophy, and by the conviction that we cannot leave it for a philosophy that would be pre-Heideggerian."

32. "De l'évasion" 375.

33. *Ibid*. 373.

34. *Ibid*. 374.

35. *Ibid*. 377.

36. *Ibid*. 378. Cf. EE 20 (20).

37. He writes elsewhere that for him this distinction is the most important lesson of *Being and Time--Le Temps et l'Autre* (TA) (Montpellier: Fata Morgana, 1979), p. 24.

38. "De l'évasion" 380. Cf. EE 21 (20).

39. "De l'évasion" 382.

40. *Ibid*. 386f.

41. *Ibid*. 390. Levinas was an attentive though critical reader of Shestov, of whom this characterization of knowledge as "impotence before the accomplished fact" is reminiscent. TIPH noted Shestov's attack on Husserl's rationalism--6, 220n. (156n.)--and a review of Shestov's book on Kierkegaard took account of his whole philosophical project--"Leon Chestov. *Kierkegaard et la philosophie existentielle*," *Revue des Etudes Juives*, n.s. 2 (1937), 139ff.

42. *Deucalion*, 1 (1946), 141-154.

43. EE 11 (15), my translation. In the new preface to the second edition of 1978, Levinas wrote that he has remained faithful to the Platonic formula, even if his terminology and operating concepts and certain of his theses have changed--EE[2] (Paris: Vrin, 1978), p. 13.

44. Cf. TI 22 (51). We will refer to EE by its French title, since the English *Existence and Existents* obscures this direction of movement.

45. EE 26ff., 93-105 (21ff., 57-64).

46. EE 125 (72f.).

47. EE 16 (18).

48. EE 124-132 (72-77).

49. EE 33 (26).

50. EE 41ff. (29ff.).

51. EE 43 (30). Consciousness is a dimension of retreat from Being: "When the biblical Jonah, the hero of impossible escapes and the invoker of nothingness and death, sees in the midst of the raging elements that his escape is blocked and his mission is unavoidable, he climbs down into the hold of the ship and goes to sleep"--EE 115 (67), my translation.

52. EE 149 (86).

53. EE 78 (49), my translation.

54. EE 55 (37).

55. EE 56 (37), my translation.

56. EE 61 (40), my translation.

57. It becomes evident in another context ("La réalité et son ombre," *op. cit.*) that Levinas disapproves of art's exoticism; it is an evasion of theoretical and practical responsibility.

58. EE 84f. (53). *L'intériorité* is "inwardness," but we will consistently translate it "interiority" to reflect its schematic relationship with *l'extériorité*, for which "outwardness" will not serve, since it suggests the "outward" form or mask rather than the nudity of the other.

59. EE 94f. (57f.).

60. EE 121f. (71).

61. EE 138f. (81).

62. "De la description à l'existence," DEHH 106f.

63. "Leon Chestov" (*op. cit.*), p. 139.

64. Levinas expressed admiration of Brunschvicg for maintaining rationalism as a critique of egoism, even the egoism of the desire for personal salvation. "I remember the *Congrès Descartes* of 1937. Already new philosophical movements were asserting themselves: existentialist thought, Catholic thought, Marxist thought. Anguish, death, care--all that was becoming very fashionable. During one session, Gabriel Marcel passionately attacked those thinkers 'destitute of any gift of the inner life,' blind to God, blind to death. Then Brunschvicg--always with that studied nonchalance--said, 'I think the death of Leon Brunschvicg worries Leon Brunschvicg less than the death of Gabriel Marcel worries Gabriel Marcel'"--"L'agenda de Leon Brunschvicg" (1949), DL 67. The sobriety and intransigent moral seriousness of rationalism is the one point to which Levinas feels "infinitely close"--DL 72.

65. DEHH 8f.

66. DEHH 42.

67. Cf. TA 25.

68. EE 60 (40).

69. EE 61f. (41).

70. EE 66 (43).

71. EE 66 (44).

72. EE 58 (38).

73. EE 161f. (94f.).

74. EE 144 (84f.), my translation.

75. EE 160f. (94).

76. EE 164 (96), my translation. *L'autrui* will always be translated "other person," to place in the highest relief the transition continually being made between the abstract *autre* and the concrete *autrui*. Cf. TA 89. When this (or "the Infinite" for *l'Infini*, see below, p. 264, n. 134) is the sole departure from an existing translation that is reproduced, it will not be specially noted.

77. (TA), originally published as "Le Temps et l'Autre" in *Le choix, le monde, l'existence*, by Jean Wahl *et. al.* (Grenoble: Arthaud, 1947), and issued in 1979 by Fata Morgana (*op. cit.*).

78. TA 33f.
79. TA 19f.
80. TA 55-64; 57.
81. TA 82.
82. TA 77-84.
83. Levinas introduces his description of fecundity with a somewhat mysterious remark on his method that will bear remembering when we discuss the method of his later work. After analyzing the dialectic of our attitude toward death in terms of Lucretius' temptation to nothingness and Pascal's desire for eternity ("These are not two distinct attitudes: we want to die and to be, at the same time") he says: "We have just described a dialectical situation. We are now going to show a concrete situation in which this dialectic is accomplished. It is impossible to explain this method here at length, even though we constantly have recourse to it. It will be seen, in any event, that it is not phenomenological all the way through"-- TA 66f. This movement of *concretization* (a movement which nevertheless reaches *beyond experience*, e.g. to the alterity of children yet unborn) is the characteristic gesture of Levinas' philosophy; and it raises the question of how one goes beyond phenomenology at the same time that one uses it. Cf. "La transcendance des mots," *Les Temps Modernes*, 4 (1949), p. 1094, where the dialectics of relation with the Other are concretely accomplished in my *voice* which, in offering speech, exposes me to the Other and ushers me into a different order.

84. TA 86.
85. TA 87.
86. "Pluralisme et transcendance," *Actes du Xme Congrès International de Philosophie*, 1 (Amsterdam: North Holland Publishing Co., 1949), ed. F. W. Beth, H. J. Pos, and J. H. Hollak, p. 383; cf. TI 254 (277).
87. (OF), *Revue de Métaphysique et de Morale*, 56 (1951), 88-98.
88. OF 91f.
89. OF 93f.
90. OF 94.
91. *Ibid.*
92. "In choosing the term 'religion'--without having uttered the word 'God' or the word '*sacred*'--our first thought has been of the sense given it by Auguste Comte at the beginning of his *Politique Positive* [the sixth chapter of the first part, on the 'religion of humanity']"-- OF 95. Cf. TI 52 (80).
93. OF 95.
94. *Ibid.*
95. As the Eleatic stranger says, "I suggest that anything has real being that is so constituted as to possess any sort of power either to affect anything else or to be affected, in however small a degree, by the most insignificant agent, though it be only once. I am proposing as a mark to distinguish real things that they are nothing but power [δύναμις]"--*Sophist* 247d, tr. Cornford.
96. OF 96.
97. OF 97.

98. OF 98. For other appreciative references to Kant see, e.g., DEHH 114, 122; TI 109, 163 (135f., 188f.); *Humanisme de l'autre homme* (HAH) (Montpellier: Fata Morgana, 1972), p. 82; AE 166 (129); and "Het primaat van de zuivere praktische rede," tr. C. P. Heering-Moorman, *Wijsgerig Perspectief op Maatschappij en Wetenschap*, 11 (1971), 178-186. For some analysis of the relation between the philosophies of Levinas and Kant, see Jan de Greef, "Ethique, réflexion et histoire chez Levinas," *Revue Philosophique de Louvain*, 67 (1969), 431-460; J. Plat, "Ethiek en Godsdienst, van Immanuel Kant tot Emmanuel Levinas," *Algemeen Nederlands Tijdschrift voor Wijsbegeerte*, 64 (1972), 15-25; Jean-François Lyotard, "Logique de Levinas," in *Textes pour Emmanuel Levinas*, ed. F. Laruelle (Paris: Jean-Michel Place, 1980), 127-148; and Edith Wyschogrod, *Emmanuel Levinas* (*op. cit.*), pp. 207ff.

Levinas' backward gesture toward Kant belongs to the logic of his polemical confrontation with Heidegger and later Hegel. In this he compares with Hermann Cohen. Henri Dussort writes (in *L'Ecole de Marbourg* [Paris: Presses Universitaires de France, 1963], 66f.) that it was not Cohen's Kantianism that made him anti-Hegelian, but his original anti-Hegelianism that turned him toward Kant. "Kant's great weakness in Hegel's eyes, his irreducible opposition between *Sein* and *Sollen*, was Kantianism's great merit for Marburg. And Cohen, a militant Jew. . . who strove to reconcile the spirit of the prophets, of Plato, and of Kant, emphasized their agreement on this fundamental point, that for them the *Good*, the full Realization, remained always ἐπέκεινα τῆς οὐσίας, that there never is a radical Incarnation. . . Hegel had reproached Kantianism for being shallow and for being a 'Jewish' philosophy (rejecting the Incarnation): Cohen turned the criticism into praise, and reversed the charge of shallowness"--137. Cf. Cohen's "Innere Beziehung der Kantische Philosophie zum Judentum," in *Hermann Cohens Jüdische Schriften*, ed. B. Strauß (Berlin: C. A. Schwetschke and Son, 1924), Vol. 1, 284-305. Hegel and Heidegger are both thinkers for whom the exclusion of a matter from thought (things-in-themselves, e.g.) represents only an inadequate thought. If the points are stressed at which Plato and Kant seem to interrupt their own systems for the sake of an outward glance at something beyond thought, they can be viewed as patrons of the critical spirit in philosophy, which both Cohen and Levinas interpret as a function of the relation with something non-given, the Other. The "Jewish" God who gives, not Himself, but the Law, is affiliated in both Cohen and Levinas with a train of thought sharply opposed to the "Christian" all-mediating incarnationism of Hegel, who assumes that the boundaries between God and (speculative) man are somehow permeable.

99. OF 98.
100. (LC), *Revue de Métaphysique et de Morale*, 58 (1953), 264-272.
101. OF 95.
102. LC 269; cf. TI 14 (43f.).
103. LC 270.
104. LC 266.
105. LC 271.
106. Cf. TI 78 (104) on creation ex nihilo.
107. ("Moi"), *Revue de Métaphysique et de Morale*, 59 (1954), 353-373.

108. "Moi" 354.
109. "Moi" 355.
110. "Moi" 356.
111. "Moi" 357.
112. "Moi" 359.
113. "Moi" 360.
114. This recalls the relationship between *Ursprung* and rationality as *Gesetzlichkeit* in Cohen--*Religion der Vernunft aus den Quellen des Judentums* (2nd ed.; Cologne: J. Melzer, 1959), pp. 5-12 (4-11); and indeed the lawful structuration of reality required by the third person will become the key to the explanation of reason in AE (see below, Chapter VI).
115. "Moi" 360.
116. "Moi" 363.
117. "Moi" 368.
118. Justice requires quantification; there could be no justice without reparations, and therein lies the "*metaphysical* meaning" of money--"Moi" 372f.
119. *Revue de Métaphysique et de Morale*, 62 (1957), 241-253; reprinted in DEHH, 165-178, and so cited.
120. DEHH 166. "Eaten by others" is a reference to Paul Valéry's *Monsieur Teste* who cries out in the Opéra after the music has stopped, "On n'est *beau*, on n'est extraordinaire que pour les autres! *Ils* sont mangées par les autres!"--*Oeuvres*, 2 (Pléiade ed.), p. 20; cited from Ad Peperzak's note to his translation of "La philosophie et l'idée de l'Infini" in *Het menselijk gelaat* (Bilthoven: Ambo, 1969), p. 249, n. 8.
121. Cf. TI 19 (48): "And to have substituted for the magical communion of species and the confusion of distinct orders a spiritual relation in which beings remain at their post but communicate among themselves will have been the imperishable merit of the 'admirable Greek people,' and the very institution of philosophy."
122. According to Levinas (in one of his sharpest published criticisms), Heidegger's subordination of the Other to the Neutrum is carried into his "later" philosophy as a pagan atheist ideology of injustice. "When Heidegger points out the forgetfulness of Being, which is veiled by the various realities it illuminates--a forgetfulness for which the philosophy descended from Socrates is blamed--while he deplores the orientation of intelligence toward technics, he maintains a regime of power more inhuman than machinism, and which perhaps does not come from the same source. (It is not certain that National Socialism arose from the mechanist reification of men, rather than from a pagan rootedness and the feudal adoration by enslaved men of the lords and masters commanding them.) . . . It is a matter of a pagan *existing*, building and cultivating in the service of Being in the midst of a familiar countryside, on a motherly earth. . . foreign to all culpability with respect to the Other Person.
   "In fact, this maternity of the earth determines the whole Western civilization of property, exploitation, political tyranny and war"--DEHH 170f.
123. DEHH 172.
124. In Victor Hugo's *Hernani*, Charles V says "Je suis une force qui va"--cited from Peperzak (ed.), *Het menselijk gelaat*, p. 216, n. 40 (in the English "Signature," p. 183).
125. DEHH 172.
126. *Ibid.*

127. DEHH 174.
128. DEHH 175.
129. DEHH 177.
130. DEHH 174.
131. DEHH 177.
132. DEHH 178.
133. TI xvif. (28).
134. One difficulty with the translation "Totality and Infinity" for *Totalité et Infini* is that it suggests two abstract principles lending themselves to logical juxtaposition; whereas "*l'Infini*," *the* Infinite, is not *l'infinité* but God—who is *not* on logical all fours with "totality." Descartes did not have an idea of "infinity," but of God (see below, p. 166). Therefore, while it is impossible not to refer to the book as *Totality and Infinity*, we will elsewhere translate *l'Infini* as "the Infinite."
135. "Signature," DL 377 (183).
136. TI ix (21).
137. TI ixf. (21).
138. TI 29 (58).
139. "Hegel's philosophy represents the logical conclusion of this fundamental allergy [to otherness] of philosophy"—"La trace de l'autre," DEHH 189.
140. TI xvi (28). Cohen's relationship to Hegel has already been noted, at least in Dussort's emphatic interpretation (see above, p. 262, n. 98). So has Rosenzweig's tribute to Cohen (see above, p. 247, n. 3). Cf. Levinas' "Franz Rosenzweig: Une pensée juive moderne," *Revue de Théologie et de Philosophie*, 98 (1965), p. 211; and "'Entre deux mondes'," DL 243f. To philosophy conceived as totalization (on the model of Thales' "All is water," culminating in Hegel's Absolute Spirit), Rosenzweig opposed Jewish existence as "*an essential event of Being*," a "*category of Being*"—DL 237—in which God, man, and world are untotalized, their relationships being a function of their intrinsic, independent motions rather than of a System to which they belong—*Der Stern der Erlösung* (*op. cit.*), Part 1, pp. 110-115 (84-88). The *Star* also criticizes at length the seclusion of the I-Thou relationship that the mystic desires with God as a *société intime* hidden from public accountability—Part 2, pp. 149-155 (203-208).
141. TI 26 (55).
142. TI 36 (65).
143. TI 29 (58).
144. TI 38f., 41 (66f., 69).
145. TI xi (22).
146. TI xif. (23).
147. TI 13 (43).
148. TI 229 (251); cf. EE 161 (94): "Neither the category of quantity nor even that of quality describes the alterity of the other, who does not simply have another quality than me, but as it were bears alterity as a quality."
149. TI 35f. (64).
150. TI 3 (33f.), my translation.
151. TI 5 (35). "An absolute adventure, in a primal imprudence, goodness is transcendence itself"—TI 282 (305).
152. TI 6 (36). The self can take a distance from itself, correct itself, but not actually leave or "apostatize" from itself.
153. TI 10, 31, 122 (39, 60, 148).

154. TI 24 (53). The resistance of interiority to totality is "necessary for the idea of the Infinite, which does not produce this separation [and pluralism] by its own force"--TI 28 (57).

155. Levinas credits Kierkegaard with catching sight of the secret of interiority (DEHH 215), but he criticizes this "egoist cry" of subjectivity still concerned for its own eternal happiness--TI 282 (305). "It is not I who resist the system, as Kierkegaard thought; it is the other"--TI 10 (40). Egoism is ultimately irresponsible; it absolves itself from the system only to see without being seen, to cheat, as though it wore Gyges' ring of invisibility (*Republic* 359d)--TI 32, 62, 148 (61, 90, 173).

156. TI 29f. (58f.).

157. TI 76, 88f. (103, 116).

158. The Other elides my *pouvoir de pouvoir*--TI 9 (39).

159. TI 11 (40f.). "Exteriority is not a negation, but a marvel"--TI 269 (292).

160. The face-to-face relation with the Other is the true *immediate*, unlike "sensation" which is always already thematized. And since the immediate is a transcendence, it cannot be integrated in any system, least of all Hegel's--TI 23, 30f. (52, 59f.).

161. TI 12f. (42f.).

162. TI 229 (251).

163. TI 5, 12 (35, 41). The term is borrowed from Jean Wahl, *Existence humaine et transcendance* (Neuchatel: Editions de la Baconnière, 1944), p. 37.

164. TI 9 (39). According to Peperzak (*Het menselijk gelaat* 249, n. 1a), the term "absolutely Other" is borrowed from Plotinus via Vladimir Jankélévitch's *Philosophie première* (Paris: Presses Universitaires de France, 1954).

165. TI 37f. (65f.).

166. TI 9, 147 (39, 172).

167. This asymmetry is no abstract requirement. "It imposes itself upon meditation in the name of a concrete moral experience: what I permit myself to demand of myself is not comparable with what I have the right to demand of the Other Person. This moral experience, so commonplace, indicates a metaphysical asymmetry: the radical impossibility of seeing oneself from the outside and of speaking in the same sense of oneself and of the others"--TI 24 (53).

168. TI 48 (75). This is the point at which Levinas acknowledges but keeps a critical distance from Buber (*I and Thou*) and Marcel (*Metaphysical Journal*)--TI 40 (68).

169. "*Imprévisibilité*"--TI 173, 212 (199, 235).

170. TI 13f. (43).

171. TI 46, 22 (73, 51).

172. TI 38, 41, 73, 146 (67, 69, 100, 171).

173. "A proposition is a sign which is already interpreted, which provides its own key. The presence of the interpretative key in the sign to be interpreted is precisely the presence of the other in the proposition, the presence of him who can come to the assistance of his discourse, the teaching quality of all speech. Oral discourse is the plenitude of discourse"--TI 69 (96).

174. TI 65 (92).

175. TI 70 (97).

176. TI 155 (180).

177. TI 178 (203).
178. TI 20 (49); *Phaedrus* 149a.
179. TI 75 (102).
180. TI 59f. (87); "Transcendance et hauteur" (TH), *Bulletin de la Société Française de Philosophie*, 56 (1962), pp. 91f.
181. TI 60 (88).
182. TI 62f. (90).
183. TI 62 (90).
184. TI 229f. (252).
185. TI 230 (252).
186. TI xvif. (28); he adds that the relations of eros, fecundity, etc. called "beyond the face" are *events* "that cannot be described as noeses aiming at noemata, nor as active interventions realizing projects, nor, of course, as physical forces being discharged into masses. They are conjunctures in being for which perhaps the term 'drama' would be most suitable, in the sense that Nietzsche would have liked to use it when, at the end of *The Case of Wagner*, he regrets that it has always been wrongly translated by action"--TI xvi, n. 1 (28, n. 2). Nietzsche asserted that the original sacred drama was "*kein Thun, sondern ein Geschehen*"--*Werke* VI/3, ed. G. Colli and M. Montinari (Berlin: W. de Gruyter, 1969), p. 26n. (174n.). Levinas would of course want to differentiate his sense of "drama" from anything in the realm of ecstatic "participation."
187. "In all this affirmation of the concrete, on which today's philosophy thrives, it is not recognized that the relation with the other person is an element of abstraction which pierces the continuity of the concrete, a relation with the Other as Other, 'denuded' in every sense of the term. For this reason one must separate the Other from the words *prochain* and *semblable*, which perpetuate so many things in common between me and the other"--TH 107.
188. Theo de Boer compares Levinas' procedure with Kant's: "Taken together, the contingency of experience and the fact of science justify the validity of Kant's categories. In the same way, human egoism, and the facts notwithstanding of self-critique and the possibility of living in society (situations in which totality is 'breached'), refer to the epiphany of the face"--*Tussen filosofie en profetie* (Bilthoven: Ambo, 1976), p. 53. However strong or weak this analogy may be with respect to the various assertions of *Totality and Infinity*, it seems certain that the formal aspects of the "logic" of pluralism are arrived at by some argumentative procedure not phenomenological; and the notion of deduction calls attention to this.
189. TI xiii (25).
190. TI 163 (189).
191. TI xiii (24).
192. TI xvii (29).
193. TI xv (27).
194. TI 52, xv (80, 26).
195. TI 55, xvf. (83, 27).
196. TI 66, 59 (93, 86).
197. TI 81 (109).
198. TI 49f. (77).
199. TI xvii (29).
200. The "curvature of intersubjective space" does not "appear," it is "effectuated"--TI 267 (291). "And if I set forth, as in a final and absolute vision, the separation and

transcendence which are the themes of this book, these relations, which I claim form the fabric of being itself, first come together in my discourse presently addressed to my interlocutors: inevitably across my idea of the Infinite the other faces me-- hostile, friend, my master, my student"--TI 53 (81).

201. TI 21 (50).
202. TI 148 (173).
203. For example, the words "exterior" and "infinite" inevitably refer to the system--Derrida (*op. cit.*), pp. 165ff. (112ff.).
204. These criticisms are drawn from Derrida.
205. TI xii (24).
206. Derrida 227f. (153).
207. Derrida 158 (107).
208. Cf. Jan De Greef, "Ethique, réflexion et histoire chez Levinas" (*op. cit.*), and "Le concept de pouvoir éthique chez Levinas," *Revue Philosophique de Louvain*, 68 (1970), 507-520, on the problem of the violence inherent in the moralization of the real world.
209. Derrida 132f. (89).
210. "Ontology without metaphysics is blind, metaphysics without ontology is empty"--de Boer (*op. cit.*), p. 55.
211. TI 265 (289).
212. TI 268, 266 (292, 290).
213. TI xi (22).
214. TI xiii, 74, 81, 170 (25, 101, 109, 196).
215. TI 179 (204).
216. TI 18 (47).
217. TI 16f. (46).
218. TH 93; cf. "Intentionalité et métaphysique," DEHH 142f.
219. TH 93.

Chapter IV

1. "Metaphysics" is not the usual term for Barth's thought, but Emil Brunner applied it in his review of first *Romans* (perhaps with an eye on the Ritschlians, to whom "metaphysics" was anathema) on account of its subject's transcendence of experience--"'Der Römerbrief' von Karl Barth," in *Anfänge* I, p. 84 (68).
2. Levinas, TI 57ff. (85f.).
3. Barth, R² 411 (425).
4. Barth, R² 254f. (271f.), my translation.
5. For Barth the truth is definitively held by Someone, but He is not me and not you: "In the Christian Church there is truly a Master and Lord, and every discussion carried on in the Church stands under notice that there is here a Master, and therefore no man can here be master. Therefore every man must be fundamentally much more ready to let himself be questioned than to question"--"Der römische Katholizismus als Frage an die protestantische Kirche," in TK, p. 331 (308).
6. According to Karl Popper, the fundamentally rational attitude is the one admitting that "I may be wrong and you may be right, and by an effort, we may get nearer to the truth"-- *The Open Society and Its Enemies* (2 vols.) (5th ed.; Princeton: Princeton U., 1966), Vol. 2, p. 225.

7. Levinas, TI 8 (38). Cf. TI 136 (162).
8. Levinas, "Langage et proximité," DEHH 224.
9. Barth, R[1] 113f., 129, 206.
10. Levinas, "Moi" 354; TI, Section 2. Unlike Barth, Levinas will retain the category of *le psychisme* (interiority) in order to transform its meaning--TI 82 (110); AE 175 (137).
11. Cf. pp. 42 and 93 above.
12. *Einführung in die evangelische Theologie* (Zurich: TVZ, 1962), p. 14 (10).
13. *Ibid.* p. 84 (104).
14. Q&R 75.
15. Q&R 69.
16. Levinas' emphasis on "events in Being" has been noted, as early as "De l'évasion." The "deductions" of TI, which refer to events, are themselves events: "In our exposition [the deduction] is indicated by expressions such as 'that is,' or 'precisely,' or 'this accomplishes that' ['*ceci accomplit cela*'], or 'this is produced as that' ['*ceci se produit comme cela*']"--TI xvii (28).
   Barth used the idea of event extensively in R[1] (e.g. 10, 60, 115, 124, 153, 195, 280) in connection with the act of God that creates faith and the new world; cf. R[2] 7 (32)--"Möchte diese Voraussetzung immer neu *geschehen*!"--and 279f. (296)-- Sonship as *Ereignis*. It is a fixed principle of his mature theology to maintain the event-character of revelation and the decision-character of faith against any proposal that "there is" (*es gibt*) a constantly available revelation or faith--KD I/1 40 (41). This so-called "actualism" or "occasionalism" of his must not be understood as an ontological solution of the problem of the relation between God and creation, but as a deferral of such a solution to maintain the difference between the personal (as divinely determined) and the ontological.
17. Barth, WGT 97 (94).
18. Barth, R[2] 198 (217); Levinas, TI 146, 173f., 240 (171, 199, 262) on the "ethical impossibility of murder."
19. The face makes murder both possible and impossible, according to Levinas--TI 240 (262). Barth applies the idea of the incognito to Christ in Jesus--R[2] 262f. (279f.), to the new man in the old man--177ff. (197ff.), to the church of Jacob in the church of Esau--325ff. (341ff.), and later to theological meaning in philosophical language (see Chapter V below). Levinas appreciates Kierkegaard's conception of the "persecuted truth" that is completely different from a known truth, a "simultaneity of Everything and Nothing, Relation with a Person at the same time present and absent--with a humiliated God who suffers, dies, and leaves those he saves in despair. A certainty that coexists with an absolute uncertainty--to the point that one can ask oneself whether Revelation itself is not opposed to the essence of this crucified truth, whether the suffering of God and the failure to recognize the truth ought not to attain their highest degree in a total *incognito*"-- "Existence et éthique," in *Noms propres* (*op. cit.*), p. 103.
20. R[2] 69, 128, 317, 398 (94, 152, 333, 412f.).
21. KD I/1 §5.2-4.
22. Levinas, TI, Preface; cf. the preface to AE, where he refers to the urgency of "*entendre un Dieu non contaminé par l'être*"--x (xlii). Barth's protest against Feuerbach is that "any man who knew that we human beings are evil from head to foot, and who bore in mind that we all die, would know that the

illusion of illusions is the notion that the being of God is the being of man. Even if he held the good God to be a dream he would certainly leave him free of identification with such as we"--TK 237 (235).

23. Cf. Levinas, TI 136, 177 (162, 202); "axiology" (i.e. of enjoyment) transcends ontology, however, since that is the self's "secret" from totality--92 (119). But at AE 158f., n. 28 (198), he shows an interest in relating the concept of value to the beyond-experience. For Barth's disparagements of "value" cf. R^2 38, 42f., 86, 306, 447f. (63, 67f., 111, 322, 463); WGT 80 (67); TK 369 (338).

24. Barth, R^2 117 (141).

25. Levinas, TI 282 (305). Barth's R^1 was a sustained attack on the pathos of individualism, on behalf of God's new world-history (see above, p. 28).

26. Barth, R^2 16 (41); Levinas, AE 160 (124): "But in the irreplaceable subject, unique and elect as responsibility and substitution, a mode of freedom that is ontologically impossible breaks apart the unbreakable essence. Substitution frees the subject from ennui, i.e. from the self-enchainment in which the ego suffocates in itself" (my translation). Barth's R^2 corrected the "ecstatic" distortion of the idea of liberation from self in R^1.

27. Levinas, TI 284 (307); Barth, KD III/2 §47.5. Barth translates the issue of resurrection into the issue of revelation in his commentary on I Corinthians, *Die Auferstehung der Toten* (Munich: Chr. Kaiser, 1924).

28. Levinas, TI 58 (86).

29. "Because--and only because--I believe, I see the problem of my humanity. As unbelieving, as unjudged, a sinner undisturbed in the dream of my likeness to God, I could deceive myself about myself. . . With the 'I believe the Church' (*credo ecclesiam*), [man] has ceased to dream; he is driven in terror out of both pure externality and withdrawn inwardness [ecstaticism and solipsism]"--Barth, TK 370 (338f.).

30. Barth, R^2 272 (292); cf. 410f. (424f.): "The fact that ethics are presented to us as a problem means that the concepts which we made use of in our conversation are, as we have so often pointed out, existential concepts; and it provides us with a guarantee that, when we repeat--somewhat tediously perhaps--the formula 'God Himself, God alone,' we do not mean by it some divine thing, or some ideal world contrasted with the visible world. We mean by the formula that unsearchable, divine relationship in which we stand as men. It is in the actual tension and movement of human life. . . that our existential concepts and formulations emerge. And it is precisely here that they emerge in their abstract contrast with everything of this world." In Levinas' AE the self is held "hostage" to the Other's welfare; cf. TI 174 (199f.).

31. Levinas, TI 177 (202f.); Barth, R^2 117 (141). Cf. KD I/1 140 (135) on Otto's "numinous"; and cf. Levinas' DL, pp. 19, 21, 23, 29, 79, 135, 243.

32. Barth, R^1 173.

33. Levinas, TI 12f. (42f.).

34. For Barth, there is such a vantage point, but only God occupies it. In this sense his pluralism can be interpreted as a dialectic with a hidden synthesis, which is quite a different matter from the pluralism of Levinas. The idea of a synthesis is always important to Barth inasmuch as God *has* triumphed

over sin, God *has* justified Himself, and Christian rhetoric ought to reflect in its own way confidence in this fact. But the victory over sin does not entail a reduction of the difference between God and man; it turns a negative difference into the positive, fruitful, normal difference between Creator and creature, so that the situation of encounter is not something short of an ultimately desirable identity, but something far better than identity. In fact, this is the burden of the shift from R¹ to R²; and its consequence is that Barth's thought is not nearly as alien to Levinas' as it would otherwise be.

35. Levinas, TI 274f. (298f.); for Barth this issue comes to hinge on preventing the dissociation of the sovereignty of God from the sovereignty of God *in His Word*--cf. "Die Souveränität des Wortes Gottes und die Entscheidung des Glaubens," *Theologische Studien*, No. 5 (1939), p. 5 (13): "For a time this was forgotten and God was separated from His Word. It was thought that men should seek God and be able to find Him apart from His Word, in order to ascribe to Him the highest, most unconditional sovereignty. But the result was that then the talk concerned something totally different from the living God and His sovereignty. I have in mind the orthodox Schoolmen of the post-Reformation time and the way they followed the pagan tradition of describing God as 'simple, absolute Being,' going on to clothe this Being with all sorts of predicates of sovereignty. The sun--namely, the sun of the Enlightenment of later centuries--showed that this sort of talk was guilty of thoughtlessness, that with this 'Being' men had described perhaps the being of man, perhaps also the being of the world. . . But they had not described our God. . ."

36. Levinas, OF 94.

37. Barth, R² 277 (294).

38. "In relation to their systems most systematisers are like a man who builds an enormous castle and lives in a shack close by; they do not live in their own enormous systematic buildings. But spiritually that is a decisive objection. Spiritually speaking a man's thought must be the building in which he lives--otherwise everything is topsy-turvy"--Kierkegaard, *Papirer* VII-A-82 (156).

39. As, concretely, the law of the State reminds the self that its freedom is conditioned--Levinas, LC 266--or the inherited written form of Scripture reminds the church that it is not left alone with itself--Barth, KD I/1 104-107 (102-105).

40. Levinas, TI 267 (291); Barth, R² 19 (44): "We suppose that we know what we are saying when we say 'God.' We assign to Him the highest place in our world: and in so doing we place Him fundamentally on one line with ourselves and with things."

41. Barth, R² 277f. (294f.); Levinas adverts in AE to the "uncondition of the hostage" (*l'incondition d'otage*)--6 (6) and *passim*.

42. Barth, R² 320 (335).

43. Barth, KD I/2 §§19, 20.

44. Levinas has made this point too--*Débats sur le langage théologique*, ed. E. Castelli (Paris: Aubier, 1969), p. 22.

45. Levinas, AE 25 (20).

46. AE 24f. (20), my translation.

47. Levinas, OF 98.

48. Death is the source of all myths--Levinas, TI 154 (179).

49. In *Die christliche Dogmatik* (CD) (Munich: Chr. Kaiser, 1927), Barth deals with the doctrine of the Trinity (i.e. of *who* God is) strictly as an articulation of revelation (Revealer, Revealed, Revelation)--§9. The Resurrection (= Revelation) of Christ signifies first of all in R^2 as the enigmatic intersection with history of One who is Other than history--6 (30); just as the first vision of eschatology, for Levinas, "reveals the very possibility of eschatology, that is, the breach of the totality"--TI xif. (23). On teaching teaching, cf. TI 41, 73, 146 (69, 100, 171).

50. Cf. Barth, KD I/2 676f. (606f.). Whereas for Barth we are primarily pupils of the Truth--N.B. a certain kind of Truth, not merely "cognitive"--for Levinas we are primarily pupils of each other: no small difference, especially in view of EE's protest against the collectivity of truth as a model of human relations--161f. (94f.). This points to the issue we have reserved for our Conclusion. However, Levinas' as well as Barth's concept of teaching implies that a fundamental disobedience or violence would be committed if the *matter* taught by another were not attended to, in faithfulness to the teaching. "But when we do take the humanity of the Bible quite seriously we must also take quite definitely the fact that as a human word it does say something specific, that as a human word it points towards a fact, an object. . . What human word is there which does not do the same? We do not speak for the sake of speaking, but for the sake of the indication which is to be made by our speaking. . . My exposition cannot possibly consist in an interpretation of the speaker. Did he say something to me only to display himself? I should be guilty of a shameless violence against him, if the only result of my encounter with him were that I now knew him or knew him better than before. What lack of love! Did he not say anything to me at all?"--KD I/2 513, 515 (464f.).

51. Barth, R^2 xff., xvi (6ff., 13).

52. Levinas, *Quatres lectures talmudiques* 14f.

53. Levinas, DL 344; cf. 212, 284. The same principle applies to the study of other philosophers; e.g., "The great interest of Rosenzweig's thought lies in the questions it leads to, rather than in the influences it has been subject to"--DL 234. "I will stick to presenting that signification of the thought of Jean Wahl that does not reduce the coherence or incoherence of the signifiers that bear it, or to their psychological genesis. It is necessary to listen to this sense without *leaning* over its tracks in order to check its logic or discover its psychology. On the contrary, it is necessary to speak of it as though we were *raising our eyes* toward a teaching. . ."--"Jean Wahl. Sans Avoir ni Etre," in *Jean Wahl et Gabriel Marcel*, by Levinas *et. al.*, ed. J. Hersch (Paris: Beauchesne, 1976), p. 15. Cf. Barth, KD I/2 806 (719): "The Bible is outwardly, so to speak, accessible only from a certain point below. Therefore we must take our stand at that point below, in order to look up to the corresponding point above."

54. Cf. the introductions to *Quatre lectures talmudique* and *Du sacré au saint* (*op. cit.*), which emphasize the normative *viva voce* presence of the inquirers to each other, and CD 345 where Barth says the evil of an "oracular" Scripture is that it would interfere with *God* speaking in person, by confusing what

the Speaker uses to speak with the Speaker Himself, and by turning revelation into a given.

55. Levinas, "La trace de l'autre," DEHH 191 (37).

56. Levinas, AE 195 (153).

57. Barth and Thurneysen, *Komm Schöpfer Geist!* (Munich: Chr. Kaiser, 1924), p. 125 (132).

58. Levinas claims that moral responsibility breaches the self's identity (adequation to self, or satisfaction with self), so that the "place" (*lieu*) of the moral self is a "non-place" or "null-site" (*non-lieu*)--as opposed to the (Heideggerian) *site* of pagan rootedness--AE 18 (14) and *passim*. He therefore embraces the charge of "utopianism"--AE 232 (184).

59. Barth, R² 427ff., 437, 479 (442ff., 452, 495); Levinas, TI 9, 21, 51 (39, 50, 78).

60. Barth, R² 370 (386).

61. Barth, KD I/2 §22.3. Barth never published a separate *Ethik*, although his ethics lectures from 1928 and 1929 appeared posthumously; he makes the same point at the beginning of these--*Ethik I*, ed. D. Braun (Zurich: TVZ, 1973), p. 13 (9f.).

62. Levinas, TI 281 (304).

63. "Goodness consists in taking up a position in being such that the Other Person counts more than myself. Goodness thus involves the possibility for the I that is exposed to the alienation of its powers by death to not be for death"--Levinas, TI 225 (247); cf. TI 153f., 216f., 251, 260, and 284 (179, 239, 274, 284, and 306f.) for this protest against the Heideggerian primacy of death. Cf. Barth, KD I/1 146 (141f.): "[D]eath is dumb. It neither questions nor answers. It is only the end. It is not really a thing outside and above our existence which can aim at our existence and smite it. The Word of God is the Word of the Lord because it comes from the point outside and above us from which death itself would not speak to us even if it could speak at all." "One man can reveal himself to another. And man can be reconciled to his destiny, even to death, and even--which is perhaps the greatest thing of all--to his fellow-man. But none of this is the act of the Son of God"--*Ibid.* 446 (424f.).

64. Barth, KD I/1 115 (113). Cf. Barth's *Die protestantische Theologie im 19. Jahrhundert* (Zurich: EVZ, 1947), and Dieter Schellong and Karl G. Steck, "Karl Barth und die Neuzeit," *Theologische Existenz Heute*, n.F. No. 173 (1973).

65. That is, an original symmetry (denied by Levinas) is presupposed as to what may be expected of myself and what of another; whereas the practical standpoint properly involves at least a second person irreducible to the first--cf. John Macmurray, *The Self as Agent* (London: Faber, 1957), Chapter 3.

66. Barth allows the truth of this--for the old man, for the church of Esau, i.e. as a function of sin and wrath (R¹ 312).

67. Levinas, TI 277 (300); Barth, R² 453 (468).

68. Barth, R² 147 (169); Levinas, TI 3 (33).

69. "Exteriority" is not a Barthian term, but God's Otherness is represented throughout R² geometrico-spatially, as the intersection of our plane from above, or the tangential intersection of a point on the perimeter of our circle--e.g. R² 5f., 170f. (29f., 191).

70. Levinas, AE 86n., 105, 116 (191, n. 3; 84; 91).

71. Barth portrays his dialectic, at the end of CD, as
Moses' staff parting by God's power the Red Sea of unqualified
human religious language (see below, p. 139). In the article
"Enigme et phénomène" Levinas writes: "Bergson has taught us
that disorder, like nothingness, is a relative idea [i.e. is
an alternate order]. Is the irruption of absolute alterity in
the Same, that of the Other Person, necessary for an absolute
disordering? . . . Jankélévitch seeks, however [*Philosophie
première, op. cit.*], to pierce order in 'glimpsing' [*entrevi-
sion*], even if the regularity of phenomena will again fill the
gap, like the waters of the Red Sea covered over the passage
that had for one night been rent in it. . . Our work owes him
a great deal"--DEHH 206 + note.
72. Levinas, AE 24 (20). "But in philosophy the fine
risk is always to be run"--*Ibid.* (my translations).
73. Barth, R² 221 (239). "[T]he problem at issue is
that of theological language, which even though it can only be
the language of the world, must still believe at root, cost
what it will, that contrary to the natural capabilities of this
language it can and should speak of God's revelation"--KD I/1
360 (341).

Chapter V

1. For further information on this period of Barth's
development, see von Balthasar, Bouillard, Busch, Monsma, and
Smart (*op. cit.*). Especially valuable sources for Barth's
dialectical theology of the 1920's are Christof Gestrich,
*Neuzeitliches Denken und die Spaltung der dialektischen Theolo-
gie* (Tübingen: J. C. B. Mohr, 1977), and T. F. Torrance (*op.
cit.*).
2. Busch 135 (123); cf. Barth to Thurneysen, Feb. 1
and 15, 1921 (RTM 56).
3. See above, p. 39.
4. "On no account will I neglect ever to take direction
from the right and to watch carefully what you do and say"--
Barth to Thurneysen, Oct. 9, 1921 (RTM 60).
5. "Das Wort Gottes als Aufgabe der Theologie," in
WGT, p. 162f. (193).
6. "Not und Verheißung der christlichen Verkündigung,"
in WGT, p. 99 (97f.).
7. Busch 139ff. (126ff.).
8. "We stand actually *between* the times, burdened with
the unhappy pietistic-rationalistic heritage of the last two
centuries, from which it is not so easy to free ourselves as
many men not closely involved imagine. And we stand before a
future which we, who are armed with only a few very modest new
approaches, must meet very cautiously"--"Wünschbarkeit und
Möglichkeit eines allgemeinen reformierten Glaubensbekenntnis-
ses," in TK, p. 100 (131). Barth criticizes Brunner's book on
Schleiermacher--*Die Mystik und das Wort* (Tübingen: J. C. B.
Mohr, 1924)--for its too-facile assumption that we can simply
identify and renounce this unhappy heritage--"Brunners Schleiermacherbuch," *Zwischen den Zeiten*, 2 (1924), 49-64.
9. Barth to Thurneysen, Feb. 5, 1924 (RTM 168).
10. Barth finds Paul applying an *exterior* standard
(revelation) to the "religious phenomena" of the Corinth community: "Where does the daemoniac start? Where does the

divinely operative cease? . . . The name *Jesus* is for Paul the criterion before which the spirits separate. He who can curse Jesus surely does not speak in the Spirit of God, whereas the name Jesus Kyrios is impossible without this Spirit"--*Die Auferstehung der Toten* 40 (77f.). Barth proposes this same standard against Harnack in their exchange of 1923, in response to Harnack's plea for scientific historical objectivity as a check on "experience"--"Ein Briefwechsel zwischen Karl Barth und Adolf von Harnack," in *Anfänge* I, pp. 323, 325f. (165, 167).

11. *Die Dogmatik der evangelisch-reformierten Kirche*, eds. H. Heppe and E. Bizer (Neukirchen: Buchhandlung des Erziehungsvereins Neukirchen, Kreis Moers, 1935), p. iii (v); cf. Busch 166f. (153f.).

12. *Ibid.*

13. WGT 167f. (200f.).

14. "Reformierte Lehre, ihr Wesen und ihre Aufgabe," in WGT, p. 180 (220f.).

15. WGT 166 (199).

16. WGT 173 (209).

17. TK 79-85 (114-119). Another feature appealed to Barth: "Acceptance of dogma among the old Reformed had nothing to do with abstract gnosis. It was wholly ethical. The *whole* man, the whole *city* was requisitioned by the 'parole de Dieu' which was confessed"--TI 101 (132).

18. "Das Schriftprinzip der Reformierten Kirche," *Zwischen den Zeiten*, 3 (1925), 215-245. Cf. Busch 170 (161). This article was substantially reproduced in §20 of *Die christliche Dogmatik*.

19. "Schriftprinzip" 215f.

20. *Ibid.* 220.

21. *Die Auferstehung der Toten* §4.

22. "Schriftprinzip" 235-240.

23. *Ibid.* 242; cf. his disapproval of Peterson's "often-repeated formula 'there is' [*es gibt*] this and that dogma, statement, theology, etc." when it stands without dialectical qualification--TI 312 (294).

24. "Schriftprinzip" 221ff.

25. *Ibid.* 218, 225f.

26. *Ibid.* 235; 228, 231f., 234.

27. *Ibid.* 221.

28. *Ibid.* 224f.

29. *Ibid.* 224.

30. *Ibid.* 243.

31. *Ibid.* 224, 244f.

32. The argument is analogous to that of CGG (see above, p. 16).

33. "Schriftprinzip" 241ff.

34. Cf. Busch 142, 156 (129, 143), on the opening of Barth's eyes in Göttingen to the Reformers.

35. CD ix; Busch 187 (174).

36. CD viii; Busch 187 (174).

37. CD 54. The Reformation, which was a struggle not for arbitrary subjective freedom but for the correct authority, is absolved from responsibility for "Cartesianism"--CD 391.

38. CD 294.

39. CD 308.

40. CD 301-318.

41. CD 109f.

42. CD 298.

43. CD 315.
44. CD 438.
45. CD 98.
46. CD 101f.
47. CD 134.
48. CD 306f.
49. CD 8.
50. CD 112.
51. CD 122f.
52. CD 255, 264.
53. CD 257.
54. CD 287.
55. Cf. GPG 22.
56. CD 18.
57. CD 32, 429.
58. CD 362-388.
59. CD 388-410.
60. CD 57.
61. CD 65.
62. CD 76.
63. Cf. KD II/1 715 (635), where Barth criticizes the timelessness of R^2's "hope."
64. CD 80f.
65. CD §§15, 16; pp. 230-284.
66. CD 170.
67. CD 211.
68. CD 217f.
69. CD 455.
70. CD 63, 126, 135ff., 157.
71. CD 268-272.
72. CD 126.
73. CD 130.
74. CD 169.
75. CD 25.
76. CD 62f.
77. CD 111.
78. *Ibid.*
79. WGT 101 (100).
80. CD 48f.
81. CD 56.
82. CD 80.
83. CD 394f.
84. CD 399; cf. 389.
85. CD 315, 296.
86. CD 71f. Cf. "Das Halten der Gebote" (1927), in *Theologische Fragen und Antworten* (TFA) (Zurich: EVZ, 1957), where with explicit reference to Kierkegaard Barth portrays the reality of our "concrete situation" as "decision" (207) and at no point strays far from this theme, perhaps to emphasize the great difference in his approach vis-à-vis his earlier pronouncement "The Problem of Ethics Today" (see below, p. 158f.)
87. §§11, 12, 13, 14, 16, 18.
88. CD 68.
89. CD 68-71.
90. CD 132.
91. CD 218.
92. See especially T. Siegfried, *Das Wort und die Existenz* (3 vols.), Vol. 1: *Die Theologie des Wortes bei Karl Barth* (Gotha: L. Klotz, 1930). "Man's contradiction" is

precisely the point which Gogarten finds crucially important. But Gogarten's desire for further clarification of the contradiction only increases Barth's distaste for the concept in KD I/1 (see below). See Gogarten's review "Karl Barths Dogmatik," *Theologische Rundschau*, n.F. 1 (1929), p. 66.

93. Two years later, in "Schicksal und Idee in der Theologie" (TFA 54-92), Barth says pointedly that "theology may in no sense and under no pretext wish to be anthropology, i.e. reflection on the reality and truth of man, because it is reflection on the reality and truth of the Word of God spoken to man"--the Word, not Existence (85).

94. CD 228.
95. CD 403-406.
96. CD 461f.
97. TFA 57.
98. TFA 54.
99. TFA 88f.
100. TFA 90ff.
101. TFA 87.
102. TFA 90.
103. TFA 69.
104. *How I Changed My Mind* 42ff.
105. "Ludwig Feuerbach," in TK, p. 212 (217).
106. Marx and Freud are not referred to personally by Barth in R^2, but his pessimism and scepticism regarding the *historical* and the *psychological* is rather allusive--"Can anyone rid me of the suspicion, amounting almost to a certainty, that the story of my life and the history of humanity could be more honestly described if the stomach rather than the head were adopted as the point of departure?"--R^2 295 (311f.); cf. 260 (277). "Everything then becomes Libido: life becomes totally erotic. When the frontier between God and man, the last inexorable barrier and obstacle, is not closed, the barrier between what is normal and what is perverse is opened"-- R^2 28 (53). Barth quotes Nietzsche several times in R^2 and borrows phrases like "beyond good and evil" and "revaluation of all values" to refer to *God's* transcendence and *God's* critique of religion.
107. TK 224 (226).
108. TK 237 (235).
109. *Fides quaerens intellectum. Anselms Beweis der Existenz Gottes* (FQI) (Munich: Chr. Kaiser, 1931). This book had an especially high place in Barth's estimation--*How I Changed My Mind* 43. Since we are interested here in the development of Barth's thought, and not in the scholarly strength or weakness of his reading of Anselm, we will look at Anselm exclusively through Barth's eyes; but cf. Manfred Josuttis, *Die Gegenständlichkeit der Offenbarung* (Bonn: Bouvier and Co., 1965), for discussion of the differences between Barth and Anselm.
110. FQI 19f. (27).
111. FQI 18 (26). This objective *Credo*, rooted in the church, explains "the characteristic absence of crisis in Anselm's theologizing"--*Ibid.*
112. FQI 74 (70).
113. FQI 2ff., 30f. (14f., 35). The quest is for the intelligibility, not the credibility, of faith's object-- 82 (78).
114. FQI 22-27, 31-36 (29-32, 35-39).

115. FQI 51f. (52).
116. FQI 60ff. (59ff.).
117. FQI 81 (77).
118. *Das Wesen des Christentums* (Berlin: Akademie-Verlag, 1956), p. 311 (199).
119. *Ibid.* 309f. (198).
120. FQI 77f. (74).
121. FQI 88 (83).
122. FQI 160ff. (140f.).
123. FQI 162 (142). For Gaunilo and Descartes, on the other hand, it is the existence of self-consciousness that is most certain.
124. FQI 167 (145f.).
125. FQI 172 (150).
126. FQI 175 (152).
127. FQI 167 (145f.).
128. FQI 173, 180 (151, 156).
129. FQI 181 (157).
130. FQI 173 (151).
131. FQI 182f. (158f.).
132. FQI 83f. (79f.).
133. Cf. WGT 50f. (298ff.).
134. FQI 4f. (15). Cf. KD II/1 740f. (656f.).
135. KD I/1 168ff. (162ff.).
136. KD I/1 169f., 171 (163f., 165).
137. KD I/1 175 (168).
138. KD I/1 339 (321).
139. KD I/1 186 (179).
140. KD I/1 262f. (249).
141. E.g., KD I/1 182, 186, 217 (175, 178f., 207). "The fact that the *Deus revelatus* is also the *Deus absconditus* and the *Deus absconditus* the *Deus revelatus*, that the Father glorifies the Son and the Son the Father, is not self-evident, i.e., intelligible *per se*, as the immanent dialectic of this or that sphere of human life, or perhaps a dialectic like the Hegelian In itself and For itself, is intelligible *per se*, i.e. resolvable into a third. If the goodness and holiness of God are neither experiences we can manufacture nor concepts we can form for ourselves but divine modes of being to which human experiences and concepts can at least respond, then their conjunction, their dialectic, in which both are only what they are, is certainly not a dialectic which we can know, i.e., achieve for ourselves, but one which we can only ascertain and acknowledge as actually taking place"--KD I/1 348f. (330).
142. KD I/1 182f. (175).
143. We are endeavoring in this section to find in the often ambiguous (for this purpose) text of KD I/1 the elements of Barth's break with dialectical theology, based on God's givenness according to the *analogia fidei*. As von Balthasar says, however, "Barth did not suddenly replace dialectics with analogy. The change cannot be isolated in any one passage, for it took place gradually. Hardly noticeable in the first volume of *Dogmatics*, Barth takes note of it in Volume 2 [I/2] (1938) . . . One will look in vain for a fully developed version of this doctrine in the earliest stages of *Dogmatics* (1932). The first volume does move far beyond the existential-anthropological cast of the *Prolegomena* [CD], seeking a purely theological foundation in the Word of God; but Christology remains in the background. Yet even in this volume we see the analogy of faith

emerging within his discussion of the Word of God, as yet unrelated to Christology" -- *Karl Barth* 116f. (93f.). This is
correct; but the present purpose is to see exactly how Barth's
thought had already changed by this point, on the hypothesis
that he learned something of the highest importance (as he himself says) in his study of Anselm. If Anselm did indeed give
him a key to his theological method, then it should be (and is)
discernible even in the first half-volume of the *Church Dogmatics*.
It is also true that much of what Barth writes in KD I/1 was
already asserted in CD or could easily be read backwards into
it, which shows that the "dialectical theology" was not merely
dialectical but a theology of the revealed Word. Were it not
for the Red Sea story placed at the end of that work, it might
even be possible to view CD as the decisive break with dialectics, and the work on Anselm as a confirming and deepening of
that break. But Barth's self-interpretation invites us to look
at the matter otherwise.

    144. KD I/1 128 (125).

    145. KD I/1 128ff. (125ff.). We defended Barth in ad-
vance on this count; see above, p. 137.

    146. KD I/1 130ff. (127ff.); Friedrich Gogarten, "Das
Problem einer theologischen Anthropologie," *Zwischen den Zeiten*,
7 (1929), 493-511, and *Ich glaube an den dreieinigen Gott* (Jena:
Diederichs, 1926).

    147. KD I/1 25ff. (27ff.); Emil Brunner, "Die andere
Aufgabe der Theologie," *Zwischen den Zeiten*, 7 (1929), 255-276.

    148. KD I/1 132 (128); Rudolf Bultmann, "The Concept of
Revelation in the New Testament" and "The Historicity of Man
and Faith," in *Existence and Faith*, tr. S. M. Ogden (New York:
Living Age Books, 1960). Cf. Bultmann to Barth, June 8, 1928,
in *Barth-Bultmann Briefwechsel 1922-1966*, ed. B. Jaspert (Zurich:
TVZ, 1971).

    149. Barth now denies that there ever has been or could
be a *philosophia christiana*--KD I/1 4 (6).

    150. KD I/1 55 (54f.); Paul Tillich, *Religiöse Verwirk-
lichung* (Berlin: Furche, 1930).

    151. KD I/1 166 (160).

    152. KD I/1 191 (184).

    153. KD I/1 152 (147).

    154. KD I/1 114 (111).

    155. KD I/1 148 (143).

    156. KD I/1 467 (444).

    157. "If we consider what [God's personhood] implies, it
will not occur to us to see in this personalising of the concept
of God's Word a case of anthropomorphism. The doubtful thing
is not whether God is person, but whether we are"--KD I/1 143
(138). "One should not say that the use of the name 'Father'
here [as eternal Father of the eternal Son] is a transferred,
improper and inadequate use. This could be said only if the
standard of what is proper here and generally were our language
or the created reality to which our language is related. If
the Creator is the standard of what is proper for the creature
and therefore for our language too, then the very reverse must
be said. . . God alone. . . is properly and adequately to be
called Father"--413 (392f.).

    158. KD I/1 348f. (329f.).

    159. KD I/1 91 (90).

    160. KD I/1 90 (89).

    161. KD I/1 93 (91f.).

162. KD I/1 107 (105).
163. KD I/1 143 (139).
164. KD I/1 146 (141). An important implication of this
relation of ours to the Word is that we participate in "real
encounter" in our arguments with each other to the extent that
the object of our discourse is *this* Object. Thus the "paradoxical fact of heresy"--i.e. the existence of different views of
the same object (in Catholicism and neo-Protestantism)--provides
the *theological* reason for dogmatic prolegomena, in a way that
philosophies or modern world-views cannot--33ff. (34ff.). This
way of starting dogmatics in KD as opposed to CD presupposes
the real givenness of, and relationship with, the Object.
165. KD I/1 63, 69, 152, 282 (62, 68, 147, 267).
166. KD I/1 27f. (29).
167. *Ibid.*; 257 (243f.).
168. KD I/1 250 (238).
169. KD I/1 96 (94).
170. KD I/1 195 (188).
171. KD I/1 9 (10).
172. KD I/1 10f. (12).
173. KD I/1 462 (440).
174. KD I/1 236ff. (225ff.).
175. KD I/1 207 (199).
176. KD I/1 216f. (207).
177. KD I/1 218 (208).
178. KD I/1 231 (220f.).
179. KD I/1 226ff. (216f.).
180. KD I/1 362 (343).
181. "Das Problem der Ethik in der Gegenwart," in WGT.
182. WGT 125ff. (136ff.).
183. WGT 136-145 (152-167).
184. "Brunner's [natural theology] was very much more
interesting in its earlier form, in accordance with Kierkegaard
and Heidegger. For, in spite of its restrained formulation, it
raised the problem of a peculiar aptitude of man for divine
revelation in a much more acute, tempting and dangerous form.
I confess that around 1920, and perhaps even later, I might
still have succumbed to it. And who knows whether one could
not find passages in the *Epistle to the Romans* in which I have
said something of the sort myself. According to Brunner's
former explanation, man's aptitude for the revelation of God
consists only in the fact that in the rational existence of man
there is a diacritical point where this existence can become
discontinuous, where it can issue in a 'negative point,' where
its most essential truth, its 'fundamental condition,' i.e.
despair, can come to light"--"Nein!," in "*Dialektische Theologie*" *in Scheidung und Bewährung 1933-1936*, ed. W. Fürst (Munich:
Chr. Kaiser, 1966), p. 247 (114f.).
185. WGT 147 (169).
186. Cf. his articles "Das Halten der Gebote" (*op. cit.*)
and "Rechtfertigung und Heiligung," *Zwischen den Zeiten*, 5
(1927), 281-309.
187. "Ludwig Feuerbach," in TK (*op. cit.*).
188. TK 238 (236). Cf. "Barth-Harnack Briefwechsel," in
Anfänge I, p. 326f. (168).
189. Barth to Thurneysen, Oct. 7, 1922 (RTM 110).
190. CD 219. Barth criticizes Gogarten for taking it
for granted that it happens, i.e. that the limit is naturally

self-evident--*Ethik I*, ed. D. Braun (Zurich: TVA, 1973), p. 73f. (44).

191. *Ethik I* 72f. (43f.).
192. *Ethik I* 73 (44).
193. D. Braun suggests that Barth has his brother Heinrich, whose *Philosophie der praktischen Vernunft* (Tübingen: J. C. B. Mohr, 1927) appeared the year before, in mind--*Ethik I* 30 (19), n. 1.
194. KD I/2 47 (42).
195. KD I/2 47f. (42f.).
196. KD I/2 442ff. (401ff.).
197. KD I/2 442 (401).
198. KD I/2 457 (414).
199. KD I/2 452f. (410f.).
200. KD I/2 459 (416f.).
201. KD I/2 473f. (429).
202. KD I/2 476 (431).
203. KD I/2 478 (433). Consider as a background to the preceding argument the identification of the Wholly Other as Jesus Christ, *deus incarnatus, as such*--*Ethik II*, ed. D. Braun (Zurich: TVZ, 1978), pp. 137, 142 (332, 335). The command of God loses none of its strangeness by assuming human form.
204. *Ethik I* 74 (45).

Chapter VI

1. For further analysis of the developments in Levinas' philosophy over part or all of this period, see Olmedo Gaviria Alvarez, "L'idée de création chez Levinas," *Revue Philosophique de Louvain*, 72 (1974), 509-538; Jan De Greef, "Le lointain et le prochain," *Tijdschrift voor Filosofie*, 31 (1969), 490-516; Ad Peperzak, review of Levinas, *Autrement qu'être ou au-delà de l'essence*, in *Philosophische Rundschau*, 24 (1977), 91-116--ET "Beyond Being," tr. M. E. Petrisko, *Research in Phenomenology*, 8 (1978), 239-261; Stephan Strasser, *Jenseits von Sein und Zeit* (The Hague: Martinus Nijhoff, 1978); and Burggraeve, de Boer, Guillot, and Wyschogrod (*Emmanuel Levinas*) (*op. cit.*).
2. De Boer 11.
3. Jan. 27, 1962, of which "Transcendance et hauteur" (TH) is a report.
4. "Violence et métaphysique," *op. cit.*
5. (AE). The adverbalization of *Autre*, "*Autrement*," detours around static ideas of either Being or the Other. "Exteriority" is no longer the formula in AE.
6. DEHH 171.
7. TH 105.
8. Descartes elsewhere grounds the existence of God on the certainty of the *cogito*--DEHH 174--and grants to God only a superlative *being*--"Dieu et la philosophie" ("Dieu"), *Le Nouveau Commerce*, Nos. 30-31 (1975), p. 109 (132).
9. René Descartes, *Meditationes de prima Philosophia*, in *Oeuvres de Descartes* (11 vols.), Vol. 7, ed. C. Adam and P. Tannery (Paris: Cerf, 1904), p. 92f. (165f.).
10. Descartes 97f. (171).
11. TI 186f. (211f.).
12. AE 185ff. (145ff.).
13. TH 107.
14. DEHH 191 (37).

15. DEHH 191f. (38).

16. DEHH 194 (40).

17. Levinas refers to Plotinus' remark (*Enneads* V.5) that all being is in the "trace" of the One--DEHH 201 (45f.). That is, the absolutely Other does have a relationship with Being, but one that calls for an extraordinary description, to match the ambiguity created by the absolution of the Other (Plotinus' One, "resting in itself") from Being.

18. DEHH 198 (43).

19. DEHH 200 (44).

20. DEHH 200 (44f.).

21. "Enigme et phénomène" (1965), in DEHH, p. 205. The terminology is taken from structuralism: "diachronics" pertain to changes and events occurring over time, "synchronics" to the systematic structure (e.g. of language, or the broader significa-cation-system of culture) that determines possibilities of meaning at every moment.

22. DEHH 209.

23. DEHH 210f.

24. DEHH 211.

25. DEHH 199 (44).

26. DEHH 202 (46).

27. *Ibid.*

28. "Enigme et phénomène," DEHH 216.

29. "Langage et proximité" (1967), in DEHH, p. 236.

30. Cf. "Le nom de Dieu d'après quelques textes tal-mudiques," in *L'analyse du langage théologique. Le nom de Dieu*, ed. E. Castelli (Paris: Aubier, 1969), pp. 156, 164ff.

31. AE x (xlii).

32. "Dieu" (1975), *op. cit.*

33. See below, Chapter VI, Section 4.

34. Cf. EE 62 (41).

35. TI 188 (213).

36. TI 267 (291); cf. 273 (296f.): "The overflowing of exteriority. . . constitutes the dimension of height or the divinity of exteriority. Divinity keeps its distances. Dis-course is discourse with God and not with equals, according to the distinction established by Plato in the *Phaedrus*. Metaphys-ics is the essence of this language with God; it leads above being."

37. TI 269 (293).

38. TI 251-261 (274-285).

39. See below, Chapter VIII.

40. AE 19 (16).

41. AE 20 (16), my translation; cf. 165, 200ff., 204 (128, 157ff., 160).

42. AE 84n. (191, n. 2).

43. AE 202 (158), my translation.

44. DEHH 224.

45. TI 174 (199f.).

46. DEHH 224f.

47. The self also transcends totality by family rela-tions (eros and fecundity).

48. TH 96 (cf. DEHH 196).

49. TH 97.

50. DEHH 229.

51. DEHH 233.

52. As in Chapter 53 of Isaiah--DEHH 196.

53. DEHH 234; cf. AE 150 (117).

54. TH 106f.
55. See AE, Chapter 1.
56. AE 132f., 130 (104, 102), my translation.
57. TI 100-103, 108ff. (127-130, 135ff.).
58. Levinas may refer to this by designating the cultural the *au-delà* and the sensible the *en-deçà*--DEHH 6 (2nd ed. Preface).
59. DEHH 205.
60. AE 187 (147).
61 There is a shorter version of this AE argument (Chapter 2) in "Langage et proximité."
62. DEHH 221.
63. *Ibid.*
64. DEHH 222.
65. The "passive synthesis" referred to is a Husserlian topic--see especially Part I of *Experience and Judgment*. On "synthesis" and "identification" as the primal work of consciousness, cf. §17f. of the *Cartesian Meditations*, and also §37ff. on the passive *genesis* that is the "history" of the passive synthesis of meanings that consciousness finds "ready-made." Levinas seems to have both of these in mind. Cf. DEHH 118 on the *"Urimpression"* in internal time-consciousness.
66. DEHH 223.
67. DEHH 226f.; cf. TI II.A.2, II.B.2.
68. DEHH 228ff.
69. AE 18 (14).
70. *Phaedrus* 251a-b; or the love-sickness of the Song of Solomon (5:8)--AE 181n. (198, n. 5).
71. AE 86n., 105, 110, 116, 227 (191, n. 3; 84, 87, 91, 180).
72. AE 81, 84, 141f., 146f., 160, 187 (64, 67, 111, 114ff., 124, 146); also "respiration" or "gasping for breath" (*essouflement, halètement*)--AE 227ff. (180ff.).
73. AE 190f. (149f.), my translation.
74. AE 187 (146f.).
75. Cf. Q&R 106.
76. AE 8 (7), my translations.
77. DEHH 199.
78. Cf. Stephan Strasser, "Antiphénoménologie et phénoménologie dans la philosophie d'Emmanuel Levinas," *Revue Philosophique de Louvain*, 75 (1977), 101-125.
79. Cf. "Enigme et phénomène," in DEHH.
80. "Réflexions sur la 'technique' phénoménologique" (1959), DEHH 111.
81. Including his doctrines of intuition, ideas, the reduction, and intersubjectivity--DEHH 112.
82. Phenomenology does not so control its agenda as to exclude "non-philosophical experiences"--cf. AE 154 (120).
83. "The role played by a given historical situation in Hegel, outside of which this or that idea is not even *thinkable*--this role is played in Husserl by the sequence of subjective steps, which is every bit as necessary and every bit as indispensable"--DEHH 117.
84. DEHH 112-122. Cf. Levinas, "De la conscience à la veille," *Bijdragen*, 35 (1974), 235-249.
85. The "new commentaries" of DEHH, pp. 111-162.
86. Originally published in 1964; included in *Humanisme de l'autre homme* (HAH) (Montpellier: Fata Morgana, 1972).
87. HAH 19.

88. HAH 20.
89. HAH 26ff.
90. HAH 29.
91. I.e. the pluralism of merely separated existences--
HAH 33.
92. HAH 35.
93. HAH 37.
94. AE 174-178 (136-140).
95. HAH 36f. "*Sens unique*" is a significant pun, since its everyday meaning is "one way" (as in "one way street"); *sens* refers to both meaning and direction. Thus the unique meaning is also a pointer, and an irreversible movement.
96. HAH 21. An "empty" signification or intention is an impossible meaning proposal, like "four-sided triangle."
97. Even in the late work "The Origin of Geometry," Husserl understood the foundation of meaning to lie in the possibility of finding the intuitive fulfillment of a proposition, while he acknowledged that propositions could be (and in some sense had to be) transmitted by non-intuitive means, such as written language.
98. AE 231 (183).
99. But Levinas also claims that his philosophy is a phenomenology, even if not by Husserl's rules--Q&R 72. The same ambiguity applies to concepts such as "reason" and "experience," which Levinas alternately claims to transcend and to embrace (as transformed). One has to attend to the definitions of the terms in each case. For example, the "phenomenology" that is embraced is defined as the discovery of new meanings in the analysis of what is thought, apart from any deductive or dialectical implication--*Ibid.* In my judgment, however, the concept of phenomenology simply will not stretch to cover Levinas' method of emphasis (see below, p. 188), inasmuch as the "bringing to light" or "evidencing" essential to the idea of *phenomenon* is replaced by something very different, a kind of witnessing rather than a making-to-appear. Cf. TI 156 (181). On the other hand, among the existing Continental schools or conceptions of philosophy, it may be that phenomenology is the most apt to Levinas' aim. But the premise of our interpretation is that Levinas' philosophy is of a different, unique type, which however defines itself by distancing itself from phenomenology. We often refer to it as "ethics" inasmuch as ethics is its optics.
100. Derrida 186 + n. (126 + n.45).
101. See Martin Heidegger, *Einführung in die Metaphysik* (3rd ed.; M. Niemeyer, 1966). "The short-of or beyond Being is not a being short of or beyond Being, but no more is it an exercise of Being--an essence--truer or more authentic than the Being of beings"--AE 57 (45), my translation.
102. AE ix (xli).
103. AE 44 (34f.), my translation.
104. Levinas refers to an "*epoché*" of disinterestedness (*désintéressement* being the altruistic beyond-Being condition), and says that ethics is a movement as radical as the transcendental reduction--"Idéologie et idéalisme," in *Démythisation et idéologie*, ed. E. Castelli (Paris: Aubier, 1971), p. 137n. (138, n. 4).
105. AE 8 (7).

106. Cf. note 21, p. 281 above. Note that Levinas' usage of "diachronic" varies from the usual in precluding its subordination to, or correlation with, the synchronic.

107. AE 213 (168), my translation.

108. According to *le beau risque* that philosophy must run--AE 24 (20).

109. AE 181f. (142f.), my translation.

110. AE 228, 198 (181, 156).

111. AE 231 (183); the mutation of the intentional or ontological to the ethical is noted at AE 146 (115) and DEHH 225.

112. AE 185ff. (145ff.).

113. Q&R 73ff. Levinas has suggested that the philosophy that seeks the architectural foundations of things may have been born in the pagan wonder at the vault of the heavens--"Sécularisation et faim," in *Herméneutique de la sécularisation*, ed. E. Castelli (Paris: Aubier, 1976), pp. 101-109. This strikes another counterpoint with Kant by implying a possible competition between the different things one can wonder at, the starry heavens above one and the moral law within one--when the wonder turns to worship.

114. Q&R 74.

115. Q&R 75.

116. TI 42 (70).

117. "De l'être à l'autre" (on Paul Celan), in *Noms propres*--ET "Being and the Other," tr. S. Melville, *Chicago Review*, 29 (1978)--pp. 61, 65f. (17f., 21).

118. "L'autre dans Proust," in *Noms propres*, p. 155.

119. "Moi" 368.

120. Derrida 124n. (84, n. 7).

121. According to the Liddell-Scott *Greek-English Lexicon*.

122. TI, section IV.

123. *Being and Time* II.1.

124. AE 212 (167), my translation.

125. HAH 99.

126. TI 122f. (148f.), my emphasis of "musts."

127. AE 233 (185), my translation and emphasis of "musts"; *l'essence* is translated "essence" throughout.

128. E.g. "Maternity. . . is the ultimate sense of this vulnerability"--AE 137 (108), meaning that one's vulnerability to being affected by the Other is so radical that the Other affects from within, "gestating," leaving no distance at all-- leaving the opposite of distance. Cf. Peperzak's review of AE (*op. cit.*), pp. 102f., 114f. (249, 259).

129. AE 229 (182), my translation; cf. 173n. (198, n. 2).

130. AE 150 (117).

131. Q&R 73, 75. (Q&R is a slightly modified version of the transcript of the conversation held with Levinas on the granting of a doctorate at Leiden University in May, 1975.) At AE 86 (68) he suggests that the very idea of an ultimate or primary meaning is ontological. This certainly heightens the ambiguity of his search for the *sens unique*.

132. EE 11 (15).

133. AE 7 (7), my translation.

134. AE 19 (16), my translation.

135. AE 166 (129), my translation.

136. AE 207 (162).

137. AE 108n. (192, n. 18).

138. *"Monstration"* appears to mean (inclusively) evidencing, showing, manifestation.

139. AE 85 (68), my translation.

140. AE 107, n. 17 (192, n. 17).

141. AE 203 (160).

142. AE 80 (63f.).

143. AE 110, 199ff. (87, 157ff.).

144. AE 6, 65 (5, 51).

145. "Exposure" being TI's "evidence that makes evidence possible"--179 (204).

146. AE 95 (75).

147. Cf. Strasser, "Antiphénoménologie" 118ff.

148. "Uniqueness here means the impossibility of getting a replacement and escaping, in which the very recurrence of the I is tied up--the uniqueness of the elect, or of the conscript who is not a voter; a passivity that does not turn into a spontaneity; a traumatic uniqueness neither assumed nor sub-sumed; an election through persecution"--AE 73 (56), my translation.

149. TI xvii (29). Heidegger represented his thought of Being as preceding the distinction between theory and practice--"Brief über den Humanismus" 116f. (301).

150. Heidegger, *Einführung in die Metaphysik* 31 (41).

151. But, as has already been noted, Levinas gives Heidegger credit for bringing a gesture of "emphasis" into philosophy--Q&R 77f.

152. Cf. Strasser, *Jenseits von Sein und Zeit*, p. 228. The responsibility of the hostage is the ultimate *Being-there*--"Dieu" 123 (140); and fear of God replaces *anxiety*--"La pensée de l'être et la question de l'Autre," *Critique*, 34 (1978), p. 194.

153. Cf. AE, Chapter 1, and "Idéologie et idéalisme."

154. Q&R 65f.

155. HAH 54f., 100 n. 9.

156. Levinas writes that his intellectual biography "is dominated by the presentiment and the memory of the Nazi horror"--"Signature," DL 374 (177).

157. HAH 11 (*King Lear* IV, 7, 53-54).

158. HAH 15.

159. AE 93 (74).

160. See especially "Humanisme et an-archie" in HAH.

161. AE 67 (52).

162. "Dieu" 117f. (145 n. 18, 137), my translation.

163. TH 110.

164. TI 51 (79).

165. Levinas calls himself only a "Sunday Talmudist," but has entered the discipline under the guidance of a master and has produced a considerable literature in this vein--"Le nom de Dieu d'après quelques textes talmudiques" 155f.

166. "Le nom de Dieu" 159, 162.

167. TI 51 (78f.).

168. TI xiif., 12 (23ff.,42).

169. This judgment must underlie his statement that the word "God" "expresses a notion that is religiously the clearest, but philosophically the most obscure of all"--*Quatre lectures talmudiques* 70. That is, one assumes that the clarity referred to is spurious. At the very least, the philosopher is in no position to accept it.

170. TI 49f. (77).

171. TI 269 (293); cf. AE 6, 120f., 148n., 155, 188, 191n., 193 (5, 94f.; 196, n. 19; 121, 147; 199, n. 21; 151), and for remarks hostile to the concept of "divinity," 68n. and 206 (190, n. 38; 162).

172. TI 76, 194 (103, 218).

173. As Derrida implies by setting a Matthew Arnold quote on Hebraism and Hellenism at the head of "Violence et métaphysique," with a James Joyce line ("Jewgreek is greekjew") at the end as a dialectical reconciliation. Levinas tries to refute in advance the suggestion that he represents a Hebraist non-philosophy challenging philosophy per se. On the other hand, Levinas can turn around and accuse the Greek tradition (as such) of ontologism or of being deaf to exteriority--"De la conscience à la veille" 242.

174. "De la conscience à la veille" 247.

175. Q&R 70.

176. "Une religion d'adultes" (1957), in DL, p. 31.

177. AE 165 (128), my translation.

178. "Dieu" 100f. (128).

179. "Dieu" 100 (128).

180. "Dieu" 102 (129), my translation.

181. "Dieu" 107 (132). This is true also of dialectical theology!--108 (132).

182. "Dieu" 110 (133). The "*in-*" of "*infini*" means *non* and *dans* at the same time--*Ibid.*

183. "Dieu" 116 (136).

184. "Dieu" 117 (137).

185. "Dieu" 122 (140).

186. "Dieu" 125 (142).

187. The philosopher is not one of those who stood at Sinai--"Ideology and Idealism" (136) (not in French version).

188. Cf. "La révélation dans la tradition juive," in *La révélation* by Levinas *et al.* (Brussels: Facultés universitaires Saint-Louis, 1977).

189. AE 105 (83).

190. EE 121f. (71); de Boer 77.

191. Q&R 63f.

192. AE 14 (11f.), my translation.

193. Cf. AE 196 (154) on "*Dieu parlant.*"

Chapter VII

1. Barth, "Das christliche Verständnis der Offenbarung," *Theologische Existenz Heute*, n.F. No. 12 (1948), p. 8f. (210f.). Cf. KD I/2 838f. (750).

2. Levinas, "Dieu" 101 (128f.), my translation and emphasis.

3. Levinas, TI 147 (172).

4. Barth, TK 372 (340).

5. Levinas, TI 23 (52).

6. "[I]t is essentially right when John of Damascus (*Ekd.* 4, 14) describes Mary's ear as the bodily organ of the miraculous conception of Christ"--Barth, KD I/2 220 (201).

7. Levinas, *Quatre lectures talmudiques* 104f.

8. "[I]n the very self-determination, without which he would not be a man, man becomes an object of the divine pre-determination. It is in this way that the circle of his existence is intersected by the circle of revelation. The grace of

revelation is not conditioned by his humanity, but his humanity is conditioned by the grace of revelation. God's freedom does not compete with man's freedom. How could it be the freedom of the divine mercy bestowed on man, if it suppressed and dissolved human freedom? It is the grace of revelation that God exercises and maintains His freedom to free man"--Barth, KD I/2 400 (364f.).

9. Levinas, TI 273 (296). Speech "cuts across" vision--TI 169 (195); cf. Levinas' critique of vision as a model of relation with reality, TI 163ff. (189ff.).

10. Levinas, TI 273 (296).

11. Hence Barth's cardinal (Reformed) principle of *Dei loquentis persona*, "God speaking in person" as the precondition of revelation in any form--KD I/1 141 (136). Hence Levinas' (Platonic) dictum that "Oral discourse is the plenitude of discourse"--TI 69 (96).

12. While Levinas and Barth are both guided in their analyses of the revelation of the Other by the structure of language spoken and heard, revelation itself is not ultimately a speech for either, or rather claims to be "speech" in a more fundamental sense than when one person utters a sentence to another in French or German. The Christian Word of God is God Himself, the whole event of Jesus Christ. For Levinas, "the face speaks"; original language is the exposure of a nudity prior to any sonic transmission.

13. Barth, WGT 168 (201); Levinas, HAH 111 n. 10.

14. Levinas, AE 60, n. 33; 70 (189, n. 33; 54).

15. Levinas, "Moi" 361.

16. For Barth's discussion of "God's time" see KD I/2, §14. There is a fulfilled present of Revelation in the life of Jesus Christ, flanked by the prophetic expectation and the apostolic recollection. But in applying this pattern to the believer's faith the present tends to evacuate: we recollect our baptism, confessions, etc., and we wait for God's Word to come, for faith to occur--but we never *have* it in the present, except with the rider "Help my unbelief!" And even the present of Revelation is empty in the sense that the event occurred incognito and the Savior was rejected.

17. Levinas, TI 244-247 (267ff.); TA 35ff.

18. Cf. Barth, "Das erste Gebot als theologisches Axiom" (1933), in TFA.

19. KD I/1 §8. "Revealedness" here is *Offenbarsein*, not *Offenbartheit*.

20. Cf. especially Barth, "Schicksal und Idee in der Theologie."

21. Levinas, Q&R 73f.

22. Barth, R² 243 (260f.).

23. Barth, R² 370f. (386f.).

24. Barth, WGT 80 (67).

25. "In what concrete attitudes to particular political patterns and realities this Christian acknowledgement will be expressed can remain a completely open question. It makes one thing quite impossible, however: a Christian decision to be indifferent; a non-political Christianity"--"Christengemeinde und Burgergemeinde," *Theologische Studien*, No. 20 (1946), p. 11 (22).

26. Levinas, TI 37 (66).

27. Levinas, DEHH 212.

28. Levinas, DL 112.

29. Levinas, HAH 11, 100f. The "youthful" capacity for discontent with established order was concretely illustrated in the Paris student protests of 1968.

30. Levinas, AE 6 (5f.). The concept of seriousness (*gravité* vs. *jeu*, *Ernst*) is of enormous importance in Barth's and Levinas' thinking, reflecting the magnitude and irreversibility of the question of the Other. One way to distinguish their claim to find the meaning of meaning from the transcendentalism that seeks systematic foundations is to call it a transcendentalism of "seriousness": ethics and theology exceed mere theory because they are more serious. Whenever the things that are known become serious, it is by virtue of a reference outside of knowledge and beyond the arbitrary concern for self.

31. Barth, KD I/1 115 (112).

32. Barth, CD 112. "Dogma" as such is a human word, which even in an eschatological attainment of perfect obedience to God's Word would not be God's Word but would make place for it--KD I/1 §7.

33. Barth, KD I/1 454 (432)--the non-knowing knowledge should regard itself as a *knowing* non-knowledge, though.

34. Barth, KD I/1 462f. (440).

35. Levinas, DL 371.

36. Barth, KD I/1 443 (422).

37. Barth, R² xiii (10).

38. Levinas, AE 233 (185).

39. Levinas, HAH 36ff.

40. Barth, KD I/1 2 (4).

41. Barth, KD I/1 195f. (188).

42. Barth, KD I/1 215f. (206).

43. Barth, KD I/1 290f. (274f.); cf. 289 (273) on the priority of *auctoritas* to *veritas*.

44. Barth, KD I/1 491 (468).

45. Levinas, TI 60 (88).

46. Levinas, TI 176 (201).

47. Levinas, TI 267 (291).

48. Fr. Christof van Buijtenen ("Emmanuel Levinas: Tussen politiek en eschatologie," *Bijdragen*, 28 [1967], 197-211) offers a perspicuous reading of Levinas' work as a "philosophical proclamation" implying a revision of the meaning of Reason.

49. See above, p. 271, n. 53.

50. Levinas, AE 20 (16).

Chapter VIII

1. Barth, "Christliche Ethik," in "Zwei Vorträge," *Theologische Existenz Heute*, n.F. No. 3 (1946), p. 6 (89f.).

2. Barth reacted in 1933 to the "practical" justifications offered by and for the German Christians: "Where in all this was the plain but critical question as to Christian *truth*: When could all this be possible? Or, is it that this question dare not be put at all in the present Evangelical Church? Has the quest for truth been totally suppressed in one jubilation or groaning by the shouts of Revolution, Reality, Life, Mastery of Destiny! and all those other bombastic slogans that stifle all Christian criticism? Has one to be dubbed a stiff-backed ecclesiastic or a dry-stick from a student's den if he permits himself to hold that the rowdiest drum-taps as such are not, in the long run, any *argument* at all? Is the 'fine thing' in

the Movement perhaps this, that thousands never openly asked first of all as regards it: What is the Christian truth? But if all this should be true at all, how profoundly and solidly we should have stayed in the 'Faith Movement' of the eighteenth and nineteenth centuries! For this is where its highest truth lay: 'never to allow the request for, and answer for, aught of truth to be made in the Church, for it would only lead to strife and intolerance, and because nothing could be settled concerning truth and untruth, but "life" alone would matter!'"--"Theologische Existenz Heute!," in *"Dialektische Theologie" in Scheidung und Bewährung 1933-1936*, p. 65 (57f.).

    3. Levinas, EE 162 (94f.).

    4. Levinas, TH 110.

    5. Cf. Ferdinand Ebner's *The Word and the Spiritual Realities* (1921) and Eberhard Grisebach's *Gegenwart. Ein kritische Ethik* (1928), besides Buber's *I and Thou* (1923).

    6. In *Qui est Jésu-Christ?*, "Recherches et débats" No. 62, (Paris: Desclée de Brouwer, 1968).

    7. That is not to say that Levinas parochially rejects the Incarnation because he is Jewish, but that the logic and concern of his philosophy is like the logic and concern of Judaism in remaining unsympathetic to important aspects of the Incarnation. Furthermore, while we will discover what look very much like a priori reasons given by Levinas against the Incarnation, he has made it clear in a private interview that he does not consider it necessary or appropriate to argue a priori against the Incarnation. He could probably agree with Michael Wyschogrod's assessment of the divergence between the Jewish and Christian "stories": "I am convinced that it is necessary to formulate the matter in these terms, to speak of stories that diverge, because too often rationalistically minded Jewish theologians have made it appear that Judaism resists incarnation on some *a priori* grounds as if the Jewish philosopher can somehow determine ahead of time just what God can or cannot do, what is or is not possible for Him, what His dignity does or does not allow. The truth is, of course, that it would be difficult to imagine anything further removed from authentic Jewish faith which does not prescribe for God some alien frame of reference but listens obediently to God's free decisions, none of which can be prescribed or even anticipated by man. If Judaism cannot accept incarnation it is because it does not hear this story, because the Word of God as it hears it does not tell it and because Jewish faith does not testify to it. And if the church does accept incarnation, it is not because it somehow discovered that such an event had to occur given the nature of God, or of being, reality, or anything else, but because it hears that this was God's free and gracious decision, a decision not predictable by man"--"Why was and is the Theology of Karl Barth of Interest to a Jewish Theologian?," in *Footnotes to a Theology*, ed. H. M. Rumscheidt (Corp. for the Publication of Academic Studies in Religion in Canada, 1974; Supplement to *Studies in Religion*), p. 99f. Cf. Levinas, DL 141.

    8. "Un Dieu homme?" 187.

    9. *Ibid.*

   10. *Ibid.* 188.

   11. *Ibid.* 189.

   12. *Ibid.* 190.

   13. *Ibid.*

14. Levinas, DL 185.

15. On the question of Barth's employment of the theological concept of Israel, see Friedrich-Wilhelm Marquardt, *Die Entdeckung des Judentums für die christliche Theologie. Israel im Denken Karl Barths* (Munich: Chr. Kaiser, 1967), and Barth's letter to Marquardt of Sept. 5, 1967, in *Briefe 1961-1968*. See especially KD II/2 §34.

16. Barth, KD I/1 336 (318f.).

17. KD I/2 98 (89).

18. KD I/2 116 (105).

19. KD I/2 98 (89).

20. KD I/2 567f. (511).

21. Barth, R^2 350 (366).

22. To define the Jew by his rejection here means to define him by the positive moral seriousness that calls for the rejection, not to impose on him the Christian scheme in which he has only a negative role.

23. This is what Levinas means by saying that the Other "as it were bears alterity as a quality"--EE 161 (94).

24. Barth, *Einführung in die evangelische Theologie* 8 (xiii).

25. Barth, "Philosophie und Theologie," in *Philosophie und christliche Existenz*, ed. G. Huber (Basel and Stuttgart: Helbing and Lichtenhahn, 1960).

26. Barth does not claim to speak for philosophers here, but only to put the case as seems right to a theologian.

27. "Philosophie und Theologie" 103.

28. Barth, *Ethik I* 72 (43f.).

29. Levinas, DL 137.

30. Levinas, Q&R 70f.

31. A sign of the clash that can come about between two serious imperatives is provided by John Smith's critique: "Followers of Barth have welcomed with enthusiasm the new freedom for theology which his thought seeks to establish, and they have made much of the idea that the theologian is free to use any philosophy or form of thought he wishes in the service of expounding and proclaiming the biblical message. As I have said above, I acknowledge the truth in the claim that the Christian theologian has a right to insist on the normative Christian content, but like Barth, who wants safeguards against philosophy, I want safeguards in order to ensure that the new freedom of theology is not, in fact, license. Here I would introduce what I call the ethics of inquiry. The responsible thinker, as doer, is bound not only by canons of logical consistency, but also by material ideals of inquiry--honesty, sincerity, and an open concern for truth which does not guarantee any position in advance. . . When we are forced to avail ourselves of a concept or principle drawn from a way of thinking [as Barth borrows working concepts from philosophy], we are not at liberty to mean by the language involved whatever we want it to mean in order to accomplish our end. . . [freedom] to use any philosophical idea in any way we please without being implicated in its consequences, on the ground that it is done in the service of the Word, violates my ethics of inquiry and suggests a license not unlike the claim of the nihilist to be 'beyond good and evil'"--"The Significance of Karl Barth's Thought for the Relation Between Theology and Philosophy," *Union Seminary Quarterly Review*, 28 (1972), p. 28.

BIBLIOGRAPHY

1. Works of Karl Barth

For a complete bibliography of Karl Barth's publications through 1966, see Charlotte von Kirschbaum's compilation in *Antwort. Karl Barth zum 70. Geburtstag am 10. Mai 1956*, edited by E. Wolf, C. von Kirschbaum, and R. Frey (Zurich: EVZ, 1956), 945-960, and the update by Eberhard Busch in *Parrhesia. Karl Barth zum 80. Geburtstag am 10. Mai 1966*, edited by E. Busch, J. Fangmeier, and M. Geiger (Zurich: EVZ, 1966), 709-723. Only works of special relevance to our study are cited here.

Many of the important shorter writings of Barth and his contemporaries are reprinted in two anthologies: *Anfänge der dialektischen Theologie* (2 vols.), edited by J. Moltmann (Munich: Christian Kaiser, 1963)--partial English translation, *The Beginnings of Dialectic Theology*, edited by J. M. Robinson, translated by K. R. Crim and L. De Grazia (Richmond: John Knox, 1968), and *"Dialektische Theologie" in Scheidung und Bewährung 1933-1936*, edited by W. Fürst (Munich: Christian Kaiser, 1966). Barth's works will be cited in these anthologies when possible. The secondary literature they contain will not be listed separately.

"Antwort an D. Achelis und D. Drews." *Zeitschrift für Theologie und Kirche*, 19 (1909), 479-486.
Die Auferstehung der Toten. Munich: Christian Kaiser, 1924. In English: *The Resurrection of the Dead*. Translated by H. J. Stenning. London: Hodder and Stoughton, 1933.
Barth-Bultmann Briefwechsel 1922-1966. Edited by B. Jaspert. Zurich: TVZ, 1971. In English: *Karl Barth/Rudolf Bultmann Letters, 1922-1966*. Translated by G. W. Bromiley. Grand Rapids: Eerdmans, 1981.
"Barth-Harnack Briefwechsel." *Anfänge der dialektischen Theologie*, Vol. 1.
Barth-Thurneysen Briefwechsel 1913-1921. Edited by E. Thurneysen. Zurich: TVZ, 1973.
Barth-Thurneysen Briefwechsel 1921-1930. Edited by E. Thurneysen. Zurich: TVZ, 1974. [Partial English translation of this and the preceding item: *Revolutionary Theology in the Making*. Translated by J. D. Smart. Richmond: John Knox, 1964.]
Briefe 1961-1968. Edited by J. Fangmeier and H. Stoevesandt. Zurich: TVZ, 1975. In English: *Letters 1961-1968*. Translated by G. W. Bromiley. Grand Rapids: Eerdmans, 1981.
"Brunners Schleiermacherbuch." *Zwischen den Zeiten*, 2 (1924), 49-64.
"Der Christ als Zeuge." *Theologische Existenz Heute*, No. 12 (1934). In English: "The Christian as Witness" and "Appendix." *God in Action*. Translated by E. G. Homrighausen and K. J. Ernst. New York: Round Table, 1936.

"Christengemeinde und Burgergemeinde." *Theologische Studien*,
No. 20 (1946). In English: "The Christian Community
and the Civil Community." *Against the Stream*. Edited
and translated by R. G. Smith. New York: Philosophical
Library, 1954.

Die christliche Dogmatik im Entwurf. Vol. 1: *Die Lehre vom
Worte Gottes. Prolegomena zur christlichen Dogmatik*.
Munich: Christian Kaiser, 1927.

"Christliche Ethik." *Theologische Existenz Heute*, n.F. No. 3
(1946). In English: "Christian Ethics." *God Here and
Now*. Translated by P. M. van Buren. London: Routledge
and Kegan Paul, 1964.

"Der christliche Glaube und die Geschichte." *Schweizerische
Theologische Zeitschrift*, 29 (1912), 1-18, 49-72.

"Das christliche Verständnis der Offenbarung." *Theologische
Existenz Heute*, n.F. No. 12 (1948). In English: "The
Christian Understanding of Revelation." *Against the
Stream*. Edited and translated by R. G. Smith. New
York: Philosophical Library, 1954.

Credo. Munich: Christian Kaiser, 1935. In English: *Credo*.
Translated by J. Strathearn McNab. London: Hodder and
Stoughton, 1936.

Einführung in die evangelische Theologie. 2nd ed. Gütersloh:
GTB/Siebenstern, 1977. In English: *Evangelical Theol-
ogy: An Introduction*. Translated by G. Foley. New
York: Holt, Rinehart and Winston, 1963.

Ethik I (Lectures given in Münster the summer semester of 1928,
repeated in Bonn the summer semester of 1930). Edited
by D. Braun. Zurich: TVZ, 1973.

Ethik II (Lectures given in Münster the winter semester of
1928-1929, repeated in Bonn the winter semester of
1930-1931). Edited by D. Braun. Zurich: TVZ, 1978.
In English [this and the preceding item]: *Ethics*.
Translated by G. W. Bromiley. New York: Seabury, 1981.

Fides quaerens intellectum. Anselms Beweis der Existenz Gottes.
Munich: Christian Kaiser, 1931. In English: *Anselm:
Fides Quaerens Intellectum*. Translated by I. W. Robert-
son. London: SCM, 1960.

Forward to *Die Dogmatik der evangelische-reformierten Kirche*.
Originally compiled by H. Heppe and newly edited by E.
Bizer. Neukirchen: Buchhandlung des Erziehungsvereins
Neukirchen, Kreis Moers, 1935. In English: *Reformed
Dogmatics*. Translated by G. T. Thomson. London:
George Allen and Unwin, 1950.

"Der Glaube an den persönlichen Gott." *Zeitschrift für Theologie und Kirche*, 24 (1914), 21-32, 65-95.

How I Changed My Mind. Richmond: John Knox, 1966.

"Jesus Christus und die soziale Bewegung." *Der freie Aargauer*,
6, Nos. 153-156 (December 23, 26, 28, 30, 1911). In
English: "Jesus Christ and the Movement for Social
Justice." *Karl Barth and Radical Politics*. Edited and
translated by G. Hunsinger. Philadelphia: Westminster,
1976.

Karl Barth's Table Talk. Recorded and edited by J. Godsey.
Edinburgh: Oliver and Boyd, 1963.

"Die Kirche und die politische Frage von heute." *Eine Schweizer
Stimme 1938-1945*. Zurich: EVZ, 1945. In English:
The Church and the Political Problem of Our Day. New
York: Scribners, 1939.

Die kirchliche Dogmatik. Zurich: EVZ, 1938-1967 (1st ed. of
    I/1 published by Christian Kaiser in Munich, 1932). In
    English: *Church Dogmatics.* Translated by G. W. Brom-
    iley, T. F. Torrance, *et al.* Edinburgh: T. and T.
    Clark, 1936-1969.
Komm Schöpfer Geist! (with Eduard Thurneysen). Munich: Chris-
    tian Kaiser, 1924. In English: *Come Holy Spirit.*
    Translated by G. W. Richards, E. G. Homrighausen, and
    K. J. Ernst. New York: Round Table, 1933.
"Die Menschlichkeit Gottes." *Theologische Studien,* No. 48
    (1956). English: "The Humanity of God." *The Humanity
    of God.* Translated by T. Wieser and J. N. Thomas.
    Richmond: John Knox, 1960.
"Moderne Theologie und Reichsgottesarbeit." *Zeitschrift für
    Theologie und Kirche,* 19 (1909), 317-321.
"Nachwort." *Schleiermacher-Auswahl.* Edited by H. Bolli.
    Munich: Siebenstern, 1968. In English: "Concluding
    Unscientific Postscript on Schleiermacher." Translated
    by G. Hunsinger. *Studies in Religion,* 7 (1978), 117-
    135.
"Nein! Antwort an Emil Brunner." *"Dialektische Theologie" in
    Scheidung und Bewährung 1933-1936.* In English: "No!"
    Natural Theology. Translated by P. Fraenkel. London:
    G. Bles, Centenary, 1946.
"Philosophie und Theologie." *Philosophie und christliche Exis-
    tenz. Festchrift für Heinrich Barth zum 70. Geburtstag
    am 3. Februär 1960.* Edited by G. Huber. Basel and
    Stuttgart: Helbing and Lichtenhahn, 1960.
Predigten 1913. Edited by G. Sauter and N. Barth. Zurich:
    TVZ, 1976.
Predigten 1914. Edited by U. and J. Fähler. Zurich: TVZ,
    1974.
Die protestantische Theologie im 19. Jahrhundert. Zurich:
    EVZ, 1947. In English: *Protestant Theology in the
    Nineteenth Century.* Translated by B. Cozens. Valley
    Forge: Judson, 1973.
"Rechtfertigung und Heiligung." *Zwischen den Zeiten,* 5 (1927),
    281-309.
"Religion und Leben" (Lecture given on October 9, 1917, in
    Safenwil). *Evangelische Theologie,* 10-11 (1952-1953),
    437-451.
Der Römerbrief. 1st ed. Bern: G. A. Bäschlin, 1919.
Der Römerbrief. 2nd ed. Munich: Christian Kaiser, 1922. In
    English (from the 6th ed.): *The Epistle to the Romans.*
    Translated by E. C. Hoskyns. London: Oxford Univer-
    sity, 1933.
"Das Schriftprinzip der reformierten Kirche." *Zwischen den
    Zeiten,* 3 (1925), 215-245.
"Die Souveränität des Wortes Gottes und die Entscheidung des
    Glaubens." *Theologische Studien,* No. 5 (1939). In
    English: "The Sovereignty of God's Word and the Deci-
    sion of Faith." *God Here and Now.* Translated by P. M.
    van Buren. London: Routledge and Kegan Paul, 1964.
Suchet Gott, so werdet ihr leben! (with Eduard Thurneysen).
    2nd ed. Munich: Christian Kaiser, 1928. (The review
    "Auf das Reiches Gottes warten" is translated as "Action
    in Waiting for the Kingdom of God," in *Action and Wait-
    ing* by Karl Barth and Christoph Blumhardt, translated

by The Society of Brothers [Rifton, N.Y.: Plough Publishing House, 1969].).

Die Theologie und die Kirche. Munich: Christian Kaiser, 1928. In English: *Theology and Church*. Translated by L. S. Smith. New York: Harper and Row, 1962.

"Theologische Existenz Heute!" *"Dialektische Theologie" in Scheidung und Bewährung 1933-1936*. In English: *Theological Existence Today*. Translated by R. Birch Hoyle. London: Hodder and Stoughton, 1933.

Theologische Fragen und Antworten. Zurich: EVZ, 1957.

"Vergangenheit und Zukunft. Friedrich Naumann und Christoph Blumhardt." *Anfänge der dialektischen Theologie*, Vol. 1.

Das Wort Gottes und die Theologie. Munich: Christian Kaiser, 1924. In English: *The Word of God and the Word of Man*. 2nd ed. Translated by D. Horton. Harper and Row, 1957.

2. Works About Karl Barth

For an exhaustive bibliography of the secondary literature on Barth up to 1977, see Manfred Kwiran, *Index to literature on Barth, Bonhoeffer and Bultmann* (*Theologische Zeitschrift*, Sonderband 7) (Basel: F. Reinhardt, 1977).

Adriaanse, Hendrik J. *Zu den Sachen selbst. Versuch einer Konfrontation der Theologie Karl Barths mit der phänomenologischen Philosophie Edmund Husserls*. The Hague: Mouton, 1974.

Althaus, Paul. "Theologie und Geschichte. Zur Auseinandersetzung mit der dialektische Theologie." *Zeitschrift für Systematische Theologie*, 1 (1923-1924), 741-786.

Bachmann, D. "Der Römerbrief verdeutscht und vergegenwärtigt" (Review of *Der Römerbrief*, 1st ed.). *Neue Kirchliche Zeitschrift*, 32 (1921), 517-547.

Bakker, Nico T. *In der Krisis der Offenbarung. Karl Barths Hermeneutik dargestellt an seiner Römerbrief-Auslegung*. Translated (from the Dutch) by W. Bunte. Neukirchen-Vluyn: Neukirchener Verlag, 1974.

Balthasar, Hans Urs von. *Karl Barth. Darstellung und Deutung seiner Theologie*. 2nd ed. Cologne: J. Hegner, 1962. In English: *The Theology of Karl Barth*. Translated by J. Drury. New York: Holt, Rinehart and Winston, 1971.

Berger, Joachim. *Die Verwurzelung des theologischen Denkens Karl Barths in dem Kerygma der beiden Blumhardts vom Reiche Gottes*. Berlin: Humboldt University (Inaugural Dissertation), 1955.

Bettis, Joseph. "Theology and Critical Theory in Marcuse and Barth." *Studies in Religion*, 7 (1978), 117-135.

Bonhoeffer, Dietrich. *Act and Being*. Translated by B. Noble. London: Collins, 1962.

Bouillard, Henri. *Karl Barth* (3 vols.). Vol. 1: *Genèse et évolution de la théologie dialectique*. Paris: Aubier, 1957.

Brinkschmidt, Egon. *Søren Kierkegaard und Karl Barth*. Neukirchen-Vluyn: Neukirchener Verlag, 1971.

Busch, Eberhard. *Karl Barth und die Pietisten. Die Pietismuskritik des jungen Karl Barth und ihre Erwiderung*. Munich: Christian Kaiser, 1978.

Busch, Eberhard. *Karl Barths Lebenslauf*. Munich: Christian Kaiser, 1975. In English: *Karl Barth*. Translated by J. Bowden. Philadelphia: Fortress, 1976.

Cushman, Robert E. "Barth's Attack upon Cartesianism and the Future in Theology." *Journal of Religion*, 36 (1956), 207-223.

Dannemann, Ulrich. *Theologie und Politik im Denken Karl Barths*. Munich: Christian Kaiser, 1977.

Delhougne, Henri. "Karl Barth et la critique feuerbachienne de l'idée de Dieu." *Mélanges de Science Religieuse*, 28 (1971), 121-163.

_____. "L'argument ontologique est il philosophique ou théologique: examen critique de la position de Karl Barth." *Revue des Sciences Religieuses*, 53 (1979), 40-63.

Fähler, Jochen. *Der Ausbruch des 1. Weltkrieges in Karl Barths Predigten 1913-1915*. Bern: P. Lang, 1979.

Gestrich, Christof. *Neuzeitliches Denken und die Spaltung der dialektischen Theologie. Zur Frage der natürlichen Theologie*. Tübingen: J. C. B. Mohr, 1977.

Giesecke, H. *Die Aufgabe der Philosophie nach der dialektischen Theologie*. Gütersloh: C. Bertelsmann, 1930.

Gogarten, Friedrich. "Karl Barths Dogmatik" (Review of *Die christliche Dogmatik*). *Theologische Rundschau*, n.F. 1 (1929), 60-80.

Härle, Wilfried. "Der Aufruf der 93 Intellektuellen und Karl Barths Bruch mit der liberalen Theologie." *Zeitschrift für Theologie und Kirche*, 72 (1975), 207-224.

Hamer, Jérome. *Karl Barth*. Translated by D. M. Maruca. Westminster, Maryland: The Newman Press, 1962.

Hendry, George S. "On Barth, the Philosopher." *Faith and the Philosophers*. Edited by J. Hick. New York: St. Martin's Press, 1964.

Hilke, Elsabeth S. *Theology as Grammar. An Inquiry into the Function of Language in the Theology of Karl Barth*. Unpublished Ph.D. dissertation, Yale University, 1976.

Hunsinger, George, ed. *Karl Barth and Radical Politics*. Philadelphia: Westminster, 1976.

Jagnow, Albert A. "Karl Barth and Wilhelm Herrmann: Pupil and Teacher." *Journal of Religion*, 16 (1936), 300-316.

Josuttis, Manfred. *Die Gegenständlichkeit der Offenbarung. Karl Barths Anselm-Buch und die Denkform seiner Theologie*. Bonn: Bouvier and Co., 1965.

Jülicher, Adolf. "Barth, Prof. Karl: *Der Römerbrief*. 2. Auflage in neuer Bearbeitung." *Theologische Literaturzeitung*, 47 (1922), 537-542.

Krüger, Gerhard. "Dialektische Methode und theologische Exegese. Logische Bemerkungen zu Barths 'Römerbrief.'" *Zwischen den Zeiten*, 5 (1927), 116-157.

_____. "Kant und die Theologie der Krisis." *Theologische Blätter*, 3 (1924), 97-105, 121-128.

Kupisch, Karl. *Karl Barth in Selbstzeugnissen und Bilddokumenten*. Stuttgart: J. F. Steinkopf, 1971.

Lange, Peter. *Konkrete Theologie? Karl Barth und Friedrich Gogarten "Zwischen den Zeiten" (1922-1933)*. Zurich: TVZ, 1972.

Loew, W. "Noch einmal Barths Römerbrief." *Christliche Welt*, 34 (1920), 585ff.

McKinnon, Alistair. "Barth's Relation to Kierkegaard: Some
    Further Light." *Canadian Journal of Theology*, 13
    (1967), 31-41.
Marquardt, Friedrich-Wilhelm. *Die Entdeckung des Judentums für
    die christliche Theologie. Israel im Denken Karl Barths.*
    Munich: Christian Kaiser, 1967.
_____. "Religionskritik und Entmythologisierung. Über einen
    Beitrag Karl Barths zur Entmythologisierungsfrage."
    *Theologie zwischen gestern und morgen. Interpretation-
    en und Anfragen zum Werk Karl Barths.* Edited by W.
    Dantine and K. Lüthi. Munich: Christian Kaiser, 1968.
_____. *Theologie und Sozialismus. Das Beispiel Karl Barths.*
    Munich: Christian Kaiser, 1972.
Maury, Pierre. "Quelques grandes orientations de la pensée de
    Karl Barth." *Bulletin de la Société Française de Phi-
    losophie*, 33 (1933).
Monsma, Peter H. *Karl Barth's Idea of Revelation.* Somerville,
    New Jersey: Somerville Press, 1937.
Mueller, David L. *Karl Barth's Critique of the Anthropological
    Starting Point in Theology.* Dissertation, Duke Univer-
    sity, 1958.
Oosterbaan, J. A. *Barth en Hegel. Leven en denken vanuit de
    verzoening* (Lecture given in Amsterdam, April 15, 1978).
    Heemstede: By the Author, 1978.
Ritschl, Otto. "Barth, Prof. D. Karl: *Die christliche Dogmatik
    im Entwurf.*" *Theologische Literaturzeitung*, 53 (1928),
    217-228.
Rumscheidt, H. Martin, ed. *Footnotes to a Theology. The Karl
    Barth Colloquium of 1972.* Supplement to *Studies in
    Religion.* The Corporation for the Publication of Aca-
    demic Studies in Religion in Canada, 1974.
_____, ed. *Karl Barth in Re-View.* Pittsburgh: The Pickwick
    Press, 1981.
Sauter, Gerhard. *Die Theologie des Reiches Gottes beim älteren
    und jüngeren Blumhardt.* Zurich: Zwingli Verlag, 1962.
Schellong, Dieter, and Steck, Karl G. "Karl Barth und die Neu-
    zeit." *Theologische Existenz Heute*, n.F. No. 173
    (1973).
Schindler, Hans. *Barth und Overbeck. Ein Beitrag zur Genesis
    der dialektischen Theologie im Lichte der gegenwärtige
    Situation.* Gotha: L. Klotz, 1936.
Schmid, Friedrich. *Verkündigung und Dogmatik in der Theologie
    Karl Barths. Hermeneutik und Ontologie in einer Theo-
    logie des Wortes Gottes.* Munich: Christian Kaiser,
    1964.
Siegfried, T. *Das Wort und die Existenz. Auseinandersetzung
    mit der dialektischen Theologie* (3 vols.). Vol. 1:
    Die Theologie des Wortes bei Karl Barth. Gotha: L.
    Klotz, 1930.
Smart, James D. *The Divided Mind of Modern Theology. Karl
    Barth and Rudolf Bultmann, 1908-1933.* Philadelphia:
    Westminster, 1967.
Smith, John E. "The Significance of Karl Barth's Thought for
    the Relation Between Theology and Philosophy." *Union
    Seminary Quarterly Review*, 28 (1972), 15-30.
Snyder, Dale N. *Karl Barth's struggle with anthropocentric
    theology.* The Hague: Wattez, 1966.

Stadtland, Tjarko J. *Eschatologie und Geschichte in der Theologie des jungen Karl Barth*. Neukirchen-Vluyn: Neukirchener Verlag, 1966.

Torrance, Thomas F. *Karl Barth: An Introduction to his Early Theology, 1910-1931*. London: SCM, 1962.

Vaart Smit, H. W. van der. "Die Schule Karl Barths und die Marburger Philosophie." *Kant-Studien*, 34 (1929), 333-350.

Walter, James S. *The development of Karl Barth's theology from the first edition of Der Römerbrief through the second edition of Der Römerbrief*. Dissertation, Claremont, 1963.

Windisch, H. "Barth, Prof. Karl: *Der Römerbrief* [1st ed.]." *Theologische Literaturzeitung*, 45 (1920), 200f.

Zuidema, S. U. "Theologie en wijsbegeerte in de 'Kirchliche Dogmatik' van Karl Barth." *Philosophia Reformata*, 18 (1953), 77-138.

3. Works by Emmanuel Levinas

For a complete bibliography of Levinas' publications and literature on Levinas up to 1977, see Roger Burggraeve, "Emmanuel Levinas: une bibliographie," *Salesianum*, 39 (1977), 633-655. This work appears again and is updated through 1981 in *Emmanuel Levinas*, Leuven (Center for Metaphysics and Philosophy of God), 1981, pp. 61-154.

L'au-delà du verset. Paris: Minuit, 1982.

Autrement qu'être ou au-delà de l'essence. The Hague: Martinus Nijhoff, 1974. In English: *Otherwise than Being or Beyond Essence*. Translated by A. Lingis. The Hague: Martinus Nijhoff, 1981.

De Dieu qui vient à l'idée. Paris: Vrin, 1982.

"De la conscience à la veille. A partir de Husserl." *Bijdragen*, 35 (1974), 235-249.

"De l'évasion." *Recherches Philosophiques*, 5 (1935-1936), 373-472.

De l'existence à l'existant. 2nd ed. Paris: Vrin, 1978. In English: *Existence and Existents*. Translated by A. Lingis. The Hague: Martinus Nijhoff, 1978.

"Dieu et al philosophie." *Le Nouveau Commerce*, Nos. 30-31 (1975), 97-128. In English: "God and Philosophy." Translated by R. Cohen. *Philosophy Today*, 22 (1978), 127-145.

"Un Dieu homme?" *Qui est Jésu-Christ?* ("Recherches et débats" No. 62). Paris: Desclée de Brouwer, 1968.

Difficile liberté. 2nd ed. Paris: Albin Michel, 1976. (The essay "Signature" is edited by A. Peperzak and translated into English by M. E. Petrisko in *Research in Phenomenology*, 8 [1978], 175-189.)

En découvrant l'existence avec Husserl et Heidegger. 2nd ed. Paris: Vrin, 1967. (The essay "La trace de l'autre" appears as "On the Trail of the Other," translated by D. J. Hoy, in *Philosophy Today*, 10 [1966], 34-47.)

"L'état de César et l'état de David." *La théologie de l'histoire. Révélation et histoire*. Edited by E. Castelli. Paris: Aubier, 1971.

"Franz Rosenzweig: une pensée juive moderne." *Revue de Théo-
    logie et de Philosophie*, 98 (1965), 208-221.
Humanisme de l'autre homme. Montpellier: Fata Morgana, 1972.
"Idéologie et idéalisme." *Démythisation et idéologie.* Edited
    by E. Castelli. Paris: Aubier, 1973. In English:
    "Ideology and Idealism." *Modern Jewish Ethics.* Edited
    by M. Fox. Translated by A. Lesley and S. Ames. Colum-
    bus: Ohio State University, 1975. (The English ver-
    sion contains Levinas' part of a discussion of this
    lecture that occurred at the 1972 "Summer Institute on
    Judaism and Contemporary Thought" in Israel, which is
    not in the French.)
"Il y a." *Deucalion*, 1 (1946), 141-154.
"Jean Wahl. Sans avoir ni être." *Jean Wahl et Gabriel Marcel.*
    Edited by J. Hersch. Paris: Beauchesne, 1976.
"Leon Chestov. *Kierkegaard et la philosophie existentielle.*"
    Revue des Etudes Juives, n.s. 2 (1937), 139ff.
"Liberté et commandement." *Revue de Métaphysique et de Morale*,
    58 (1953), 264-272.
"Martin Buber, Gabriel Marcel et la philosophie." *Revue Inter-
    nationale de Philosophie*, 32 (1978), 492-511.
"Martin Heidegger et l'ontologie." *Revue Philosophique de la
    France et de l'Etranger*, 57 (1932), 395-431. Reprinted
    with slight alteration in *En découvrant l'existence
    avec Husserl et Heidegger.*
Het menselijk gelaat. Edited by A. Peperzak. Translated by A.
    Peperzak and O. de Nobel. Bilthoven: Ambo, 1969.
"Le moi et la totalité." *Revue de Métaphysique et de Morale*,
    56 (1954), 353-373.
"Le nom de Dieu d'après quelques textes talmudiques." *L'analyse
    du langage théologique. Le nom de Dieu.* Edited by
    E. Castelli. Paris: Aubier, 1969.
Noms propres. Montpellier: Fata Morgana, 1976. (The essay on
    Paul Celan, "De l'être à l'autre," is translated as
    "Being and the Other: On Paul Celan" by S. Melville in
    the *Chicago Review*, 29 [1978], 16-21. The essay "Martin
    Buber et la théorie de la connaissance" appears as
    "Martin Buber and the Theory of Knowledge" in *The Phi-
    losophy of Martin Buber*, edited by P. A. Schilpp and
    M. A. Friedman [La Salle, Illinois: Open Court, 1967].)
"L'ontologie est-elle fondamentale?" *Revue de Métaphysique et
    de Morale*, 56 (1951), 88-98.
"La pensée de l'être et la question de l'Autre." *Critique*, 34
    (1978), 187-197.
"La pensée de Martin Buber et le judaïsme contemporain." *Mar-
    tin Buber. L'homme et le philosophe.* Brussels: Edi-
    tions de l'Institut de Sociologie de l'Université Libre
    de Bruxelles, 1968.
De Plaatsvervanging. Edited and translated by T. de Boer.
    Baarn: Het Wereldvenster, 1977. (This is an extensive-
    ly annotated presentation of Levinas' essay "La substi-
    tution," which originally appeared in *Revue Philoso-
    phique de Louvain*, 66 [1968], 487-508, and is incorpo-
    rated in *Autrement qu'être ou au-delà de l'essence*,
    Chapter IV.)
"Pluralisme et transcendance." *Actes du Xme Congrès Interna-
    tional de Philosophie*, 1, 381ff. Amsterdam: North
    Holland Publishing Company, 1949. Edited by F. W. Beth,
    H. J. Pos, and J. H. Hollak.

Quatre lectures talmudiques. Paris: Minuit, 1968.
"Quelques réflexions sur la philosophie de l'hitlérisme."
    Esprit, 2 (1934), 199-208.
Question to Martin Buber, translated by R. Rosthal, in *Philo-
    sophical Interrogations* (23-26). Edited by S. and B.
    Rome. New York: Holt, Rinehart and Winston, 1964.
"Questions et réponses." *Le Nouveau Commerce*, Nos. 36-37 (1977),
    61-86. (This is a slightly changed version of the
    transcript of a colloquy at Leiden in May, 1975, on his
    receipt of a doctorate from Leiden University.)
"La révélation dans la tradition juive." *La révélation*. Brus-
    sels: Facultés universitaires Saint-Louis, 1977.
Du sacré au saint. Cinq nouvelles lectures talmudiques. Paris:
    Minuit, 1977.
"Sécularisation et faim." *Herméneutique de la sécularisation*.
    Edited by E. Castelli. Paris: Aubier, 1976.
"Sur les *Ideen* de M. E. Husserl." *Revue Philosophique de la
    France et de l'Etranger*, 54 (1929), 230-265.
Le Temps et l'Autre. 2nd ed. Montpellier: Fata Morgana, 1979.
La théorie de l'intuition dans la phénoménologie de Husserl.
    Paris: Alcan, 1930. In English: *The Theory of Intui-
    tion in Husserl's Phenomenology*. Translated by A.
    Orianne. Evanston: Northwestern University, 1973.
Totalité et Infini. The Hague: Martinus Nijhoff, 1961. In
    English: *Totality and Infinity*. Translated by A.
    Lingis. Pittsburgh: Duquesne University, 1969.
"La transcendance des mots. A propos des 'Biffures' de Michel
    Leiris." *Les Temps Modernes*, 4 (1949), 1090-1095.
"Transcendance et hauteur." *Bulletin de la Société Française
    de Philosophie*, 56 (1962), 89-113.
"Transcendance et mal." *Le Nouveau Commerce*, No. 41 (1978),
    55-75.

4. Works About Emmanuel Levinas

See Roger Burggraeve's bibliography cited at "Works by
Emmanuel Levinas."

Adriaanse, Hendrik J. "Het rationale karakter van de wijsbe-
    geerte van Levinas." *Nederlands Theologisch Tijdschrift*,
    29 (1975), 255-263.
Blanchot, Maurice. "Connaissance de l'inconnu." *L'entretien
    infini*. Paris: Gallimard, 1969.
————. "Tenir parole." *L'entretien infini*. Paris: Galli-
    mard, 1969.
Boer, Theo de. *Tussen filosofie en profetie. De wijsbegeerte
    van Emmanuel Levinas*. Baarn: Ambo, 1976. (An earlier
    version of one chapter appeared in English: "Beyond
    Being. Ontology and Eschatology in the Philosophy of
    Emmanuel Levinas," *Philosophia Reformata*, 38 [1973],
    17-29.)
Bouckaert, Luk. "Ontology and Ethics. Reflections on Levinas'
    Critique of Heidegger." *International Philosophical
    Quarterly*, 10 (1970), 402-419.
Buijtenen, Christof van. "Emmanuel Levinas: Tussen politiek
    en eschatologie. De redelijkheid van een wijsgerige
    verkondiging." *Bijdragen*, 28 (1967), 197-211.

Burggraeve, Roger. *Emmanuel Levinas' metafysisch-ethische herdefiniëring van het subject vanuit joodse en filosofische achtergronden*. Dissertation, Leuven, 1981.

Decloux, S. "Existence de Dieu et rencontre d'Autrui." *Nouvelle Revue Théologique*, 86 (1964), 706-724.

De Greef, Jan. "Le concept de pouvoir éthique chez Levinas." *Revue Philosophique de Louvain*, 68 (1970), 507-520.

_____. "Empirisme et éthique chez Levinas." *Archives de Philosophie*, 33 (1970), 223-242.

_____. "Ethique, réflexion et histoire chez Levinas." *Revue Philosophique de Louvain*, 67 (1969), 431-460.

_____. "Levinas et la phénoménologie." *Revue de Métaphysique et de Morale*, 76 (1971), 448-465.

_____. "Le lointain et le prochain." *Tijdschrift voor Filosofie*, 31 (1969), 490-518.

Derrida, Jacques. "Violence et métaphysique. Essai sur la pensée d'Emmanuel Levinas." *L'écriture et la différance*. Paris: Seuil, 1967. In English: "Violence and Metaphysics." *Writing and Difference*. Translated by A. Bass. Chicago: University of Chicago, 1978.

Duval, Raymond. "Exode et altérité." *Revue des Sciences Philosophiques et Théologiques*, 59 (1975), 217-241.

_____. "Parole, expression, silence." *Revue des Sciences Philosophiques et Théologiques*, 60 (1976), 226-260.

Féron, Etienne. "Ethique, langage et ontologie chez Emmanuel Levinas." *Revue de Métaphysique et de Morale*, 82 (1977), 64-87.

_____. "Le temps de la parole." *Exercises de la patience*, 1 (1980), 19-32.

Gans, Stephen. "Ethics or Ontology. Levinas and Heidegger." *Philosophy Today*, 16 (1972), 117-121.

Gaviria Alvarez, Olmedo. "L'idée de création chez Levinas. Une archéologie de sens." *Revue Philosophique de Louvain*, 72 (1974), 509-538.

Goud, Johan F. "Über Definition und Infinition: Probleme bei der Interpretation des Denkens des Emmanuel Levinas" [review of Burggraeve's dissertation]. *Nederlands Theologisch Tijdschrift*, 36 (1982), 126-144.

Guillot, Daniel E. "Emmanuel Levinas. Evolución de su Pensamiento." *Liberación Latinoamericano y Emmanuel Levinas*. By Enrique Dussel and Daniel E. Guillot. Buenos Aires: Bonum, 1975.

Heering, H. J. "Levinas' Godsconceptie." *Nederlands Theologisch Tijdschrift*, 29 (1975), 277-284.

_____. "Het primaat der praktische rede in nieuwe vorm." *Algemeen Nederlands Tijdschrift voor Wijsbegeerte*, 64 (1972), 4-14.

Keyes, Charles D. "An Evaluation of Levinas' Critique of Heidegger." *Research in Phenomenology*, 2 (1972), 121-142.

Laruelle, François, ed. *Textes pour Emmanuel Levinas* [by Lyotard, Peperzak, Wyschogrod, et. al.]. Paris: Jean-Michel Place, 1980.

Lawton, Philip N. "Levinas' Notion of the 'There is.'" *Tijdschrift voor Filosofie*, 37 (1975), 477-489; and *Philosophy Today*, 20 (1976), 67-76.

_____. "Love and Justice: Levinas' Reading of Buber." *Philosophy Today*, 20 (1976), 77-83.

Loeff, J. J. "De Ontmoeting als Thora." *Nederlands Theologisch Tijdschrift*, 29 (1975), 286-292.
Luijk, H. van. "Het Godsbegrip bij Emmanuel Levinas." *Neder-lands Theologisch Tijdschrift*, 29 (1975), 267-277.
Peperzak, Adrien. "Emmanuel Levinas: *Autrement qu'être ou au-delà de l'essence.*" *Philosophische Rundschau*, 24 (1977), 91-116. In English: "Beyond Being." Trans-lated by M. E. Petrisko. *Research in Phenomenology*, 8 (1978), 239-261.
Plat, J. E. "Ethiek en godsdienst, van Immanuel Kant tot Emmanuel Levinas." *Algemeen Nederlands Tijdschrift voor Wijsbegeerte*, 64 (1972), 15-25.
Smith, Steven G. "Reason as One for Another: Moral and Theo-retical Argument in the Philosophy of Levinas." *Journal of the British Society for Phenomenology*, 12 (1981), 231-244.
Strasser, Stephan. "Antiphénoménologie et phénoménologie dans la philosophie d'Emmanuel Levinas." *Revue Philosophique de Louvain*, 75 (1977), 101-125.
_____. "Buber und Levinas. Philosophische Besinnung auf einen Gegensatz." *Revue Internationale de Philosophie*, 32 (1978), 512-525.
_____. "Le concept de 'phénomène' chez Levinas et son impor-tance pour la philosophie religieuse." *Revue Philos-ophique de Louvain*, 76 (1978), 318-342.
_____. "Emmanuel Levinas' strijd tegen de westerse traditie en het nieuwe spreken over God." *Nederlands Theologisch Tijdschrift*, 29 (1975), 209-226.
_____. *Jenseits von Sein und Zeit.* The Hague: Martinus Nijhoff, 1978.
Tallon, Andrew. "Emmanuel Levinas and the Problem of Ethical Metaphysics." *Philosophy Today*, 20 (1976), 53-56.
Wyschogrod, Edith. *Emmanuel Levinas. The Problem of Ethical Metaphysics.* The Hague: Martinus Nijhoff, 1974.
_____. "God and 'Being's Move' in the Philosophy of Emmanuel Levinas." *The Journal of Religion*, 62 (1982), 145-155.
_____. "The Moral Self: Emmanuel Levinas and Hermann Cohen." *DAAT*, No. 4 (1980), 35-58.

5. Other Works

Barth, Heinrich. "Gotteserkenntnis." *Anfänge der dialek-tischen Theologie*, Vol. 1.
_____. *Philosophie der praktischen Vernunft.* Tübingen: J. C. B. Mohr, 1927.
Brunner, Emil. "Die andere Aufgabe der Theologie." *Zwischen den Zeiten*, 7 (1929), 255-276.
_____. *Die Mystik und das Wort.* Tübingen: J. C. B. Mohr, 1924.
_____. "Nature and Grace." *Natural Theology.* Translated by P. Fraenkel. London: G. Bles, Centenary, 1946.
Buber, Martin. *I and Thou.* Translated by R. Gregor Smith. 2nd ed. New York: Charles Scribners Sons, 1958.
Bultmann, Rudolf. "The Concept of Revelation in the New Testa-ment." *Existence and Faith. Shorter Writings of Rudolf Bultmann.* Translated by S. M. Ogden. New York: Living Age Books, 1960.

Bultmann, Rudolf. "The Historicity of Man and Faith." *Existence and Faith* (see preceding entry).

Cohen, Hermann. *Hermann Cohens Jüdische Schriften* (2 vols.). Edited by B. Strauß. Berlin: C. A. Schwetschke and Son, 1924.

_____. *Religion der Vernunft aus den Quellen des Judentums*. 2nd ed. Cologne: J. Melzer, 1959. In English: *Religion of Reason out of the Sources of Judaism*. Translated by S. Kaplan. New York: F. Ungar, 1972.

Comte, Auguste. *System of Positive Polity* (3 vols.). Vol. 1. Translated by J. H. Bridges. London: Longmans, Green, and Co., 1875.

Descartes, René. *Meditationes de prima Philosophia*. *Oeuvres de Descartes* (11 vols.), Vol. 7. Edited by C. Adam and P. Tannery. Paris: Cerf, 1904. In English: *Meditations on First Philosophy*. *The Philosophical Works of Descartes* (2 vols.), Vol. 1. Translated by E. S. Haldane and G. R. T. Ross. Cambridge: Cambridge University, 1911.

Dussort, Henri. *L'Ecole de Marbourg*. Paris: Presses Universitaires de France, 1963.

Ebner, Ferdinand. *The Word and the Spiritual Realities*. Translated by H. J. Green. Dissertation, Northwestern, 1980.

Feuerbach, Ludwig. *Das Wesen des Christentums*. Berlin: Akademie-Verlag, 1956. In English: *The Essence of Christianity*. Translated by G. Eliot. New York: Harper and Row, 1957.

Gogarten, Friedrich. "Das Problem einer theologischen Anthropologie." *Zwischen den Zeiten*, 7 (1929), 493-511.

_____. *Ich glaube an den dreieinigen Gott*. Jena: Diederichs, 1926.

Grisebach, Eberhard. *Gegenwart*. *Ein kritische Ethik*. Halle: M. Niemeyer, 1928.

Heidegger, Martin. "Brief über den Humanismus." *Platons Lehre von der Wahrheit. Mit einen Brief über den Humanismus*. Bern: Francke, 1947. In English: "Letter on Humanism." Translated by E. Lohner. *Philosophy in the Twentieth Century* (4 vols.), Vol 3. Edited by W. Barrett and H. D. Aiken. New York: Random House, 1962.

_____. *Einführung in die Metaphysik*. 3rd ed. Tübingen: M. Niemeyer, 1966. In English: *Introduction to Metaphysics*. Translated by R. Manheim. New Haven: Yale University, 1959.

_____. *Being and Time*. Translated by J. Macquarrie and E. Robinson. New York: Harper and Row, 1962.

Herrmann, Wilhelm. *Ethik*. 4th ed. Tübingen: J. C. B. Mohr, 1909.

Husserl, Edmund. *Cartesian Meditations. An Introduction to Phenomenology*. Translated by D. Cairns. The Hague: Martinus Nijhoff, 1973.

_____. *Experience and Judgment*. Edited by L. Landgrebe. Translated by J. S. Churchill and K. Ameriks. Evanston: Northwestern University, 1973.

_____. *Ideas*. Translated by W. R. Boyce Gibson. New York: Macmillan, 1931.

_____. *Logical Investigations*. Translated by J. N. Findlay. New York: Humanities, 1970.

Husserl, Edmund. "The Origin of Geometry." *The Crisis of European Sciences and Transcendental Phenomenology*. Translated by D. Carr. Evanston: Northwestern University, 1970.

Jankélévitch, Vladimir. *Philosophie première. Introduction à une philosophie du "presque."* Paris: Presses Universitaires de France, 1954.

Kant, Immanuel. *Critique of Practical Reason*. Translated by L. W. Beck. Indianapolis: Bobbs-Merrill, 1956.

_____. *Religion Within the Limits of Reason Alone*. Translated by T. M. Greene and H. H. Hudson. La Salle, Illinois: Open Court, 1934.

Kelkel, Lothar, and Schérer, René. *Husserl: Sa Vie, Son Oeuvre*. Paris: Presses Universitaires de France, 1964.

Kierkegaard, Søren. *Papirer*. 2nd ed. Edited by N. Thulstrup. Copenhagen: Gyldendal, 1968- . In English: *The Journals of Søren Kierkegaard*. Edited and translated by A. Dru. London: Oxford University, 1938.

_____. *Philosophical Fragments*. Translated by D. Swenson and H. V. Hong. Princeton: Princeton University, 1962.

Kirk, G. S., and Raven, J. E., eds. *The Pre-Socratic Philosophers*. Cambridge: Cambridge University, 1957.

Macmurray, John. *The Self as Agent*. London: Faber, 1957.

Marcel, Gabriel. *Metaphysical Journal*. Translated by B. Wall. Chicago: H. Regnery, 1952.

Nietzsche, Friedrich. *Der Fall Wagner. Werke* VI/3. Edited by G. Colli and M. Montinari. Berlin: W. de Gruyter, 1969. In English: *The Case of Wagner*. Translated by W. Kaufmann. New York: Random House, 1967.

Otto, Rudolf. *The Idea of the Holy*. Translated by J. W. Harvey. 2nd ed. London: Oxford University, 1950.

Overbeck, Franz. *Christentum und Kultur. Gedanken und Anmerkungen zur modernen Theologie*. Edited by C. A. Bernoulli. Basel: Benno Schwabe and Co., 1919.

Palmier, Jean-Michel. *Les écrits politiques de Heidegger*. Paris: L'Herne, 1968.

Plato. *Collected Dialogues*. Edited by E. Hamilton and H. Cairns. Many translators. Princeton: Princeton University, 1961.

Popper, Karl. *The Open Society and Its Enemies*. 5th ed. Princeton: Princeton University, 1966.

Rosenzweig, Franz. *Der Stern der Erlösung*. 3rd ed. Heidelberg: Lambert Schneider, 1954. In English: *The Star of Redemption*. Translated by W. W. Hallo. Boston: Beacon, 1972.

Sartre, Jean-Paul. *Being and Nothingness*. Translated by H. Barnes. New York: Philosophical Library, 1956.

Schleiermacher, Friedrich. *The Christian Faith*. Edited and translated by H. R. Mackintosh and J. S. Stewart. Philadelphia: Fortress, 1928.

_____. *On Religion. Speeches to Its Cultured Despisers*. Translated by J. Oman. New York: Harper and Row, 1958.

Spiegelberg, Herbert. *The Phenomenological Movement*. 2nd ed. The Hague: Martinus Nijhoff, 1976.

Thurneysen, Eduard. *Christoph Blumhardt*. Munich: Christian Kaiser, 1926.

_____. *Dostojewski*. Munich: Christian Kaiser, 1921. In English: *Dostoevsky*. Translated by K. R. Crim. Richmond: John Knox, 1964.

Tillich, Paul. *Religiöse Verwirklichung*. Berlin: Furche, 1930.

Tolstoy, Leo. *War and Peace*. Translated by C. Garnett. New York: Random House, n.d.

INDEX OF PERSONS

Steven G. Smith holds a B.A. degree from Florida State University and graduate degrees from Vanderbilt and Duke Universities. He is presently Assistant Professor of Philosophy and Religion at North Carolina Wesleyan College.